D1558379

Henry VIII

Significant Figures in World History

Charles Darwin: A Reference Guide to His Life and Works,
by J. David Archibald, 2019.

Leonardo da Vinci: A Reference Guide to His Life and Works,
by Allison Lee Palmer, 2019.

Michelangelo: A Reference Guide to His Life and Works,
by Lilian H. Zirpolo, 2020.

Robert E. Lee: A Reference Guide to His Life and Works,
by James I. Robertson Jr., 2019.

John F. Kennedy: A Reference Guide to His Life and Works,
by Ian James Bickerton, 2019.

Florence Nightingale: A Reference Guide to Her Life and Works,
by Lynn McDonald, 2019.

Napoléon Bonaparte: A Reference Guide to His Life and Works,
by Joshua Meeks, 2019.

Nelson Mandela: A Reference Guide to His Life and Works,
by Aran S. MacKinnon, 2020.

Winston Churchill: A Reference Guide to His Life and Works,
by Christopher Catherwood, 2020.

Catherine the Great: A Reference Guide to Her Life and Works,
by Alexander Kamenskii, 2020.

Golda Meir: A Reference Guide to Her Life and Works,
by Meron Medzini, 2020.

Karl Marx: A Reference Guide to His Life and Works,
by Frank Elwell, Brian Andrews, and Kenneth S. Hicks, 2020.

Eva Perón: A Reference Guide to Her Life and Works,
by María Belén Rabadán Vega and Mirna Vohnsen, 2021.

Adolf Hitler: A Reference Guide to His Life and Works,
by Steven P. Remy, 2021.

Sigmund Freud: A Reference Guide to His Life and Works,
by Alistair Ross, 2022.

Henry VIII: A Reference Guide to His Life and Works,
by Clayton Drees, 2022.

Henry VIII

A Reference Guide to His Life and Works

Clayton Drees

ROWMAN & LITTLEFIELD
Lanham • Boulder • New York • London

Published by Rowman & Littlefield
An imprint of The Rowman & Littlefield Publishing Group, Inc.
4501 Forbes Boulevard, Suite 200, Lanham, Maryland 20706
www.rowman.com

86-90 Paul Street, London EC2A 4NE, United Kingdom

British Library Cataloguing in Publication Information Available

Library of Congress Cataloging-in-Publication Data

Names: Drees, Clayton J., author.
Title: Henry VIII : a reference guide to his life and works / Clayton Drees.
Other titles: Henry 8th.
Description: Lanham : Rowman & Littlefield Publishing Group, [2022] I Series: Significant figures in world history I Includes bibliographical references and index. I Summary: "Henry VIII: A Reference Guide to His Life and Works captures his eventful life, his works, and his legacy. It features a chronology, an introduction, a comprehensive bibliography, and the dictionary section lists entries on all the locales, events and personalities associated with King Henry" —Provided by publisher.
Identifiers: LCCN 2021047735 (print) I LCCN 2021047736 (ebook) I ISBN 9781538122839 (cloth) I ISBN 9781538122846 (epub)
Subjects: LCSH: Henry VIII, King of England, 1491–1547—Encyclopedias. I Great Britain—History—Henry VIII, 1509–1547—Encyclopedias.
Classification: LCC DA332 .D74 2022 (print) I LCC DA332 (ebook) I DDC 942.05/1—dc23/eng/20211008
LC record available at https://lccn.loc.gov/2021047735
LC ebook record available at https://lccn.loc.gov/2021047736

∞™ The paper used in this publication meets the minimum requirements of American National Standard for Information Sciences—Permanence of Paper for Printed Library Materials, ANSI/NISO Z39.48-1992.

Contents

Preface

When compiling lists of prominent figures in history, heads of state usually spring to mind first because their decisions and actions often have affected profoundly the lives of the people they ruled. European sovereigns—especially those whose reigns predate today's constitutional monarchies—exercised much greater and more autocratic power over their realms and subjects than we in our modern democracies could ever imagine. In particular, kings (and occasionally queens regnant) of England mostly enjoyed such unchecked regal authority from the medieval period to the advent of the British parliamentary state in more recent times. Despite their great power, however, the English rulers of bygone ages were still human beings, possessed of the same hopes, desires, needs, weaknesses, and flaws that characterize us all. Like any individual from any era, they were studies in human contrast, at times displaying genius, mercy, and kindness while at others revealing their greed, arrogance, and cruelty for all to see. Henry VIII was such a king. He fascinates us today because, despite his famously explosive temper, his overbearing bluster, and his appalling disregard for human life, he also proved himself at times to be a caring husband, a loyal friend, a compassionate ruler, and a pious believer.

Perhaps the most obvious contrast in the life of this well-known English king manifested itself in his dramatically changing physical appearance over time. At the start of his reign, Henry VIII was an athletic, handsome, and energetic young man who far preferred physical activity to the drudgery of Crown administration. He was by all accounts an accomplished dancer, tennis player, and wrestler who also loved to joust in the tiltyard, practice archery at the butts, and hunt wild boar and deer on horseback in his royal parks. By the time he reached his early 40s, however, years of excessive feasting and drinking, a sedentary lifestyle, and many broken marriages had taken their toll. King Henry became dangerously corpulent, and plagued as well by painful gout, ulcerated legs, and (probably) an advanced case of syphilis, his death came far too swiftly in 1547 for a formerly fit man who had not yet reached his 56th birthday.

Henry VIII's personality also allows us to study the many contrasting sides of this complex sovereign. Early in life, the Tudor king was a jovial, boisterous, fun-loving, and spontaneous youth who often ran with a group of exuberant noble rascals he affectionately called his "henchmen." The 20- and 30-something Henry was quick with a joke or a song, cheerfully rewarded courtiers who pleased him, and delighted in disguising himself to deceive and "amaze" his pageant audiences. Later in life, however, and plainly alarmed by his own obesity and many ailments, the Tudor king became increasingly argumentative, morose, and quick to anger. Many scholars believe that a serious 1536 jousting accident, when the king crashed to earth and lay comatose for two hours, may have precipitated this rather sudden shift in the royal personality. Whatever the cause, the Henry VIII who ruled England in the 1540s was a very different man from the youthful and carefree monarch who had frolicked and laughed his way through the first two decades of his reign.

In another sense, we can learn much about the contrasting nature of Henry VIII from the way he related to and treated his many wives. The young Tudor king seems to have genuinely loved—or at least befriended and trusted—Queen Katherine of Aragon and then turned quite bitterly against her when she failed to give him his coveted male heir and tried to block his attempts to replace her. Likewise, King Henry was at first infatuated with and deeply loved Anne Boleyn, only to reject and then condemn her to death when her willfulness and nagging displeased him. He clearly cared the most for his third spouse, Jane Seymour, who finally gave him a son but who did not long survive the child's birth. However, he cared nothing for the unattractive Anne of Cleves, though he treated her kindly as his "sister" and supported her financially through the end of his reign. Henry VIII's fifth queen, Katherine Howard, initially delighted him with her amorous affections but soon prompted his disgust and her own execution with her scandalous infidelities. Finally, Katherine Parr played nursemaid to the aged and infirm Tudor king but had to beg for his mercy to survive his profound aversion to her evangelical religious views. As a historical testament to the vagaries of human relationships, surely his six wives experienced the full measure of happiness and hatred, of love and loathing from the enigmatic Henry VIII.

The contrasts that characterized the private and wedded life of King Henry tended to inform his religious innovations and regard for his royal advisors as well. The Tudor king was famously conservative in matters of religion, inspiring Pope Leo X to name him "Defender of the Faith" for his written assault on the reformist doctrines of Martin Luther. Yet Henry was also quite willing to break free from Rome a dozen years later to establish the Church of England, with himself as its supreme head. Then, having unwittingly allowed certain Protestant beliefs to take root in his Church, King Henry abruptly launched a conservative religious reaction in the 1540s that brought much of the old Roman faith back to England.

The Tudor king also proved most unpredictable when it came to choosing and dismissing his chief Crown ministers. Henry elevated Thomas Cardinal Wolsey, Sir Thomas More, and Thomas Cromwell to great heights of wealth, prestige, and power, only to turn on and destroy each of them in turn for (what he believed were) their failures to carry out his will. Indeed, King Henry VIII was a man of many moods, contrasts, and insecurities, one whose multifaceted character and volatile disposition defined the early Tudor age and helped make him a compelling subject for historical biography today.

When friends and colleagues asked me about this encyclopedia project, I told them my plan was to treat "all things Henry VIII" within its pages. Like the other volumes in this Rowman and Littlefield Reference Guide series, my offering on the famous Tudor king opens with a detailed chronology of important events in Henry's life and reign. A biographical entry on Henry VIII himself then follows as an introduction, one that considers the possible motivations and aspirations of the man and highlights his most important achievements and spectacular blunders. The main body of the book features 152 entries on the events, places, queens, ministers, foreign rivals, nobles, scholars, trends, and institutions that were associated with King Henry from the years before his birth, through the nearly 38 years of his reign, to the subsequent regimes of his three royal children and successors. Cross-references appear in bold in the text of most entries to guide readers to related subjects elsewhere in the encyclopedia. An extensive but selective bibliography closes out the volume to provide suggestions for further research in manuscript archives (both British and American) and among published primary works, modern secondary sources (arranged by topic), and general starting-point links to reliable internet websites as well.

My interest in English history, and particularly in King Henry VIII and the Tudors, is doubtless grounded in the three years I lived in Surrey in southern England as a boy. My parents were wise enough to enroll me in an English "public" (American private) school, where I wore my knee socks and macintosh (raincoat) uniform, played rugby and cricket, and learned to read and translate the Latin classics. While living in the United Kingdom, my family visited cathedrals, castles, and other historic sites, all of which fired my imagination and led to a lifelong love of the English past. Those boyhood experiences lived on to become a history double major (with economics) in college and then carried into graduate school, where I focused on Tudor England as my primary field of study. As a history professor at Virginia Wesleyan University in Virginia Beach for the past 30 years, I have authored and published two monographs that are squarely anchored in the early Tudor period. My approach to Henry VIII has always been one of love and hate; I have admired him over the years as a Renaissance scholar, jolly bon vivant, and resolute man of action yet have despised him at the same time as a bully, tyrant, scoundrel, and narcissist. I hope I have achieved some semblance of love-hate balance in bringing this storied English king to life in these pages.

I wish to thank my friend and colleague Ronald H. Fritze, who was kind enough to mention my name to Rowman and Littlefield as a qualified author for this work. I am also grateful to my wife, Val—herself a published fiction author—for her support and helpful suggestions during the three years it took me to write this book. I am indebted to the British Library, the National Archives (formerly the Public Record Office), the Hampshire Record Office, Oxford's Corpus Christi College, and the Lambeth Palace Library in the United Kingdom as well as the Library of Congress and the Huntington Library in the United States, for their generous assistance and ready access to their collections. Finally, my deepest gratitude extends to Professors Peter O'Malley Pierson, Christiaan Lievestro, and Robert L. Woods, who introduced me to the fascinating world of early modern Europe and inspired me to become the teacher and scholar I am today. This encyclopedia is dedicated to them.

Chronology

1485 22 August: At the Battle of Bosworth Field near Leicester, King Richard III died bravely in combat trying to defeat the army of Henry Tudor, the Earl of Richmond, who claimed the English throne as the last surviving Lancastrian heir from the Wars of the Roses. Henry Tudor was crowned King Henry VII on the battlefield by some of his officers. **30 October:** Henry VII was formally crowned king of England at Westminster Abbey outside London. **November:** The first Parliament of Henry VII's reign met at Westminster to proclaim his right to rule England by royal descent (dubious), God-given victory in battle, and a promise to govern wisely. King Henry also had Parliament attaint more than 100 Yorkist enemies of treason in order to confiscate their estates to the Crown.

1486 18 January: Henry VII married Elizabeth of York, the daughter of the Yorkist King Edward IV, to unify the hostile factions of Lancaster and York from the Wars of the Roses. The lavish wedding ceremony took place in Westminster Abbey. **20 September:** Prince Arthur, Henry VII's heir and the elder brother of the future Henry VIII, was born in Winchester.

1487 16 June: Henry VII defeated the invasion force of Lambert Simnel, insurgent pretender to the English throne, at the Battle of Stoke. Simnel was captured and put to work as a scullery (dishwasher) in the royal kitchens and later rose to become the king's falconer.

1489 23 November: Princess Margaret, the elder sister of the future Henry VIII, was born at Westminster Palace. She would grow up to wed King James IV of Scotland and eventually produced with him the Stuart line of succession to the English throne. **29 November:** Henry VII designated his son Arthur Tudor as his principal heir by creating him Prince of Wales.

1491 28 June: Prince Henry (VIII) Tudor was born at Greenwich Palace to King Henry VII and Queen Elizabeth of York. **Early July:** Bishop Richard Fox of Exeter baptized the infant Prince Henry in the chapel of the Observant Friars at Greenwich.

1494 1 November: Henry VII created Prince Henry Duke of York as the second heir in line to the Tudor succession and granted him several other titles and honors, as well.

1495 17 May: Prince Henry was made a companion knight of the Garter six weeks before his fourth birthday. **July:** Prince Henry's formal education began under tutors Bernard André and John Skelton. At this tender age, he began to study Latin grammar and other European languages and was taught to avoid vice and distrust corrupt counselors.

1496 18 March: Princess Mary, Prince Henry's younger (and favorite) sister, was born at Richmond Palace, west of London. She would grow up to marry Henry VIII's best friend, Charles Brandon, the Duke of Suffolk.

1497 10 August: Henry VII formally betrothed his eldest son and heir, Prince Arthur, to Princess Katherine of Aragon, the youngest daughter of King Ferdinand of Aragon and Queen Isabel of Castile. This royal match secured a Spanish alliance for England and also won important international recognition for Tudor royal claims. **7 September:** Perkin Warbeck, another false pretender from Flanders, landed in Cornwall with a small force to challenge Henry VII's claim to the English throne. **5 October:** Warbeck surrendered to King Henry's troops at Beaulieu Abbey in Hampshire and was imprisoned in the Tower of London.

1499 19 May: Prince Arthur was "married" to Katherine of Aragon, with the Spanish ambassador Roderigo de Puebla standing in as Katherine's proxy at Bewdley Manor near Worcester. **23 November:** Perkin Warbeck was publicly hanged, drawn, and quartered at Tyburn in London as punishment for his failed coup attempt against King Henry VII two years earlier.

1501 2 October: Princess Katherine of Aragon arrived at Plymouth in England for her wedding to Prince Arthur. **October–November:** Katherine of Aragon traveled by stages under escort through Devonshire, Somerset, Hampshire, and Surrey to London. **14 November:** Archbishop Henry Deane of Canterbury married Prince Arthur to Katherine of Aragon (both aged just 15 years) in an opulent ceremony at St. Paul's Cathedral in London.

1502 2 April: Prince Arthur died, possibly from the lingering effects of the sweating sickness or perhaps from consumption. With his elder brother's premature death, Prince Henry now became the principal royal heir of the House of Tudor.

1503 11 February: Queen Elizabeth of York, Prince Henry's mother, died from the physical complications of a difficult pregnancy and childbirth. **June:** Henry VII betrothed his son and heir, Prince Henry, to his brother's widow, Katherine of Aragon. **8 August:** Princess Margaret Tudor married King James IV of Scotland at Holyrood Abbey in Edinburgh. **26 December:** Pope Julius II granted a dispensation

for Prince Henry to marry Arthur's widow, Katherine of Aragon. The dispensation was based on Deuteronomy 25:5, an Old Testament passage that urged men to "take in" and protect (in effect, marry) their brother's widow.

1504 18 February: Henry VII created Prince Henry the new Prince of Wales, thus formally naming his only surviving son as the next in line to the Tudor throne.

1505 27 June: Prince Henry publicly objected to his proposed marriage with Katherine of Aragon before the bishops of Winchester and Durham and the Earl of Surrey (among others) in London. Prince Henry ostensibly rejected the match because Princess Katherine was six years his senior, but King Henry VII probably orchestrated the incident because of a dowry dispute with the Spanish king. Prince Henry's objections were later withdrawn.

1507 28 June: Prince Henry took part in his first public jousting tournament on his 16th birthday. He remained an enthusiastic and successful tiltyard competitor for most of the rest of his life.

1509 21 April: King Henry VII died at Richmond Palace of consumption, thus placing Prince Henry on the English throne as King Henry VIII just two months prior to his 18th birthday. **23 April:** King Henry VIII ordered the arrest of Edmund Dudley and Richard Empson on charges of treason for their role in collecting Henry VII's hated benevolence and recognizance fees. **11 June:** King Henry VIII married Katherine of Aragon, his brother's widow, in a sumptuous ceremony at Greenwich Palace. **24 June:** Archbishop William Warham of Canterbury crowned Henry VIII and Katherine of Aragon king and queen of England at Westminster Abbey outside London. **29 June:** Lady Margaret Beaufort, Henry VIII's grandmother and an important advisor and confidante of his father, Henry VII, died at Westminster Palace. **November:** Thomas Wolsey, a brilliant priest, talented administrator, and ambitious opportunist, entered royal service as King Henry VIII's almoner (charity director).

1510 **31 January:** Queen Katherine delivered a stillborn daughter following the first of her six pregnancies. **17 August:** Henry VIII had his father's unpopular Crown ministers Edmund Dudley and Richard Empson executed on Tower Hill to win the enthusiastic approval of most of his subjects.

1511 **1 January:** Queen Katherine gave birth to a sickly prince, who died 52 days later. **October:** Thomas Wolsey joined King Henry's royal council as a secretary. **17 November:** Diplomats representing King Ferdinand of Spain signed the Treaty of Westminster to formalize a military alliance with England against France.

1512 **April:** Thomas Wolsey became the de facto chief minister of Henry VIII. **Summer:** Naval raids launched against France and an ill-fated ground incursion from Spain against Gascony all ended in disaster. **Autumn:** Thomas Wolsey and Bishop Richard Fox of Winchester began assembling an English force of 40,000 men with arms, supplies, and horses to invade France the following year.

1513 **30 June:** King Henry set sail with his invasion force for France. **August–September:** The English army besieged and captured the French towns of Thérouanne and Tournai. **13 August:** Henry VIII personally led a force of mounted English troopers to victory over a squad of French cavalry in a skirmish later known as the Battle of the Spurs. **9 September:** Ordered by Queen Katherine of Aragon to northern England with an army, Thomas Howard, the Earl of Surrey, defeated a Scottish invasion force at the Battle of Flodden. Thousands of Scottish soldiers perished, along with King James IV of Scotland himself. **17 September:** Queen Katherine gave birth to a premature prince, who soon died. **22 October:** King Henry returned to England with most of his army to put an inconclusive end to his first French invasion.

1514 **September:** Representatives of King Louis XII of France signed the Treaty of London peace accord with England to end recent hostilities between the two kingdoms. **9 October:** Princess Mary Tudor (aged 18 years) married Louis XII (aged 52 years) as required by the Treaty of London to become queen of France. **31 December:** King Louis XII died from the lingering effects of gout and syphilis. Mary Tudor, now the dowager queen of France, was thus freed from her unhappy union with Louis to marry again.

1515 **1 January:** François I succeeded Louis XII as king of France. **8 January:** Queen Katherine of Aragon gave birth to a stillborn prince. **February:** French Dowager Queen Mary Tudor married her English beau Charles Brandon, Duke of Suffolk, King Henry VIII's best friend. **18 November:** Pope Leo X made Thomas Wolsey a cardinal of the Roman Church and a member of the papal curia. **22 December:** King Henry created Cardinal Wolsey lord chancellor of England, the highest administrative office in the land and one that befitted the prestige and duties of a royal chief minister.

1516 **18 February:** Queen Katherine of Aragon gave birth to a healthy princess, whom she and King Henry named Mary Tudor. This daughter was destined to be the only surviving child of their marriage and would later grow up to rule England as Queen Mary I in the 1550s.

1517 **1–5 May:** The "Evil" May Day riots occurred in London to protest the presence and commercial activities of foreign traders in the capital. The Duke of Norfolk suppressed the uprising and put 15 of its ringleaders to death. **July:** The deadly "sweate" (sweating sickness) broke out in London, prompting most members of King Henry's royal court to flee to safety in the countryside.

1518 **Summer:** King Henry began his extramarital affair with mistress Elizabeth Blount. **November:** The town of Tournai, captured by the English during Henry VIII's first French invasion of 1513, was returned to France by the terms of the Treaty of London. **10 November:** Queen Katherine's final pregnancy ended in the birth of a frail princess, who died after three days.

1519 King Henry began his extramarital affair with mistress Mary Boleyn at some point during this year. Mary Boleyn was the elder sister of the king's future queen Anne Boleyn and later bore a son who may have been Henry VIII's bastard child. **Summer:** Mistress Elizabeth Blount gave birth to a bastard prince named Henry Fitzroy, the only illegitimate child King Henry ever acknowledged as his own. **28 June:** Despite attempts by King Henry of England and King François of France to claim the imperial throne for themselves, Charles V of Spain was elected Holy Roman Emperor instead.

1520 **Spring:** Cardinal Wolsey began preparing for a summer summit with the French king François I to take place near the English-held town of Calais in France. **26–29 May:** King Henry met for the first time with Emperor Charles V at Dover Castle to discuss a possible alliance against France. **7–24 June:** Henry VIII met with King François of France at the decorous Field of Cloth of Gold summit. A sumptuous prefabricated village (festooned with glittering cloth of gold) was erected to house thousands of courtiers and stage colorful ceremonies, lavish feasts, and competitive sporting events. Other than demonstrating the magnificence of the English and French kings and their courts, the conference itself achieved very little. **10–14 July:** Henry met again with Emperor Charles in Flanders to formalize their alliance and begin planning for an upcoming invasion of France.

1521 **May:** The *Assertio septem sacramentorum*, King Henry's defense of Rome's seven sacraments against the teachings of the German reformer Martin Luther, was completed, published, and submitted to Pope Leo X. **17 May:** Edward Stafford, the Duke of Buckingham, was beheaded for allegedly plotting against Henry VIII and Cardinal Wolsey. Wolsey probably fabricated the charges against Buckingham because he resented the way the arrogant duke had treated and insulted him. **10 October:** Pope Leo granted Henry the title "Defender of the Faith" for his *Assertio* treatise

that supported the sacramental doctrines of the Roman Church.

1522 **January–February:** Anne Boleyn, mistress Mary Boleyn's younger sister, returned from France to accept a place in Queen Katherine's household as a lady-in-waiting. **4 March:** Anne Boleyn made her first court appearance playing the part of Perseverance in a royal pageant entitled "Chateau Vert" at Cardinal Wolsey's York Place residence in London. **27 May:** Emperor Charles V arrived in Dover to complete arrangements with King Henry for their forthcoming joint invasion of France the following year. **19 June:** The Treaty of Windsor was signed to formalize England's alliance with the empire against France.

1523 **August–October:** Charles Brandon, the Duke of Suffolk, led an army of 10,000 men across the English Channel and advanced quickly on Paris, but an absence of the emperor's promised reinforcements and unusually stormy weather forced the duke's withdrawal, thus ending King Henry's second French invasion. **19 November:** Despite Cardinal Wolsey's repeated attempts to bribe his way onto the papal throne, the Medici cardinal Clement VII was elected pope instead.

1524 Anne Boleyn probably first attracted the amorous notice of King Henry at court at some point during this year, partly because his Spanish queen, Katherine of Aragon, was nearing (at age 39) the end of her childbearing years.

1525 **24 February:** Emperor Charles V decisively defeated a French army at the Battle of Pavia in Italy and took King François prisoner. Charles soon accepted the French ruler's promises of money and territory and released him, only to discover later that François's promises had been (predictably) insincere. **March:** Cardinal Wolsey imposed "amicable grants" on members of the English nobility and gentry to pay off war debts from the recent 1523 French invasion. **26 April:** King Henry suspended the amicable grant policy after riots of protest erupted across England.

16 June: Fearing that he might never sire a legitimate male heir, Henry VIII recognized his bastard son Henry Fitzroy and created him Duke of Richmond.

1526 Spring: William Tyndale's English translation of the New Testament began to arrive in England. Cardinal Wolsey condemned the vernacular Bibles as heretical and did his best to round up and destroy as many of the offending Scriptures as he could.

1527 April: In order to free him to marry again, Henry VIII sent scholars to the Continent in search of legal and scriptural precedents to annul the king's union with Queen Katherine of Aragon. **6 May:** Unpaid and hungry imperial troops sacked Rome while Emperor Charles was away in Spain. Pope Clement VII took refuge in the Castel Sant'Angelo outside Rome but remained a virtual prisoner of the emperor's army. **June:** Hearings began in England on the "Great Matter" to annul King Henry's marriage to Queen Katherine of Aragon. The case for annulment was based on Leviticus 20:21, an Old Testament passage that condemned unions between a man and his brother's widow as sinful.

1528 May–August: When the sweating sickness returned to London, King Henry sent Anne Boleyn away from court to safety at Hever Castle, her ancestral home in Kent. **29 September:** Lorenzo Cardinal Campeggio arrived in England to represent Pope Clement at the trial King Henry was planning to invalidate his marriage with Queen Katherine. Campeggio and Wolsey began gathering evidence to support the king's case for annulment. **November:** As the sweating sickness began to abate, King Henry recalled Anne Boleyn to London and then sent his increasingly resentful and estranged queen Katherine of Aragon away from court.

1529 31 May: Campeggio's and Wolsey's legatine (papally authorized) court met at Blackfriars' Abbey outside London to begin the Great Matter annulment trial. **18 June:** Queen Katherine of Aragon appealed her case

directly to Pope Clement in Rome to override the jurisdiction of the legatine court. **Autumn:** Recognizing the queen's right to appeal her case to the pope, Cardinal Campeggio adjourned the legatine court and returned to Rome. **26 October:** An angry and frustrated Henry VIII replaced Cardinal Wolsey as lord chancellor with Sir Thomas More. **30 October:** King Henry stripped Wolsey of all his administrative offices and estates and banished him from court.

1530 March: King Henry ordered Cardinal Wolsey to go to his northern archepiscopal diocese of York, a place the former lord chancellor had never even visited. **Summer:** Henry VIII granted the lawyer and former Wolsey secretary Thomas Cromwell a seat on his royal council. **29 November:** Recalled to London by Henry VIII to face probable treason charges, Cardinal Wolsey (probably) suffered a heart attack and died at the Abbey of St. Mary in Leicester at the age of just 55 years.

1532 18 March: The House of Commons petitioned King Henry in its "Supplication against the Ordinaries" to address popular grievances of corruption against the English clergy. **15 May:** In the "Submission of the Clergy," the English Convocation of Bishops agreed to pay a huge fine to the Crown and accepted Henry VIII as the "supreme lord of the Church as far as the law of Christ allows." **16 May:** Unable to live with his king's usurpation of church authority, Sir Thomas More surrendered his chain of office and resigned as lord chancellor of England. **23 August:** William Warham, the archbishop of Canterbury, died at the age of 82. **1 September:** Henry VIII made Anne Boleyn the Marquess of Pembroke in her own right, a rare gift of nobility for an unmarried woman. **December:** Probably as a show of gratitude for his gift, Anne Boleyn finally shared her bed with the king and was soon with child.

1533 26 January: King Henry secretly married Anne Boleyn at Whitehall Palace in order to legitimize the child she carried. **30 March:** Henry VIII named Thomas Cranmer, a reform-minded cleric and scholar, to become the next archbishop of Canterbury. **7 April:** Parliament passed the Act in Restraint of Appeals to divert appeals of church court cases from the pope in Rome to the archbishop of Canterbury. **23 May:** Archbishop Cranmer annulled King Henry's marriage to Katherine of Aragon at his Dunstable residence in Bedfordshire. **1 June:** King Henry formally married the unpopular Anne Boleyn and had Archbishop Cranmer crown her queen of England at Westminster Abbey. **25 June:** Mary Tudor, King Henry's youngest and favorite sister, died from the lingering effects of sweating sickness at the age of just 38 years. **7 September:** To her new royal husband's great disappointment, Queen Anne Boleyn gave birth not to his coveted male heir but instead to Princess Elizabeth at Greenwich Palace.

1534 24 March: Parliament passed the Act of Succession naming the children of King Henry and Queen Anne Boleyn as heirs to the English throne. All English subjects were required by the act to swear an oath acknowledging the new succession and denigrating the pope as the "bishop of Rome." **April:** Henry VIII appointed Thomas Cromwell to the post of personal royal secretary, thus effectively making him his chief minister. **17 April:** King Henry had Bishop John Fisher of Rochester and former lord chancellor Sir Thomas More arrested for refusing to swear the Oath of Succession. **26 September:** Pope Clement VII died, clearing the way for the election of Pope Paul III as his successor the following month. **3 November:** Parliament passed the Act of Supremacy naming King Henry the "supreme head of the Church of England" and granting him wide powers of ecclesiastical control. Like the Act of Succession, the Supremacy Act required an oath of acceptance and obedience from all English subjects. **Late November:** Parliament passed the Act of Treasons naming seditiously spoken words as traitorous offenses for the first time in English history.

1535 January: Cromwell launched the *Valor Ecclesiasticus* survey to assess and record the value of England's monasteries. The idea was to sell off their lands, buildings, and possessions and use the proceeds to replenish the royal treasury. **21 January:** Henry VIII named Thomas Cromwell his vicegerent in spirituals, an office that granted control over most Church of England affairs to the royal secretary and chief minister. **22 June:** Bishop John Fisher was beheaded at age 65 for refusing to acknowledge King Henry's supremacy over the Church of England. **6 July:** Not refusing but simply maintaining his silence, Sir Thomas More was also beheaded at age 57 for his failure to acknowledge King Henry's supremacy over the Church of England.

1536 7 January: Katherine of Aragon died at age 50, possibly from cancer, at Kimbolton House in Cambridgeshire. **24 January:** Henry VIII suffered a serious fall from his horse during a jousting tournament in the tiltyard at Greenwich Palace. He injured his legs and remained unconscious for several hours. When he awoke, the king had become more impatient, judgmental, and short-tempered than before, character traits that dominated his personality for the rest of his life. **29 January:** Queen Anne Boleyn's final pregnancy ended in a miscarriage. **11 March:** Thomas Cromwell ordered the smallest of England's monasteries dissolved and their lands and possessions confiscated to the Crown. **2–5 May:** Accused by her royal husband of marital infidelity and incest, Queen Anne Boleyn and several male courtiers were arrested and imprisoned in the Tower of London. **15 May:** Queen Anne Boleyn was convicted of treasonous adultery and was condemned to death in a court presided over by her uncle the Duke of Norfolk. **19 May:** Brought to England at her own request, a French swordsman beheaded Queen Anne Boleyn within the precincts of the Tower of London. **30 May:** King Henry married his third wife and consort, Jane Seymour, at Whitehall Palace. **July:** At Thomas Cromwell's urging, Convocation of English Bishops passed the Ten Articles of Faith to introduce more reformed doctrines into the Church of England. **2 July:** Henry VIII appointed Cromwell his lord privy seal, an important administrative officer with the power to certify royal summonses, writs, and grants.

22 July: Henry Fitzroy, the 16-year-old Duke of Richmond and King Henry's bastard son and heir presumptive, passed away, possibly from the effects of consumption. October: The Pilgrimage of Grace, an uprising against the Crown's religious reforms and dissolution of the monasteries, began in the English Midlands and northern shires under the leadership of a clothing merchant named Robert Aske.

1537 May: The Duke of Norfolk suppressed the Pilgrimage of Grace and arrested and jailed its principal leaders. 12 July: Robert Aske, the inspirational leader of the Pilgrimage of Grace, was slowly suffocated to death by hanging in chains from the keep of York Castle. 12 October: Queen Jane Seymour gave birth at Hampton Court Palace to Prince Edward Tudor, King Henry's long-awaited son and male heir. 24 October: Queen Jane Seymour died at Hampton Court Palace following complications from Prince Edward's birth. The king had her buried in a tomb in St. George's Chapel at Windsor Castle, where he himself would be laid to rest just 10 years later.

1538 Spring: The dissolution of England's medium-sized and larger monasteries continued. Eventually some 800 religious houses were closed, and the monks and nuns were given modest pensions to begin new lives in the secular world. September: The agents of Thomas Cromwell destroyed St. Thomas à Becket's shrine in Canterbury Cathedral as part of an effort to eliminate what reformers believed was "idol worship" in the Church of England.

1539 April: Thomas Cromwell sponsored publication of the Great Bible, translated into English by Miles Coverdale and John Rogers, and ordered its distribution to parish churches throughout the realm. 16 May: Annoyed by the steps Cromwell had taken to reform English religion, Henry VIII had Parliament pass the Act of Six Articles to restore certain Roman Catholic doctrines and practices to the Church of England.

1540 6 January: Talked into the match by Thomas Cromwell, King Henry married the German princess Anne of Cleves (whom he found repugnant) at Greenwich Palace. April: The closure of the largest and last of England's monasteries was completed, and the Crown seized their lands and goods. 10 June: Angry about his marriage to Anne of Cleves and feeling betrayed by Cromwell's reformation of his church, King Henry ordered his chief minister arrested and attainted of high treason. 8 July: King Henry had his marriage to Anne of Cleves invalidated on grounds of nonconsummation. 28 July: Thomas Cromwell was beheaded on Tower Hill as a traitor and heretic. On the same day, King Henry married his fifth wife and consort, the 19-year-old Katherine Howard, in a private ceremony at Oatlands Manor in Surrey.

1541 8 October: Margaret Tudor, queen dowager of Scotland and King Henry's sister, died near Perth in Scotland of a reported "palsy" at age 51. November: After hearing of her many alleged infidelities, Henry VIII had Queen Katherine Howard arrested along with several courtiers accused of having been her lovers. 10 December: Francis Dereham and Thomas Culpepper, two of Queen Katherine Howard's alleged lovers, suffered traitors' deaths at Tyburn.

1542 13 February: After practicing head placement on the executioner's block the preceding night, Queen Katherine Howard was beheaded within the precincts of the Tower of London. 24 October: Some 3,000 English border guards attacked and routed a large Scottish invasion force of 18,000 men at the Battle of Solway Moss. 14 December: Emotionally crushed by his army's defeat at Solway Moss, King James V of Scotland died of "melancholy," leaving the infant Mary Stuart as his royal successor.

1543 12 July: King Henry married his sixth and last queen, Katherine Parr, at Hampton Court Palace. August: Queen Katherine Parr engaged the religiously reform-minded Roger Ascham and John Cheke to tutor King Henry's younger children, Princess Elizabeth and Prince Edward.

1544 May: The depleted royal treasury was refilled by debasing the English coinage, a desperate financial act that in turn caused rampant inflation. **14 July:** Henry VIII appointed Queen Katherine Parr his regent to rule England during his upcoming invasion of France. **Late July:** King Henry led an English army of 40,000 men into northern France. **18 September:** After a lengthy siege, Henry VIII and his English troops occupied the fortified French stronghold of Boulogne. **30 September:** King Henry returned to England, leaving the Dukes of Suffolk and Norfolk with token forces to garrison and defend the captured town of Boulogne in France.

1545 20 July: King Henry watched from the shoreline as his prized battleship *Mary Rose* sank in Portsmouth Harbor sailing to its first engagement against the French. **22 August:** Charles Brandon, the Duke of Suffolk and King Henry's friend and brother-in-law, died after a prolonged illness at Guildford in Surrey and was buried in St. George's Chapel in Windsor Castle. **6 November:** Queen Katherine Parr published her devotional work *Lamentations of a Sinner*. **24 December:** Henry VIII, in his final speech to Parliament, called for religious unity in England and ordered both conservatives and reformers to stop their theological bickering.

1546 13 July: Having been accused by religious conservatives at court of Protestant "heresies," Queen Katherine Parr begged King Henry for clemency and was forgiven. **16 July:** Anne Askew, a former housewife and courageous evangelical believer, was burned at the stake in Smithfield outside London as a heretic. **November:** Suddenly turning against the religiously conservative faction at court, Henry VIII dismissed Bishop Stephen Gardiner of Winchester from his seat on the privy council. **12 December:** Thomas Howard and his son Henry, respectively the Duke of Norfolk and the Earl of Surrey, were accused of treason for displaying the royal arms on their family crest and were both imprisoned in the Tower of London.

1547 19 January: Henry Howard, the Earl of Surrey, was beheaded as a traitor on Tower Hill. **28 January:** King Henry VIII died at 2:00 a.m., aged 55 years, at Whitehall Palace. Because the king was now dead, Thomas Howard, the Duke of Norfolk, escaped execution by the automatic pardon of royal succession. **16 February:** King Henry's remains were laid to rest in a tomb beside the grave of Queen Jane Seymour in St. George's Chapel at Windsor Castle. **20 February:** Henry VIII's nine-year-old son and heir, Prince Edward Tudor, was crowned King Edward VI of England at Westminster Abbey.

Introduction

Henry VIII, king of England (born 1491, reigned 1509–47), is one of England's best-known rulers today, partly because of his six famous marriages and partly because of the religious revolution he precipitated as a result of one of those marriages. Most students of English history remember "Great Harry" as a larger-than-life monarch, an overweight, blustering, lusty, and arrogant fellow who cast a long, tyrannical, and sometimes bloody shadow over the age in which he lived. The reality of this king, however, differs somewhat from his popular image. Born the second son of a very insecure new monarch, Henry inherited a "hand-me-down" throne from his deceased older brother, Arthur, and married a "hand-me-down" wife, Katherine of Aragon, the widow his brother left behind at his premature death. Henry thus became king of England as an unintended replacement for Arthur and seems to have developed an unhealthy streak of personal insecurity as a result. He was by all accounts a skilled jouster, a graceful dancer, a learned humanist, a practiced musician, and a biblical scholar, but these talents were often obscured by a violent temper and a fragile ego that needed constant approbation. Henry VIII longed to achieve the same kind of military glory as had his namesake Henry V, but his repeated invasions of France over the course of three decades brought him nothing but unfulfilled hopes and an empty royal treasury. His desperate quest to ensure the Tudor succession only brought him a fair amount of matrimonial heartache, a sickly male heir, and two daughters he thought unworthy to rule. A conservative Roman Catholic most of his life, King Henry also presided over an evangelical (or Protestant) reformation he really never wanted but half-heartedly accepted in order to achieve his dynastic, financial, and geopolitical ends. However, despite the many personal disappointments Henry VIII suffered during his reign, the early Tudor era in the end proved transformative, as England emerged from the late-medieval "age of faith" to take its place in the intellectually curious and dynamic "light" of the European Renaissance.

Prince Henry Tudor was born on 28 June 1491 at Greenwich Palace to King Henry VII and Queen Elizabeth of York. Prince Henry had three siblings who lived to maturity, including his brother Arthur (b. 1486); his sister Margaret (b. 1489); and his youngest sister, Mary (b. 1496). The first Tudor king and his consort were well pleased with the birth and survival of these offspring, for their two sons represented heirs to carry on the Tudor dynasty, while their daughters would serve as diplomatic pawns to solidify alliances with other kingdoms.

Henry VII needed this royal brood as a kind of insurance policy because his legal and dynastic claims to the English throne were very weak indeed. In 1485, as Henry Tudor, Earl of Richmond, he defeated and killed the last Yorkist king, Richard III, at Bosworth Field and was proclaimed King Henry VII on the battlefield. Aware that his military victory did not legitimize his hold on power, however, the new Tudor king strengthened his thin royal pedigree and his sons' future claims to the English throne by marrying Richard III's niece,

Elizabeth of York, now his queen and the mother of his children. Thus Prince Henry, the future King Henry VIII, was born the second son of the new royal House of Tudor at a time when the realm of England was enjoying its first extended period of peace and stability since the onset of the Wars of the Roses some 36 years before.

The education that young Henry received befitted a Tudor prince who, as Henry VII's second son, was destined not for the English throne but for the archiepiscopal see of Canterbury, England's highest church office. Prince Henry, styled the Duke of York since his birth, began his study of Latin, the Vulgate Bible, and the works of classical Roman authors at around age five. He learned under the tutelage first of Bernard André, a blind humanist scholar, and then John Skelton, a poet and cleric who composed his *Speculum principis* as a moral guide for the young duke. Henry was also trained during these early years in music, riding, and the arts of warfare and the hunt, and by age 10, he had grown into a tall, athletic, and rather handsome youth.

Meanwhile, King Henry VII concluded an alliance with Spain that called for the marriage of Prince Arthur, the young Duke of York's older brother, to Katherine of Aragon, the youngest daughter of King Ferdinand and Queen Isabel of Spain. Princess Katherine arrived in England in October 1501 and was wed to Prince Arthur the following month, but the 15-year-old Tudor heir lived for only 199 more days before succumbing to what many modern scholars now believe was consumption, or today's tuberculosis. The somewhat sudden demise of his brother thus made the 11-year-old Henry the presumptive heir to the Tudor throne and bestowed upon him the title Prince of Wales to signify that honor. Henry VII also began at this time to consider remarrying Katherine of Aragon, the widow of Arthur, to his next surviving son, even though the dowager princess (as Katherine was now styled) was six years his senior. Because such a union was considered incestuous in the early 16th century, the elder Tudor was careful to obtain a dispensation from Pope Julius II to allow his remarriage scheme to move forward.

King Henry's plans were nearly scuttled, however, when the youthful Prince Henry formally recoiled from the prospect of marriage to Katherine in spring 1505. His objection to the match was ostensibly based on their difference in age, but many scholars now believe that King Henry VII was behind his son's truculent display on this occasion. By 1505, the aging Tudor ruler was busy negotiating a better alliance (and more useful marriage for Prince Henry) with officials of the Holy Roman Empire, so he needed his son to appear to have repudiated his proposed union with the dowager princess from Spain. Whatever the real reason for the delay, the royal wedding between Henry and Katherine of Aragon would eventually take place as originally planned shortly after the old king's death in 1509.

When King Henry VII breathed his last on 21 April 1509, his athletic, handsome, and well-educated 17-year-old heir succeeded him as King Henry VIII. In an attempt to win the instant and widespread approval of his subjects, the new king had lawyers Edmund Dudley and Richard Empson, his father's wildly unpopular royal officials, arrested just a few days after his accession to the throne. Dudley and Empson had attracted the ire of England's noble and gentry classes because Henry VII had employed them to collect "benevolences" and "recognizances," extortionate hostage payments meant to ensure loyalty and obedience to the Crown. The two men were tried for and convicted of treason in July 1509 and were publicly beheaded some 16 months later. King Henry also carried out his father's plan to "recycle" Katherine of Aragon within the Tudor family when he married her on 11 June 1509 at Greenwich Palace amid much royal splendor. The fact that Katherine was too closely related to Henry as his brother's widow was cast aside by the scriptural passage Deuteronomy 25:5, which called upon brothers to "take in" and care for their siblings' widows. When Queen Katherine was clearly with child by November 1509, all was right with King Henry's world, and the future of the House of Tudor seemed secure.

Hoping to glory in the same sort of military success as had his predecessor King Henry V, the new Tudor monarch began planning and preparing for an invasion of France only three years into his reign. When two poorly conceived raids on Brittany and Gascony met with disaster, the bellicose King Henry decided to lead an all-out campaign to conquer northern France himself and ordered his chief advisors Thomas Wolsey and Bishop Richard Fox of Winchester to recruit, equip, victual, and prepare transport for a large invasion force of some 40,000 men. The royal fleet set sail for the French coast in June 1513; by July, King Henry's army had captured the towns of Thérouanne and Tournai, and by August, he and his mounted escort had defeated a troop of French cavalry in a skirmish the king later dubbed the "Battle of the Spurs." No significant territorial or political gains resulted from this brief invasion, however, and so hostilities ended when Bishop Fox and Wolsey negotiated the Treaty of London with King Louis XII of France in 1514. If Henry VIII's hopes for military glory were thus left unfulfilled by this little war, its drain on his royal treasury squandered the large fortune his father had left him and set in motion the king's seemingly endless quest to replenish its resources.

While King Henry was away making war on France, he left Queen Katherine behind as his trusted regent to rule in his place, a duty she deftly executed while keeping her husband informed by letter of important developments at home. When King James IV of Scotland invaded England to take advantage of Henry's absence, she ordered Earl Thomas Howard of Surrey (the future second Duke of Norfolk) to halt the incursion, which he did with devastating effect (James IV was killed) at the battle of Flodden Field in August 1513. Queen Katherine was far less successful, however, when it came to providing her husband and the House of Tudor with a male heir. Between January 1510 and November 1518, Henry's Spanish queen was pregnant at least six (and probably more) times; a few pregnancies ended in miscarriages; some children were stillborn; two lived for a few days or weeks before dying; and one, Mary, survived to maturity. This inability to produce a male heir hung like a dark cloud over the royal couple and led to King Henry's increasing involvement in extramarital affairs as the 16th century passed from its second to its third decade.

The gregarious, flamboyant, and irrepressible Henry VIII loved to ride with the hunt, display his jousting prowess, and take part in masques and pageants, but he had little stomach for governmental detail and tedious paperwork and so turned these chores over to others as soon as he could find men competent enough to do the work. One such was the cleric Thomas Wolsey, the son of an Ipswich butcher and a brilliant Oxford graduate who served noble and episcopal masters as chaplain before entering Henry VIII's service as his royal almoner (distributor of charity) in 1509. Demonstrating tireless administrative abilities and thus freeing the king to enjoy more pleasurable pursuits, Wolsey was appointed to Henry's royal council in 1511 and then proved himself indispensable by overseeing all aspects of the king's massive 1513 invasion of France. When the war ended, a grateful Henry VIII rewarded his devoted servant with the title of lord chancellor, making him the king's chief minister, while in 1515, Pope Leo X elevated Wolsey to a seat on the papal curia by granting him a cardinal's hat. The ambitious cleric from Ipswich then set about empowering and enriching himself as few common-born Englishmen had ever done. By 1514, he was bishop of Tournai and Lincoln and archbishop of York, and he later acquired the lucrative episcopal sees of Durham and Winchester, along with the abbey of St. Alban's. Many of these church positions brought manor houses and even palaces to Wolsey, and he had his opulent new Hampton Court residence built outside London in a bid to project the kind of majesty his new Crown and church titles demanded. By 1520, foreign ambassadors and English courtiers alike had dubbed Wolsey the *alter rex*, the "other king," because his wealth and power rivaled even that of the king himself.

As King Henry's chief minister, Cardinal Wolsey clearly recognized his master's belligerent tendencies and wisely understood that further conflict with other European powers would only lead to economic disruption and an empty treasury. Believing that face-to-face meetings between the rulers of Europe's rival kingdoms might help avert such conflicts, Wolsey arranged for a summit between Henry and King François I of France during the summer of 1520. A neutral site was chosen for the meeting on the border of the pale (surrounding territory) of Calais, the English-held town in France, and preparations were begun to create a prefabricated village capable of accommodating thousands of attendees. Palaces, banquet halls, jousting lists, and guest tents were erected using imported bricks, lumber, and many different fabrics, including cloth of gold, so-called because of the tiny strands of hammered gold woven into more base materials like linen or wool. This extravagant textile gave its name to the summit—the Field of Cloth of Gold—that commenced on 7 June 1520 with the arrival of the English and French kings, along with their huge retinues of courtiers and servants and several thousand horses. Although Henry and François engaged for 16 days in carefully choreographed displays of manly friendship, little of substance was achieved, and when the Frenchman bested his English counterpart in a wrestling match, the summit came to an abrupt end. Within weeks of this showy meeting, King Henry met with Holy Roman Emperor Charles V to discuss their forthcoming joint invasion of France.

Henry VIII had always been a devoted son of the Roman Church, and by 1521, he was becoming increasingly offended by the reformed teachings of the German monk Martin Luther, whose movement of "protest" against the pope and his church was gaining momentum in northern Europe. Perhaps hoping to earn an appellation like "Catholic majesty" or "Christian king," which graced the titles of other European rulers, King Henry called on his own extensive scriptural knowledge and several learned English theologians to compose an attack on Luther's doctrine of the sacraments. This tract, entitled *Assertio septem sacramentorum*, or "The Assertion of the Seven Sacraments," defended the traditional seven sacraments of the Roman Church, denounced Luther's insistence on only two, and won for Henry the epithet "Defender of the Faith" from Pope Leo X. Scholars have debated ever since its 1521 appearance exactly how much of the *Assertio* was Henry's composition and how much may have been the work of advisors like Cardinal Wolsey, Thomas More, and Bishop John Fisher of Rochester. Regardless of the true identity of the treatise's author(s), however, it was the insecure king of England—as ever—who claimed the credit and the laudatory new title from the pope for himself.

Following the inconclusive Field of Cloth of Gold summit of 1520, King Henry rushed to forge a pact with Holy Roman Emperor Charles V for a coordinated attack on their mutual enemy France. The emperor arrived in England for an extended stay in May 1522, was lavishly fêted in Winchester and London, and then signed the Treaty of Windsor with Henry the next month that pledged reciprocal military assistance when their expected French campaign commenced. In summer and autumn 1522, King Henry sent Thomas Howard, the Earl of Surrey (and future third Duke of Norfolk), to raid the Breton coast and ravage Picardy with ships and ground troops, but disease forced the English invaders to withdraw to their Calais base. Charles Brandon, the Duke of Suffolk and Henry's close friend and brother-in-law, renewed the offensive the following year and advanced to within 60 miles of Paris, but no aid was forthcoming from the emperor, and Suffolk was forced to break off the campaign once more. When King Henry sent £20,000 to help fund a final imperial push into southern France in 1525—an assault that also failed—an empty English royal treasury persuaded the once-bellicose Tudor king to sue for peace. Cardinal Wolsey, charged with replenishing the royal coffers, demanded "amicable grants" (friendly monetary contributions) from the English nobility, gentry, and even some commoners, but this policy only incited riots in Kent and the Midlands and had to be abandoned. Thus did King Henry's second invasion of France end in both military futility and a desperate financial crisis for the Crown.

By the mid-1520s, Queen Katherine of Aragon had reached the age of 40, and having borne just one surviving child, the Princess Mary, Henry VIII's consort was unlikely at this point to conceive and bear any more children. This state of affairs greatly alarmed the king, for England had never been ruled in all her history by a queen regnant. Henry firmly believed that a son must be his royal successor, or else the House of Tudor (with its tenuous claim to the throne through Henry VII) might face another round of civil wars that could be disastrous for the kingdom and her people. In addition to his dynastic concerns, King Henry's roving eye had recently fallen on the sister of one of his mistresses, Anne Boleyn, a Kentish-born woman about half Queen Katherine's age who had just returned to England from service as a lady-in-waiting at the French court. The king had previously enjoyed an affair with Mary Boleyn in the early 1520s, but by 1525–26, he was increasingly captivated by the French fashions, manners, and accent of her sister Anne. When the younger Boleyn sister refused his advances and insisted that Henry wed her before he might bed her, the king saw an opportunity not only to satisfy his lust but also to sire the male heir he believed was essential to carry on the Tudor royal line. First, of course, he had to free himself from his first marriage to Queen Katherine, an enterprise that was to prove very complicated and frustrating and would end up altering the course of English history in the bargain.

Henry VIII's subsequent efforts to secure a "divorce" (actually, an annulment) from Katherine of Aragon in order to marry Anne Boleyn became known euphemistically across England and the rest of Europe as the king's "Great Matter." King Henry began this process by first trying to invalidate his marriage with his Spanish queen. Attempting to override the biblical verse that had allowed them to wed in the first place, the king found a contradictory passage, Leviticus 20:21, that condemned unions between brothers and sisters-in-law as "unclean" and "barren." Henry next enlisted the aid of his chief minister Cardinal Wolsey, who, as a member of the papal curia, was in a position to persuade Pope Clement VII to annul the English royal marriage from Rome. Wolsey was prevented from attempting this diplomatic overture, however, when the unpaid imperial army of Charles V sacked Rome

and handed the pope over to the emperor, who, as Katherine of Aragon's nephew, now blocked any chance for a papal annulment. Two years passed, and with Pope Clement finally free from the emperor's custody, Wolsey convinced him to send his envoy, Lorenzo Cardinal Campeggio, to England to try King Henry's marriage-annulment case. Wolsey and Campeggio heard testimony on the Great Matter through the summer of 1529, but when Queen Katherine threatened to appeal her case to Pope Clement himself, Campeggio ended the trial and made preparations to return to Rome. An outraged King Henry then turned on his once-trusted chief minister and, banishing him from court, was likely preparing treason charges against him when Wolsey died in Leicester in November 1530.

Now more desperate than ever to set aside his Spanish queen, Henry VIII sent English scholars to universities across Europe in search of legal precedents to justify his case for annulment. He also bullied the House of Commons in Parliament and the Southern Convocation of Bishops into passage of the Supplication of the Ordinaries and the Submission of the Clergy, both measures that distanced the English Church from Rome and granted new powers of ecclesiastical control to King Henry. Meanwhile, Anne Boleyn must have surrendered herself to the king near the end of 1532, for she turned up pregnant in January 1533. Her condition both surprised and delighted Henry, who hastily arranged for a secret wedding at Whitehall Palace to ensure the legitimacy of their unborn child. These events now launched a rush of activity on the part of the king and his new chief advisor, Thomas Cromwell, to secure the desired royal annulment and, in the end, to separate England completely from the Roman Church once and for all.

Thus did the Henrician Reformation begin, not as a theological dispute with the Holy See and its pope, but as a strategic policy to sidestep papal authority and allow the king of England to achieve his dynastic and matrimonial ends. Shortly after his secret marriage to Anne, Henry VIII appointed the religious reformer Thomas Cranmer as his new archbishop of Canterbury. He then had Thomas Cromwell persuade Parliament in April 1533 to pass the Act in Restraint of Appeals, which redirected all religious appellate cases from the pope to Cranmer. Finally, he submitted his annulment case to his new archbishop, who dutifully pronounced in the king's favor in May 1533. With his first wife and queen now discarded, Henry publicly married Anne Boleyn and had her crowned queen of England in June 1533. His disappointment was profound, however, when in September of that year his new consort presented him not with the son he had hoped for but with a daughter, the Princess Elizabeth.

This setback notwithstanding, Henry VIII now sought to complete his kingdom's break with the Roman Church, a schism that had begun as a by-product of his celebrated Great Matter. With Thomas Cromwell guiding the way, Parliament passed the Act of Succession in March 1534 to name the children of Henry and Anne as heirs to the throne, and quickly added the Act to Punish Heresy to give the Crown control over matters of religious doctrine. In November 1534, Parliament made the split with Rome permanent by passing the Act of Supremacy, which named Henry VIII as the "supreme head of the Church of England." The Henrician Reformation did not end with these statutes, however. In 1535, the king made Cromwell his vicegerent-in-spirituals, an office that granted him de facto control over matters of doctrine and practice in the English Church. After prevailing upon Convocation of Bishops to approve his mostly reformed Ten Articles of Faith, Cromwell began to close and sell off all the monasteries in England (to replenish the royal treasury) and then introduced an English translation of the Bible (called the Great Bible) into every parish church in the land.

These religious changes were generally accepted quietly, and at times even eagerly, by a population of English believers who were quite fed up with the greed, corruption, and arrogance of the Roman clergy and their popes. Some stubbornly loyal defenders of the Catholic Church, such as Sir Thomas More, the former lord chancellor, and Bishop John Fisher of Rochester, the trusted confessor of the king's grandmother Lady Margaret Beaufort, attempted to resist Henry VIII's break with

Rome and paid for their intransigence with their lives. Small groups of Carthusian and Benedictine monks from across England also refused to recognize the royal supremacy and were hanged, drawn, and quartered as traitors for their "crimes" against the Crown. In addition, a great popular movement known as the "Pilgrimage of Grace" erupted in the Midlands in 1536–37 to protest the closing of the monasteries and the introduction of Cromwell's Ten Articles, but this revolt was savagely suppressed as well, and its leaders similarly put to death as traitors. Despite such sporadic instances of dissent, however, only 329 men and a few women perished as "martyrs" to the Henrician Reformation, a remarkably small number for a kingdom with a population of some 3,500,000 souls by 1535.

As this religious transformation was taking place, the king's marriage to Anne Boleyn was beginning to unravel. Her next two pregnancies ended in miscarriages, while her nagging of her philandering husband and the plots of her enemies at court to see her undone all began to erode Henry's love for his second consort. In May 1536, Queen Anne was convicted of having carried on romantic affairs with courtiers and even her own brother, George, and was beheaded as a traitor, thus freeing the king to wed his new lady-love, Jane Seymour, just 11 days later. It was the demure, charming, and acquiescent Jane who finally gave Henry what he had wrecked two marriages and rejected the Roman Church to achieve: a male heir to carry on the Tudor royal line. The queen Henry VIII claimed he loved best, however, became gravely ill and then died just two weeks after giving birth to Prince Edward in October 1537. Thomas Cromwell next convinced the king to marry the daughter of a Lutheran prince, Anne of Cleves, but Henry found the buxom German so unattractive he never consummated their union and then divorced her six months later. His fifth wife was a pretty teen named Katherine Howard, whose numerous affairs with various men at court led to her execution on the block just 19 months after Henry wed her. His sixth and last wife, Katherine Parr, was a learned, pious, and twice-widowed woman of 31 years who served King Henry in his declining years as a companion and nurse-maid. Like Anne Boleyn, Katherine Parr sympathized with the Protestant movement on the Continent and made sure that at least two of Henry's royal children, Edward and Elizabeth, were educated in the reformed faith. She survived the death of the old king in 1547 and then married her former suitor Thomas Seymour, the brother of Queen Jane, only to die in childbirth in September 1548 at age 36.

By the late 1530s, King Henry was no longer the jaunty, athletic, and handsome man he had been at his accession in 1509. Early in 1536, he suffered a serious jousting accident that left him comatose for several hours, and although he recovered, his legs were permanently damaged, and his usually jovial demeanor turned angry and cruel. By the time he reached age 50, Henry was obese from constant feasting and too little exercise, and he had contracted syphilis, gout, and a host of other maladies that presented as ulcerated sores, a foul odor, and a vicious temper. Because he blamed his chief minister for the disastrous match with Anne of Cleves, the king became distrustful of Thomas Cromwell and began to back away from his counsels by 1540. In addition, Henry had since childhood always embraced the basic tenets of the Roman faith—if not its pope or monasteries—and he had not realized how reformed (Lutheran) the Church of England had lately become under his vicegerent's guidance. Encouraged by Cromwell's court enemies Bishop Stephen Gardiner of Winchester and Thomas Howard, Duke of Norfolk, the king turned on his chief minister, had him convicted of treason and heresy, and ordered him beheaded in July 1540.

Henry VIII effectively become his own chief minister and vicegerent-in-spirituals during the final seven years of his reign and led a religious backlash in the Church of England that restored many of the key doctrines and sacraments of the old Roman Church. The 1539 Act of Six Articles, dubbed the "whip with six strings" by its Protestant critics, brought back the Catholic teachings on transubstantiation, auricular confession, clerical celibacy, and private masses and added savage new heresy penalties to help enforce the changes.

In 1543, Henry authorized publication of the *King's Book*, which reaffirmed the seven sacraments, masses for the dead, and salvation by good-works doctrines of the old religion. Perhaps seeking to weaken her influence with the king, Gardiner and Norfolk actually threatened heresy charges against the reform-minded Katherine Parr, but the queen wisely threw herself on Henry's mercy, and he chose to forgive rather than behead his last wife. He did, however, have six individuals—three reformers and three Catholic priests—executed in 1540 for transgressions against the newest version of the English Church. Clearly the supreme head of that church was as confused about religious truth at this time as were the believers over whom he ruled.

In truth, King Henry regretted the discord his reformation had unleashed among the various religious factions in his kingdom and urged his subjects to cease their quarrelling and try to find common theological ground. In a 1545 speech to the House of Commons, the king scolded his evangelical and conservative listeners and, accusing them of engaging in euphemistic "mumpsimus and sumpsimus" debates, warned them to resolve their doctrinal differences or risk his unrestrained wrath.

In addition to his insistence on English religious unity, Henry VIII had never given up on his dream to conquer France by the 1540s, despite his advancing age, failing health, and lack of financial resources. A massive Scottish raid temporarily distracted Henry from his latest French adventure, but a much smaller English force met and completely routed the Scots on 24 November 1542 at Solway Moss. When a depressed James V of Scotland died from a fever just three weeks after the battle, the English king was now free to organize his French campaign and soon signed another pact with Emperor Charles V for a joint military action against their mutual enemy. An English invasion force numbering some 30,000 men under the Duke of Norfolk advanced from Calais in spring 1544 to besiege the town of Monteuil, but bad weather and stout French resistance thwarted this initial thrust. Then King Henry himself arrived in France to lead an assault on Boulogne, which finally fell several months later but at great cost in English lives and treasure. When Emperor Charles halted his own invasion from Flanders and made a separate peace with the French, the king of England was forced to abandon his own operations and returned to London with the bulk of his army at the end of 1544. Although Boulogne remained in English hands until 1550 (when it was returned to France by treaty), Henry VIII's third French invasion ended with the same lack of military success and great expense as had his first two such campaigns.

By 1545, it was becoming apparent to most observers at the English court that Great Harry, the mighty monarch who had ruled England for nearly four decades, was nearing the end of his life. In a frantic bid to replenish his finances once again, the ailing king resorted to the ill-advised policy of currency debasement, or the cutting of silver coins with base alloys, a practice that temporarily increased the Crown's cash flow but also ignited a state of hyperinflation soon thereafter. Meanwhile King Henry, probably embittered by his obesity and many painful diseases, had Thomas Howard, the Duke of Norfolk, and his son, the Earl of Surrey, arrested in 1546 on charges of treason for displaying the royal insignia on their family crest. Surrey was beheaded in mid-January 1547, leaving his father, Norfolk, to await the same fate in the Tower of London.

The execution of the senior Howard never came to pass, however, because at age 55, King Henry VIII breathed his last on 28 January 1547, thus granting Norfolk the customary pardon of the royal succession. Henry's massive corpse was embalmed and lay in state in Westminster for 10 days and was then borne on an enormous hearse in a lavish procession to Windsor Castle. There, the king's remains were interred in the chapel of St. George, next to the grave of Queen Jane Seymour, on 14 February 1547. King Henry's death left England in the impressionable and inexperienced hands of his nine-year-old son and heir, Edward VI, whose brief reign soon began under the watchful eye of his uncle and lord protector Edward Seymour, the Earl of Hertford and soon-to-be Duke of Somerset.

It is probably fair to say that future generations will recall both the positive achievements and the disruptive, sometimes dangerous, and even bloody moments of his reign when assessing the legacies of King Henry VIII. The second Tudor king of England was physically imposing and multitalented, but he was emotionally insecure and unabashedly narcissistic at the same time. Because his father's claim to the English throne was so tenuous, the son launched a desperate quest to provide the Tudor succession with a male heir, a process that ultimately destroyed his first two marriages and ignited the historic break with Rome. When one considers the many wasteful wars, suppressed revolts, and executed enemies and rivals to his throne, the number of English subjects who perished under the hand of Henry VIII during his reign can likely be counted in the tens of thousands.

And yet, the bellicose, colorful, and devil-may-care Tudor king also presided over an age that bequeathed several important innovations to England and to the English-speaking world. For example, King Henry's second chief minister, Thomas Cromwell, streamlined the clumsy royal council by paring down its numbers to create a more efficient privy council of 12–15 members. Cromwell also initiated the kingdom's first census by ordering the recording of births, marriages, and deaths in English parishes, and he pioneered the use of parliamentary statutes to ensure popular support for his more radical religious and political programs. Perhaps most significantly, King Henry and Thomas Cromwell together engineered the rejection of the Roman Church and the establishment in its place of the Church of England, a moderate "middle-way" form of Protestantism that in turn spawned the Baptist, Methodist, and Episcopal denominations a few centuries later. Despite the fame that his six marriages and able chief ministers have garnered over the years, the most permanent and influential legacy of Great Harry will always be the Church of England that, almost by accident, was born as an unintended consequence of the king's need for a male successor to carry on the royal House of Tudor.

The Dictionary

ACT IN RESTRAINT OF APPEALS (1533).

This was a **parliamentary** statute passed in early April 1533 at the behest of Henry VIII and his chief minister, **Thomas Cromwell**, during the early stages of the **Henrician Reformation**. This act overturned the long-held right of King Henry's subjects to appeal cases previously decided in English ecclesiastical courts to the jurisdiction of a higher papal court in Rome. The act also offered in its preamble the earliest description of England as an "empire," a device inserted by Cromwell to enhance the authority of his royal master in the British Isles and even in France. Most significantly, it cleared the way for the newly installed archbishop of Canterbury, **Thomas Cranmer**, to annul King Henry's marriage to Queen **Katherine of Aragon** without further obstruction from the pope.

The need for a way to cut off appeals of church court cases to Rome first arose in 1529 from a hearing in England to determine the validity of Henry VIII's matrimonial union with his first queen. During the trial, as **Lorenzo Cardinal Campeggio** (the pope's emissary) and **Thomas Cardinal Wolsey** heard evidence from Henry's canon lawyers, Queen Katherine suddenly demanded that her case be transferred to Rome for adjudication by Pope **Clement VII** himself. King Henry was outraged, but Cardinal Campeggio acknowledged the Spanish queen's right to appeal her case to the pope and then declared an abrupt end to the trial proceedings. His action effectively delayed resolution of King Henry's "**Great Matter**" for several years and impressed Wolsey's then

secretary Thomas Cromwell that the time had come to renounce papal authority in England once and for all.

When King Henry bigamously wed his second wife, **Anne Boleyn**, in January 1533, the need to bypass the pope to annul his first marriage became ever more urgent. Thomas Cromwell, by this time a royal secretary, began drafting a bill in winter and spring 1533 to end ecclesiastical court appeals to Rome and then asked civil and canon lawyers and the king himself to review its text. Realizing the potential propaganda value of the bill, Cromwell first insisted in its preamble that the dominions of Henry VIII—England, **Wales**, **Calais**, and **Ireland**—formed a far greater political entity than just a single kingdom. His draft bill proclaimed, "[T]his realm of England is an empire, . . . governed by one supreme head and king having the dignity and royal estate of the imperial crown."

With this founding principle in place, Cromwell's bill went on to restrict much of the Roman pontiff's authority in England and then reserved the right of episcopal appointment to the English monarchy alone. Most importantly, the bill stipulated that final appellate jurisdiction over ecclesiastical matters in England would henceforth revert to the archbishop of Canterbury, who, since March 1533, was the evangelical reformer Thomas Cranmer. After Parliament passed the Act in Restraint of Appeals early in April 1533, Archbishop Cranmer withdrew to his Dunstable estate, where he duly annulled the king's first marriage and validated his second union with Anne Boleyn one month later.

ACT OF SIX ARTICLES (1539). This **parliamentary** statute, officially entitled "An Act Abolishing Diversity in Opinions," essentially closed the door on evangelical reform in the Church of England and inaugurated in its place the reactionary final phase of the **Henrician Reformation.** By the late 1530s, Henry VIII was growing weary of the ceaseless theological bickering between rival religious factions in England and thought to silence the debates and unify believers by better defining certain points of doctrinal contention in the English Church. Instead of entrusting this task to **Thomas Cromwell,** his vicegerent in spirituals (chief church administrator) since 1535, the king turned to more conservative individuals at court to help him carry out his program of religious revision. The resulting Six Articles of Faith restored many of the old Roman teachings, brought back the draconian heresy laws, and initiated a conservative theological retrenchment in England that lasted for the remainder of Henry VIII's life.

By late 1538, it appeared that the forces of Roman Catholicism in Europe might soon unite to isolate and perhaps even invade England as a renegade heretic kingdom. At the urging of Pope **Paul III,** the representatives of **François I** of France and Emperor **Charles V** signed the Treaty of Toledo in January 1539, a pact requiring both rulers to dissolve their diplomatic and commercial contacts with England. King Henry genuinely feared an imminent invasion at this point and spent lavishly on coastal fortifications and warship construction to strengthen his kingdom's defenses. Meanwhile Thomas Cromwell, having done his best since 1535 to introduce Lutheranism into the English Church, advised his Tudor master to seek an alliance with the Protestant princes of Germany to counter the Catholic threat from abroad. A German delegation duly arrived in April 1539 to negotiate the treaty, but after they insisted that Henry VIII fully reform his church along Lutheran lines, the still-conservative English king flatly refused and sent the foreign envoys packing a few weeks later. While Cromwell continued to pursue a Protestant alliance, King Henry thought he might better discourage a Franco-imperial invasion by simply restoring many of the old teachings and practices of Rome to the English Church instead.

Accordingly, he ordered Cromwell to clarify and even rework some of the more ambiguous points of evangelical theology that had emerged in England since passage of the **Ten Articles of Faith** by **Convocation of Bishops** in 1536. The vicegerent in spirituals at first promised to obey but then procrastinated, prompting an exasperated Henry VIII to hand the task of doctrinal revision over instead to Bishop **Stephen Gardiner** of Winchester and his more conservative supporters at court. Gardiner devised six topics of religious inquiry and had his "old church" ally **Thomas Howard,** the third Duke of Norfolk, submit them in May 1539 to Parliament for its consideration. With King Henry often in attendance, the House of Lords debated Gardiner's six questions about eucharistic real presence, communion in both kinds, the need for chastity and/or celibacy among the **clergy,** and the validity of private masses and auricular confession under divine law. Discussions between the reformist and conservative factions in Parliament were lively, heated, and frequently vitriolic, but with undoubted pressure from the king of England himself, the Act Abolishing Diversity in Opinions became law in June 1539.

Commonly called the Act of Six Articles (or the "Whip with Six Strings" by its evangelical detractors), this statute enjoyed the backing of England's representative Parliament and so superseded the more Lutheran Ten Articles that had been approved by Convocation of English Bishops in 1536. Cromwell's dream of fully reforming the Church of England was now dead, and although he continued to work toward a German Protestant alliance, the marriage of Henry VIII to **Anne of Cleves** he arranged to forge that agreement backfired and led instead to his downfall and execution in 1540. From the summer of 1539 onward, the religiously conservative party of Gardiner and Norfolk ruled supreme at court. They convinced King Henry to reinstate the old 15th-century heresy statutes, yet despite the nearly 500 evangelical believers rounded up and interrogated under these harsh laws, only 6 brave souls eventually suffered death at the stake for their faith when all was said and done. When Henry VIII breathed his last late in January 1547, his more radically reform-minded successor **Edward VI** had the Six Articles repealed early in his reign to launch a new phase of Lutheran and, later, even Calvinist reformation in the Church of England.

ACT OF SUCCESSION (1534). This **parliamentary** statute settled the royal succession on the heirs of King Henry VIII and Queen **Anne Boleyn** and made refusal to acknowledge the new line of succession an act of treason. In addition, the Act of Succession further weakened the authority of the pope in England and helped prepare the ground for King Henry's final break with Rome later the same year. Concerned that some might not accept his new queen or their children's royal claims, the king insisted that all his subjects swear an oath to acknowledge the provisions of the succession statute. Most English men and women complied and took the oath, but the few who resisted often ended up in prison or died on the block as traitors. When Henry VIII remarried after Anne Boleyn's fall and execution in 1536, he had Parliament replace the earlier succession law with another naming his children with **Jane Seymour** as his newly designated royal heirs.

The anxiety King Henry felt about the Tudor succession stretched back to the 15th-century **Wars of the Roses**, which were fought to determine whether the Houses of York or Lancaster possessed the strongest claim to the English throne. The first Tudor ruler, **Henry VII**, fathered a brood of royal offspring to secure the succession for his own descendants, but his son Henry VIII had managed by the mid-1520s to produce just one daughter, the Princess **Mary** Tudor, with his Spanish queen **Katherine of Aragon**. Because a queen regnant had never ruled in England before, the second Tudor king feared that if Mary remained his sole royal heir, her claim to the throne might be challenged and another bloody civil war might erupt again. Although Henry did have an illegitimate son named **Henry Fitzroy** by this time, he knew that his family's right to

wear the English Crown would never be secure until he sired a true Tudor prince within the bounds of lawful matrimony.

The opportunity to do just that arose in the mid-1520s, when the king became infatuated with Anne Boleyn, one of Queen Katherine's attending ladies. Initially pursuing her as a possible mistress, Henry soon realized that she might bear him his coveted male heir if he could only free himself from his first wife to marry Anne in her place. Accordingly, King Henry ordered his lord chancellor **Thomas Cardinal Wolsey** to seek an annulment of his marriage with Queen Katherine from Pope **Clement VII**. When the Roman pontiff refused to grant Henry's request—he was at the time a virtual prisoner of Emperor **Charles V**, Queen Katherine's nephew—the English king dismissed and exiled Wolsey and then began to explore other ways to achieve his ends.

Still disgusted with the pope and his church a few years later, Henry VIII bullied his bishops into accepting his ecclesiastical lordship in England with the **Submission of the Clergy** in 1532. When Mistress Boleyn was found to be with child early in 1533, the need to set Queen Katherine aside suddenly became much more urgent. Acting quickly, King Henry secretly married Anne and then had his new chief minister, **Thomas Cromwell**, push the **Act in Restraint of Appeals** through Parliament to transfer matrimonial annulment authority from Rome to the archbishop of Canterbury. After filling this vacant office with the reform-minded **Thomas Cranmer**, the king prevailed on his new archbishop to invalidate his first marriage in May 1533 so he could openly and formally wed (and then crown) his second queen the following month. The king was deeply disappointed, however, when Anne did not produce a son but instead gave birth to the Princess **Elizabeth** in September 1533.

Although a baby girl was not the heir he desired, Henry was well aware that most of his subjects were still loyal to his discarded Spanish wife and her daughter, Mary, while they roundly detested the upstart Boleyn woman, who had now taken Queen Katherine's place. Sensing the need to enforce recognition of his new consort and their infant daughter, Henry VIII ordered Cromwell to bring a succession bill to the House of Commons for that body's consideration in March 1534. This long, rambling document declared Anne Boleyn to be the "most dear and entirely beloved lawful wife" of the king and named their "lawful children" as the rightful heirs of "this imperial crown of the realm." The bill further demoted Katherine of Aragon to the lesser title of dowager princess—in effect, the widow of King Henry's brother **Arthur** Tudor—and relegated her teenaged daughter, Mary, to the status of royal bastard. Styling the pope "bishop of Rome," the bill also denounced the ecclesiastical powers the pontiff had formerly exercised in England as "contrary to the great . . . grants of jurisdiction given by God immediately to emperors, kings and princes" in their own domains.

Most ominously, all subjects of Henry VIII were now to "make a corporal oath . . . to observe, fulfill, maintain [and] defend . . . the whole effects and contents of this present act . . . [or] be taken and accepted for offender . . . of high treason." Composed by Lord Chancellor **Thomas Audley** and the Dukes of Norfolk and Suffolk, this final clause was meant to enforce obedience to the statute by threatening those who resisted its oath with treason. After the Act of Succession was passed into law by Parliament on 23 March 1534, Crown agents went forth across the kingdom to read its provisions aloud and administer its required oath to one and all. Bishop **John Fisher** of Rochester outright refused the oath and was subsequently arrested, tried for treason, and executed in June 1535. Ready enough to accept the new line of succession, Sir **Thomas More** could not endorse the act's diminution of papal authority in England and, maintaining his silence when asked to take the oath, was also eventually arrested and put to death as a traitor. When Queen Anne Boleyn herself fell afoul of her royal husband and followed Fisher and More to her death in May 1536, King Henry had another legal instrument passed to replace Princess Elizabeth in the Tudor line of succession with the son he hoped his third queen, Jane Seymour, would soon give him.

ACT OF SUPREMACY (1534). This important statute of **Parliament** completed the separation of the English Church from Rome and replaced the pope with King Henry VIII as the "supreme head" of all Christian believers and religious institutions in England. Formally entitled "An Act Concerning the King's Highness to Be Supreme Head of the Church of England and to Have Authority to Reform and Redress All Errors, Heresies and Abuses in the Same," this revolutionary directive confirmed the king's sovereignty over the English **clergy** and granted him the power to determine orthodox doctrine and enact canon laws within his church and his kingdom. In addition, the act passed the title of supreme head along to King Henry's successors and appropriated control over the vast wealth of the English Church to the Crown. All of this was done, the statute concluded, to ensure the "pleasure of Almighty God, the increase of virtue in Christ's religion, and the peace, unity and tranquility of this realm." Although it ran to just 307 words in length, this short but mighty law became one of the most significant legal instruments ever enacted by Parliament in the constitutional history of England.

By the mid-1520s, **Katherine of Aragon** had failed to give Henry VIII a male heir, and because he was by then infatuated with **Anne Boleyn**, the king began to seek a way to set aside his first queen so he might wed and then sire a prince with his younger new paramour. All efforts by Henry and his lord chancellor **Thomas Cardinal Wolsey** to achieve these ends came to nothing, however, causing the king to explode in anger and send his chief minister away to his death in 1529–30. Still resentful a few months after Wolsey's demise, King Henry launched a campaign to tighten his control over the English clergy, replenish his royal treasury, and restrict the power of the pope all at the same time. In January 1531, he levied an enormous fine of £100,000 on the Southern **Convocation of Bishops** for having violated an old 14th-century statute and accepted Wolsey as the pope's representative in England. The Tudor king also ordered the assembled bishops to recognize him as the "sole protector and supreme head of the

English Church," a device they only approved 16 months later after inserting the qualifying phrase "as far as the law of Christ allows." Although this 1532 **Submission of the Clergy** thus initiated the separation of the English Church from Rome, a few more years and further matrimonial, political, and ecclesiastical maneuvers were still required before it could be fully achieved.

By this time, Mistress Anne had finally allowed Henry into her bed and was soon pregnant, so the king bigamously married her in a secret ceremony in January 1533 to ensure the legitimacy of the royal child she carried. Henry VIII's new chief minister, **Thomas Cromwell**, meanwhile oversaw passage in Parliament of the **Act in Restraint of Appeals**, which transferred ecclesiastical appellate jurisdiction from the pope in Rome to the English archbishop of Canterbury. When the king appointed the reform-minded **Thomas Cranmer** to the vacant See of Canterbury in March 1533, the new archbishop obligingly annulled Henry's first marriage and validated his second secret union with Anne Boleyn just two months later. Then, during the summer and autumn of 1533, Henry VIII formally married and crowned his new consort, Pope **Clement VII** excommunicated the English king, and Queen Anne gave birth to a daughter named **Elizabeth**. The **Act of Succession** that followed in March 1534 not only required an oath of allegiance to the heirs of King Henry and his second queen, but it also denounced the authority that the "bishop of Rome" had in times past exercised in England. Thus, the stage was set for the final break of the Tudor king and the English Church from the ecclesiastical dominion of Rome and its pontiff.

Because the English bishops had already recognized the king as the leader of their church and most papal powers in King Henry's realm had now been swept aside, little remained except to formalize the reality of England's split from Rome in statute law. Thomas Cromwell, ever the parliamentary manager, began drafting a supremacy bill in summer and autumn 1534 that he then submitted to the House of Commons for its consideration when that body next met. Getting right to the point, the bill initially insisted that "King's Majesty justly and rightfully is . . . the supreme head of the Church of England," thus simply confirming this title as an established fact and deliberately dropping the phrase "as far as the law of Christ allows" from the episcopal submission of 1532.

In addition, the supremacy bill acknowledged the king's right to "repress . . . and amend" all theological deviance in the land and transferred the "profits and commodities" of the *Anglicana Ecclesia* to the Crown. As if to sever any remaining ties to Rome, the bill finally invalidated all "foreign laws [and] foreign authority" that threatened the independent dominion of the English Church and its supreme head. After Parliament passed the bill into law in November 1534, Cromwell had it published and widely disseminated with an addendum requiring oaths of assent from all of King Henry's subjects. The enactment of the Act of Supremacy marked the final separation of the English Church from Roman obedience and formally launched the religious revolution that came to be known as the **Henrician Reformation**.

ACT OF TREASONS (1534). This statute of **Parliament** added spoken words for the first time as a traitorous offense to the English law of treason that formerly had included only seditious activities against the Crown. The need for such an addition surfaced during the trial of **Elizabeth Barton**, the so-called Holy Maid of Kent, who had publicly prophesied the king's death but had otherwise never undertaken any form of subversive action. **Thomas Cromwell**, Henry VIII's secretary and chief minister, eventually resorted to a rare act of attainder to convict and execute Barton, prompting him to introduce and guide this revised treason bill through the House of Commons just seven months after her death. The "spoken words" clause of the 1534 treason law was considered draconian and needlessly harsh by the royal councilors of King Henry's successor **Edward VI** and so was repealed by his government shortly after the young king's accession in 1547.

The most important piece of treason legislation in the constitutional history of England was that enacted under Edward III in 1352. Because King Edward faced few threats of revolt and his regime was so stable, his treason law limited rather than broadened the statutory definition of traitorous activity. Six specific provisions confined treason to imagining the king's death, violating the queen or a princess, counterfeiting the royal coinage or seal, waging war against the king, joining the king's enemies, and murdering royal ministers. All these forms of treason required that some act or deed be committed and were punishable by death and confiscation of property. The act failed, however, to mention conspiracies against the Crown, plots to incite revolts, or the use of inflammatory speech to threaten the monarchy.

Between the 14th-century and the Tudor era, the original treason statute was applied more flexibly at times, as the kingdom struggled through periods of revolt, civil war, and dynastic change. A revised act of 1397 conveniently omitted the traitorous "action" requirement, while later Lancastrian rulers simply interpreted the 1352 phrase "imagine the king's death" to include verbal expressions of treason. The **Wars of the Roses** saw the clause "accroaching the king's power" used to indicate the spread of hatred for the king through provocative speech. Still, by the accession of King Henry VIII in 1509, there existed no formal parliamentary statute—by this time recognized as the "law of the land"—that specifically named threatening remarks as treason.

Under the English **judiciary**, accused traitors were ordinarily tried before the Court of King's Bench or the local assizes (circuit courts), but commissions of oyer and terminer could be issued to round up and try the leaders of popular revolts or public disturbances. **Nobles** enjoyed the privilege of trial by their peers, usually a court made up of royal councilors or members of the House of Lords. If all else failed, the Crown could seek a parliamentary act of attainder against its enemies. Attainders carried charges of treason to validate the confiscation of property from landed rebels and so were most often called on when dynasties changed or civil wars ended.

The legal case that prompted Henry VIII's chief minister to rush a revised treason law through Parliament late in 1534 involved a young serving-class nun named Elizabeth Barton, who claimed to have visions foretelling King Henry's doom if he set aside Queen **Katherine of Aragon** in order to wed **Anne Boleyn**. Widely known as the "Holy Maid of Kent" or the "Nun of Canterbury," Barton's visionary piety attracted a large commonfolk following along with such important dignitaries as Bishop **John Fisher** of Rochester and Gertrude **Courtenay**, the Marchioness of Exeter. Curious, even such notable figures as Sir **Thomas More**, **Thomas Cardinal Wolsey**, Archbishop **William Warham**, and King Henry VIII himself all interviewed her at least once. After three volumes of the Holy Maid's most damning and subversive prophecies appeared in print, Cromwell had Barton and her principal supporters arrested and tried for treason by a commission of oyer and terminer in autumn 1533. When the commissioners refused, however, to convict the Holy Maid of high treason on her spoken words alone, Cromwell and Lord Chancellor **Thomas Audley** turned to a parliamentary act of attainder to send the young nun and four of her closest adherents to their deaths in April 1534.

Owing to the legal frustrations of the Barton case, the king's chief minister submitted draft legislation for a revised statute of treason to the House of Commons the following November. The bill's preamble defined *treason* as a crime against the entire realm, not just the king, while its first article named as traitors those who might "maliciously wish, will or desire by words" any harm to the sovereign or his subjects. The law passed both chambers of Parliament with little opposition and was soon put to use silencing opposition to the **Henrician Reformation**. In early summer 1535, the revised act helped convict both Thomas More and Bishop John Fisher of high treason for their refusals to swear the Succession and Supremacy oaths [*see* ACT OF SUCCESSION (1534); ACT OF SUPREMACY (1534)].

ANNE OF CLEVES, QUEEN OF ENGLAND
(1515–57). This uncultured and naïve young

woman became Henry VIII's fourth queen to seal the terms of a foreign alliance, but the Tudor king disliked her from their first meeting and soon found a pretext to have their brief union annulled in summer 1540. Anne of Cleves has often been described as a "footnote" in English history because her time as queen-consort was so short and her impact on the Henrician age was so negligible. However, the quiet and uncomplaining Anne did indirectly bring about the fall of the king's mighty chief minister **Thomas Cromwell**, and unlike most of Henry's other queens, she survived her husband to live out her days as an honored member of the later Tudor royal family.

Anne of Cleves was born in Düsseldorf in summer or early autumn 1515 to John de la Marck III, Duke of Cleves, and his wife, Maria, the Duchess of Jülich-Berg in her own right. Anne grew up in her mother's Berg Castle on the lower Rhine River, where she lived a sheltered life devoid of much exposure to humane learning or to the social graces of a grand ducal court. Anne's father, John of Cleves, was a reform-minded admirer of the Dutch scholar **Desiderius Erasmus**, who deplored papal and clerical corruption but who refused to break with Rome as had Martin Luther in eastern Germany. Nevertheless, the Duchy of Cleves established a strong connection to the Lutheran world in 1526, when Anne's older sister Sibylle married Elector Frederick of Saxony, Martin Luther's protector and an important leader of the embryonic Protestant movement. The following year, Duke John betrothed his 12-year-old daughter Anne to Francis, duc de Lorraine, but the arrangements were never finalized, and so the proposed wedding never took place. When Anne's father died early in 1539, her brother William, an avowed Lutheran and an enemy of the Emperor **Charles V**, became the next duke of Cleves and the guardian of his sister Anne at the same time.

Meanwhile in England, Henry VIII's third (and perhaps best-loved) queen, **Jane Seymour**, had died in October 1537 after giving birth to the healthy prince and heir the English king had long coveted and had finally sired after breaking away from the Roman Church. Already contemplating remarriage within months of Queen Jane's death, King Henry considered several potential foreign brides, such as Christina of Denmark (who turned him down), a few French princesses, and even (briefly) Anne of Cleves herself. This last match could not go forward, however, until the old Catholic Duke of Cleves died and was replaced by his Lutheran son William, who was more open to a union with the schismatic Tudor king than his conservative father had been. Negotiations for Anne's hand might still have foundered had not King **François I** of France and Emperor Charles V, Henry VIII's two greatest European rivals, unexpectedly signed a treaty of mutual détente in Toledo in January 1539. This pact forced England to search for allies of her own, and hopeful that King Henry might befriend other Protestant rulers on the Continent, chief minister Thomas Cromwell urged his royal master to pursue a match with Anne of Cleves in earnest during the spring of 1539.

Agreeable but not overly enthused by the idea, Henry dispatched his court artist **Hans Holbein** the Younger to Germany to paint a portrait of Mistress Anne so he could judge the lady's physical attributes for himself. Initially satisfied, the English king ordered his diplomats to sign a marriage pact with Cleves in October 1539, which then launched preparations to bring the 24-year-old Anne to England to become Henry's fourth wife and queen. Although he had guardedly approved what he saw in Holbein's portrait, the king was woefully unaware that his intended bride was poorly educated, shy, simplistic, and ignorant of the nuances of fashionable court etiquette. Worse still, Anne could only speak her native German, her habits of personal hygiene were below Tudor court standards, and her full-breasted figure did not generally accord with King Henry's taste in women. This unfortunate woman, so ill-suited to wed the gregarious, cultured, and domineering king of England, gradually made her way to **Calais** and then crossed the English Channel into Kent just after Christmas in 1539.

Still hoping that Cromwell had procured for him an attractive and vivacious new bride, the king disguised himself among a group of courtiers and surprised Mistress Anne with gifts in Rochester where she was staying on New Year's Day 1540. Rather than express delight at Henry's romantic and chivalrous gesture—something his earlier and more sophisticated wives would have done—Anne recoiled in horror and had to be left alone with her German attendants to recover her composure. Henry for his part was not well pleased, either, confessing to Cromwell afterward that Anne resembled a Flemish mare and then bluntly declaring, "I like her not!" Although the king received her graciously enough at the nearby palace of **Greenwich** and then married her there on Twelfth Night (6 January) following, he could not bring himself to consummate their union and instead (reportedly) played cards with his befuddled new consort for the rest of their wedding night together.

Their "marriage," such as it may have been, was destined to last just a little over six months. Queen Anne seems to have been satisfied by the platonic attentions shown to her by her husband, telling her ladies that he kissed her each night and morning and called her "sweetheart" and "darling" whenever he took leave of her. It is possible that poor ignorant Anne believed these kisses could lead to pregnancy, a notion she may have formed on her own during her isolated upbringing in her mother's castle on the Rhine. Meanwhile, King Henry did his best to avoid the company of his unattractive and boring queen, going off frequently to hunt with his circle of male courtiers and only deigning to have Anne by his side at formal court functions and banquets. A month after their wedding, the king and queen traveled by barge up the Thames River from Greenwich to the **Tower of London**, where cannons discharged to welcome the pair to the capital. Henry provided Anne with jewels, gowns, and her own household of more than 130 attendants, including some Germans but mostly English ladies of **noble** birth. Among them was the teenaged **Katherine Howard**, soon to catch the eye of the king and become his fifth wife and queen.

As King Henry wearied of Anne, he blamed Cromwell for the disaster of his union with her and had charges of treason and heresy drawn up that soon led to the former chief minister's execution on the block in early July 1540. At around the same time, the English king had his marriage with Anne of Cleves formally annulled by Archbishop **Thomas Cranmer** and the **Convocation of Bishops** within a few days of Cromwell's death. Designating her his "beloved sister," Henry VIII generously settled several manors and an income of £3,000 per annum on his former spouse, and over time, they even became passably good friends. Anne of Cleves survived her royal husband and presided over her own German-style court during the reigns of **Edward VI** and **Mary I** until she died at the age of 42 following a lengthy illness in Chelsea.

ANTICLERICALISM. *See* CLERGY, PARISH OR SECULAR (c. AD 600–).

ARAGON, KATHERINE OF. *See* KATHERINE OF ARAGON, QUEEN OF ENGLAND (1485–1536).

ARTHUR (TUDOR), PRINCE OF WALES (1486–1502). The eldest son and royal heir of King **Henry VII** and Queen **Elizabeth of York**, Prince Arthur symbolized the union and the future of the Houses of York and Lancaster/Tudor after the **Wars of the Roses** had finally ended one year before his birth. In an attempt to construct an alliance network with other European powers, his father married Prince Arthur in 1501 to **Katherine of Aragon**, the youngest daughter of **Ferdinand and Isabel** of Spain. Scholars have debated whether Arthur was sickly through much of his short life, but in any case, he died in 1502 at age 15 and left his consort, Katherine, a youthful widow. A papal dispensation was subsequently secured to allow Arthur's younger brother Henry VIII to marry Katherine, but doubts lingered about whether Arthur and his Spanish bride had ever consummated their union. King Henry later used these doubts to set Katherine aside for **Anne Boleyn**, an affair that ultimately sparked the **Henrician Reformation** and tore England away from the Church of Rome.

Prince Arthur was born on 20 September 1486 within the confines of St. Swithun's

Priory in Winchester, Hampshire. His father, King Henry VII, named his infant son after the mythical King Arthur, hoping to evoke memories of ancient British rulers in an effort to solidify his questionable Tudor claim to the English throne. Bishop John Alcock of Worcester baptized the young prince four days after his birth in Winchester Cathedral. King Henry soon ennobled Arthur as the Duke of Cornwall and a few years later created him Prince of Wales as the principal heir of the House of Tudor. Traditionally, Arthur has been seen as frail and weak, perhaps because of his premature birth after his mother's pregnancy of just eight months, but many sources from his early childhood describe him as tall for his age and generally quite healthy. King Henry employed Winchester College educator John Rede, poet laureate Bernard André, and royal physician **Thomas Linacre** to tutor his young heir in ancient and modern languages, the classics, history, and philosophy, all subjects at which the prince reportedly excelled. As he grew older, Arthur was showered with other titles and offices, such as Earl of Chester, knight of the **Garter**, and warden of the Scottish and Welsh Marches.

To legitimize his shaky hold on the English throne and to strengthen his hand against his French enemies, Henry VII decided to pursue an alliance with Spain as the time approached for Prince Arthur to marry. King Ferdinand and Queen Isabel of Spain, who had loosely united their respective kingdoms of Aragon and Castile through their marriage in 1469, had a pretty, teenaged daughter named Katherine of Aragon who was just one year older than the Tudor Prince of Wales. Preliminary negotiations resulted in the Treaty of Medina del Campo (1489), and the young royals were duly betrothed in 1497 and married in 1499, on both occasions by proxy. Katherine arrived in England in early October 1501 and was escorted in stages by Bishop **Richard Fox** of Winchester to London, where, on 14 November 1501, Arthur and his Spanish bride married in a lavish ceremony at St. Paul's Cathedral. Whether the teenaged couple consummated their union at that or any other time remains a mystery to this day. Within a month of their wedding, the young newlyweds took up their married residence at Ludlow Castle on the Welsh frontier. In March 1502, both Katherine and Arthur fell ill with what their physicians believed was a noxious airborne "vapour" but that may have been consumption (tuberculosis) or even the dreaded **sweating sickness**, or "sweate." Katherine recovered, but Prince Arthur died on 2 April 1502.

King Henry and Queen Elizabeth were stricken with grief and ordered that requiem masses and mourning dirges be sung for the repose of Prince Arthur's soul. He was buried several weeks later in Worcester Cathedral, where a tomb chest and a chantry chapel were built to mark his grave and provide a sanctified place for the many funerary masses his father endowed for him. Dowager Princess Katherine was now left a widow in a strange land at the tender age of 16 years, but within months of Arthur's death, King Henry began to contemplate her remarriage to his younger son Henry, then Duke of York but soon-to-be Prince of Wales in the wake of his brother's death. King Henry secured a papal dispensation for the potentially incestuous match based on the biblical passage Deuteronomy 25:5, which exhorted the brother of a deceased man to take in the latter's widow. Prince Henry briefly balked at his impending marriage to Katherine in 1505, but upon his father's death and his own accession to the throne in 1509, he duly took his brother's widow as his first wife and queen. When Henry VIII sought to free himself from this union two decades later, he argued (among other points) that Arthur had in fact consummated his marriage to Katherine in 1501, thus invalidating and even cursing as incestuous his (Henry's) own union with her according to Leviticus 20:21. When the pope refused to grant his requested "divorce" (annulment) from Katherine, Henry VIII eventually broke with the Roman Church and established his own Church of England, with himself as its "supreme head." *See also* THE GREAT MATTER (c. 1526–33).

ASCHAM, ROGER (c. 1515–68). One of England's most prominent Renaissance scholars, this gifted but irascible intellectual served the House of Tudor as schoolmaster to two of Henry VIII's children and royal heirs. He is also remembered today for his reformed religious beliefs and for his use of elegant English prose to compose works on the education of the body and the mind. A teen prodigy at **Cambridge University**, Ascham taught courses there and then traveled widely on the Continent as a diplomatic secretary before returning to England in his later years. As a royal tutor, Ascham largely shaped the educational experience of Princess **Elizabeth** Tudor and lived on to serve her as a Latin secretary when she became queen.

Roger Ascham was the third son of John and Margaret Ascham and was born in the northern Yorkshire village of Kirby Wiske sometime between 1514 and 1516. His father, John, was a steward in the household of Lord Henry Scrope of Bolton, but his mother's origins and background were obscure and mostly elude us today. Young Roger received his earliest tuition at the Kirby Wiske village school, where he soon attracted the attention of Sir Humphrey Wingfield, a local **gentry** squire. Sir Humphrey took Ascham into his household, where he introduced the lad to ancient languages, classical literature, and the sport of archery. At age 15, Ascham entered St. John's College at Cambridge University and, studying with **John Cheke**, the school's regius (royally appointed) professor of Greek, Ascham progressed quickly and became an outstanding classical scholar in his own right. During his student days, he also developed his own elegant prose style in both English and Latin, and his penmanship was so graceful the university administration asked him to write all its official correspondence. He earned his baccalaureate degree in 1534 and his master of arts three years later. He then accepted a teaching fellowship in Greek at St. John's College at the young age of 23.

While at Cambridge, Ascham adopted the ideas of the emergent Lutheran and Calvinist movements as his own and soon found himself embroiled in heated theological debates with members of the university's more conservative community. Ascham was brilliant and passionate but also ambitious and hot-tempered, characteristics that aroused hostility and jealousy in his rivals and made life uncomfortable for him at Cambridge. Determined to escape academia, he published *Toxophilus* in 1545, an elegantly crafted dialogue in English on fitness and sport that especially promoted his lifelong fascination with archery. He dedicated his little book to Henry VIII and presented it to him at **Greenwich Palace**, a gesture that pleased the king greatly and earned him much royal favor and a pension of £10 per annum. When King Henry and Queen **Katherine Parr** hired John Cheke in 1544 to educate **Edward** Tudor, Prince of Wales, the new royal tutor convinced them to add his old friend Roger Ascham to the boy's pedagogical team the following year. In 1546, Queen Katherine asked him to read her religious treatise *Lamentations of a Sinner*, and although he did not comment on her prose writing style, he found much in the book's evangelical and self-deprecating message to admire.

Despite his many earlier accomplishments, Ascham achieved his greatest fame during the two decades that followed the death of King Henry VIII in 1547. With the teenaged Princess Elizabeth now resident in Katherine Parr's household, the widowed queen engaged Ascham for two years to sustain and expand on the excellent education her stepdaughter had already received. In 1550, Ascham was appointed secretary to Sir Richard Morrison, the English ambassador to the Holy Roman Empire, and so he lived at Augsburg and traveled extensively across Europe over the next three years. He returned to England in 1554 to accept a position as Latin secretary to the Catholic Queen **Mary I**—a surprise given his reformist religious views—and then married Margaret Harleston and with her produced seven children. During his final years, his former pupil Queen Elizabeth I retained his services as a royal secretary while he composed the greatest English prose work of his career, *Schoolmaster*, between 1563 and 1567. In this educational treatise, Ascham outlines the gently persuasive methods he believed private tutors should employ when instructing young men of privilege in the Latin language. The book had to await posthumous publication in

1570, however, for Ascham contracted a virulent fever and, passing away in late December 1568, was laid to rest in the parish church of St. Sepulchre-without-Newgate in London.

ASKEW, ANNE (1521–46).

Anne Askew (alternately Ayscough) was a willful young woman who died at the stake as a heretic for resisting Henry VIII's return to the traditionalist doctrines of Rome near the end of his reign. The educated daughter of a **gentry** family, Askew abandoned her Catholic husband in her early 20s to seek out communities of evangelical believers in London. There she came into contact with peripheral members of the household of Queen **Katherine Parr**, who was herself a confirmed religious reformer. Askew's indirect association with Parr in turn attracted the hostility of Henry VIII's more conservative ministers, who at that moment were scheming to turn the aging king against his Protestant queen. Thus caught between contending political and religious factions at court, Askew endured imprisonment, interrogation, and torture—and recorded her trials in her "examinations"—before courageously surrendering her life in the flames as a martyr to her faith.

Anne Askew was born in Stallingborough, Lincolnshire, and was the second daughter and one of five offspring of Sir William Askew and his wife, Elizabeth Wrottesley Askew. The Askews were relatively prosperous and apparently educated all their children, including Anne, whose articulate prose style was much in evidence in her later *Examination* memoirs. As a teen, she very likely witnessed the **Pilgrimage of Grace** uprising in Lincolnshire, and she was probably well aware of **Parliament**'s passage of the **Act of Six Articles**, a statute that restored much Roman doctrine and practice to the English Church in 1539. Anne doubtless bristled at these changes, for she had already rejected the old church and embraced instead the radical new teachings of the leading religious reformers on the Continent. When she turned 18, her father insisted she wed a Catholic farmer—the former fiancé of her deceased sister—but the match was ill suited, and despite producing two children together, Anne left her home and marriage in

1543 to make contact with other like-minded religious dissidents in London.

Once in the capital, Askew joined with a community of evangelical believers, among whom were some of Queen Katherine Parr's attending ladies: Anne Parr (the queen's sister), Katherine Willoughby, and Anne Stanhope. Askew's brother Edward meanwhile held a servant's position in the household of Archbishop **Thomas Cranmer** of Canterbury, the kingdom's most prominent Protestant prelate. Arrayed against this reformist party were such religious conservatives as Bishop **Stephen Gardiner** of Winchester; Lord Chancellor **Thomas Wriothesley; Thomas Howard**, third Duke of Norfolk; and Bishop **Edmund Bonner** of London. These individuals and their allies were intent on isolating King Henry from his reformist sixth queen and his archbishop and believed they might uncover damning evidence against them both by interrogating Anne Askew and some of her associates.

She was duly arrested and charged with heresy in March 1545 for denying eucharistic transubstantiation, a traditionalist Roman tenet that had been reaffirmed in England six years earlier under the Act of Six Articles. City and episcopal officials questioned Askew at the London Guildhall, but no witnesses could be found against her, and she soon regained her freedom. Apprehended again more than a year later, Mistress Anne this time found herself jailed in Newgate Prison and was there interrogated by Bishop Gardiner, Bishop Bonner, and Lord Chancellor Wriothesley. She stubbornly refused, however, to name any of her evangelical brethren or connect Queen Katherine to any alleged acts of heresy. Frustrated by Askew's intransigence, Gardiner ordered her transferred to the **Tower of London** and there tortured on the rack to help loosen her tongue. Sir Anthony Kingston, constable of the tower, refused to carry out Gardiner's illegal directive to torture a woman, so Wriothesley and Sir **Richard Rich**, then solicitor general and the man responsible for condemning Sir **Thomas More** a decade earlier, stepped in to turn the wheel of the rack themselves. Anne Askew bravely bore her torments and, still refusing to utter any incriminating word against her reformist associates or the queen, was finally condemned to death as an obdurate heretic in late June 1546. Weak form her ordeal in the tower, Mistress Askew traveled in a chair to her execution site at Smithfield. There, chained to the stake and praying for her soul, she was offered a pardon by Wriothesley if she would but recant her "errors." Defiantly refusing to do so, Anne Askew perished in the flames on 16 July 1546 and was later proclaimed a Christian martyr by the Protestant polemicist John Foxe in 1563.

Anne Askew left a fascinating account of her trials in 1545–46 in two surviving memoirs known as her *Examinations*. These works, penned by Askew while incarcerated and undergoing interrogation and torture in London, are autobiographical in nature and offer a rare glimpse into the spirituality, motivation, and fortitude of a courageous young woman. Within a year of her death, the evangelical apologist John Bale edited and published Askew's *Examinations*, and although he may have changed portions of the text to suit his mostly male reading audience, Bale did help to rescue the essentials of Askew's work from obscurity. Today her *Examinations* stand as a testament to the devotion and inner strength of a woman who, unwilling to compromise her religious convictions, gave her life as a martyr rather than betray her faith.

ASSERTIO SEPTEM SACRAMENTORUM (DEFENSE OF THE SEVEN SACRAMENTS; 1521).

A religious treatise attributed to King Henry VIII, the *Assertio* was penned and published in response to the *Babylonian Captivity of the Church*, which Martin Luther, the great German reformer, issued in 1520. The *Assertio* opened with two chapters that didn't seem to fit with the rest of the book, a rambling and at times vitriolic apology for Roman Catholic doctrines. The *Assertio* earned for the English king the title Defender of the Faith from the pope, a distinction still borne by British monarchs despite their nearly 500-year separation from the Holy See of Rome.

By the time Martin Luther launched the Protestant Reformation with his *95 Theses against Indulgences* in 1517, the 26-year-old King Henry VIII of England had only ruled his island kingdom for a mere eight years. In those early days, he viewed himself not only as a learned theologian but as a committed son of the Roman Church as well. With youthful zeal, King Henry began in spring 1518 to compose a rebuttal to Luther's *95 Theses*, but the distracted king's enthusiasm soon waned, and he abandoned the project after penning only a few short chapters entitled "On Indulgences" and "On Papal Authority." Many scholars now believe that these draft essays, set aside almost as soon as they were written, were then resuscitated three years later and inserted as the ill-fitting opening chapters of a new treatise in defense of Rome's seven sacraments.

It seems that **Thomas Cardinal Wolsey**, King Henry's lord chancellor since 1515 and certainly one of his spiritual mentors as well, encouraged his Tudor master to take up the quill in defense of the Roman Church once again in 1521. Wolsey presented the king with a copy of Luther's *Babylonian Captivity of the Church*, a venomous assault on clerical corruption [*see* CLERGY, PARISH OR SECULAR (c. 600–)]; papal authority; and, most particularly, the sacramental system that aided Catholics in their pursuit of eternal life. The king was outraged, and unlike his earlier attempt to challenge the German reformer, Henry warmed to his task and plunged into drafting the *Assertio* in earnest during the spring of 1521. Wolsey doubtless promised some assistance with the project—the finished treatise reads more like a "team effort" than a royal monograph—and so recruited such theologians as John Longland (soon to become bishop of Lincoln) and Edward Lee (later archbishop of York) to conduct research and rough out portions of the text. It has long been generally believed that Sir **Thomas More**, Bishop **John Fisher** of Rochester, and even Wolsey himself had a hand (or two) in the composition of the *Assertio*, but More and Fisher commented on the work from afar, and Wolsey was too busy with affairs of state to have been involved.

On 12 May 1521, Cardinal Wolsey led a procession of clerics and dignitaries through the streets of London to the square in front of St. Paul's Cathedral. There Bishop Fisher preached a lengthy sermon against Luther, whose writings were piled up and set ablaze; Wolsey then announced that King Henry himself would soon produce his own polemic against the Protestant heretic. The *Assertio septem sacramentorum* was published in July 1521 and soon became a best-seller of sorts, appearing in some 20 editions and multiple languages during the 16th century. Bearing a dedication to Pope **Leo X**, a copy (bound in tooled leather and gold piping) was forwarded to the pontiff a few months later. Pope Leo duly rewarded the English king with the title *Defensor Fidei*, or Defender of the Faith, an appellation that set Henry VIII on an equal footing with the "most Christian Majesty" **François I** of France and the "most Catholic Majesty" **Charles V** of Spain. Although Henry would famously break with Rome in the early 1530s over the pope's refusal to annul his marriage to Queen **Katherine of Aragon**, the king of England never relinquished his new title and passed it along to his royal heirs, who still sport the dignity today.

AUDLEY, THOMAS, LORD CHANCELLOR OF ENGLAND, FIRST BARON AUDLEY OF WALDEN (1488–1544).

This trusted Crown minister exercised great political and judicial power as speaker of the House of Commons in **Parliament** and as lord chancellor of England during the later years of King Henry VIII's reign. He supported the campaign to suppress the English **monasteries** in the late 1530s and enriched himself by acquiring many of the confiscated monastic properties, either as rewards for his service or at bargain prices. Audley also presided over (or took part in) many of the most sensational trials of the early 16th century, including those that found Sir **Thomas More**, Bishop **John Fisher**, Queen **Anne Boleyn**, **Thomas Cromwell**, and Queen **Katherine Howard** guilty of treason. He was twice married, but his baronial title became extinct in 1544 when he died at age 56 without male issue.

Thomas Audley was born into the family of Geoffrey Audley in Earls Colne, Essex, and studied at Buckingham (now Magdalene) College at **Cambridge University** before entering the **Inns of Court** in London around 1510 to study law. Four years later, he accepted the office of town clerk in Colchester and then became a justice of the peace for Essex in 1520. Audley was subsequently elected to the House of Commons in Parliament in 1523 and a few years later joined Thomas More, Thomas Cromwell, and other future Tudor statesmen as a legal secretary in the household of **Thomas Cardinal Wolsey**. When Wolsey fell from royal favor, Audley distanced himself from his former master to become chancellor of the Duchy of Lancaster and then speaker of the House of Commons (reportedly at King Henry's request) in 1529. In the latter role, Speaker Audley helped guide the Supplication against the Ordinaries [*see* SUBMISSION OF THE CLERGY AND SUPPLICATION AGAINST THE ORDINARIES (c. 1531–32) through the House in 1531–32, a petition that anticipated England's complete break with the Church of Rome a few years later.

As an enthusiastic agent of the royal will, Thomas Audley worked tirelessly with Henry VIII's new chief minister Thomas Cromwell to free the Tudor king from his marriage to Queen **Katherine of Aragon**. In January 1533, a grateful king chose his loyal speaker of the House to succeed Cardinal Wolsey and Sir Thomas More as lord chancellor of England. Over the next few years, Audley had a hand in all the major events of the **Henrician Reformation**, including the resolution of Henry's matrimonial affairs and Parliament's passage of the statute laws that finally separated the English Church from Rome. When Bishop John Fisher of Rochester and Audley's old political rival Sir Thomas More refused to swear oaths to uphold those new statutes, the lord chancellor presided over the trials that convicted both men of treason and sent them to the block in summer 1535. Within a year of their deaths, Queen Anne herself fell afoul of her royal husband and suffered through another Audley tribunal before facing her own execution for infidelity and treason.

Despite his dutiful service to the Crown, Thomas Audley did far less than most other government officials over the years to elevate his social standing and increase his personal wealth. This situation changed when Cromwell became the king's vicegerent in spirituals (a religious superintendent of sorts), then closed England's monasteries during the late 1530s and sold off their lands to refill a depleted royal treasury. The lord chancellor assisted Cromwell with the monastic dissolution and was thus in a good position to snap up several of the confiscated religious estates for himself. When the king bestowed the Barony of Walden on him in 1538, he finally possessed enough property and status to enter the ranks of the titled **nobility**. The year 1538 also saw his childless first marriage end with the death of his wife, Christina Barnardiston, but he quickly married Elizabeth Grey, the daughter of a powerful landowning family, who gave him two daughters but no sons to inherit his title or lands.

Meanwhile, as the lead Tudor prosecutor, Thomas Audley presided over or took part in the treason trials that condemned the **Pilgrimage of Grace** ringleaders to death in 1537. After Thomas Cromwell arranged the king's loveless fourth marriage to **Anne of Cleves**, Henry called upon his lord chancellor to set aside the new queen and then to try and execute Cromwell as a traitor and heretic in 1540. Audley similarly managed the treason trials of Queen Katherine Howard and her alleged lovers and sent them all to their deaths 18 months later. Quite pleased with his work, King Henry invited his loyal servant to become a knight companion of the Order of the **Garter** in 1540.

The aging lord chancellor was by this time enjoying an annual income of some £800 and was financially secure enough to loan the king £4,000 in 1542. Some modern scholars believe that Audley may have authored *A Booke of Orders for the Warre both by Sea and Land*, a small treatise intended to advise Henry VIII on preparations for his forthcoming **French invasion of 1544–45**. Baron Thomas Audley of Walden resigned his lord chancellor's chain of office on 21 April 1544 and died nine days later at his home in Aldgate, London. His family interred his remains in an ornate black marble tomb in the parish church of St. Mary the Virgin in Saffron Walden, the seat of Audley's barony located some 15 miles south of Cambridge.

B

BARNES, ROBERT (1495–1540). One of Tudor England's best-known reformist preachers and martyrs, Robert Barnes began his career as a monastic friar in the Roman Church but quickly fell away to embrace the evangelical teachings of the Protestant Reformation. A prominent contributor to discussions of Lutheran theology in Cambridge, Barnes knew and was friendly with many of the great religious figures of his age. As his doctrinal views became more radicalized during the 1520s, he attracted heresy charges from the English ecclesiastical authorities and endured close confinement before escaping into exile on the Continent. Barnes returned to England in the 1530s, but his passionately reformist sermons continued to exasperate the religious conservatives who seized control of the English Church in 1540. Despite King Henry's pressure to recant his "errors," Barnes remained true to his faith and ended his life in the flames as a heretic at the age of just 45 years.

Robert Barnes was born around 1495 in Bishop's Lynn (later King's Lynn), a seaport and market town in the county of Norfolk, but beyond this, little is known of his parentage or early life. He entered the religious house of the Augustinian friars in Cambridge as an adolescent, then studied at Louvain University in **Flanders** under the great Dutch humanist **Desiderius Erasmus**. Returning to Cambridge in the early 1520s, Barnes became the prior of his Augustinian house and introduced his fellow friars there to the Renaissance "new learning" he had discovered and embraced at

Louvain. One of the young friars who took up this course of study was Miles Coverdale, the scriptural linguist who was later to produce the translated **Great Bible** for the Church of England. After earning his doctorate in theology from **Cambridge University** in 1523, Barnes began meeting on a regular basis with other scholars at the White Horse Inn near King's College to discuss the revolutionary religious ideas of Martin Luther. Notable among his White Horse associates were **Thomas Bilney, Hugh Latimer, Stephen Gardiner, William Tyndale**, John Rogers, and Coverdale, all of whom would go on to play significant roles in the **Henrician Reformation** of the 1530s and beyond.

Robert Barnes first came to the notice of the church hierarchy in England after he preached a provocative sermon in the parish church of St. Edward King and Martyr in Cambridge on Christmas Eve 1525. Although he began by simply chastising England's corrupt **clergy**, Dr. Barnes grew bolder in the pulpit and went on to condemn traditional church teachings and the opulent worldliness of **Thomas Cardinal Wolsey** as well. Bishop **Cuthbert Tunstall** of London wasted little time in summoning Barnes to the capital, where he was examined by both bishop and cardinal and threatened with death at the stake if he did not recant his "errors." The intimidated preacher agreed, and with Wolsey, Tunstall, and other prelates looking on from an elevated dais, Barnes retracted his recent sermon and performed public penance at Paul's Cross marketplace in London in February 1526. He lived under house arrest for the next two years at the Augustinian friary in the capital, but he soon busied himself distributing copies of Tyndale's English New Testament rather than spending his time in penitential meditation as his accusers had commanded. Transferred in 1528 to another monastery in Northampton, Barnes pulled off a daring escape and made his way to Antwerp and then to Wittenberg to live in exile at the epicenter of the Lutheran Reformation.

With plenty of time on his hands, Dr. Barnes now produced the two most important written works of his career and had them both published in Antwerp in 1531. His *Articles of the Christian Church* essentially explains Martin Luther's religious program to English believers, while his *Supplication unto the Most Gracious Prince Henry VIII* seeks to discredit the heresy charges that Wolsey and Tunstall brought against him five years earlier. King Henry and his royal secretary **Thomas Cromwell** were intrigued and, seeking a spokesman to champion the coming break with Rome, invited Barnes to return to England under a safe conduct late in 1531. He did so but did not stay long because Sir **Thomas More**, then Henry VIII's lord chancellor, was at that moment making life uncomfortable for anyone who dared to criticize the Roman Church. Barnes again fled overseas to Hamburg, where he proved useful to Cromwell as an ambassador to the Lutheran princes of northern Germany. He returned to England in 1534 and dedicated his *History of the Popes* to King Henry, but this gesture and his many pleas to Cromwell for offices and patronage only yielded a few minor appointments and little additional income. Cromwell finally hired Barnes in 1539 to negotiate Henry VIII's marriage with **Anne of Cleves** in Germany, a diplomatic mission whose very success only led (ironically) to the king's great unhappiness and Barnes's spectacular fall from royal favor just seven months later.

With the religiously reactionary **Act of Six Articles** already in place by 1539, Dr. Barnes ignored the new statute and delivered (with fellow reformist divines William Jerome and Thomas Garrett) several more Lutheran sermons at Paul's Cross during Lent in spring 1540. All three preachers denounced the conservative Bishop Stephen Gardiner of Winchester and condemned the Roman doctrine of salvation by good works as contrary to Holy Writ. Gardiner complained to the king, who insisted that Barnes apologize and withdraw his earlier Lenten remarks, but the preacher only partially complied in a follow-up sermon with halfhearted and ambiguous retractions. Feeling disrespected, King Henry ordered Barnes, Jerome, and Garrett imprisoned in the **Tower of London** in April 1540, and although Cromwell soon had all three men released, they were jailed again in mid-June following the arrest and confinement of Cromwell himself. With Henry's great chief minister now unable to protect them, Barnes and his fellow preachers were attainted of treason by **Parliament** and died together at the stake in Smithfield on 13 July 1540 as "detestable heretics." The Protestant apologist John Foxe later memorialized them in his 1563 *Acts and Monuments* as three of the greatest martyrs in the history of the English Church.

BARTON, ELIZABETH, THE HOLY MAID OF KENT (c. 1506–34).

A young woman of obscure origin, Elizabeth Barton won considerable renown in her own time for the strange fits and saintly visions she claimed were sent to her from heaven. She attracted the notice of **Thomas Cromwell**, Henry VIII's secretary and chief minister, when her visions became subversive critiques of Crown policy during the turmoil of the king's "**Great Matter**." Because Cromwell had difficulty silencing the Holy Maid under existing English law, he had to resort to unusual measures to put her to death and then corrected a glaring omission in the **Act of Treasons** to avoid such complications in the future.

Elizabeth Barton was born and raised in a small Kentish hamlet and by age 16 was employed as a servant in the household of the archbishop of Canterbury's estate manager. By the mid-1520s, Barton began to experience convulsive seizures and facial contortions, and she emitted voices from deep within that seemed to foretell future events. One such voice summoned her to a tiny chapel, where, followed by a large crowd of curious onlookers,

Barton was "cured" of her strange malady during a three-hour ordeal in May 1525. Archbishop **William Warham**, who may already have met Barton, quickly pronounced her "cure" miraculous, appointed Edward Bocking (monk) and Richard Masters (priest) as her spiritual advisors, and ordered the young servant to enter the convent of St. Sepulchre in Canterbury as a nun.

Although her fits and grimaces had by now subsided, Barton continued to utter visionary prophecies, whose seeming sanctity was attracting a large following by the late 1520s. Widely known as the "Holy Maid of Kent" or the "Nun of Canterbury," she claimed that demons were tormenting her and saints were sending her messages, letters, and even articles of clothing. Sir **Thomas More**, Henry VIII's soon-to-be lord chancellor, interviewed Barton twice and politely dismissed her, but Bishop **John Fisher** of Rochester believed her instead to be "honest and virtuous." Gertrude Courtenay, the wife of Marquis **Henry Courtenay** of Exeter, asked the maid's prayers for a full-term pregnancy and safe delivery. **Thomas Cardinal Wolsey** also met with her at least once, as did a curious King Henry VIII himself, while an even wider group of important individuals and families were at least acquainted with her reputation and some of her visionary claims.

Elizabeth Barton's revelations were all fairly innocent at first, but by 1532, they were evolving into political commentaries on the king's Great Matter, or his attempt to reject his first queen so he might marry another. Perhaps coached by Bocking and Masters, the Holy Maid predicted Henry VIII's overthrow if he wed **Anne Boleyn** and added later that he faced eternal damnation—and his subjects, a great plague—if the king went forward with his plans. Other Barton visions saw Cardinal Wolsey burning in hell, Anne Boleyn's father offering bribes to the pope, and King Henry as an abomination in the eyes of God. As if these remarks were not damning enough, a series of printed works then appeared that threatened to spread knowledge of the maid's inflammatory visions to a much wider audience. Probably authored by Edward Bocking or other Barton adherents, the *Cure Book* (1527),

the *Nun's Book* (1529), and a third volume (seized before its release) catalogued the Holy Nun's various prophecies and were composed in rhymed verses to facilitate their memorization and recitation. The appearance and dissemination of these publications thus signaled to Thomas Cromwell that the time had come to find a way to silence Elizabeth Barton and her circle of supporters.

The master secretary had the young nun and five of her closest advisors arrested and taken to the **Tower of London** for questioning in the autumn of 1533. Barton quickly confessed that she was a fraud and that Edward Bocking was behind most of her provocative statements, but Cromwell knew he needed to make a public example of her to suppress the damage she had already caused. He therefore displayed Barton and several of her followers on high scaffolds in London and Canterbury to discredit their claims and humiliate them before large crowds of jeering onlookers. Then Cromwell summoned a commission of oyer and terminer (an emergency court) of specially selected **nobles**, judges, and prelates to try the Maid of Kent and her adherents on charges of high treason. Bocking, Masters, and the other members of her inner circle were easy to condemn because they had clearly performed treasonous actions by publishing the Barton books, but the nun herself had only spoken subversive words, an offense excluded from the English statute of treason then in force. Cromwell was obliged instead to seek a **parliamentary** act of attainder to convict the Holy Maid and, once obtained, used it to send the hapless Barton and four of her supporters to the scaffold to suffer traitors' deaths on 21 April 1534. Within seven months of their executions, Cromwell had Parliament pass a revised act of treason—one that now included spoken words as a traitorous offense—thus closing the legal loophole that had nearly allowed the dangerous Maid of Kent to escape the hangman's noose.

BEAUFORT, LADY MARGARET, COUNTESS OF RICHMOND (1443–1509). Four times married and the mother and grandmother of Tudor kings, Margaret Beaufort shrewdly manipulated 15th-century dynastic politics in England yet cultivated a reputation for personal piety and educational patronage toward the end of her life, as well. After frequently switching sides during the **Wars of the Roses**, Beaufort encouraged and enabled her son Henry Tudor to seize the English throne as **Henry VII** in 1485. The countess of Richmond then became his principal confidante and royal advisor, all the while wielding great power and influence at court and across the kingdom. Having seen Henry VII secure his family's claim to the Crown of England, Lady Margaret died just two months after her son, to leave a peaceful, stable, and prosperous England to her grandson Henry VIII.

Margaret Beaufort was born on 31 May 1443 (or possibly 1441) at Bletsoe Manor in Bedfordshire. She was the daughter of John Beaufort, the Duke of Somerset who, as a great-grandson of King Edward III, possessed a distant claim to the English throne himself. Following his botched military campaign in France, Somerset fell out with King Henry VI and then died in 1444, either from an illness or perhaps (as some sources suggest) from suicide. As the deceased duke's heiress, the infant Margaret now was suddenly a youthful but coveted prize on the marriage market. She became a ward of William de la Pole, the Duke of Suffolk, and at the tender age of three years was "married" (symbolically) to Suffolk's son John so Pole could retain control over her vast inheritance. In 1450, John de la Pole and the Beaufort girl were more formally wed, but Henry VI dissolved this union three years later (she was still far too young) and then handed her wardship over to his Tudor half-brothers. Edmund Tudor, the Earl of Richmond, married the adolescent Beaufort heiress in 1455, and two years later, their son Henry Tudor was born. Margaret's delivery was difficult (she was only 14), however, and as a result, she was unable to conceive for the rest of her life. In the meantime, her husband, Edmund Tudor, died of the plague while campaigning in **Wales**, thus freeing Margaret (now the dowager countess of Richmond) to marry again.

This she did in 1458, after Jasper Tudor (Edmund's surviving brother) arranged a match between his teenaged sister-in-law and Sir Henry Stafford, the second son of the Duke of Buckingham. In 1461, Edward of York seized the English throne, forcing Lancastrian supporters Margaret, her son Henry Tudor, and her husband to leave court, while Jasper Tudor fled into exile abroad. The new King Edward IV gave Lady Margaret's Beaufort lands to his brother George, Duke of Clarence, and handed custody of little Henry Tudor over to his Welsh ally Lord William Herbert. When Clarence rebelled against and was defeated and captured by his brother, the Countess of Richmond briefly reclaimed her son from Herbert but soon had to send the boy into exile with his uncle Jasper in France. In 1471, Lady Margaret lost her third and best-loved husband, Sir Henry Stafford, when he fell at the Battle of Barnet. The next year, she married her fourth spouse, the Yorkist client Lord Thomas Stanley, a union that allowed her to make peace with Edward IV and Queen Elizabeth Woodville and then return to court once more.

The unexpected death of 40-year-old King Edward brought his younger brother Richard of Gloucester to the throne as King Richard III in 1483. Lady Margaret meanwhile remained at the Yorkist court and served Anne Neville, King Richard's queen, as one of her attending ladies. Although Richard III is widely blamed today for the murder of his two nephews in the **Tower of London**, Lady Margaret Beaufort might also have arranged their deaths to clear a path to the throne and legitimize the relatively weak royal pretensions of her beloved son Henry Tudor. After she helped finance the Duke of Buckingham's unsuccessful revolt against King Richard in autumn 1483, the angry Yorkist ruler placed the scheming Lady Margaret under house arrest in the custody of her husband, Lord Stanley. She continued plotting to replace Richard III with her son, however, enlisting the support of Queen Dowager Elizabeth Woodville and spending what resources she possessed to raise mercenary troops in France for Henry Tudor's forthcoming invasion. Her son's army finally landed in England and defeated Richard's forces (and killed the king himself) at Bosworth Field in August

1485. Margaret's husband, Lord Stanley, who had turned against Richard III during the battle at the last moment, placed the dead king's battered crown on Henry Tudor and proclaimed him King Henry VII.

Once her son had successfully seized the English throne, Margaret Beaufort presided over the Tudor court as "My Lady, the King's Mother," and was authorized to sign her name "Margaret R" as if she were the actual queen. She saw that Henry VII married **Elizabeth of York**, the daughter of Edward IV, in order to strengthen the royal bloodlines of the children this union of Tudor and York would soon produce. She later helped negotiate the marriages of her grandchildren **Margaret** Tudor to King **James IV** of Scotland and Prince **Arthur** Tudor to **Katherine of Aragon**, thus also securing alliances with these important neighboring kingdoms.

Lady Margaret became devoutly religious later in life and appointed Bishop **John Fisher** of Rochester her confessor and spiritual advisor in the 1490s. As a pious daughter of the Roman Church, the Countess of Richmond gave generously from her considerable fortune (now restored to her) to found Christ's and St. John's Colleges at **Cambridge University**. As a scholar in her own right, she also translated the *Imitatio Christi* of Thomas à Kempis, and she financially supported William Caxton's printing operation in Westminster to make thousands of books more available to English readers. Having witnessed the undisputed passage of her son's Crown to her teenaged grandson Henry VIII two months earlier, Lady Margaret Beaufort breathed her last on 29 June 1509 and was laid to rest in the Henry VII Chapel of Westminster Abbey.

BILNEY, THOMAS (c. 1495–1531). A diminutive but passionate religious reformer, Thomas Bilney experienced an emotional conversion to evangelical Christianity early in life and went on to preach and distribute English Bibles in East Anglia and the region around London. Bilney was a regular member of the White Horse Inn coterie in Cambridge, where he and other early-Tudor-era reformers discussed the innovative religious ideas then trickling into

England from the Continent. Much of what we know today about Thomas Bilney comes to us from John Foxe, whose *Acts and Monuments* (1563) presents the dissident priest as one of England's most important Protestant martyrs. Arrested as a suspected heretic in 1527, he recanted his "errors" but was so consumed by guilt he returned to Norwich and took up his evangelical proselytizing once more. Bilney was finally arrested again, convicted of heresy, and died at the stake for his faith in August 1531 at age 36. Through his discussions at the White Horse Inn and his preaching of reformist theology, Thomas Bilney helped prepare English believers for the coming of the **Henrician Reformation** in 1533–34.

Thomas Bilney was born in the village of East Bilney (or perhaps in nearby Norwich) in East Anglia, most likely in 1495. We know next to nothing about his early life, but his parents probably came from sturdy yeoman or artisan stock, and we do certainly know that they both outlived their son by several years. Young Thomas seems to have loved books and reading and presumably acquired a solid grammar-school education before going on to Trinity Hall at **Cambridge University** to study canon and civil law while still in his teens. During these collegiate years, the precocious Bilney came across a copy of **Desiderius Erasmus**'s Greek-to-Latin New Testament and, reading from St. Paul's first letter to Timothy 1:15, experienced an almost mystical epiphany that instantly changed his life's calling from the law to the service of God. The bishop of Ely ordained him in 1519, he earned his legal degree the following year, and then he accepted a teaching fellowship at Trinity Hall.

The newly consecrated priest and university fellow was of such small stature that many who knew him called him "Little Bilney." His contemporaries believed he rarely slept more than four hours each night, and he reportedly hated swearing and especially music so much that he prayed fervently for the offending sounds to stop whenever they drifted his way. Around 1522, Bilney began frequenting a tavern near King's College in Cambridge called the White Horse Inn, a place where other like-minded university scholars were congregating to discuss the latest religious ideas from the Continent. Many of their conversations focused on Martin Luther, the German reformer whose revolutionary doctrines were making their way into England despite the best efforts of **Thomas Cardinal Wolsey** to keep them out. The men who conversed with Bilney at the White Horse included **Hugh Latimer**, **Robert Barnes**, **Stephen Gardiner**, **William Tyndale**, Miles Coverdale, John Rogers, Nicholas Ridley, and Matthew Parker, among others. Conservatives hostile to the White Horse group dubbed their meeting place "Little Germany" to ridicule the mostly Lutheran ideas under discussion there.

By the mid-1520s, Thomas Bilney was delivering sermons in Cambridgeshire and East Anglia that condemned the corrupted Roman clergy, false saints' relics, idolatrous images, and meaningless pilgrimages. In 1526, Cardinal Wolsey interrogated Bilney and made him promise to abandon his Lutheran beliefs, but by the following year, the diminutive cleric had broken his promise and was preaching his evangelical message once more. In Ipswich, his offended congregants dragged him from the pulpit of St. George's Church and turned him over to local episcopal officials, who had him taken to the capital and locked away in the **Tower of London** in November 1527. Wolsey convened an examination board that included Archbishop **William Warham** of Canterbury, Bishop **Cuthbert Tunstall** of London, and Sir **Thomas More**, and together they convicted Bilney of heresy, persuaded him to abjure his heterodox ideas, forced him to do public penance, and then released him early in 1529.

Little Bilney returned to Cambridge but was so deeply aggrieved by his recent confession and abjuration that he resolved to make amends by going "up to Jerusalem" in March 1531 to begin anew his preaching mission, this time in Norwich. Barred from area churches, he renounced his earlier submission to the London prelates, delivered reformist sermons to curious crowds in open fields, and distributed copies of William Tyndale's English Bible wherever he went. Bishop Richard Nix of Norwich had Bilney arrested, charged, and convicted as a relapsed heretic and, sentencing

him to death, watched as the courageous little preacher was burned alive at the stake in the **Lollards'** Pit (site of heresy executions) in Norwich. What was left of Bilney's remains were quietly gathered up and scattered, leaving no trace of his final resting place for his admirers to find and venerate.

BISHOPS. *See* CONVOCATION OF BISHOPS (c. AD 690–).

BLOUNT, ELIZABETH OR BESSIE (c. 1497–1540). An early mistress of Henry VIII, Elizabeth, or Bessie, Blount gave birth to **Henry Fitzroy**, the only illegitimate child King Henry ever openly acknowledged and the heir presumptive to the Tudor throne until he died in 1536. Blount was a royal attendant at the court of Queen **Katherine of Aragon** and decades later served as lady-in-waiting to King Henry's fourth wife and queen, **Anne of Cleves**. After Fitzroy's birth, Blount married twice and bore six more children before her own untimely death at age 42, possibly from some sort of respiratory disease.

Born around 1497–98 in Shropshire, Elizabeth Blount was the daughter of Katherine (Pershall) and Sir John Blount, a soldier in the Tudor royal bodyguard who was later to serve with Henry VIII's army during his **French invasion of 1513–14**. Elizabeth, called Bessie by most who knew her, was a distant cousin of William Blount, Lord Mountjoy, a mentor to the future Tudor king in his youth and, beginning in 1512, a chamberlain in the service of Queen Katherine. Probably through his influence, Bessie became a maid of honor to the Spanish queen and, as a lovely blond teenager, soon attracted the roving eye of Henry VIII himself. Mistress Blount was not just a pretty face, for her unusual level of education, beautiful singing voice (she wrote her own music!), vivacious charm, and graceful dancing ability were all qualities sure to draw the attentions of the high-spirited young king. Henry and Bessie likely met at a New Year celebration they both attended early in 1514, and it cannot have been long before they were involved in a serious affair together. The king gave Blount a house called Blackmore near

Chelmsford in Essex, one wing of which they used as a regular meeting place and that royal courtiers referred to as "Jericho" to keep its true purpose from Queen Katherine.

By October 1518, Mistress Blount was obliged to remove herself from court because she was pregnant with King Henry's child, so she took up residence at Blackmore and there gave birth to an illegitimate Tudor son on 15 June 1519. When news of the birth reached him, Henry was overjoyed that he had finally sired a son, a feat he had been unable to achieve with his Spanish queen. Insisting that the infant be named Henry Fitzroy (Norman-French for "son of the monarch"), the king openly claimed the boy as his own and from the start took a special interest in him.

Having now produced a royal bastard, Bessie's affair with King Henry was effectively over, and it fell to **Thomas Cardinal Wolsey** to find an appropriate husband for her. Within two years of Fitzroy's birth, Blount married Gilbert Tailboys, a gentleman in Wolsey's household whose father, Sir George Tailboys, had also served with King Henry's French invasion force in 1513–14. Bessie brought several properties in the Midlands and Yorkshire with her to the marriage as a dowry from Wolsey, and after the couple had three children of their own, Gilbert was created Baron Tailboys in 1529. He died the following year, however, leaving the still-attractive Bessie a fairly well-to-do and thus very desirable widow. In 1531, King Henry, still quite fond of his former mistress, gave her a gilt silver cup weighing more than two pounds as a New Year gift. Lady Tailboys was then courted by Leonard Grey, the brother of **Thomas Grey**, the Marquis of Dorset, but she deflected his advances to wed another, this time a younger man named Edward Fiennes, Lord Clinton, in 1534. Although their union was blessed with three more children, tragedy struck in summer 1536, when Henry Fitzroy, Bessie's royal bastard, died at age 17 of either consumption (tuberculosis) or pneumonia. Bessie Clinton briefly served as lady-in-waiting to Anne of Cleves, before her own death from consumption in autumn 1540. *See also* BOLEYN, MARY (CAREY; c. 1499–1543); POPINCOURT, JANE OR JEANNE (c. 1484–c. 1530); SHELTON, MARGARET OR MADGE (c. 1505–c. 1553); STAFFORD, ANNE, LADY HASTINGS, COUNTESS OF HUNTINGDON (c. 1483–1544).

BOLEYN, ANNE, QUEEN OF ENGLAND (c. 1504–36). The second wife and queen of King Henry VIII, Anne Boleyn is best remembered today for the central role she played in the king's **"Great Matter,"** the royal matrimonial crisis that in turn touched off the **Henrician Reformation.** The daughter of an ambitious lord on the rise at the Tudor court and the sister of one of Henry VIII's early mistresses, Anne captured the king's heart while offering him a chance to beget the male heir he had always desired. During her brief reign as King Henry's royal consort, Queen Anne wielded considerable influence at court and was able to promote her reformed views on religion with the king and some of his ministers and associates. Although Queen Anne was ultimately unable to give her husband his coveted male heir and died partly as a result of that failure, she did give birth to Princess **Elizabeth** Tudor, who would eventually grow up to preside over an English "golden age" as Queen Elizabeth I.

Anne Boleyn's birth year has never been firmly established, but most scholars believe she drew her first breath at Blickering Hall in Norfolk sometime between 1501 and 1507. Her father was **Thomas Boleyn,** a **gentry** landowner with estates in the southeast of England who, descended from wealthy merchants and their aristocratic wives, eventually rose to become the Earl of Wiltshire and of Ormond. Anne's mother was Elizabeth Howard, one of the daughters of **Thomas Howard,** the Earl of Surrey and future second Duke of Norfolk. With such ancestry, Anne Boleyn could claim a few drops of royal blood in her veins, a fact that made her even more attractive as a prospective match on the **noble** marriage market.

While Anne was growing up at Hever Castle in Kent, the fortunes of her father were soaring at the Tudor court. A fluent linguist, a polished wit, and an irrepressible gallant, Thomas Boleyn served both the first two Tudor monarchs as a personal attendant, trusted diplomat, and royal escort. His growing prominence at court also paved the way for the rise of his children. In 1513, Anne was sent to Brussels to serve in the household of **Margaret of Austria**, the daughter of Holy Roman Emperor **Maximilian I** and his ruling regent in the Netherlands. Anne's sister **Mary Boleyn** accompanied King Henry's younger sister **Mary** Tudor to France in 1514, and Anne traveled south the following year to join her sibling as a lady-in-waiting to Queen Claude in Paris. There the adolescent Anne learned important lessons about French fashions, dances, and social graces, all skills that soon made her the most noticeable figure in any room she entered.

As King Henry VIII prepared for his second **French invasion**, Anne was forced to withdraw from the French court and return to her native England during the winter or early spring of 1522. Sophisticated and cosmopolitan, Mistress Boleyn immediately became a royal attendant to Queen **Katherine of Aragon** and took up residence with the rest of the Spanish queen's staff at **Westminster Palace** in London. Though not classically beautiful, Anne boasted gorgeous jet-black hair and lively, entrancing eyes that, combined with her coquettish French manners and infectious energy, often drew the attentions of all the young men who knew or wished to know her.

One such was **Henry Percy**, heir to the Earldom of Northumberland and a ward of **Thomas Cardinal Wolsey**, King Henry's lord chancellor. Percy very likely met Anne in the spring or summer of 1522, and it was not long before the two fell in love and reached some sort of "understanding" (or even drew up a formal contract) with their future marriage in mind. Wolsey did his best to break up the young couple, but having failed in the attempt, he summoned Lord Percy's father, the old Earl of Northumberland, to threaten his son into abandoning the Boleyn girl. In 1524, Anne also entertained a brief dalliance with **Thomas Wyatt**, a poet and family neighbor from Kent, but they were in these early years never more than just close friends.

By the time Lord Percy had moved on from Mistress Boleyn in the mid-1520s, King Henry was nearing the end of his affair with Anne's sister Mary, who may have borne the king two children (this is disputed) during their four years together. Sometime in 1525–26, Henry's roving eye fell on the vivacious Anne, and he was soon in amorous pursuit of the woman he assumed would become his next lover and mistress. Well aware of how Henry had treated her sister, however, Anne Boleyn demurely refused the king's advances and insisted that they be married before allowing him into her bed. By 1527, King Henry was quite besotted with the younger Boleyn sister, but he also began to realize that, if he could in fact wed her, she might then bear the son and heir Queen Katherine had never been able to give him. Accordingly, Henry now worked strenuously to free himself from Katherine so he might marry again, a campaign his English subjects euphemistically called the king's Great Matter.

Once Anne had recovered completely from the deadly **sweating sickness** in summer 1527, the king moved forward with his plan to secure a papal annulment of his union with his Spanish queen. Unfortunately for Henry, Pope **Clement VII** was at this moment a prisoner of Emperor **Charles V**, Queen Katherine's nephew, and so was unwilling to hear the English king's case against his wife. After King Henry sent teams of scholars to the Continent to research canon law rulings on marital annulment, the pope suddenly relented and dispatched **Lorenzo Cardinal Campeggio** in 1528–29 to hear Henry's cause with Cardinal Wolsey in England. When Queen Katherine countered with a plan to appeal her own case to Rome, however, Campeggio abruptly adjourned the court, thus leaving the Great Matter unresolved and the hopes of Henry and Anne temporarily dashed.

Cardinal Wolsey's failure to secure the king's desired annulment swiftly led to his downfall and death in 1530, opening the door for **Thomas Cromwell** to join the royal council, then to become King Henry's principal secretary, and finally to acquire the privy seal as the king's chief minister. Meanwhile, Henry created Anne Boleyn Marquess of Pembroke late in 1532, an honor never before granted to a woman in her own right, and one she soon repaid by finally sharing her bed with the king. When Anne's resulting pregnancy became known to him, King Henry hastily married her in a secret ceremony at **Whitehall Palace** to ensure the legitimacy of her hoped-for male child. In spring 1533, Cromwell pushed the **Act in Restraint of Appeals** through **Parliament** to overrule the authority of the pope. Then the king appointed religious reformer **Thomas Cranmer** to the vacant primacy of Canterbury and ordered him to pronounce the long-desired annulment of his marriage with Katherine in May 1533. The following month, Anne Boleyn and King Henry VIII were formally wed—and Anne crowned queen of England—before she gave birth three months later to a baby girl named Elizabeth.

King Henry's disappointment at the birth of a daughter was profound, but in March 1534, he had Cromwell pass the **Act of Succession** through Parliament to name his children with Queen Anne as true heirs to the Tudor throne. At this early point in her reign, Anne went out of her way to protect certain Lutheran reformers from conservative bishops and royal councilors, and she persuaded her husband to read a copy of **William Tyndale**'s *Obedience of a Christian Man*. By autumn 1534, Anne was with child again, but this time her pregnancy miscarried, causing her husband to turn away from her in frustration and mounting dissatisfaction. Queen Anne also proved quite unpopular with her English subjects (many called her the "ogle-eyed whore") when she appeared to celebrate the deaths of such rivals as Katherine of Aragon, Sir **Thomas More**, and Bishop **John Fisher** of Rochester. When the king was seriously injured in a **jousting tournament** in January 1536, his queen, now pregnant for a third time, went into premature labor and gave birth to a stillborn and grossly malformed son. King Henry recovered from his injuries, but he was by now thoroughly disenchanted with Anne Boleyn and was actively searching for a way to set her aside.

That opportunity presented itself in spring 1536, when some of the queen's most bitter enemies, led by Thomas Cromwell, began to plot against her. At first, Cromwell pressured Henry Percy, now the Earl of Northumberland, into admitting that he and Anne had shared a premarriage contract in 1523—thus nullifying her union with the king—but the sickly lord refused to confirm any such thing. Cromwell then had six men arrested who were suspected of carrying on affairs with the queen, including her Flemish minstrel Mark Smeaton, the poet Sir Thomas Wyatt; her own brother **George Boleyn**; and a member of the king's inner circle, Sir **Henry Norris**. Under torture, or perhaps the threat of it, Smeaton the minstrel confessed, and so Anne was arrested in early May 1536 and locked away in the **Tower of London**. There she went through a show trial for treason, and with her own uncle the Duke of Norfolk presiding, the inevitable sentence of death was pronounced upon her. Remembering from her days in France that beheading by a sword seemed easier than by an English axe, Queen Anne asked that a French executioner be provided, and King Henry granted her request. After her brother George and four of her alleged lovers had died two days before (Wyatt was imprisoned and later released), Anne Boleyn bravely met her end on 19 May 1536. Just 11 days after his second queen's execution, Henry VIII married his third wife and queen, **Jane Seymour**.

BOLEYN, GEORGE, SECOND VISCOUNT ROCHFORD (c. 1505–36). The only surviving son of Sir **Thomas Boleyn**, the Earl of Ormond and Wiltshire, George Boleyn was the brother of **Mary Boleyn**, one of Henry VIII's mistresses, and **Anne Boleyn**, King Henry's second wife and queen. George Boleyn inherited the Barony of Rochford from his father and became an influential young gentleman at court and a skilled diplomat in France once his sister Anne attracted and then wed the second Tudor king. Though married himself, he and his spouse remained childless, a fact that has prompted some modern scholars to suggest (without much proof) that George Boleyn was either gay or bisexual. He was accused of incestuous relations with his sister Queen Anne, and both were beheaded for treason in May 1536.

George Boleyn was born around 1505 at Blickling Hall in Norfolk to Thomas Boleyn and his wife, Elizabeth Howard Boleyn. George's father came from **gentry** roots, but his mother was a daughter of the powerful Howard family, the early-16th-century claimants of the title and estates of the Duchy of Norfolk. Of his four siblings, only Mary and Anne survived to adulthood, while his two brothers died in infancy. Like his father before him, George was educated for a diplomatic career and so studied French, Latin, Italian, the classics, poetry, court etiquette, and all the social graces needed to move with ease in a world of privilege. Unlike his older sisters, George remained in England during his youth, which made possible his presentation at court by his father during the Christmas season of 1514–15. He may have attended **Oxford University** as a young man, though there is no evidence from university records to substantiate this. In 1525, he married **Jane Parker Boleyn**, the woman who was destined to produce no offspring for her husband and whose testimony would later help condemn him to a traitor's death with his sister Anne.

George Boleyn was thought intelligent, witty, charming, and urbane by most of his contemporaries, although some noted how arrogant and self-absorbed he could be as well. An outstanding athlete, he quickly attracted Henry VIII's favor by challenging his sovereign at bowls, tennis, archery, and the **joust**, and when he married in 1525, the king presented him with Grimston Manor in Norfolk as a wedding gift. The following year, the young courtier became a gentleman of the king's privy chamber, but the cost-saving **Eltham Ordinances** of **Thomas Cardinal Wolsey** soon saw him ousted from this influential position. Undaunted, Boleyn continued to ascend the ladder of royal favor as King Henry's infatuated gaze fell ever more longingly on his sister Anne. Surviving a bout of the deadly **sweating sickness** in June 1528, Henry VIII took George on as esquire of the king's body the following autumn and then showered his rising protégé with controlling interests in several palaces, castles, and hospitals around southern England. The Tudor king knighted young Boleyn in 1529, and when Sir Thomas Boleyn came into the Earldoms of Ormond

and Wiltshire in the same year, he passed the title of Viscount Rochford along to his only son and heir.

By now one of Henry VIII's most trusted lieutenants, Lord Rochford the diplomat represented the English Crown on six embassies to France between 1529 and 1535. His early missions sought support for King Henry's rejection of Queen **Katherine of Aragon**, but after 1533, he worked to secure French acceptance of his sister Anne Boleyn as England's rightful new queen. In September 1533, he occupied an honored place at the christening of his royal niece Princess **Elizabeth** Tudor, and later the same year, he attended his first **Parliament** as a member of the House of Lords. Lord Rochford's religious sympathies were very clearly aligned with the Lutheran reformers on the Continent, views he shared with his sister Queen Anne more openly as the **Henrician Reformation** gained momentum in England. Eloquent and persuasive, George Boleyn argued the case for Crown control of the English Church during the **Submission of the Clergy** crisis in 1532 and later supported the condemnation of Sir **Thomas More** and the **Carthusian martyrs** of 1535 for refusing to acknowledge the **Act of Succession**.

The spring of 1536 saw Henry VIII growing weary of his second queen, and angered by the recent failure of her third pregnancy, his everwandering eye now fell on the acquiescent and demure **Jane Seymour**, one of Anne Boleyn's ladies-in-waiting. Meanwhile, Henry's chief minister, **Thomas Cromwell**, a committed opponent of the Boleyns, sensed his master's displeasure with Queen Anne and so began to plot with other Boleyn enemies to engineer her downfall. After gathering (or perhaps fabricating) "evidence" of the queen's alleged infidelities with several men at court, Cromwell had six of them—including Anne Boleyn's own brother George—arrested and brought to the **Tower of London** in early May 1536. Only one of the accused actually confessed, but all five of the men arrested with George Boleyn were found guilty of adultery with the queen and were accordingly condemned to death at their trial on 12 May. Lord Rochford and his sister Anne were tried separately on 15 May, and based on damning testimony from George's wife, Jane Boleyn, and despite a spirited self-defense by each sibling, both were convicted of treason for having committed incest together. After delivering a lengthy and prosaic scaffold speech, George and four of the queen's alleged lovers were executed on Tower Hill on 17 May 1536. As queen of England, Anne Boleyn was accorded more privacy and so died as a traitor within the protective walls of the tower two days later. Lord Rochford's remains were laid to rest shortly after his execution in the parish church of St. Peter ad Vincula within the tower precincts.

BOLEYN, JANE (PARKER), VISCOUNTESS ROCHFORD (c. 1505–42).

The wife of **George Boleyn**, Viscount Rochford, and the sister-in-law of **Anne Boleyn**, Henry VIII's second queen, Jane Boleyn played key roles in the downfall not only of her Boleyn relatives but King Henry's fifth wife and queen, **Katherine Howard** as well. Jane Boleyn, known better today as Lady Rochford, lived much of her adult life at the center of the Tudor court as lady-in-waiting to four of the king's royal wives. Apparently unhappy in her own marriage to George Boleyn, she is widely thought to have testified against him at his trial and thus helped send him to a traitor's death on the block. Because she had much to lose if he died, however, Jane attempted to avoid involvement in her husband's trial altogether but was pressured to provide damaging evidence against him and his sister by their enemy **Thomas Cromwell**. Lady Rochford somehow survived the Boleyn downfall but later became an enabler of the adulterous Katherine Howard and so went to the block herself at the young age of just 37 years.

Jane Parker was born around 1505 to Henry Parker, 10th Baron Morley, and his wife, Alice St. John Parker, at one of their estates (Morley, Hingham, or Hockering) in the county of Norfolk. Given an education suitable to a daughter of **noble** rank, Jane learned reading and writing; music; needlework; dance; courtly manners; and the rudiments of French, Spanish, and Italian. She appeared at the Tudor court for the first time before her 15th birthday and reportedly accompanied King Henry, Queen **Katherine of Aragon**, and their entourage to France for the **Field of Cloth of Gold** summit meeting with the French king in summer 1520. Although no known portrait of Jane Parker survives, she was probably a graceful dancer and attractive in appearance, for she was chosen to perform (along with Anne and **Mary Boleyn**) in the fanciful *Château Vert* **pageant** at court during the state visit of Emperor **Charles V** in 1522.

Around the beginning of 1525, Jane married George Boleyn, the son of Sir **Thomas Boleyn** of Norfolk, who was elevated to the peerage as Viscount Rochford later the same year. Her father, Lord Morley, and Henry VIII both provided Jane with a handsome dowry of some £1,300, while the king gave the couple Grimston Manor in Norfolk to serve as their principal residence away from court. Their union may not have been a happy one, however, for George was a serial philanderer who enthusiastically seduced widows and teenaged virgins alike without scruple or remorse. As the king became ever more enchanted with Anne Boleyn in the later 1520s, the fortunes of the entire Boleyn family, including those of George and Jane, began to rise accordingly. When King Henry bestowed the Earldoms of Ormond and Wiltshire on Thomas Boleyn in 1529, he passed his former title, Viscount Rochford, to his son George, which then ennobled Jane as Viscountess or Lady Rochford in her turn. The couple also acquired Beaulieu Palace in Essex at this time, a sumptuous home once owned by Princess **Mary** Tudor before she and her mother, Katherine of Aragon, were banished from court.

When Henry VIII finally married Anne Boleyn in 1533, Lord and Lady Rochford naturally attended the ceremony, and Jane Boleyn then joined the new queen's household as a lady-in-waiting. The birth of a daughter and two miscarried pregnancies did not further endear Anne to her royal husband, however, and within three years of their marriage, the king was already looking for a way to set her aside. Thomas Cromwell, King Henry's chief minister, had early on been an ally of the religiously reformist Anne Boleyn, but the two fell out as Henry's interest in her waned. Eager to please his royal master, Cromwell began to construct a case of criminal infidelity against the queen that promised to bring about her total destruction. His agents arrested her brother George Boleyn and five other courtiers and had charges of treasonous adultery with Queen Anne drawn up against them in spring 1536. All six men were interrogated closely, but only one—Anne's Flemish minstrel Mark Smeaton (who was probably tortured)—confessed to improper relations with the queen, while the others strenuously and even eloquently denied any wrongdoing. In order to strengthen his case of incest against George Boleyn, Cromwell pressed Lady Rochford to testify that her husband and his sister had frequently been alone together, though she denied any knowledge of what had transpired between them. Requiring more direct evidence than this, Cromwell put a more damning spin on Jane Boleyn's testimony and ultimately used it to condemn both George and Anne Boleyn to death as traitors. They died in May 1536, leaving Lady Rochford a destitute widow but freeing the king to wed again just 11 days after his second queen's execution.

Having "cooperated" with Cromwell's investigation in this way, Jane Boleyn's fortunes rose again, and she became a lady-in-waiting to King Henry's third queen, **Jane Seymour**, a post that soon rescued her from the penury of her recent widowhood. While resident at court once more, Lady Rochford (as she was still known) helped restore Princess Mary Tudor to the favor of her royal father and his demure new bride. These happier times did not long endure, however, for Queen Jane died from childbirth complications in October 1537 after producing her husband's long-awaited male heir. Jane Boleyn promptly retired to her father-in-law's Norfolk estate of Blickling Hall, but she was summoned again early in 1540 to take up her accustomed position as lady-in-waiting to Henry VIII's fourth queen, the naïve German princess **Anne of Cleves**. When this royal union unraveled six months later, Lady Rochford decided to remain at court rather than withdraw to a comfortable—and safe—existence in the countryside.

Now the most experienced household attendant to serve England's previous three queens, Jane Boleyn naturally accepted an appointment in the same capacity when the aging Tudor monarch married his fifth queen, Katherine Howard, in July 1540. The new royal consort, though faithful to King Henry at first, had a promiscuous past and soon turned to more virile lovers to satisfy the marital needs that her corpulent, ulcerous, and often inattentive royal husband could not. Loyal to her new mistress, Lady Rochford facilitated and then covered up the queen's illicit trysts with the likes of **Thomas Culpepper**, a gentleman of King Henry's privy chamber, and probably also with Francis Dereham, Katherine's former tutor. Rumors of the queen's indiscretions gradually reached Lord Chancellor **Thomas Audley** and Archbishop **Thomas Cranmer**, who, following a thorough investigation, informed King Henry and then had Culpepper and Dereham jailed and racked in the **Tower of London** in November 1541. Henry VIII was deeply aggrieved by his wife's apparent infidelities and ordered her and Lady Rochford seized and held under house arrest to await their respective fates. Queen Katherine tried to deny the allegations against her and then begged her husband for mercy, but Jane Boleyn was quickly transferred to the tower, where she suffered a complete mental and emotional collapse. Culpepper and Dereham suffered traitors' deaths in mid-December 1541, while Queen Katherine Howard and Lady Jane Boleyn, Viscountess Rochford, both died on the same scaffold and block within minutes of each other on 13 February 1542.

BOLEYN, MARY (CAREY; c. 1499–1543). One of King Henry VIII's more famous mistresses, this "other Boleyn girl" was the elder sister of **Anne Boleyn**, Henry's second wife and queen. Mary Boleyn spent four of her teen years at the French court, where she earned a reputation for loose morals and easy availability. After her return to England, Mary engaged in a four-year affair with the English king and possibly bore him two illegitimate children in the process. She was wed to Sir William Carey just before her relationship with

Henry VIII began, and when Carey died, she married William Stafford and had two more children by him before her own death in her 43rd year.

Although the details about Mary Boleyn's early life are sketchy at best, most scholars agree that she was probably born at Blickling Hall in Norfolk—not at the more impressive Hever Castle in Kent—sometime around 1499 or 1500. **Thomas Boleyn**, her father, boasted an aristocratic ancestry, was a popular and dashing figure at court, and eventually became the Earl of both Wiltshire and Ormond in 1529. Mary's mother was Elizabeth Howard, the daughter of **Thomas Howard**, the Earl of Surrey and future second Duke of Norfolk. As were all the Boleyn children, Mary was groomed for a life at court, and by her mid-teens, she had mastered the French language and proper court etiquette. Thus suitably trained, young Mistress Boleyn accompanied **Mary** Tudor, King Henry's favorite sister, to Paris in August 1514 to marry the toothless old French monarch **Louis XII**.

Fortunately for the pretty new queen of France, her aged husband died within three months of their wedding, which released her to wed her childhood beau **Charles Brandon**, King Henry's closest friend and the future Duke of Suffolk. When the happy newly-weds returned to England in May 1515, Mary Boleyn stayed behind and was soon joined by her sister Anne as ladies-in-waiting to Queen Claude, the consort of King Louis's successor **François I** of France. Over the next four years, Mary had several affairs with various members of the French nobility, and briefly entered into a romantic dalliance with the virile young French king himself. She soon acquired a promiscuous reputation and was ridiculed (or celebrated!) as a "great slut" or a "hackney" (a horse with multiple riders) by some of her French lovers. When her father arrived in Paris as Henry VIII's ambassador, he quickly packed his lascivious daughter off to England in 1519 to avoid any further scandals.

In February 1520, the somewhat tarnished but still attractive Mary was wed in an arranged match to Sir William Carey, a distant Tudor relation who was at the time attached to the household of **Thomas Cardinal Wolsey**. It is likely that King Henry had already noticed Mary, for he attended her wedding to Carey and gave the couple a modest marriage gift of 6s.8d. It was not long, however, before Sir William's new wife and the English king were involved in an amorous relationship of their own. In March 1522, both Boleyn sisters (Anne had just returned from France) appeared in a chivalrous **pageant** at court entitled *Château Vert*, in which Mary played an allegorical nymph named Kindness, while Anne represented the virtue Perseverance. This was probably the first time that Henry laid eyes on the younger Boleyn girl, but he was by then already enjoying the favors of her older sister Mary.

Between 1521 and 1525, King Henry and his Boleyn paramour often met at Penshurst Place, a small manor house owned by Mary's father and located just west of the family seat at Hever Castle in Kent. By 1523, Mary Boleyn was pregnant—either by the king or her husband, the evidence has never been clear—and she subsequently gave birth to a daughter, whom she and Sir William Carey named Katherine. Meanwhile, Sir Thomas Boleyn took advantage of his daughter's royal favor to gather in honors and titles, including membership in the **Order of the Garter** in 1522 and an appointment as Viscount Rochford in 1525. In that year, Mary found herself with child again and gave birth this time to a son, whom the Careys named Henry, perhaps as a nod to the boy's true father. As was often the case with King Henry, he began to lose interest in Mary once she became pregnant for the second time. In 1525, he ended their affair but generously compensated her husband for his stoic forbearance and discretion during the previous four years.

The **sweating sickness** carried off Sir William Carey in 1528, the year that Henry VIII launched his campaign to set aside Queen **Katherine of Aragon** so he might wed Anne Boleyn in her place. By this time, young Henry Carey was beginning to bear a noticeable resemblance to the king, and it was perhaps for this reason that the boy was placed in wardship to his aunt Anne Boleyn, who in turn arranged for his education with a prominent tutor named Nicholas Bourbon. In 1532, Mary accompanied King Henry and her younger sister to **Calais** for a summit meeting with the French king, and she was present at Anne's coronation in London in June 1533. The following year, the widowed Mary married William Stafford, the younger son of a minor Essex landowner, whose fortune was so meager the couple probably wed primarily for love. Their lives together were so destitute that Mary was reduced to asking **Thomas Cromwell** for financial assistance, but King Henry's chief minister generally ignored her pleas. Though never close as girls, Queen Anne helped the Staffords with gifts and money until her own arrest and execution, along with brother **George Boleyn**, in May 1536. Mary Boleyn Stafford died of unknown causes in July 1543. *See also* BLOUNT, ELIZABETH (BESSIE; c. 1497–1540); POPINCOURT, JANE OR JEANNE (c. 1484–c. 1530); SHELTON, MARGARET OR MADGE (c. 1505–c. 1553); STAFFORD, ANNE, LADY HASTINGS, COUNTESS OF HUNTINGDON (c. 1483–1544).

BOLEYN, THOMAS, EARL OF WILTSHIRE AND ORMOND, VISCOUNT ROCHFORD (c. 1477–1539).

Hailing from a relatively obscure **gentry** family in Norfolk, Sir Thomas Boleyn rose to great prominence and wielded considerable influence at the Tudor court when King Henry VIII rejected his first queen to marry Thomas's daughter **Anne Boleyn** in 1533. Sir Thomas was also a loyal and capable servant of the Crown in his own right as a diplomat, government minister, royal councilor, and member of **Parliament**. He fathered **Mary Boleyn**, one of King Henry's early mistresses, and **George Boleyn**, who was implicated in the alleged treason of his sister Queen Anne and was executed with her in 1536. Sir Thomas Boleyn's life exemplified the kind of meteoric rise and precipitous collapse that could and often did befall many ambitious gentlemen at the volatile court of King Henry VIII.

Thomas Boleyn was one of 10 children born at Blickling Hall in Norfolk to Sir William Boleyn and his wife, Lady Margaret Butler Boleyn. Thomas's father was descended from a family of successful tradesmen, but his mother

was a daughter of the **noble** house of Ormond, an earldom with significant land holdings in **Ireland**. Sometime before the turn of the 16th century, Thomas married Elizabeth Howard, the daughter of **Thomas Howard**, second Duke of Norfolk, thus joining the Boleyns to one of the wealthiest and most powerful families in England. Together Thomas and Elizabeth Boleyn produced five children, three of whom—Mary, Anne, and George—survived to adulthood and became important figures in the reign of Henry VIII. Their father educated not only his son but his daughters as well, insisting they all learn fluent French, palace etiquette, music, dance, and hunting skills to prepare them for potential careers at court.

Thomas Boleyn began his own ascent as a courtier by joining the escort troop that accompanied Princess **Margaret** Tudor to her wedding with King **James IV** in Scotland in 1503. At the accession of the teenaged Henry VIII in 1509, Boleyn accepted a knighthood in the Order of the Bath and then became better known to the young king when they clashed in a celebratory **joust** at **Greenwich Palace** in 1511. The next year, King Henry granted Sir Thomas several estates in Kent, appointed him constable of Norwich Castle, and then sent him off as a diplomat to the court of **Margaret of Austria**, the Duchess of Savoy, who ruled the Netherlands for her father, Emperor **Maximilian I**. Anne Boleyn accompanied her father on this occasion and remained in the Netherlands as a lady-in-waiting to the duchess after Sir Thomas left to ride with King Henry on his **French invasion of 1513–14**. In 1514, both Mary and Anne Boleyn traveled to Paris to wait first upon Princess **Mary** Tudor and then upon Queen Claude of France. When Sir Thomas's eldest daughter acquired a promiscuous reputation there, however, her embarrassed father quietly fetched her home to the family estate at Hever Castle in Kent in 1519.

By now a member of King Henry's inner circle of dashing courtiers, Sir Thomas Boleyn helped arrange and then attended the **Field of Cloth of Gold** summit meeting with King **François I** in June 1520. That brief Anglo-French detente quickly broke down, however, and so Boleyn was reassigned to Germany as

England's ambassador at the imperial court of Emperor **Charles V** in 1521. Around this time, Henry VIII entered into an intimate relationship with Sir Thomas's eldest daughter, Mary, an affair that moved a grateful sovereign to knight the senior Boleyn into the **Order of the Garter** in a demonstration of singular royal favor in 1523. By this time, Boleyn's younger daughter, Anne, had also returned from France, and it was not long before her lustrous dark hair, enchanting eyes, and coquettish French manners stole the fancy of the Tudor king away from her older sister. By 1525, Henry VIII was in hot pursuit of Mistress Anne, and once again wishing to show his appreciation, the king elevated Sir Thomas to the peerage as Viscount Rochford. As Henry's infatuation with Anne grew ever deeper, the titles and offices Sir Thomas accumulated grew more prestigious, valuable, and influential as he became the Earl of Ormond, the Earl of Wiltshire, and King Henry's lord privy seal between 1529 and 1530.

During the period of Anne Boleyn's rise to marriage with King Henry in 1533, the Earl of Wiltshire was active in the background of the Tudor court as a diplomat, a religious reformer, and a member of the House of Lords. In 1527, he traveled to Paris to secure the signature of King François on a new Anglo-French treaty, and in 1530, he joined an ill-fated embassy to treat with the emperor and the pope—then newly allied together—for an annulment of Henry VIII's first marriage. Clearly sympathetic to the Lutheran movement in Germany, Wiltshire refused to kiss the foot of Pope **Clement VII** on this occasion and so guaranteed the failure of his mission. In 1532, he publicly denounced the pope and the Roman bishops in England during the **Submission of the Clergy** dispute but then took part in the examination of the evangelical preacher **John Frith** in London prior to that reformer's death at the stake for heresy in 1533.

In April 1536, the Earl of Wiltshire was forced to help investigate the men accused of adultery with his daughter Queen Anne, and when all were duly convicted of treason, the patriarch of the Boleyn family watched as two of his children were beheaded the following

month. Thomas Boleyn understandably retreated from court after the execution of his daughter and son, but he survived to help suppress the **Pilgrimage of Grace** uprising with the Duke of Norfolk in 1536, and he was sufficiently restored to royal favor by autumn 1537 to attend the christening of Prince **Edward VI** at **Hampton Court Palace**. Sir Thomas Boleyn, Earl of Ormond and Wiltshire, died in March 1539 and was laid to rest in St. Peter's Church in Hever, Kent. His tomb inside the church is today marked by a beautiful brass effigy clad in the robes of a Garter knight.

BONNER, EDMUND, BISHOP OF LONDON

(c. 1500–1569). Another example of a conservative English bishop who survived the **Henrician Reformation,** Edmund Bonner played a major role in the reactionary religious settlement that dominated the final years of Henry VIII's reign. A humanist scholar and a brilliant lawyer, Bonner enjoyed active service as a Crown agent and diplomat in addition to his career as a prominent bishop. As a younger man, he held the Roman papacy in contempt and even entertained reformist religious views for a time, but later in life, he returned to the Church of Rome and eventually helped persecute Protestant heretics in his diocese under Queen **Mary I**. He was twice incarcerated under two different Tudor rulers for his religious conservatism and ended his days in a Southwark prison across the Thames from his home diocese of London.

Edmund Bonner was born around 1500 in Hanley, Worcestershire, to Elizabeth Frodsham Bonner, although the identity of his father remains uncertain to this day. Some scholars believe he was the natural son of Elizabeth's legal husband, Edmund Bonner, a sawyer, but others suggest that George Savage, a rector of Davenham Parish in Cheshire, may have been the boy's real father. In any case, the teenaged Edmund Bonner enrolled in Broadgates Hall (now Pembroke College) at **Oxford University,** where he completed his baccalaureate degree in civil and canon law and then entered holy orders as a priest in 1519. After earning a doctoral degree in civil law six years later, Bonner joined the household of **Thomas**

Cardinal Wolsey, whom he served as a chaplain and legal assistant during the late 1520s. Ever loyal, Bonner was with his patron when the "Great Cardinal" died in November 1530 in Leicester on his way back to London.

Surviving Wolsey's fall, Bonner became a Crown diplomat and was dispatched by Henry VIII to Rome in January 1532 to help secure a papal annulment of the English king's first marriage to Queen **Katherine of Aragon.** He remained on the Continent over the next few years to dissuade the pope from excommunicating King Henry and then to convince Emperor **Charles V** to recognize his royal master's second marriage to **Anne Boleyn.** Although neither mission proved successful, Bonner received lucrative rewards for his efforts that included various church livings in Durham, Yorkshire, the Midlands, and East Anglia and an archdiaconal appointment in Leicester. A religious conservative at heart, Bonner nevertheless despised Pope **Clement VII** and at least outwardly supported Henry VIII's supremacy over the English Church. In 1535, he authored a preface to Bishop **Stephen Gardiner**'s *De vera obedientia*, a little tract that urged all loyal English subjects to reject papal authority and accept King Henry as the true lord of their breakaway church.

The king was well pleased with Bonner and made him a royal chaplain in absentia, which allowed Henry to post his faithful ambassador overseas to the French and imperial courts in 1537–38 once more. While in France, Bonner helped push the publication of the **Great Bible** through hostile Catholic presses in Paris and was again duly rewarded for his service with an appointment as the new bishop of Hereford. He was too busy abroad to return for his consecration to the diocese, however, and within a year was translated instead to the wealthier and more prominent see of London. This prize was too grand to pass up, and he hurried back to England for consecration to his new diocese early in 1540. By that time, **Parliament** had passed the **Act of Six Articles,** which restored to the English Church most of the traditional doctrines and ceremonies of Rome. This more conservative religious climate suited Bonner well, and he

enthusiastically hunted down and prosecuted evangelical believers in his diocese, attracting the enmity of many Londoners in the process. In 1546, he initiated heresy proceedings against **Anne Askew,** an outspoken reformist from Lincolnshire, but then turned her over to Crown officials **Thomas Wriothesley** and **Richard Rich** to be tortured on the rack and finally burned at the stake.

The royal favor and good fortune that Bishop Bonner had so far enjoyed completely evaporated upon the death of King Henry VIII in late January 1547. His successor, **Edward VI,** though still a child, felt nothing but scorn for the old Roman Church and was supported in these views by the powerful men who now dominated his royal council. When Bonner refused to uphold the new king's supremacy over the English Church, he was deprived of his episcopal office and locked away in the Marshalsea debtor's prison in Southwark for the duration of Edward's reign. In August 1553, Queen Mary pardoned Edmund Bonner, and now restored to his London diocese as bishop, he zealously set about persecuting Protestant heretics as he had once done under Henry VIII. Directly responsible for the burning deaths of 113 evangelical Londoners and indirectly involved as a Crown judge in dozens more, Bonner earned the epithet "Bloody Bonner" just as his Catholic royal mistress was later dubbed "Bloody Mary." His reputation as a merciless persecutor followed him into the reign of the reformist Queen **Elizabeth I,** who deprived Bonner of his episcopal miter and crozier for a second time and then had him returned to the Marshalsea prison in Southwark. He died there on 5 September 1569 and was buried in the nearby chapel of St. George in the middle of the night to prevent angry Londoners from disturbing his entombment.

BRANDON, CHARLES, FIRST DUKE OF SUFFOLK, FIRST VISCOUNT LISLE (1484–1545).

This accomplished courtier, royal councilor, and military commander grew up in the royal Tudor household and so became a great friend and the brother-in-law of Henry VIII. Sharing the same love of adventure and athletic competition with the young king, Brandon later led English armies in all three of Henry's **French invasions** and served the Crown as an international diplomat on several occasions as well. The first Duke of Suffolk is perhaps best remembered today as the husband of King Henry's younger sister **Mary** Tudor, who always cared deeply for her brother's friend and who jumped at the chance to marry him following the death of her first husband, the king of France. Brandon encouraged Henry VIII to replace his first queen, **Katherine of Aragon**, with **Anne Boleyn**; supported the separation of England from the Roman Church; and enriched his land holdings when the English **monasteries** were dissolved between 1536 and 1539. Of all the men who knew and served the first two Tudor rulers, only Charles Brandon succeeded in cultivating a close and lasting friendship with Henry VIII over the course of their lifetimes together.

Charles Brandon was born the only surviving son of Sir William Brandon of Soham, Cambridgeshire, and his wife, Elizabeth Bruyn Brandon, the heiress of a minor **gentry** family from Essex. Sir William Brandon was famous in his own right because, as the Tudor standard-bearer at the Battle of Bosworth, he was killed defending Henry Tudor (the future **Henry VII**) from the furious last onslaught of King Richard III in August 1485. Grateful for his father's battlefield courage and sacrifice, King Henry took the infant Charles Brandon into his royal household and there raised the boy as a favored stepson. Thus Brandon grew up beside both **Arthur** Tudor and his younger brother Henry, receiving the same humanist education and learning the finer points of court etiquette and knightly prowess in the company of the two royal princes. An athletic and precocious teenager, Charles Brandon was skilled at the **joust** and took part in the tournament Henry VII sponsored to celebrate the marriage of Prince Arthur to Katherine of Aragon in 1501. King Henry continued to favor Brandon as a young adult, adding him to his household guards and appointing him a squire of the king's body in 1506–7. Apparently irresistible to women, Brandon had already married (then lost or discarded) two wives and had fathered several children both inside and outside

of wedlock by the time the first Tudor king breathed his last in April 1509.

When Henry VIII succeeded his father at age 17, he quickly surrounded himself with a group of boisterous young courtiers he affectionately called his "henchmen." These men, who included Sir **Nicholas Carew**, Sir **Henry Norris**, and of course Charles Brandon, all hunted, jousted, danced, and seduced their way around the Tudor court in the company of their high-spirited Tudor master. Henry had always looked up to the older Brandon and soon rewarded his friend by naming him master of the king's horse in 1512 and ennobling him as the first Viscount Lisle in 1513. Later that year, Lord Lisle accompanied King Henry on his first French invasion and led a successful assault on the main gate of Tournai that persuaded the town's garrison to surrender. Impressed, Henry welcomed Brandon into the chivalrous Order of the **Garter** late in 1513 and then created him the first Duke of Suffolk early the following year.

After the war in France, Suffolk returned to the Tudor court, where he fell in love with Henry's pretty sister Mary, a teenager who had long been infatuated with the dashing 30-something duke herself. Despite their budding romance, Mary's brother shipped her off in October 1514 to wed the aged and decrepit **Louis XII** of France to fulfill the terms of an earlier peace treaty. A few months later, Suffolk managed to join a diplomatic mission to France in order to reconnect once more with Mary, by then the neglected consort of the repulsive old French king. Brandon's arrival in Paris coincided with the death of King Louis, and afraid that Henry VIII might seek another arranged state match for his sister, the couple hastily married in a secret ceremony in March 1515 before embarking for England a few weeks later.

King Henry was of course furious that Brandon and Mary had wed without his permission, but he gradually forgave them (after they agreed to pay a huge fine) and then attended their more formal nuptials at **Greenwich Palace** in May 1515. The happy couple accompanied the king to the **Field of Cloth of Gold** summit meeting outside **Calais** five years later, but Henry VIII decided to invade France again in 1523 and nominated Suffolk to serve as his principal field commander. In 1524, the king named his brother-in-law Earl Marshal of England—the highest military rank in the land—despite the fact that Suffolk had nearly blinded Henry accidentally in a jousting mishap a few months earlier. Because of their great friendship, Suffolk supported Henry's campaign to set aside Katherine of Aragon in favor of Anne Boleyn, even though he later admitted that he found the entire affair quite distasteful. Suffolk took great pleasure, however, in the downfall of **Thomas Cardinal Wolsey** and Queen Anne, both of whom he had intensely disliked and with whom he had often crossed political swords. Suffolk's wife gave him two living daughters before her premature death at age 37 in June 1533, which freed the duke to wed 14-year-old Katherine Willoughby (his former ward and now his fourth wife) later the same year.

By the time Henry VIII had taken his own third wife, Charles Brandon was attempting to withdraw from the tumultuous Tudor court and retire with his young bride to his estates in East Anglia. Yet, when King Henry ordered the dissolution of England's religious houses in the late 1530s, Suffolk eagerly emerged from his seclusion to acquire as much of the confiscated church land as he could. Unexpectedly, however, the Crown's closure policy sparked a massive revolt in Lincolnshire and Yorkshire known as the **Pilgrimage of Grace** in autumn 1536. This popular uprising protested the shuttering and sale of the monasteries that had always been an important part of daily life in the rural English Midlands. King Henry called his old friend out of retirement to lead an armed force against the insurgents, but before he could intercept them, most of the rebel host had already melted away. Suffolk still put some 60 of the ringleaders to death and then turned operations over to **Thomas Howard**, the third Duke of Norfolk, who eliminated any lingering resistance and carried out another 180 executions to bring the Pilgrimage to a bloody conclusion.

Satisfied once again with his friend's loyal service, Henry VIII invited Suffolk back to court in the late 1530s and immediately appointed him to the newly reorganized and more compact privy council. As his trusted advisor, the duke accompanied Henry to Kent to surprise his intended fourth queen, **Anne of Cleves**, and so was present when the king recoiled in disgust upon meeting his German bride-to-be for the first time in January 1540. Six months later, Suffolk was instrumental in arranging the annulment that freed his friend from his loveless union with the unattractive Queen Anne. At age 60, Suffolk again commanded English troops in France when Henry VIII invaded that realm for the last time in the **French invasion of 1544–45**. After his return to England, the duke's health deteriorated rapidly, and he died in Guildford, Surrey, on the 60th anniversary of his father's heroic action and death at the Battle of Bosworth. Suffolk had requested a simple burial in a church at Tattershall near Lincoln, but the king interred his remains instead at Windsor Castle in the chapel of St. George, the principal meeting chamber of the knights of the Garter. When Henry VIII himself passed away just 17 months later, his will provided for his own burial near the tomb of his lifelong friend in the same chapel at Windsor.

BUTTS, SIR WILLIAM (c. 1486–1545). A royal physician of the early Tudor age, William Butts treated members of King Henry VIII's immediate family as well as the families of many prominent lords and prelates during his lengthy and successful medical career. When the **sweating sickness** ravaged the realm in the 1520s, an alarmed king sent Butts to Kent to ensure the health of his lady-love **Anne Boleyn**. Butts was a committed reformer in his religious beliefs who defended fellow Protestants and tried to convert those conservatives who opposed the **Henrician Reformation**. As a member of King Henry's inner circle, Butts enjoyed unprecedented royal access and at times used his influence to promote the careers of others he admired and respected.

William Butts was born around 1486, either in the London suburb of Fulham or perhaps in Norfolk in East Anglia, but little is otherwise known of his parentage or his early life. He was educated at **Cambridge University**, earning his baccalaureate degree in 1506, his master's degree in 1509, and his medical doctorate in 1518. By the mid-1520s, Butts was already a practicing physician whose growing list of clients included many members of the **gentry** and **nobility**. One of his early patients was **Thomas Cardinal Wolsey**, who, impressed with the results of Butts's treatment, recommended him to his master, Henry VIII. The king obviously shared Wolsey's assessment of Butts's medical talents because when the "sweate" struck southern England in summer 1527, he dispatched the man he called his "second best" physician (his best doctor was unavailable) to attend Anne Boleyn at her Hever Castle family estate in Kent. Henry was overjoyed to learn that Lady Anne had survived her illness, and he immediately placed the man who had brought about her cure on a £100 annual retainer for life.

The good doctor soon found himself treating the likes of Princess **Mary** Tudor, King Henry's daughter by **Katherine of Aragon**; **Henry Fitzroy**, the king's illegitimate son by his mistress **Bessie Blount**; **Thomas Howard**, third Duke of Norfolk; King Henry's third wife and queen, **Jane Seymour**; and several members of Anne Boleyn's family, including her father, **Thomas Boleyn**, the Earl of Wiltshire, and her brother **George Boleyn**, Lord Rochford. In addition, Dr. Butts's proximity to royalty occasionally gave him the chance to influence state affairs, as when he tried (unsuccessfully) to reconcile Cardinal Wolsey with King Henry in 1529. No friend of the Roman Church, however, the royal physician knew well and championed the careers of religious reformers **Hugh Latimer** and **John Cheke**, and he tried to convince the monks of Syon Abbey to accept King Henry's supreme lordship over the English Church. Anne Boleyn relied on him to recommend reformist scholars to serve her, and he was a close associate of both **Thomas Cranmer**, the archbishop of Canterbury, and **Katherine Parr**, King Henry's sixth and final queen.

Butts was admitted into the prestigious College of Physicians in 1529, and he was knighted later in his career for his great service to the House of Tudor. Around the age of 30, he married Margaret Bacon of Cambridgeshire and by her fathered three sons named William, Thomas, and Edmund. In 1540, it was Dr. Butts who assured King Henry that his failure to consummate his union with **Anne of Cleves** was entirely due to her inability to arouse him sexually. Butts's portrait was painted in 1543 by no less an artist than **Hans Holbein** the Younger and is today on display in Montacute House in Somersetshire. When the good doctor died in November 1545 and was buried in All Saints' parish church in Fulham, his friend John Cheke (by then employed as a tutor to Henry VIII's children) composed an epitaph in Latin for his tomb.

C

CALAIS (c. 997–1558). Situated only 20 miles across the English Channel from the coastal town of Dover, this strategically important fortified port, located in the northernmost corner of the kingdom of France, was an English possession for more than 200 years and provided its rulers with a convenient staging ground for invading armies and diplomatic meetings. The only French territory to remain in English hands following the end of the Hundred Years' War in 1453, Calais was the launch site for three of King Henry VIII's **French invasions**, served as headquarters for the **Field of Cloth of Gold** summit meeting, and played host to King Henry and **Anne Boleyn** during the final stages of their courtship in 1532.

The origins of Calais can be traced back to Roman times, when Gaius Julius Caesar mounted his successive invasions of Britannia from Celetum in the first century BC. During the early medieval period, Calais was a tiny fishing village located on a small island in the midst of marshland. In 997, the Count of **Flanders** claimed Calais and enclosed the settlement with earthen walls and a moated ditch. In 1181, the town was issued a charter of incorporation by the Count of Boulogne, and eight years later, King Richard the Lionheart passed through Calais on his way to the Third Crusade. Realizing its strategic importance, a later Count of Boulogne erected more permanent stone walls and enlarged the town's harbor in 1224. Little more was heard from Calais until after the Battle of Crécy in 1346, when the victorious King Edward III decided to capture the town for England. Following a long and vicious siege, Edward threatened to massacre the entire population of Calais unless several of its leading citizens surrendered themselves to his wrath. Six town leaders, or burghers, stepped forward to save Calais and were in turn spared by the English king, an episode later memorialized by Auguste Rodin in his famous ensemble sculpture *The Burghers of Calais* in 1895. Dating from its seizure in 1347, Calais would remain in English hands for the next 211 years.

By the 15th century, Calais was sending representatives to sit in the English **Parliament**, and it became an important wool export center when the staple trade association established warehouses and inns there. Desirous of greater royal control over the port, the Crown created the lucrative and much-coveted captaincy of Calais to represent its interests there and coordinate its defenses in the event of French or Burgundian attacks. A few of the more important men to hold this office during the early Tudor period were Sir Richard Nanfant; Lord William Sandys; **Arthur Plantagenet**, Lord Lisle; and Sir Edward Wotton.

Within a few years of his accession, the young and energetic Henry VIII used Calais as the initial landing site for his French invasion force of some 40,000 men in June 1513. The invasion itself accomplished little—King Henry only captured two towns and fought in a brief skirmish—and within five months, the English army had withdrawn to Calais and thence back to England. Two more futile English invasions of France were launched later from Calais in 1523–24 and 1544–45. In 1520,

Calais became the staging ground for the glittering Field of Cloth of Gold summit meeting between Henry VIII and King **François I** of France, but as with all the English king's invasions, little of real substance was achieved. In 1532, King Henry brought Anne Boleyn to his French enclave in hopes of meeting with and persuading François to confer public recognition of their relationship. A few meetings did in fact take place between the two rulers, but no French recognition was forthcoming, and after four weeks in Calais, the Tudor party returned empty handed to England. Within two months of their visit to Calais, Anne Boleyn was with child, and King Henry secretly wed her to ensure that the child she carried would be born within the bonds of marriage. Calais remained in English hands until the end of the reign of King Henry's daughter Queen **Mary I**, when François duc de Guise recaptured the town for France in 1558.

CAMBRIDGE UNIVERSITY (1209–). England's second-oldest institution of higher learning, Cambridge University was founded quite unintentionally by a band of educational refugees in the early 13th century. Like its sister school **Oxford University**, Cambridge evolved from a loose collection of semiautonomous colleges into one of Europe's premier universities by the late 15th century. Alongside Oxford, Cambridge paved the way for the *studia humanitatis*, or new learning of humanism, to take root in England by quietly and then openly embracing the study of Greek letters during the reigns of the first two Tudor kings. Cambridge also became a hotbed of Lutheran dissent during the 1520s and, in direct opposition to religiously conservative Crown and church officials, helped plant the earliest doctrinal seeds of the **Henrician Reformation** in England. Many luminaries of the Tudor age were educated at Cambridge University, while Tudor royals, magnates, and even prominent commoners founded or endowed colleges there as well.

The town of Cambridge emerged during the Anglo-Saxon period as an important trading center on the River Cam in the fenland region of the eastern Midlands. A castle overlooking the Cam already existed by 1086, and by the early 12th century, the area had become home to the episcopal diocese of Ely and to several monasteries, convents, and hospitals. In the early 13th century, Cambridge was a bustling and prosperous market town that was licensed to host three large trade fairs each year. In 1209, two groups of Oxford University scholars (undergraduate students) sought refuge from violent Oxford townsmen and fled either to nearby Reading or to more distant Cambridge. Those who went to Cambridge (possibly natives of the place) elected to remain there and soon invited some of the more learned area monks and secular priests into town to teach lessons in Latin grammar, Christian theology, and rudimentary mathematics. This embryonic Cambridge educational community continued to attract many more students, until their numbers warranted the creation in 1225 of a learning administration, or *universitas*, under the direction of a supervising chancellor. By the mid-13th century, the student-scholars were mostly living in *collegia* townhouses and tended to congregate together according to their shared place of origin or course of study. They took common meals in dining hall *refectoria*, worshipped in collegiate chapels, and invited professors or "masters" (typically Dominican or Franciscan friars) into their living quarters to deliver lectures on the seven liberal arts.

King Henry III chartered Cambridge University in 1231, and Pope Gregory IX authorized its graduates to teach courses anywhere in Europe two years later. The first few Cambridge *collegia* no longer exist; the oldest surviving school at the university is Peterhouse, founded by Bishop Hugh de Balsham of Ely in 1284. By the time of Henry VIII's accession to the throne in 1509, there were 12 colleges operating in Cambridge. University Hall was founded in 1326 but changed its name to Clare College a dozen years later to honor its principal benefactor, Lady Elizabeth de Clare. Henry VI provided the founding endowment for King's College in 1441, while his consort, Margaret of Anjou, did the same for Queen's College seven years later. Bishop **John Fisher** of Rochester, the chaplain and confessor of

Henry VII's mother, Lady **Margaret Beaufort**, persuaded her to endow both Christ's and St. John's Colleges at Cambridge in 1505 and (posthumously) in 1511. Perhaps inspired by his grandmother's example, Henry VIII himself founded Trinity College in 1546, today one of the university's largest and by far its wealthiest school.

Aside from procuring funds for and overseeing collegiate foundations, Bishop Fisher was also instrumental in opening Cambridge University to the study of Greek just after the turn of the 16th century. King Henry VII appointed Fisher chancellor of the university in 1504, and interested in bringing the previously prohibited *studia humanitatis* to England, he invited the noted Dutch scholar and humanist **Desiderius Erasmus** to Cambridge to offer informal lessons in Greek language and classical texts to interested students. Thanks in part to the establishment of a chair in Greek studies at Oxford University by Bishop **Richard Fox** and to the support Henry VIII gave to Fox's bold educational initiative, Bishop Fisher was able to endow his own Greek chair at St. John's College in Cambridge in 1523.

At around the same time, a circle of Cambridge University academics, such as **Robert Barnes**, **Hugh Latimer**, **Thomas Bilney**, **William Tyndale**, and others, were beginning to meet regularly (and secretly) at the White Horse Inn in Cambridge. They gathered to discuss the revolutionary ideas of the German reformer Martin Luther, whose controversial teachings had recently been condemned as heretical by King Henry and **Thomas Cardinal Wolsey**. Although this group of scholarly dissidents was small, they introduced England to Lutheran theology and so helped prepare the way for the coming English Reformation in the 1530s.

Some of the most important Tudor-era figures to attend or graduate from Cambridge University included archbishop of Canterbury **Thomas Cranmer**; Duke **Edward Seymour** of Somerset; royal tutors **John Skelton**, **Roger Ascham**, and **John Cheke**; historian **Edward Hall**; and Lord Chancellors **Thomas Audley** and **Thomas Wriothesley**.

CAMPEGGIO, LORENZO CARDINAL (c. 1473–1539). An eyewitness to some of the greatest religious upheavals of the early 16th century, Lorenzo Cardinal Campeggio is best remembered in English history for the role he played in the "divorce" (annulment) trial of **Katherine of Aragon** in 1529. Aside from this association with Henry VIII's "**Great Matter**," Campeggio served five different popes as a nuncio (diplomat) or legate (legal representative) in Germany, Italy, and England for nearly 30 years. He was also a respected humanist scholar and an ecclesiastical reformer who worked tirelessly to heal the schism between Rome and the breakaway Protestants, unfortunately without much success. Although he undertook many important assignments during his career, Campeggio failed to accomplish most of them because he was arrayed against powerful religious and political forces that in the end defeated his best intentions and efforts.

Lorenzo Campeggio was born in Bologna between 1472 and 1474 and was one of five children in the family of well-known attorney and legal professor Giovanni Campeggio. Young Lorenzo learned the rudiments of the law from his father in Padua and then earned his doctorate in civil law at the University of Bologna in 1500. He also married around this time and managed to sire five children of his own before his wife's untimely death in 1509. One year later, Campeggio entered holy orders and rose so quickly within the hierarchy of the Roman Church that in 1512, Pope Julius II created him bishop of Feltre and appointed him notary of an important papal court. During the next five years, Campeggio was resident in Germany trying (unsuccessfully) to persuade Holy Roman Emperor **Maximilian I** to undertake a crusade against the Ottoman Turks, but upon his return to Rome in 1517, he was granted a cardinal's hat in compensation for his diligent service to the pope. In April 1518, Pope **Leo X** sent him to England to recruit Henry VIII for the crusade, a mission that also failed when **Thomas Cardinal Wolsey** stripped Campeggio of his legatine powers and tried to block his access to the king. Despite Wolsey's attempts to isolate him, King Henry was sufficiently impressed with the learning and dignity of the Italian cardinal to grant him the bishopric of Salisbury in absentia.

By late 1519, Cardinal Campeggio was back in Rome and soon took part in the papal conclave that elected the pious Dutch monk Adrian VI as the new pope early in 1522. Unlike the Medici pontiffs who preceded and succeeded him, Adrian was an ascetic and saintly man who was determined to clean up the many corruptions that plagued the Roman Church of his day. Eager to assist in this effort, Cardinal Campeggio recommended many ecclesiastical reforms in his *De depravato statu ecclesiae* that included abolition of clerical pluralism and absenteeism, restoration of episcopal investiture rights to Rome, more careful vetting of candidates for high church office, and limitation of indulgence sales for papal profit. Within 20 months of his election, however, Pope Adrian died and was replaced by another son of the House of Medici, Pope **Clement VII**. Campeggio then took possession of the see of his hometown Bologna before going off once again as the new papal legate in Germany.

There he encountered the hostile Lutheran movement, but rather than condemn the reformers outright, he tried to reconcile them to the Roman Church at the Diet of Nuremburg in 1524. What little progress Campeggio was able to make in this regard was quickly overturned by the great Peasants' Revolt of 1524–25, a bloody upheaval that made Pope Clement decide to recall his oft-thwarted cardinal back to the Vatican. He was still there when the unpaid armies of Emperor **Charles V** attacked and sacked **Rome** in 1527. He hid with the terrified pontiff in the Castel Sant'Angelo while imperial troops looted the papal palaces and *camera* (treasury) inside the city. Once Pope Clement escaped from the emperor's grasp the following year, he was free to send Campeggio back to England on another legatine mission to help judge the very delicate matter of King Henry's longed-for annulment of his marriage to Queen Katherine of Aragon.

The aging Italian cardinal arrived in England in October 1528 with orders to convince the English king to reconcile with his wife, to prevail upon Queen Katherine to enter a convent, or (failing all else) to draw out the proceedings and avoid rendering any decision at all. After Wolsey had joined him to preside over the trial, the two cardinals collected evidence, interviewed witnesses, and delayed matters for so long that King Henry finally lost patience and demanded that his annulment case be heard forthwith. The trial therefore commenced in June 1529 at the Blackfriars Monastery outside London, but when the queen first pleaded with her husband and then threatened to appeal her case to the pope in Rome, Campeggio abruptly adjourned the proceedings on 23 July before any verdict could be reached. King Henry was apoplectic with rage and had Campeggio detained at Dover for two weeks as the old cardinal tried to make his way back to Rome.

The remainder of Campeggio's life was somewhat less eventful than had been the case in his earlier years. In 1530, he was present in his episcopal city of Bologna for the coronation of Charles V as Holy Roman Emperor, and he returned to Germany with that ruler later that same year to attend the Diet of Augsburg, where, for all intents and purposes, the Protestant split from Rome was made permanent. When Pope Clement died a few years later, Campeggio attended the conclave that elected the fifth and final pope he would serve, Paul III, in autumn 1534. After the English **Parliament** stripped him of his diocese of Salisbury at Henry VIII's behest, he sat on the papal commission that excommunicated the English king in 1535. The sickly 66-year-old prince of the church finally died on 19 July 1539 and was buried in the church of Santa Maria in the Trastevere district of Rome, although some of his remains were later translated to a church in his native Bologna.

CAREW, SIR NICHOLAS (1496–1539). A

courtier, diplomat, **Garter** knight, and Henry VIII's master of horse, Nicholas Carew was one among many young favorites with whom the king surrounded himself during the early and middle years of his reign. As a dashing member of King Henry's inner circle of so-called henchmen, Carew attended his royal master at lavish court entertainments, **jousting tournaments**, and hunting expeditions during the course of his 25-year public career. He was implicated, however, in an alleged plot by Yorkist descendants to overthrow the House of Tudor, and condemned as a traitor, he died under the headsman's axe on Tower Hill in March 1539.

Nicholas Carew was born in Beddington, Surrey, into the family of Sir Richard Carew, whose loyal service to King **Henry VII** had earned him a knighthood and an appointment as a sheriff in Surrey by 1501. At age 18, Nicholas accompanied Henry VIII on his **French invasion of 1513–14** and, distinguishing himself during the English siege of Thérouanne, became a squire of the king's body and was rewarded with an annuity and several estates in Surrey. At the end of 1514, Carew married Elizabeth Bryan, the daughter of one of Queen **Katherine of Aragon**'s chamber attendants. Three years later, Henry VIII knighted his young courtier and bestowed upon him the honorific office of king's cupbearer. Oddly, the royal council twice banished Sir Nicholas from court in 1518 and 1519 for being overly "familiar" with the king, but he was soon restored to favor and joined the English contingent at the **Field of Cloth of Gold** summit meeting with King **François I** outside **Calais** in June 1520.

His gracious service at the French conference helped launch his career as a foreign diplomat, for Carew was soon with King Henry a few weeks later to negotiate a military and trade pact with Emperor **Charles V** in **Flanders**. Later in the 1520s, the Tudor king authorized Sir Nicholas to carry important dispatches and a Garter knighthood to King François in Paris, and he attended another meeting with the emperor in Bologna near the end of that decade. As one of the king's rowdy "henchmen," a group of spirited youths who included **Charles Brandon**, Duke of Suffolk; Sir Francis Bryan; and Henry Guildford, among others, Henry VIII regarded Carew as a sort of friend worthy of royal trust and reward. In due course, the king granted Sir Nicholas the lucrative office of master of horse and promoted his election to the prestigious Order of the Garter in the early 1530s.

These signal honors were ultimately insufficient to shield the ambitious knight from the capricious and dangerous politics that swirled around the Henrician court at this time. Always thought to have sympathized with the deposed Queen Katherine, Carew eagerly helped bring about the downfall of Queen **Anne Boleyn** in 1536 and worked to promote King Henry's third marriage to **Jane Seymour**. Two years later, his privileged position at court began to erode, however, when Henry Pole, Lord Montague, and **Henry Courtenay**, Marquis of Exeter—both descended from the House of York—were arrested and sent to the **Tower of London** for plotting to overthrow the Tudor regime. Royal agents soon found a letter in Exeter's household that also implicated Sir Nicholas Carew in the plot, a discovery that led to his own arrest, trial, and conviction as a traitor in February 1539. A few weeks later, he went to his death on the block, more a victim of the political vagaries of the Tudor court than from any real threat he may have posed to the rule or the person of his royal patron.

CARTHUSIAN MARTYRS (1535–40).

As one of the most austere, pious, and respected religious houses in Tudor England, the Carthusian **monastery** of the Charterhouse in London remained true to the Roman Church during the **Henrician Reformation** of the mid-1530s. Led by their prior John Houghton, the Carthusians tried to sidestep Henry VIII's rejection of papal authority, but the Crown required the acquiescence of all English landowners and **clergy**, and the holy monks of the Charterhouse were no exception. Nearly 20 Carthusians from three different religious houses (plus a few other clerics and laymen) either suffered a grisly traitor's death, were publicly hanged from city walls, or were imprisoned and allowed to starve to death in one of the most shamefully barbaric episodes of King Henry VIII's reign.

The Carthusian order of monks was originally founded by St. Bruno in the Chartreuse Mountains of France (hence the order's name) in 1084 and came to England in the late medieval period, when nine houses were established across the realm between 1341 and 1414. The Carthusians were cloistered monks who lived in communal monasteries and who shared food, labor, and prayer with their brethren in almost total silence. Each monk lived in a hermit-like cell; wore rough woolen habits over hair shirts; and consumed simple meals of bread, vegetables, and water each day. The largest and most prominent of the Carthusian monasteries was the Charterhouse, a complex of buildings located in the Smithfield district of London, where decades later hundreds of Protestant martyrs would die as heretics under Queen **Mary I**. In an age when many monastic communities were acquiring reputations for licentiousness, worldliness, and vice, most English believers greatly esteemed the monks of the Carthusian order as models of sanctity and pious self-sacrifice.

When **Parliament** passed the **Act of Supremacy** in November 1534, all the wealthier and more influential subjects of Henry VIII were expected to swear allegiance to their sovereign (and not the pope in Rome) as supreme head of the breakaway English Church. A few weeks later, the king's chief minister, **Thomas Cromwell**, prevailed upon Parliament to pass the **Act of Treasons**, a vicious new law that accounted spoken words as acts of treason to help enforce acceptance of the royal supremacy statute. Anticipating resistance from the Carthusian community, Cromwell sent his agents Thomas Bedyll and John Rastall to the London Charterhouse to persuade the monks there to submit to the required oath. Prior John Houghton and his Carthusian brethren refused to comply, however, citing Scripture to support their unwavering adherence to the Petrine Succession of the pope in Rome. Exasperated, Cromwell himself visited the Charterhouse but was met with the same intransigence, so he ordered the arrest of Houghton and two other Carthusian priors, Robert Lawrence and Augustine Webster, along with a Brigittine brother of Syon Abbey, Dr. Richard Reynolds, and a local parish priest named John Hale.

Cromwell interrogated the five clerics and then put them on trial on 29 April 1535 in the Court of King's Bench at Westminster Hall for denying King Henry's supremacy over the English Church. With **Thomas Howard**, the third Duke of Norfolk (and ironically a committed Catholic himself) presiding as judge, all five of the accused were found guilty of treason and were condemned to death by hanging, drawing, and quartering, a gruesome sentence that was carried out at Tyburn on 4 May 1535. The slaughter had only just begun at this point, however, for on 19 June following, three more Carthusian brothers named Humphrey Middlemore, William Exmew, and Sebastian Newdigate died as convicted traitors at Tyburn in the same horrific manner. Almost two more years passed before another group of four Charterhouse monks were taken north and hanged from chains along the curtain walls of York on 11 May 1537, perhaps as a warning to believers in that region who thought to resist the supremacy oath themselves. Eighteen days later, seven more Carthusians were chained to pillars in standing positions at Newgate Prison in London and were left there in excruciating pain to die of starvation. The final Carthusian brother to die for his faith was William Horne, who endured an agonizing traitor's death on 4 August 1540 along with five other Catholic laymen, monks, and priests.

Thus did the brave Carthusian monks give their lives as steadfast sons of Rome for refusing to accept Henry VIII's supremacy over the English Church. Along with Sir **Thomas More** and Bishop **John Fisher**, both of whom died on the block within weeks of the first Carthusian executions in 1535, all these men represented some of the most noteworthy opposition faced by the king and his chief minister in their quest to bring the Henrician Reformation to England. Pope Leo XIII beatified all the Carthusian martyrs in 1886, and in 1970, Pope Paul VI canonized the first three to perish at Tyburn—Houghton, Lawrence, and Webster—as saints in the Roman Church.

CAVENDISH, GEORGE (c. 1499–1562). A gentleman usher, undersecretary, and courier messenger in the service of **Thomas Cardinal Wolsey**, Cavendish is mostly remembered today for his groundbreaking biography *The Life and Death of Cardinal Wolsey*, which he completed in manuscript form near the end of his life in 1558. Cavendish certainly drew for some source material on certain extant descriptions of Henry VIII's chief minister, but he mostly relied on his own recollections of Wolsey's household and character to construct this intensely personal work. The intimacy, realism, and humanity of the portrait Cavendish painted of his master helped set new standards for biographical narrative over the course of many future centuries.

George Cavendish was born close to the turn of the 16th century as the fourth child and eldest son of Alice and Thomas Cavendish of Cavendish Hall in Suffolk. George's father was a **gentry** landholder and an official of the royal exchequer in London; he was an ancestor of the ducal Cavendish family of Devonshire and Newcastle, and he was also related to a younger Thomas Cavendish, the famed navigator and privateer of the 1580s. George's younger brother William grew up to wed Bess of Hardwick, one of the most ambitious, fiery, and colorful figures of the later Elizabethan age. When George was still a lad, he enrolled at **Cambridge University**, but he did not stay to complete a degree. He was married twice, the first time (briefly) to a daughter of the Spring family of Lavenham, Suffolk, and then (around 1524) to Margery Kemp, a niece by marriage of Sir **Thomas More**.

As "clerk of the pipe" in the exchequer, Thomas Cavendish was known well enough in royal court circles to introduce his eldest son to Cardinal Wolsey, who soon took young George into his service as a gentlemen-usher sometime around 1522. In this role, Cavendish was a personal attendant, or "body man," to the cardinal, helping prepare Wolsey's many progresses, entertainments, and diplomatic receptions in the opulent style his master favored. He also acted as a courier or advance agent for the cardinal's frequent trips abroad to France or Italy, and he became over time an undersecretary who assisted with Wolsey's voluminous correspondence and made copies of official documents for storage in the chancellery archive.

During these years in Wolsey's household, Cavendish came to know both Thomas More and **Thomas Cromwell**, both lawyers who served the cardinal as secretaries in the 1520s

but who went on to distinguished careers before dying on the block some years later. Cavendish also befriended Wolsey's ward **Henry Percy** at this time and so observed firsthand the young lord's romance with Mistress **Anne Boleyn** before his master, the cardinal, intervened to end their relationship in 1523. Six years later, Wolsey's loyal servant was also on hand to witness the annulment trial of Queen **Katherine of Aragon**, which failed in its purpose and instead resulted in the fall from favor and eventual death of the "Great Cardinal" himself. Ever devoted to his disgraced master, Cavendish was questioned by the royal council in the wake of Wolsey's demise. He demonstrated such loyalty and integrity on that occasion that the councilors released him without penalty and allowed him to withdraw to his family estate of Glemsford in western Suffolk.

We hear little else from George Cavendish until the appearance of his famous *Life and Death of Cardinal Wolsey* in the late 1550s. The decision to compose his own biography of Wolsey likely came in response to the scurrilous treatment the fallen cardinal had received in the earlier histories of **Edward Hall** and **Polydore Vergil**. As he began work on his book in 1554, Cavendish certainly consulted these and other extant sources, but he principally relied on the careful notes he had taken during his years in the cardinal's household to rough out the details of his subject's life and career. The former gentleman-usher applied a nuanced, familiar, and surprisingly balanced hand to Wolsey's life, depicting him as an arrogant and venal bully at times yet displaying his vulnerability, generosity, and sense of compassion at others. Cavendish is guilty of some factual and time-sequence errors in his book, but these can be forgiven in light of the lively and captivating prose he used to tell his story, now regarded as one of the most reliable primary sources we possess of the early Tudor age. When Cavendish completed his biography in 1558, it circulated in manuscript form for nearly 80 years until its first print publication as *Thomas Wolsey, his Lyffe and Deathe* in 1641. George Cavendish died in relative obscurity from unknown causes in 1562.

CHAPUYS, EUSTACE, IMPERIAL AMBASSADOR (c. 1490–1556).

Over the course of a distinguished diplomatic career, Eustace Chapuys represented the Holy Roman Emperor **Charles V** at the English court of King Henry VIII. His diplomatic dispatches and other correspondence from England to the imperial government in Europe are among the most revealing and detailed primary sources we possess today for daily happenings at the Tudor court. As an ambassador, it was imperative that Chapuys remain as neutral as possible in his reports so his own opinions would not cloud the judgment or influence the decisions of imperial officials back home. Despite this need for objectivity, Chapuys was a devout Roman Catholic who clearly supported the cause of Queen **Katherine of Aragon** during the crisis of the king's "**Great Matter**" and who opposed the **Henrician Reformation** when it took place in England during the 1530s.

Eustace Chapuys was born around 1490 in the town of Annecy, then located in the Duchy of Savoy in northwestern Italy. He was the second son and one of six children born to Louis Chapuys, a judicial clerk, and his wife, Guigone Dupuys Chapuys, who may have been related to Savoyard nobility. Young Eustace began his undergraduate education at the University of Turin in 1507, then studied for a time in southern France, before earning a doctorate in canon and civil laws at the Sapienza University of Rome in 1515. After entering into holy orders two years later, Chapuys accepted a position on the secretarial staff of the bishop of Geneva and went on to represent the interests of Duke Charles de Bourbon at the Spanish court of Emperor Charles V until the duke's death during the sack of **Rome** in 1527. The emperor quickly took Chapuys into his own diplomatic service, and because he had traveled to England in 1526, he was appointed the resident imperial ambassador to that kingdom in 1529, a post he would occupy (with brief interruptions) for the next 16 years.

Chapuys arrived in England at a very inauspicious time, for Henry VIII was in the midst of a campaign to free himself from Queen Katherine of Aragon in order to marry **Anne Boleyn**, the younger woman he hoped would give him the healthy male heir his first wife could not. Chapuys was specifically sent to England by the emperor at the bidding of Queen Katherine—who was also the emperor's aunt—so the Savoyard diplomat might use his background in canon law to defend the legality of the Spanish queen's marriage to King Henry. Throughout the tribulations of the Great Matter, Chapuys championed the cause of Queen Katherine and her daughter, Princess **Mary** Tudor. He carried messages back and forth from Katherine to the imperial court, prepared legal briefs to protest King Henry's annulment proceedings, and tried to preserve as much royal dignity and estate for the queen and her daughter as possible. When Katherine died early in 1536, Chapuys reported in his dispatches his belief that the heartbroken queen had been poisoned.

By that time, Henry VIII had split from Rome to create the Church of England, an act of reformation the devoutly Catholic Chapuys vigorously opposed. His loyalty to the deceased Queen Katherine naturally made him an enemy of Henry's second wife, Queen Anne, but when she was accused of incest and treason, Chapuys was convinced she was innocent. In addition, the earnest Savoyard continued to support Princess Mary long after her mother's death and helped persuade Henry VIII (with assistance from his third wife, Queen **Jane Seymour**) to reconcile with his daughter late in 1536. Chapuys was also involved in negotiations between the English king and Charles V for a joint invasion of France in 1543, but by this time, the aging imperial ambassador was suffering from gout, and as his health declined further, he sought permission to retire from active diplomatic service. In July 1545, he finally left England to settle in **Flanders** near the University of Louvain, where he founded his own college and established a scholarship to support English students. Eustace Chapuys died in January 1556 and was laid to rest in the chapel of his Louvain college.

CHARLES V, HOLY ROMAN EMPEROR (1500–1558; r. 1519–1556; a.k.a., CARLOS I, KING OF SPAIN, r. 1516–1556).

The first true global emperor in European history,

Charles V ruled over a vast collection of territories that included Germany, Spain, Burgundy, **Flanders**, and parts of Italy, along with overseas possessions in the New World and the Philippines. Charles was a fierce defender of Roman Catholicism against Lutheran reformers in Germany and Muslim Turkish invaders in eastern Europe. He also fought many bitter wars against his French archrival King **François I** for control of lands in central and southern Europe. Although Charles was betrothed to or negotiated for the hand of Henry VIII's sister and later his daughter, none of these unions ever took place. Despite these failed overtures, the emperor was allied with King Henry against France on two different occasions, in 1520–22 and again in 1544. Charles twice broke his promises to the English king, however, which in the end caused the collapse of their attempted Anglo-imperial entente. Having briefly taken custody of the pope in Rome in 1527–28, the emperor "persuaded" him to withhold the requested annulment of Henry VIII's first marriage as well. Charles V won significant victories over all his enemies during the course of his long reign, but exhausted by the effort and unable to subdue any of them completely, he abdicated his imperial and Spanish thrones in 1556 and died two years later.

Charles Habsburg was born on 24 February 1500 in the Flemish town of Ghent to Philip the Fair (son of Holy Roman Emperor **Maximilian I**) and his consort, Joanna la Loca ("the Mad"), the eldest daughter of **Ferdinand and Isabel** of Spain. He grew up in Brussels, where he received a traditional Catholic education from Adrian of Utrecht (later Pope Adrian VI) and learned to read and speak French, Spanish, Italian, Latin, and some German. Despite his slight build and pale complexion, Charles preferred the outdoor rigors of hunting and **jousting** to scholarly pursuits. Early on, he developed a reticent and overly cautious personality that mistakenly suggested a dull mind and slow wit to some contemporary observers. In 1506, Charles was promised in marriage to **Mary** Tudor, the pretty daughter of King **Henry VII** of England, and two years later, the young royals formally became betrothed by proxy in

a ceremony at **Greenwich Palace**. When old King Henry died in 1509, however, his son and successor Henry VIII delayed the wedding of Mary and Charles so long that Emperor Maximilian eventually lost patience and sought another match for his grandson elsewhere in Europe.

In the meantime, Charles had inherited the Duchy of Burgundy following the death of his father, Philip, in 1506. Still a mere child of six years, he relied on his aunt **Margaret of Austria** to administer his Burgundian dominions in the Netherlands until he declared his majority in 1515. The following year, Charles acceded to the throne of Spain and traveled there to take up residence for a time and learn the customs and culture of his new subjects. He also entered into diplomatic talks with Henry VIII in 1518 to marry the English king's infant daughter **Mary** Tudor, but these discussions broke off upon the death of Charles's grandfather Emperor Maximilian. Aided by significant support from his aunt Margaret and the Fugger banking house of Augsburg, the teenaged king of Spain bribed his way to unanimous election as Holy Roman Emperor in 1519.

The early 1520s were eventful years for the young man who now ruled half of Europe and vast overseas territories on two other continents as well. Already signatories to the Universal Peace Treaty of London in 1518, Emperor Charles and Henry VIII of England decided two years later to meet in person for the first time to take stock of one another. Accordingly, King Henry played host to Charles V in England during 26–31 May 1520, and each man having earned the respect of the other, they agreed to a second tryst in Flanders in another six weeks' time. Then, after Henry met inconclusively with King François I at the grand **Field of Cloth of Gold** summit near **Calais** in June, the Tudor king hurried off to his rendezvous with the emperor at Gravelines to begin planning for a joint Anglo-imperial invasion of France.

Charles visited King Henry in England again in May 1522 and signed the Treaty of Windsor to formalize their alliance and initiate preparations for their upcoming French campaign. When Henry VIII sent a sizeable army into northern France in summer 1523, however, the emperor's promised troops never made an appearance, and the English invaders were forced to withdraw. As a result, the English king gained little from this (his second) invasion of France, except for a nearly empty royal treasury and a loss of trust in his erstwhile imperial ally.

Ever the self-appointed champion of the Roman Church in Europe, Charles V faced a different sort of enemy when the reformist monk Martin Luther launched his religious revolution in Germany in 1517. Luther criticized indulgence sales, debated learned Roman theologians, and published (among other works) his *On the Freedom of a Christian* before Emperor Charles summoned him to answer for his "errors" at the imperial Diet of Worms in 1521. Luther managed to escape from the Catholic authorities at Worms and went into hiding in Saxony to carry on his work of religious reform. Thus thwarted by Luther's disappearance, Charles shifted his focus to geopolitical and territorial concerns in Italy against rival encroachments by the French. The emperor achieved a stunning victory and captured King François I of France at Pavia in 1525, only to accept a ransom payment and many promises in exchange for the Valois king's release the following year.

In 1527, Charles ordered a force of mercenaries to attack his enemies in central Italy, but the hungry and unpaid troops carried out a destructive sack of **Rome** and took Pope **Clement VII** hostage instead. With the pontiff now in his power, the emperor forced Clement to deny the requested annulment of Henry VIII's marriage to **Katherine of Aragon**, who happened to be Charles's aunt. Charles V's chance intervention in papal policy at this juncture ultimately determined the outcome of King Henry's marital affairs and in turn helped launch the **Henrician Reformation**.

The Holy Roman Emperor continued to struggle against the forces of Lutheran reform in northern Germany, the French threat in central Europe and Italy, and the invading Ottoman Turks in the Balkans during the next two decades of his reign. While turning back a Turkish advance on Vienna in 1532, he tried to reach doctrinal compromise with the Protestants at the Diets of Augsburg (1530) and Regensburg (1541). The religious divide was too great, however, and grew even wider when the reformers defiantly formed the Schmalkaldic League of Lutheran Princes in the mid-1540s. Charles also planned another French invasion in 1543 and, inviting Henry VIII to join him, offered to return the province of Gascony to England if Anglo-imperial forces managed this time to conquer France. An aging and sickly King Henry saw his last chance for military glory and agreed to join forces with the emperor, but when the campaign got underway in 1544, Charles made a separate peace with King François and thus abandoned his English allies for the second time.

After Emperor Charles defeated (but did not destroy) the Lutheran princes at Mühlberg in 1547, his health began to deteriorate, and by 1550, he was searching for ways to reduce the overwhelming cares of imperial rule. Realizing that the Protestant split from the Roman Church was now permanent, Charles agreed to the Peace of Augsburg in 1555 with the Schmalkaldic League. This measure authorized the ruler of each principality in the Holy Roman Empire to determine what form of Christianity (Lutheran or Catholic) his subjects would follow, thus establishing religious pluralism for the first time in any European kingdom. One year later, an exhausted Charles abdicated both his thrones, handing the empire over to his brother Ferdinand and Spain (with its valuable overseas colonies) to his son Philip II, who at that time was also king of England thanks to his marriage to Henry VIII's daughter Queen Mary I. In 1557, he retired to the monastery of San Jerónimo de Yuste in Spain. Emperor Charles V died a year later of malaria at the age of just 58 years and was eventually laid to rest in an elaborate tomb at the Escorial Palace outside Madrid.

CHEKE, SIR JOHN (1514–57). An enthusiastic advocate and practitioner of humanist scholarship, John Cheke (sometimes spelled Cheeke) did much to win acceptance of evangelical doctrines and helped institutionalize the study of Greek at **Cambridge University** during the later reign of Henry VIII. Through his humanistic work in ancient linguistics, Cheke discovered the true pronunciation of Attic Greek, which until then was generally and awkwardly mispronounced everywhere in England and on the Continent as well. King Henry and his last wife and queen, **Katherine Parr**, hired Cheke to provide Prince **Edward** Tudor (later Edward VI) and Princess **Elizabeth** Tudor (later Elizabeth I) with a sound humanist and reformed (Protestant) education. He fell afoul of the Catholic authorities in Marian England, was threatened with a heretic's death at the stake, recanted his beliefs, and then died an emotionally broken man at a relatively young age.

John Cheke was born in Cambridge to Peter and Agnes Cheke, whose own families originally hailed respectively from Northamptonshire and the Isle of Wight. John was one of six children and the only son of his father, who served the Cambridge University community as an esquire bedell, a marshal or master of ceremonies responsible for leading academic processions. Young John acquired the elements of Latin grammar and then entered St. John's College at Cambridge, where he earned his baccalaureate degree in 1529, became a teaching fellow in 1530, and then graduated with his master's degree in 1533. Cheke became fascinated with the ancient Greek language while studying at St. John's and developed an unusual affinity for its translation and especially for its authentic pronunciation. Henry VIII even granted financial patronage to the young scholar in the late 1520s to help him with his educational and scholarly expenses. With the winds of evangelical Lutheranism blowing through Cambridge, Cheke rejected the Roman Church during his student days and embraced the reformed doctrines that would later dominate his personal and devotional life.

By the mid-1530s, John Cheke was tutoring such Cambridge students as William Cecil (later Lord Burghley and Cheke's brother-in-law) and **Roger Ascham**, who was destined with Cheke to assist with the education of Henry VIII's royal children. Alongside his friend Thomas Smith, Cheke taught lessons in the proper pronunciation of Attic Greek diphthongs—and even sponsored a play by Aristophanes in that style—but he was hotly opposed in this by Bishop **Stephen Gardiner** of Winchester, who was himself a noted humanist scholar. In 1540, King Henry bestowed on Cheke the title of regius professor of Greek at Cambridge, and two years later, an admiring sovereign created young Cheke (he was not yet 30 years old) a canon of Christ Church College at **Oxford University**, Cardinal **Wolsey**'s former collegiate foundation.

Impressed with his command of classical learning and his evangelical religious leanings, Queen Katherine Parr prevailed upon her royal husband to engage John Cheke in 1544 as the principal tutor to King Henry's son and heir, Edward, the Prince of Wales. Cheke took over this important post from Dr. Richard Cox, who had earlier supervised the prince's education but who now was obliged to leave the royal household at **Hampton Court** to take up his duties as the new chancellor of Oxford University. Cheke based his program of tuition for the prince on the same classical and scriptural texts as those studied in earlier years by the Princess **Mary** Tudor and the king's bastard son **Henry Fitzroy**. After reading from the histories and orations of Cato the Elder as well as some of Aesop's fables, Prince Edward took on the *Satellitium* of Juan Luis Vives; the *Colloquies* of **Desiderius Erasmus**; and the works of other ancient authors, such as Cicero, Plutarch, Pliny the Younger, Herodotus, and Thucydides. Less familiar with more modern European languages, Cheke brought in his nephew Jean Belmain, a Huguenot, to teach the young Tudor prince the essentials of French. During his tenure as a royal tutor, Cheke was also an active scholar who published translations of the Greek writings of St. John Chrysostom and Plutarch after dedicating them to his patron Henry VIII.

Following the old king's death in late January 1547, the youthful Edward VI granted Cheke the dignity of schoolmaster of the king, showered him with gifts of rich manors, and then knighted his trusted former teacher in 1552. Ever the religious progressive, Cheke prepared Latin translations of Archbishop **Thomas Cranmer**'s 1549 *Book of Common Prayer* and *Defense of the True Sacrament* to help hasten the further reformation of the

English Church. He threw his support behind the Protestant pretender Lady Jane Grey immediately after King Edward's death in 1553, but when Catholic Mary Tudor quickly made good on her own royal claim, Cheke was forced to flee into exile on the Continent. While living abroad, he penned scathing critiques of Queen Mary's restoration of the Roman Church in England and her ill-considered marriage to Prince Philip of Spain. His polemics prompted Philip to order Cheke's arrest and incarceration in the **Tower of London**, where, threatened with burning alive if he did not renounce his evangelical beliefs, Cheke submitted in autumn 1556 and was released to live out his days in the house of a friend in London. Aggrieved by the recantation of his reformist views, John Cheke died a dispirited and melancholy man of just 43 years on 13 September 1557 and was buried in the Church of St. Alban in Wood Street, London.

CLEMENT VII, POPE (1478–1534; r. 1523–34). When he first became pope, this Medici kinsman of Pope **Leo X** only planned to safeguard the papal state from foreign domination and restore his family to power in his native Florence. Pope Clement, however, failed to grasp the bigger picture and so badly misunderstood the magnitude of the issues facing the Roman Church during his pontificate. He switched sides with impunity during the Italian wars of the 1520s, and he refused to take steps to deal with the surging momentum of the Lutheran Reformation in Germany. Perhaps most disastrously, Clement VII completely mishandled Henry VIII's request for an annulment of his marriage to **Katherine of Aragon**, a failure that ultimately drove the Tudor king away from Rome to declare himself supreme head of his own church in England.

Born out of wedlock to Giuliano de' Medici and his mistress Foiretta Gorini in Florence, Giulio de' Medici grew up in the household of his uncle Lorenzo de' Medici Il Magnifico because his father was assassinated one month before his birth in the Pazzi conspiracy of late April 1478. Giulio collected several minor church livings during his youth, and after his cousin was elected to the throne of St. Peter

as Leo X in 1513, the ambitious Medici cleric quickly accepted appointments from the new pope as the absentee bishop of Worcester (England), the cardinal archbishop of Florence, and the vice chancellor of the Holy See itself. Leo X died in 1521, and Giulio de' Medici lost the ensuing papal election to Adrian VI, but when that pious Dutch pontiff also passed away, the door was left open for the election of the Florentine cardinal as Pope Clement VII in November 1523.

The new pope almost immediately found himself embroiled in the ongoing wars between France and the Holy Roman Empire and, always hoping to back the winning side, supported King **François I**'s Italian invasion until that headstrong French ruler was defeated and captured by Emperor **Charles V** outside Pavia in 1525. François made many promises to win his freedom from Charles but then reneged on them all and joined Venice, Florence, and Pope Clement in the League of Cognac in May 1526 to oppose further imperial ambitions in Italy. In spring 1527, an annoyed emperor sent a force of mercenaries from Milan to stir up trouble in the Papal States, but they attacked and then plundered the city of Rome instead, driving Clement and a small detachment of Swiss Guards to the nearby fortress of Castel Sant'Angelo for safety. The pope soon fell into the hands of the occupying imperial troops and became the prisoner of Emperor Charles until he paid an enormous indemnity and was finally freed in December 1527.

Meanwhile, the teachings of Martin Luther were spreading rapidly across Germany despite their condemnation at the Diet of Worms in 1521, but Pope Clement was too distracted by events in Italy to pay much attention to this new threat from the north. In June 1526, the Diet of Speyer overturned the anti-Lutheran measures enacted at Worms, which emboldened the reformers to create their own rival churches rather than simply settle for an overhaul of the existing Church of Rome. Charles V and other loyal Catholics called for a general council of church leaders to address the Protestant challenge, but Pope Clement discounted the gravity of the problem and in the end took no action at all.

It was just after the sack of **Rome** in May 1527 that **Thomas Cardinal Wolsey** arrived from England with a request that Clement annul Henry VIII's marriage to Katherine of Aragon, the Spanish queen who had failed to produce the English king's much-coveted male heir. During the summer and autumn of 1527, however, Charles V still retained custody of the pope and prevented him from granting King Henry's annulment because Queen Katherine was the emperor's aunt. When Clement finally gained his freedom, he sent **Lorenzo Cardinal Campeggio** to England in 1528 to try (with Wolsey) the king's case for annulment, but Queen Katherine threatened to appeal for papal justice to Rome, thereby ending the proceedings abruptly and without resolution. Campeggio left for the Continent, Wolsey was disgraced and died, and King Henry began to explore ways to separate himself and his kingdom from the Roman Church and its holy father.

As a typical son of the House of Medici, Clement VII was an enthusiastic patron of the arts who commissioned Michelangelo Buonarroti, Raphael Sanzio, and Benvenuto Cellini to create gorgeous masterworks for the papacy in the high Renaissance style of the day. Indeed, Michelangelo painted his great *Last Judgment* fresco in the Sistine Chapel for Clement, while Cellini (who fought for the pontiff at the siege of Castel Sant'Angelo in 1527) fashioned several golden medallions to adorn the papal palace in Rome. Also an avid student of the past, the Medici pope patronized the historical writings of Niccolò Machiavelli and Francesco Guicciardini as well. Clement VII died suddenly (perhaps from a poisoned mushroom) after a banquet on 25 September 1534 and was buried in the basilica of Santa Maria sopra Minerva in Rome.

CLERGY, PARISH OR SECULAR (c. AD 600–).

The parish clergy were for the vast majority of English believers the principal church representatives in their daily lives, both before and after the **Henrician Reformation**. These priests differed from England's "regular" clergy or monks, who lived in isolated communities according to a lifestyle code known in Latin as a *regula*, or rule. Rather, secular clergy (from the Latin *sæculum*, or of this world) were those who ministered to the spiritual needs of common layfolk in village and town parishes all over England. They lived on meager incomes generated by parishioner tithes and fees they collected from sacramental services and intercessory masses. Parish priests enjoyed "benefit of clergy," which protected them from criminal prosecution in royal or shire courts, and they were generally valued and respected by the lay communities they served. By the dawn of the Tudor age, however, anticlericalism was beginning to gain momentum among England's lay believers due to the increasing worldliness and corruption they often observed in all ranks and orders of their clergy.

Since the early Middle Ages, the secular clergy in England had been responsible for holding religious services (the Catholic mass), administering the grace-giving sacraments, maintaining the physical fabric of their churches and living quarters, and operating elementary schools for local youngsters. Many of these priests occupied beneficed parishes that, complete with small glebe farms, also entitled them to collect tithes (portions of congregants' wealth) in the form of agricultural produce or (later) monetary assessments. Secular clerics were appointed to beneficed livings by bishops, monastic foundations, or even local **nobles** in whose gift or advowson the parish was held.

The late-medieval religious community in England featured three priestly ranks: the rector, who kept all parish income and glebe produce for his own support; the vicar, whose tithes were appropriated and then partially returned by his appointing patron; and the curate, who simply earned a small stipend from the rector or vicar he was hired to assist. The average income of a beneficed parish priest (rector or vicar) in the 16th century was between £10 and £15 per annum, or between $11,000 and $16,500 in modern American currency, while curates only averaged £2 to £5 yearly, or just $2,200 to $5,500 American. The English parish clergy were so impoverished in early-Tudor times that many began to charge additional fees for weddings, christenings, and burials, while others accepted endowed income to say intercessory masses for the souls of the wealthy deceased.

Such extra financial charges from their secular priests only served to irritate English layfolk, who naturally felt that the provision of sacraments and the celebration of masses were well within the normal range of required clerical duties. Believers were also angry because whenever men of the cloth committed crimes, they could claim "benefit of clergy," be tried, and usually were only lightly punished in lenient ecclesiastical courts. In addition, many beneficed clerics were absentees who hired poorly paid curates to serve their parish congregations while they went off to study at university or earn extra money as cathedral canons or prebendaries (paid choristers). Others collected several beneficed livings and so were not only pluralists but also absentees because they could not reside and work in multiple parishes at the same time.

A popular Tudor-era joke charged that few English priests were sufficiently educated to carry out their regular sacerdotal duties. Some possessed such scant knowledge of Latin that they mumbled "hocus pocus" instead of the proper eucharistic blessing *hoc est corpus meum* when celebrating mass. Perhaps worst of all, many parish clergymen ignored their vows of chastity and lived with women—or even married them—and then had families that further strained their meager resources. All these abuses led to a resurgence in the early 16th century of the **Lollards**, a group of homegrown English heretics who had made it their business to criticize the secular parish clergy since the late Middle Ages.

Indeed, soon after Henry VIII became king in 1509, learned voices were also being raised against the clerical corruption that seemed to worsen in England and on the Continent each year. **Desiderius Erasmus**, the great Dutch scholar and humanist, attacked the worldliness of all Europe's clergy in his satirical *In Praise of Folly* in 1509, sentiments that his friend Sir **Thomas More** echoed in *Utopia*, the perfect fictional society he described a few years later. Many in Christendom blamed general clerical vice on the shameful example of

the Renaissance popes in Rome, who were less concerned with the spiritual welfare of their flock than with papal revenues and territorial expansion. Anticlericalism had reached such a fever pitch in England that, when **Parliament** named Henry VIII the supreme head of the English Church in 1534, only the most loyal sons of Rome were willing to stand against the change.

Many members of the nobility and **gentry** supported England's split from Rome because they gained access to the vast landed wealth of the church they had coveted for so long. Most commoners were simply fed up with clerical corruption, however, and hoped the emergent Church of England would bring with it much-needed reform. As it happened, the parish clergy were left largely unaffected by the religious changes that took place in England in the 1530s. It was true that **Great Bibles** were installed in every parish and the content of sermons was partially controlled, but Parliament's Supplication against the Ordinaries [*see* SUBMISSION OF THE CLERGY AND SUPPLICATION AGAINST THE ORDINARIES (1531–32)] was primarily aimed at the abuses of bishops and not lowly priests. Once the reformist chief minister **Thomas Cromwell** was executed in 1540, Henry VIII restored much of the conservative English Church he had always preferred, and the parish clergy quietly returned to many of their former wayward habits through the end of the old king's reign. *See also* HUNNE, RICHARD (c. 1480–1514); MONASTERIES, DISSOLUTION OR SUPPRESSION OF THE (1535–40); SHRINES AND PILGRIMAGES (c. AD 650–1539).

COINAGE OF HENRY VIII (1400–1550). The basic currency units of the United Kingdom that circulated prior to the introduction of Britain's decimal system in 1971 were the same denominations (though issued entirely in the form of coins) in use during the reigns of the first two Tudor monarchs. By the time of King **Henry VII's** accession in 1485, the principal monetary unit of the English economy had for many centuries been the pound sterling, a familiar denomination that continues in use even today. Originally in the medieval period, the designation of a pound represented a full pound (weight) of silver. The term *sterling* was adopted in the early 15th century to describe the purity level of silver used to make up a monetary pound. Because high-quality silver came to England from the Hartz Mountains in eastern Europe, currency-grade silver was known at first as "easterling," a term then corrupted over time to *sterling*.

Of course, silver coins that actually weighed a full pound were too heavy and clumsy to carry about or use in daily commercial transactions, so during the early Tudor era, the pound sterling served mostly as a unit of monetary account. One pound sterling in the 16th century was worth approximately $1,100 in today's American money, or around £750 in the currency of the modern United Kingdom. Because officials used a checkered tablecloth (like an abacus) to add up the sums of pounds collected from subsidy (tax) measures, the royal treasury eventually became known as the exchequer, while promissory notes written against treasury currency holdings came to be known as cheques, or checks. In Tudor times, the pound sterling was subdivided (as it was until 1971) into 20 shillings, while each shilling was divided into 12 pennies, or pence. The symbol for the pound sterling has long been £, a shortened form of lb. that derives from the Latin *libra pondo*, or pound in weight. The symbol for shillings was simply the letter *s* (or sometimes a number-slash-hyphen, as in 6/-), while pence were designated by the letter *d* from the Roman penny, or *denarius*.

Because a pound of sterling silver was far too awkward to use as a daily medium of exchange, King Henry VII had gold sovereigns minted that equaled the silver pound in value but were much lighter and easier to carry. By 1525, the value of gold had risen so steeply that sovereign coins had to be revalued at 22 and later at 30 shillings each. The earliest silver shillings were also issued by the first Tudor ruler in 1502 and were called testons (from the Latin *testa*, or head) because they featured a profile portrait of the reigning monarch on their obverse side. When Henry VIII became king in 1509, he did not replace his father's image on English shillings until 1526!

For most commoners, the standard coins in circulation in Tudor England were the silver groat (worth 4d.) and the silver half-groat (worth tuppence, or 2d.). Halfpenny or farthing (a quarter penny) coins were so small they were difficult to handle, so regular silver pennies were usually cut into halves and quarters to create smaller denominations. Other coinage values common in Tudor times included the mark (13 shillings), the angel (a half-mark, or 6s.6d.), the half- and quarter-angels, and so forth. Henry VIII began issuing small golden quarter-angels in 1544 in response to the rampant inflation his coinage debasement policies were causing. Royal (sometimes called ryal or noble) coins worth 10s. each were introduced in the 1490s, while the crown (5s.) and half-crown (2s.6d.), both of which survived until 1971, made their first appearances in England under Henry VIII.

As a point of comparison, the currencies and exchange rates of foreign kingdoms and states in 1520 were: the Venetian ducat = 4s.6d., the French ecu d'or = 4s.4d., the imperial gold carolus = 6s.10d., and the Florentine florin = 3s.3d.

COLET, JOHN, DEAN OF ST. PAUL'S CATHEDRAL (c. 1466–1519).

This learned and intellectually precocious churchman was one of the most renowned humanist scholars, progressive scriptural exegetes, and creative educationalists of the pre-Reformation period in England. Eager to immerse himself in the *studia humanitatis* then flourishing on the Continent, Colet traveled to Italy and there met many of the great thinkers of the Florentine Renaissance. He also knew and exchanged ideas with England's earliest "new-learning" scholars, and he developed a close friendship with **Desiderius Erasmus**, the prominent Dutch humanist and religious reformer. Colet was famous for the novel way he interpreted the epistles of St. Paul and, as dean of London's largest cathedral, delivered hundreds of sermons during his career on Christian morality, clerical austerity, and the nature of faith and grace. Before his untimely death at age 52, he founded St. Paul's School in London to train young **clerics** to reform a

Roman Church he considered overly corrupt and worldly.

John Colet was born in either 1466 or 1467 to Sir Henry Colet, a well-to-do member of the Mercers' Company of London, and his wife, Christian Knyvet Colet, who was distantly related to the powerful Grey and Stafford families of East Anglia. Although Christian Colet endured no fewer than 22 pregnancies during her marriage to Sir Henry, her son John was the only child to survive beyond infancy. As a youth, he very likely studied at St. Anthony's School in Threadneedle Street, London—the same institution **Thomas More** later attended—and then entered Magdalen College at **Oxford University** to begin his liberal arts education in 1483. Seven years later, he earned his master's degree, and inspired by his Oxford mentors **William Grocyn** and **Thomas Linacre**, two of England's greatest early humanists, he set off for Italy to take in the classical studies of the Renaissance for himself. In Florence, Colet visited the Platonic Academy, made the acquaintance of philosophers Marsilio Ficino and Giovanni Pico della Mirandola, and heard the fiery sermons of the puritanical Fra Girolamo Savonarola from the pulpit of Santa Maria della Fiore. By the time he returned to England in 1496, John Colet had decided on a career in the church, but he was determined to bring the lessons he had learned in Italy to his reading of the Scriptures and the exemplary life of spirituality he intended to lead.

Once again based in Oxford, the 30-year-old Master Colet began offering lectures to the university community on the epistles of St. Paul. His unusual exegetical approach dismissed the line-by-line analysis of the medieval Scholastic philosophers, instead examining the apostle's letters within their historical context and as reflections of the character and spiritual devotion of St. Paul himself. His lectures drew large crowds of students, faculty fellows, and even senior church officials; when Erasmus visited Oxford in 1499, he heard Colet speak and rushed to introduce himself to the promising young theologian from London. It was at this time in his life that Colet also developed lasting friendships with Thomas More and the future bishop **John Fisher**, two

of England's leading intellectual figures of the early 16th century. Ordained into holy orders in 1498, the young priest soon acquired the beneficed parishes of All Saints in Stepney and St. Dunstan-in-the-East in London, but he preferred to live the simple *imitatio Christi* and never became an abusive pluralist like so many of his clerical contemporaries.

In 1504, Colet was appointed dean of St. Paul's Cathedral in London, an administrative post he was destined to occupy for the rest of his life. The following year, his father died and left his only son a small fortune, which Colet committed to the foundation of a grammar school for boys on a site near the Thames River just north (and bearing the name) of St. Paul's Cathedral. By 1510, the campus fabric had been constructed, and in 1518, the founder completed a set of governing statutes that authorized the Mercers' Company (and not the **clergy**) to manage his school. Colet also reduced restrictive regulations at St. Paul's School, insisting that the boys read improving books and follow positive role models rather than submit to strict regimentation and discipline. St. Paul's went on to become one of the premier grammar schools in all England and still operates today as the highly selective Christian institution John Colet envisioned more than five centuries ago.

During the first years of Henry VIII's reign, Dean Colet continued to deliver his innovative sermons on the Pauline epistles, but he also folded in his pacifist views on Christian statecraft and on salvation by faith alone. After he denounced the use of images in places of worship and the excessive wealth of the Roman Church in 1510, Bishop Richard Fitzjames of London accused Colet of **Lollard** heresy, but the charges were soon dropped as unfounded by Archbishop **William Warham** of Canterbury. When talk of the outspoken London dean reached Henry VIII himself, the king commanded Colet to preach before the assembled royal court at **Greenwich Palace** on the eve of his great **French invasion of 1513–14**. Holding nothing back, Colet admonished Henry for making war on another Christian realm, an opinion he had already shared by letter with Pope Julius II, Emperor **Maximilian I**, and King

Louis XII of France. The Tudor king was more amused than angry and, as later reported by Erasmus, soon forgot this scolding by the dean of St. Paul's to prepare for his coming campaign overseas.

John Colet contracted the dreaded **sweating sickness** three times in 1518–19 and finally succumbed to its ravages on 16 September 1519. As a man of the cloth who never formally rejected the Roman Church, Colet intriguingly made no mention in his will of the Virgin Mary or the saints, and he left no money to endow masses for the repose of his soul. He was laid to rest in an elaborate tomb in St. Paul's Cathedral that still features his likeness in stone looking down on a grisly skeletal effigy at the base of the monument.

CONVOCATION OF BISHOPS (c. AD 690–).

The term *convocation*, derived from the Latin for calling together, has referred since medieval times to the regular meeting of all the English bishops (with their subordinate **clergy**) in the two administrative regions of Canterbury (Southern Province) and York (Northern Province). Summoned by the respective archbishop in each province, Convocation has met continually over the centuries to discuss and act on matters of ecclesiastical law, church governance, and grants of financial assistance to the Crown. When necessary, the two convocations (but mostly the larger, more important Southern Convocation) have issued injunctions or episcopal decrees that have then been handed down to the secular clergy for implementation in their various parishes in each diocese. The Southern Convocation of Bishops played a significant role in the **Henrician Reformation** by surrendering a great deal of ecclesiastical power to the Crown in 1532 and by accepting King Henry VIII as the head of the English Church in the **Act of Supremacy** of 1534.

It was Archbishop Theodore of Canterbury, the seventh-century-AD "primate of all England," who fully integrated the English Church into the Roman organizational scheme by recognizing bishops as the chief governing officials in smaller administrative units called sees or dioceses. Theodore further grouped these dioceses into a single large province and then regularly called their bishops together in Convocation to deal with matters of importance to the English Church. Three northern sees separated from those in the south of England and **Wales** to form the Northern Province in 1225. Later, the bishops of both provinces invited other ranking churchmen—subordinate diocesan clerics and abbots—to participate in Convocation meetings as well. The bishops met in an upper house of Convocation under the direction of the archbishops of Canterbury or York, while the other clerics gathered in a lower house and elected their own chairman. Because these church prelates met in their own deliberative and legislative bodies, they lost the right over time to attend sessions of the House of Lords in **Parliament**, as had originally been authorized by the Magna Carta in 1215.

During the 14th and 15th centuries, episcopal administration in the Northern and Southern Provinces emerged into the form generally practiced in England by the time Henry VIII acceded to the throne in 1509. The Tudor kings actually nominated their own candidates to fill vacant bishoprics, but their appointments were subject to routine and nearly always automatic confirmation from worldly and distracted popes in Rome. English bishops also presided over their own courts that, independent from the Crown **judiciary**, dealt with matters that early-Tudor society considered essentially religious in nature. These tribunals took two forms: consistory courts, which heard cases involving defamation, will probate, marriage contracts, clerical crime, and heresy, and audience courts, which mostly confirmed ordinations and appointments to diocesan administrative posts. In addition, bishops were responsible for conducting visitations of parish churches and monastic houses to ensure that proper standards of building maintenance and clerical morality were upheld. To keep a record of all these proceedings, clerical scribes took down accounts of all the court rulings, disciplinary injunctions, diocesan visitations, and sacramental dispensations of their bishops in great, leather-bound vellum or parchment registers.

Many prelates also served the Tudors as royal minsters, so they were frequently absent from their sees and typically left most of their administrative duties to assistant churchmen, such as archdeacons and deans, or to secular officials known as chancellors and vicars general. Because only bishops could perform the sacraments of confirmation and ordination, absentees usually employed suffragans—clerics of true episcopal rank whose "dioceses" were defunct or located in Muslim lands—to serve as substitute bishops in their place. Resident in their dioceses or not, all English prelates were beneficed with revenues they collected from their episcopal estates. These financial returns were in many cases quite substantial, inspiring some greedy career churchmen to chase translations to ever-richer dioceses or else become pluralists with beneficed incomes from multiple sees. One of Tudor England's most notorious pluralists was **Thomas Cardinal Wolsey**, Henry VIII's lord chancellor, who was variously and often simultaneously archbishop of York and bishop of Tournai, Bath and Wells, Lincoln, Durham, and Winchester. Needless to say, Wolsey could not minister to the faithful in all of these dioceses at once. In fact, he never even visited most of them, even though he continued to collect the considerable revenues their episcopal lands generated over the course of his avaricious career.

As they had been doing since medieval times, English bishops continued to meet in Convocation into the reigns of the first two Tudor kings. Both **Henry VII** and Henry VIII often approached the larger and richer Southern Convocation for financial contributions to support Crown initiatives, requests that the assembled bishops came over time to expect and rarely ever contested. Meanwhile, anticlerical attitudes among the English laity were on the rise by the early 1520s, partly as a reaction to the wealth and corruption of the clergy but partly also from a desire (on the part of the **nobility** and **gentry**) to acquire some of the church's vast property holdings for themselves. Annoyed by the bishops' continuing loyalty to the pope in Rome, Henry VIII took advantage of popular hostility toward the church to extort the **Submission of the Clergy** from Southern Convocation in 1532. This measure approved the payment of an enormous fine to the Crown, ceded important religious powers to the king, and then recognized Henry as supreme lord over the English Church "as far as the law of Christ allows."

At around the same time, the House of Commons passed a list of grievances known as the Supplication against the Ordinaries that threatened to eliminate or severely restrict the rights and privileges of the English clergy. King Henry gave the Southern Convocation a chance to respond to these complaints, and led by Archbishop **William Warham** of Canterbury, the bishops issued their Answer to the Supplication in April 1532. Parliament and the king simply ignored Convocation's rebuttal, however, prompting Sir **Thomas More** to resign his chain of office as lord chancellor and effectively subordinating the English bishops and clergy to the authority of the Tudor monarchy. The Southern Convocation's role in accepting both submission and supplication marked the beginning of England's complete break from the Roman Church, one that found final expression in the Act of Supremacy just two years later.

COURTENAY, HENRY, FIRST MARQUIS (MARQUESS) OF EXETER, SECOND EARL OF DEVON (c. 1498–1538).

This influential English lord was a descendant of the royal House of York and was closely related to and a trusted friend of Henry VIII. Courtenay's wife, Gertrude, aroused the king's displeasure when she became obsessed with **Elizabeth Barton**, the "Holy Maid of Kent," and then remained loyal to Henry's discarded first queen and wife, **Katherine of Aragon**. The great wealth and vast estates of the Marquis of Exeter also attracted the hostility of **Thomas Cromwell**, King Henry's chief minister and the prime architect of the **Henrician Reformation**. With the dissolution of the English **monasteries** in the later 1530s, Exeter joined a revolt in Devon and Cornwall against the reformed policies of the king and Cromwell. Arrested with his family and convicted on charges of treason, the Marquis of Exeter suffered execution late in 1538 at the age of only 40 years.

Henry Courtenay was the sole surviving son of William Courtenay, first Earl of Devon, and his wife, Katherine of York, who was a younger daughter of King Edward IV and Queen Elizabeth Woodville. Henry Courtenay's mother was thus the sister of **Elizabeth of York**, **Henry VII**'s queen, which made the Courtenay boy the first maternal cousin of the future King Henry VIII. As a royal relation, Henry Courtenay was raised and educated in the same privileged household as the other Tudor children, where he soon became good friends with the king's only surviving son, Henry, by then Prince of Wales and the heir to his father's throne. When he was just six years old, Courtenay's father fell afoul of Henry VII for alleged plots against the Crown and was jailed in the **Tower of London** until his release and sudden death in 1511. That year, the adolescent Henry Courtenay inherited his father's Earldom of Devon, a title that elevated the lad to the peerage and qualified him for command in the Tudor armed forces. The young earl fought with the king's **navy** during his **French invasion of 1513–14** and then married a teenaged bride, who passed away just a few years later. In 1519, Devon took as his new wife one of Katherine of Aragon's ladies-in-waiting, Gertrude Blount, who was the daughter of the Spanish queen's chamberlain William Blount, Lord Mountjoy.

The year 1520 was an eventful year for the youthful Earl of Devon. After King Henry made him a gentleman of the privy chamber and appointed him to the royal council, Devon accompanied his cousin to his **Field of Cloth of Gold** summit meeting with the French king in **Calais** in June of that same year. Along with **Charles Brandon**, the Duke of Suffolk and Henry VIII's brother-in-law, Courtenay joined the inner circle of dashing young courtiers who regularly hunted, **jousted**, and reveled in the company of the king. When **Edward Stafford**, the third Duke of Buckingham, was executed for treason in 1521, Devon took his place as a companion knight in the prestigious Order of the **Garter** and acquired some of the attainted duke's confiscated properties as well. In 1525, King Henry created his friend and cousin Marquis (sometimes spelled *Marquess*) of Exeter,

and now among the highest-ranking and wealthiest men in the realm, Courtenay ruled supreme over the English West Country at the young age of only 27 years.

Ever loyal to his kinsman the king, Exeter at first supported Henry's bid to cast aside Katherine of Aragon, but he was never fond of the woman his cousin proposed to wed in her place, **Anne Boleyn**. More dangerously, Exeter's wife, Lady Gertrude Courtenay, vocally opposed the king's rejection of Queen Katherine (her former mistress) and then became an open adherent of Elizabeth Barton, the nun from Kent whose visions of Henry VIII's demise bordered on treason. To punish Lady Gertrude, King Henry forced her to act as godmother to Queen Anne Boleyn's infant daughter, **Elizabeth**, at that child's christening in September 1533. When the king sought to rid himself of his second queen three years later, however, the Marquis of Exeter served on the commission that found Anne Boleyn guilty of treasonous adultery and then condemned her to death.

Exeter's own end came just two years later in the wake of the king's and Thomas Cromwell's reformation of the English Church and their policy to close the kingdom's monasteries. Having always remained quietly loyal to the Roman Church, the marquis and his wife resented the religious changes that Cromwell had wrought and worried that his immense influence over Henry VIII might lead to their own fall from royal favor. For his part, Cromwell greatly feared the close kinship and friendship that Exeter had enjoyed over the years with the king and believed that the marquis's downfall was the only way to secure his own position at court. Having corresponded for years with members of the Pole family, the strongest Yorkist claimants to the English throne, Exeter attempted to raise the men of Devon and Cornwall in a revolt against the suppression and sale of all the monastic houses in southwestern England. Cromwell's agents arrested him, along with his wife; son; and the brothers and mother of **Reginald Cardinal Pole**, the exiled leader of conservative opposition to the English Reformation. After enduring several weeks in the Tower of London, Henry Courtenay was tried and convicted of treason and was quickly beheaded with a sword (not the usual axe and block) along with Henry Pole on Tower Hill on 9 December 1538. All of Exeter's estates were confiscated to the Crown, but Lady Gertrude and their son Edward survived in the Tower and were eventually released some 15 years later. *See also* POLE, MARGARET, COUNTESS OF SALISBURY (1473–1541).

COVERDALE, MILES. *See* GREAT BIBLE (1539).

CRANMER, THOMAS, ARCHBISHOP OF CANTERBURY (1489–1556). Widely recognized as the theological architect of the English Reformation, Thomas Cranmer annulled Henry VIII's marriage to **Katherine of Aragon** and then validated his subsequent union with **Anne Boleyn** to bring an end to the king's "**Great Matter.**" Cranmer also assisted in making the vernacular English Bible available to the subjects of Henry VIII, and he composed an original litany (form of prayer) that is still in use today as part of the Anglican worship service. Most famously, the evangelical archbishop compiled and edited the earliest editions of the *Book of Common Prayer* during the reign of King Henry's successor **Edward VI**. Steadfastly opposed to Queen **Mary I**'s restoration of the Roman Church in England, Cranmer endured imprisonment in the **Tower of London** and in Oxford before his conviction on charges of heresy led to his fiery death at the stake early in 1556. Today he is admired as the first Protestant archbishop of Canterbury and the most prominent of the nearly 300 Marian martyrs to surrender their lives for their faith.

Thomas Cranmer was born the second son of Thomas Cranmer and Agnes Hatfield Cranmer in the village of Aslockton in Northamptonshire on 2 July 1489. His father, a member of the English **gentry**, was not a wealthy man, so son Thomas naturally looked forward to a future career in the priesthood. Little is known of Thomas Cranmer's early life, but he very likely acquired the solid grammar-school education required to enroll in the newly founded Jesus College at **Cambridge University** in 1503. There he followed

a typically medieval course of study to earn his baccalaureate degree in 1511 and then began a graduate program that exposed him to the more humanistic writings of Jacques Lefèvre d'Étaples and **Desiderius Erasmus**. After completing his master's degree in 1515, he accepted a teaching fellowship at Jesus College. Around the same time, Cranmer married a young woman named Joan, but because he was training for the priesthood he was dismissed from his fellowship and his quarters at his alma mater. Joan died in childbirth one year later, however, a loss that allowed Cranmer to seek and obtain reinstatement at Jesus College once more. In 1520, he was ordained a priest, and in 1526, he earned his doctoral degree in divinity.

By 1529 Henry VIII's Great Matter, his attempt to set aside his first queen to wed another, had reached a crisis point after **Thomas Cardinal Wolsey** had failed to procure a marriage annulment for his Tudor master from the pope. During a discussion that year with two Crown officials, Cranmer suggested that English scholars be sent to seek out scriptural support for the royal annulment from theologians at Europe's leading universities, an idea that greatly appealed to the increasingly desperate King Henry. Cranmer thus accompanied this scholarly team abroad and spent the next few years in France, Italy, and Germany consulting with divinity professors and carrying out diplomatic missions for the English Crown. Having previously accepted the position of chaplain to **Thomas Boleyn**, the Earl of Wiltshire and Anne Boleyn's father, the two men met with Pope **Clement VII** in 1530 in Rome but carefully avoided discussion of the annulment issue. Later meeting with Lutheran clerics in Germany in 1532 and apparently still frustrated by his priestly vows, Cranmer took another wife, this time a German woman named Margaret, to whom he secretly remained married for the rest of his life.

Archbishop **William Warham** finally died in 1532, and as Anne Boleyn was soon with child while **Parliament** considered repudiating papal authority in England, Henry VIII named Thomas Cranmer his next archbishop of Canterbury early in 1533. For several months,

Cranmer studied scriptural and canon law precedents for annulment, then dissolved King Henry's marriage to Queen Katherine and validated his second union with Anne Boleyn, all in May 1533. Although the new archbishop enjoyed a cordial relationship with Henry's second queen, he was ordered to annul her marriage with the king when she fell spectacularly from royal favor and was executed for treason in May 1536. In 1540, Cranmer again freed his royal master from an unpleasant marriage with **Anne of Cleves**, while in 1542, he had to preside as archbishop at the adultery and treason trial of Queen **Katherine Howard**. A studious and quiet man by temperament, Thomas Cranmer clearly found his involvement in these matters distasteful, but after 1534, he was in no position to refuse the wishes of the newly proclaimed supreme head of the Church of England.

As a theologian, Thomas Cranmer was an evangelical Christian whose religious views lined up somewhere between the teachings of Martin Luther and those of the more radical John Calvin of Geneva. In the late 1530s, he supported the efforts of **Thomas Cromwell**, Henry VIII's chief minister and vicegerent in spirituals (ecclesiastical coordinator), to produce a **Great Bible** in English and have copies placed in every parish church in the kingdom. In 1544, the archbishop composed a prayer litany that exhorted God, Christ, the angels, and the saints to deliver the faithful from evil and to grant all good Christians mercy and peace, a device still recited in Church of England services today. Following enactment of the reactionary **Act of Six Articles** in 1539, Cranmer faced allegations of heresy from religious conservatives like Bishop **Stephen Gardiner** of Winchester and **Thomas Howard**, third Duke of Norfolk, but the enduring affection and support of King Henry saved him (for the time being) from the dangers of a trial and possible death at the stake.

When his great patron Henry VIII breathed his last in 1547, Cranmer continued to serve his successor Edward VI as archbishop of Canterbury. Thomas Cranmer is perhaps best known today for creating the 1549 and 1552 editions of the *Book of Common Prayer*, a volume that fully reformed the Church of England mass by simplifying clerical vestments, emphasizing scriptural readings and sermons, and providing prayers and hymns in plain English. King Edward himself died in his teens of consumption (tuberculosis) and was succeeded by his half-sister Mary in 1553. After promising her subjects religious toleration, the new queen broke her word, restored the Roman Church in England, and then ordered the arrest of hundreds of Protestants as heretics. The most prominent target of this campaign was Archbishop Cranmer, who soon found himself imprisoned in the Tower of London and then in Oxford to await trial. Following the burning deaths of his fellow bishops **Hugh Latimer** and Nicholas Ridley and finally convicted of heresy himself early in 1556, Cranmer at first renounced his "errors" and signed multiple testaments to that effect, but his conscience rallied, and he tore up the offending recantations rather than betray his faith. On 21 March 1556, he perished at the stake in Oxford but not before thrusting his right hand into the raging fire as punishment for having signed his earlier confessions. The courageous deaths of Cranmer, Latimer, and Ridley are today commemorated by the Martyrs' Monument, which was erected in the 1840s at the Oxford intersection of St. Giles, Magdalen, and Beaumont Streets, across from the entrance to Balliol College and near to the site where all three men perished in the flames.

CROMWELL, THOMAS, EARL OF ESSEX, LORD PRIVY SEAL, VICEGERENT IN SPIRITUALS (1485–1540).

Arguably the most powerful man (aside from King Henry VIII himself) in early-Tudor England, Thomas Cromwell served the second Tudor monarch as his chief minister during the crucial years of the **Henrician Reformation** and launched a so-called revolution in government that greatly streamlined and in many ways modernized Crown administrative practices. Cromwell followed the kind of meteoric rise from humble beginnings to great power and wealth that typified many political careers in the Tudor age. Born into an artisan's family, he acquired military experience and a legal education on the Continent before accepting employment in the household of **Thomas Cardinal Wolsey**, Henry VIII's first chief minister. When the "Great Cardinal" fell from royal favor and died in 1530, Cromwell sidestepped his patron's fate and rose to join King Henry's royal council a few years later. For the next eight years, Cromwell presided over one of the greatest periods of political and religious transformation in English history. His revolution in government featured better royal revenue management, a smaller and thus more effective privy council, improved informant networks, and creation of an early English census system. As King Henry's vicegerent in spirituals, Cromwell also oversaw the separation of the English Church from Rome, the dissemination of an English **Great Bible**, the dissolution of the **monasteries**, and the introduction of the partially reformed **Ten Articles of Faith**. King Henry's trust in him began to fade, however, with the **Anne of Cleves** match in 1539. When Cromwell's enemies seized this opportunity to discredit him with the king, he was arrested on charges of treason and heresy and was beheaded in July 1540.

Thomas Cromwell was born sometime around 1485 to Katherine and Walter Cromwell, the latter a blacksmith, brewer, and tavern owner in Putney, Surrey. As a young man, Thomas left England to join the French army as a mercenary soldier and saw action in the Italian wars before mustering out to become an apprentice banker in Florence. There he established a textile export business of his own and then relocated to **Flanders** to connect with and sell his wares to English cloth merchants. At some point during these early years, Cromwell acquired some legal training (perhaps he was self-taught), and he mastered a working knowledge of several European languages as well. Around 1515, he returned to England where he married Elizabeth Wyckes, a local Putney girl he may have known since childhood. Together they had three children, only one of whom, Gregory, survived to outlive his father. Cromwell's wife and their two daughters all died in 1529, possibly of the dreaded **sweating sickness**.

After undertaking mercantile embassies to Rome in 1516 and 1518, Cromwell established himself as a successful London cloth merchant and practicing lawyer in 1520. He then took a seat in the House of Commons in **Parliament** in 1523 and was elected to Gray's Inn the next year as a senior solicitor. By this time, he had attracted the notice of Thomas Cardinal Wolsey, King Henry VIII's chief minister, who invited Cromwell to join his household staff as a lawyer and secretary. There he met and cultivated relationships with such men as **Thomas More**, **George Cavendish**, and **Thomas Audley**, all of whom would go on to influence English affairs of church and state in the years to come. When Wolsey failed to secure the marriage annulment King Henry sought from the pope, the Great Cardinal fell precipitously from royal favor, was banished from court, and died from a possible heart attack at a monastery in Leicester in 1530. Cromwell had wisely separated himself from Wolsey before his fall from grace, however, and was thus in position to take his patron's place as a trusted advisor to the Tudor king when the opportunity presented itself.

In summer 1531, Henry VIII added Thomas Cromwell to his royal council, an appointment that coincided with the ongoing crisis in Crown affairs known euphemistically as the king's "**Great Matter.**" Since the late 1520s, King Henry had been trying to set aside his first wife, **Katherine of Aragon**, because he longed for the son she could not give him and because he was infatuated with a younger court lady named **Anne Boleyn**. The road to an annulment from Pope **Clement VII** was by this time blocked, leaving the king increasingly desperate to free himself from his first marriage so he might father a male heir with Anne. Many scholars now believe it was probably Thomas Cromwell who first suggested a break with Rome so Henry VIII could set himself up as the head of his own Church of England. Such a move would then allow the king to bypass the authority of the papacy and pronounce for himself (through a deputy) an annulment of his union with Katherine. In addition, Cromwell apparently persuaded King Henry to utilize parliamentary statutes to achieve this end, sensing that English believers would more readily accept a split with the Roman

Church if brought about by the men who represented their various counties in the House of Commons.

Thus, Thomas Cromwell began accomplishing his master's Great Matter by initiating a legislative breach with Rome between 1532–34 that over time evolved into a full-scale reformation. To prepare the ground for his radical program, Cromwell first packed the House of Commons with his supporters and then threatened the English bishops with financial ruin. These measures ensured passage of the Supplication against the Ordinaries and the **Submission of the Clergy** (1532), both of which handed a great deal of authority over the English Church to Henry VIII. In early 1533, Cromwell sponsored passage of the **Act in Restraint of Appeals**, which transferred final jurisdiction of ecclesiastical court cases from the pope to the archbishop of Canterbury. This authorized Archbishop **Thomas Cranmer** to pronounce King Henry's long-awaited "divorce" from Queen Katherine and opened the door for his quick remarriage to Anne Boleyn. Finally, in November 1534, Cromwell completed the break from Rome with passage of the **Act of Supremacy**, naming the Tudor king "supreme head in earth of the Church of England . . . united to the imperial crown of this realm."

Impressed with his handling of religious matters, a grateful Henry VIII granted Cromwell the title vicegerent in spirituals in 1535, an office that entrusted full authority over the English Church to the lawyer from Putney. The king was unaware, however, that Cromwell harbored secret Lutheran sympathies that now inspired him to reform the Church of England along more evangelical lines. He sent his agents out to assess the monetary value of England's monasteries, recorded these amounts in the *Valor Ecclesiasticus*, and then systematically closed some 800 monastic houses (1536–39) and used the proceeds from their sale to enrich the royal coffers. He persuaded the **Convocation of Bishops** to approve the Ten Articles of Faith (1536), which reduced the official sacraments of the English Church from seven to three and adopted a modified form of Luther's "justification by faith" as the approved salvation doctrine. In addition, he commissioned Miles Coverdale and John Rogers to produce an English translation of the Bible, based on the earlier translation by **William Tyndale**, and had it published as the Great Bible (1539) and placed in every parish church in the land.

Thomas Cromwell has also been recognized for launching a revolution in government by overhauling old medieval institutions and inventing new administrative practices to help the Crown function more efficiently. He was the first to use parliamentary statute laws to achieve revolutionary changes in church and state, knowing that the preambles he carefully drafted for these laws would be read aloud to the people in public squares across the realm. To manage the great flow of royal revenues pouring in from various sources, Cromwell created courts of augmentations (monastic income), first fruits and tenths (clerical fees), wardships (feudal dues), and general survey (income from royal lands). In the absence of any police force, he set up a system of paid informants and spies to help him keep order in a turbulent age. Amazingly, of some 900 individuals Cromwell had arrested and interrogated for noncompliance with his religious changes, only 329 were executed, while the others were all acquitted, released, or pardoned. Already King Henry's lord privy seal by 1536 and elevated to the Earldom of Essex in April 1540, Cromwell also reduced the size of the royal council to create a privy council (12–15 members) and established parish registers across England to record births, marriages, and deaths as an early form of population census.

Cromwell's ultimate downfall began in 1539–40, when he convinced his Tudor master to marry the German princess Anne of Cleves, who was so unattractive to Henry that he refused to consummate their union and divorced her six months later. The king's resulting displeasure with his chief minister opened the door for Cromwell's many enemies at court, including **Thomas Howard**, third Duke of Norfolk, and **Stephen Gardiner**, bishop of Winchester, to accuse him of usurping royal authority and introducing heretical (reformed) doctrines into the English Church. Cromwell was convicted by act of attainder in the House of Lords in late June 1540 and, after he was stripped of his many titles and properties, was beheaded on Tower Hill one month later.

CULPEPPER, THOMAS (1514–41).

A royal courtier and favorite of Henry VIII, Culpepper was distantly related to two of the Tudor king's queens and carried on a scandalous affair with one of them that ended with his execution. As a gentleman of the royal privy chamber, he enjoyed open access to nearly every aspect of court life and took full advantage of his privileged position to profit from his influence with Henry VIII and other members of the king's inner circle. The handsome Culpepper was involved with Lady **Katherine Howard** while the future queen was still in her teens and later spent considerable time with her again when the aging Henry VIII began to neglect his young consort. Although Culpepper may have been innocent of the adulterous charges brought against him, he nevertheless (and almost inevitably) suffered a traitor's death with other alleged lovers of the queen in December 1541.

Thomas Culpepper was born the second of three sons (and the second of those sons named Thomas) to Alexander and Constance Harper Culpepper in the village of Bedgebury in Kent in 1514. He was a fifth cousin of Joyce Culpepper, the mother of the future queen Katherine Howard, and was thus distantly related to **Anne Boleyn** through her Howard family connections as well. Little is known of the younger Thomas's upbringing or education, although he seems at least to have learned several European languages that later proved useful in aristocratic circles at the Tudor court. He was energetically athletic and a successful tiltyard **jouster**, and he cut a dashing figure in a wide array of close-fitting, expensive, and fashionable outfits. The historical record first mentioned Culpepper in 1535, when he accepted employment as a personal attendant in the household of **Arthur Plantagenet**, Viscount Lisle, who was at the time lord deputy of the English-held town of **Calais** in France. Lisle's wife, Honor, was quite taken with her husband's attractive young valet and later sent him her colors to wear as her champion during an invitational jousting tournament.

Culpepper returned to England in summer 1537 and, catching the eye of Henry VIII with his charm, wit, and grace, soon accepted the coveted position of privy chamber gentleman to the king a few months later. He also began at this time to acquire multiple estates of his own, including a dissolved monastery in Kent; seven manors in Essex, Gloucestershire, and Wiltshire; and a townhouse in London with 15 rooms.

While Thomas Culpepper continued to bask in the glow of royal favor, Katherine Howard arrived at court late in 1539 to begin service as a lady-in-waiting to Henry VIII's expected fourth wife and queen, **Anne of Cleves**. Aged just 18 years at the time, Lady Katherine was already an experienced courtesan, whose previous lovers included her former music teacher Henry Mannox and an ambitious gentleman named Francis Dereham. Culpepper and the Howard girl met for the first time at court and quickly became enamored of one another, after which the impetuous Thomas professed his love for her and then (very probably) enjoyed more intimate relations with her as well. The two were briefly separated when Culpepper traveled to Calais to help escort Anne of Cleves to England, but when King Henry first beheld his new bride in January 1540, he was revolted by her appearance and likened her to a Flemish mare. He married her anyway but refused to sleep with her and then began to search about his court for a more attractive woman to satiate his frustrated sexual urges. The lustful royal gaze soon fell on Katherine Howard, who had in the meantime resumed her affair with Thomas Culpepper. The Tudor king flirted with Lady Katherine, showered her with gifts, and finally had the **Convocation of Bishops** annul his unhappy union with Queen Anne early in July 1540 so he could wed the still-teenaged Howard girl a few weeks later.

As queen of England, Katherine Howard had the good sense at first to avoid Thomas Culpepper and devote herself completely to fulfilling the every desire of her obese, sickly, and rapidly aging royal husband. In spring 1541, Henry's various ailments flared up and plunged him into fits of depressed rage, which in turn caused the king to ban his pretty young wife from his presence and his bed. Now frustrated herself, Queen Katherine brought her old amour Francis Dereham to court as her personal secretary and took up again with the alluring Thomas Culpepper, with whom she regularly met in her private bedchamber and other locations through the summer and autumn of 1541. Salacious rumors of the queen's indiscreet behavior soon flew around the Tudor court, prompting the arrest of Dereham and Culpepper and their interrogation at the **Tower of London**. Both men confessed under torture to sexual intimacy with Katherine Howard, but they insisted their illicit liaisons with her had taken place before her marriage to the king. Unconvinced, the royal privy council, led by **Thomas Howard**, the third Duke of Norfolk and Queen Katherine's uncle, sentenced both Dereham and Culpepper to die as traitors by hanging, drawing, and quartering at Tyburn. King Henry commuted Culpepper's sentence to beheading, and kneeling on the scaffold without the customary block in place, he was executed on 10 December 1541 with a single stroke of the headsman's axe. His and Dereham's heads were displayed on pikes along the side rails of London Bridge as a discouraging example to other would-be traitors.

D

DARCY (OR DACRE), THOMAS, BARON TEMPLEHURST (c. 1467–1537). This prominent magnate enjoyed a long and distinguished career serving the first two Tudor kings as a military commander, international diplomat, and royal councilor. With most of his principal estates located in the kingdom's northern shires, Darcy spent much of his life in that region administering justice, raising royal troop levies, and most crucially securing the northern marches against Scottish raids and invasions. Lord Darcy was a committed son of the Roman Church who refused to condone Henry VIII's rejection of Queen **Katherine of Aragon** in the late 1520s and who later opposed the suppression of the **monasteries** during the subsequent **Henrician Reformation**. Darcy took a leading role in the **Pilgrimage of Grace** rebellion in 1536–37 and was executed on the block for treason in his 70th year.

Thomas Darcy was born the only son and heir of Sir William Darcy, a minor **gentry** landholder with estates in Richmondshire, Yorkshire, and Lincolnshire. As a young man, Thomas was knighted when he came into possession of his family's lands at his father's death in 1488. He was married twice, first to Dousabelle Tempest, who gave him four sons before her untimely death around 1498. Two years later, he wed Edith Sandys, the widow of Lord Ralph Neville, who brought her young son, Ralph (and his inherited wealth), with her into the Darcy household. In 1497, Sir Thomas Darcy rode with **Thomas Howard**, the Earl of Surrey (later the second Duke of Norfolk) to repel an invasion of England by King **James IV** of Scotland, service that earned him elevation to the peerage as the first Baron Darcy of Templehurst (the principal family seat) a few years later. At the same time, Darcy was busy supporting King **Henry VII** in the north country as the constable of Bamburgh Castle, the captain of the border town of Berwick, and the warden of the east marches along the Scottish frontier. At the accession of King Henry VIII, Lord Darcy was honored with a knighthood in the prestigious Order of the **Garter** in 1509.

In 1511, Darcy volunteered to lead a force of 1,200 English archers to Spain to support an invasion of France by King **Ferdinand of Aragon**, but his men proved quarrelsome, and his little army languished in Cádiz for two weeks before returning to England. Darcy next accompanied Henry VIII on his own **French invasion in 1513–14**, where he took part in—and was injured during—the siege and capture of Thérouanne. Upon their return to England, a grateful king appointed Lord Darcy to his royal council, where he met and became friendly with **Thomas Wolsey**, the soon-to-be cardinal of the church and Henry's chief minister. Over the next decade, Darcy carried out numerous administrative tasks for the Crown, and in 1523, he led a force of some 1,750 soldiers on a punitive expedition into Scotland. Although he did not support Henry VIII's campaign to set aside Queen Katherine (declaring that such authority only rested with the pope), Lord Darcy dutifully turned on Cardinal Wolsey in 1529 by helping draw up the list of charges that led to his old friend's downfall.

Always a devout adherent of the Roman Church, Thomas Darcy became increasingly alarmed as the Henrician Reformation gradually evolved from a marriage and succession crisis into a fully reformed English Church and the dissolution of most of the kingdom's monasteries. By the mid-1530s, he and Lord John Hussey, another disaffected northern baron, plotted with imperial ambassador Eustace Chapuys to convince Emperor Charles V to invade England, though nothing ever came of this scheme. When the Pilgrimage of Grace uprising got underway in autumn 1536, however, Darcy found himself siding with the rebels in opposition to the religious reforms of Thomas Cromwell, King Henry's new chief minister and vicegerent in spirituals. As Pilgrimage leader Robert Aske led his followers to Pontefract Castle, then under Darcy's command, the Yorkshire baron surrendered the royal fortress to the insurgents without hesitation and quickly joined the protest movement himself. He then helped Aske draft the 24 articles of grievance that the Pilgrimage's emissaries presented to Henry VIII two months later. Despite the pardon the king offered if he came to London, Darcy chose to remain in the north of England until he was arrested and taken to the Tower of London to await trial. In May 1537, he was convicted of high treason and was sentenced to a grisly traitor's death, but his noble rank spared him that horror, and he was more mercifully beheaded on 30 June following.

DENNY, SIR ANTHONY (1501–49). As yeoman of the wardrobe (the king's private living quarters) and groom of the royal stool (restroom attendant), Sir Anthony Denny was Henry VIII's closest confidant and in some ways the power behind the throne during the final years of the Tudor king's long reign. Denny oversaw settlement of royal household expenses and gambling debts, was keeper of Westminster Palace, and duplicated King Henry's signature on writs, grants, summonses, and other official Crown documents. Although he was in sympathy with the religious reform party in England, he kept his more radical theological views to himself during Henry VIII's period of conservative reaction in the 1540s. Sir Anthony attended the old king on his deathbed, witnessed and helped execute

Henry's will, served on the privy council of his successor Edward VI, and only lived another 25 months before following Henry VIII to the grave himself at age 48.

Anthony Denny was born the second surviving son of Sir Edmund Denny, an official of the royal exchequer, and his second wife, Mary Troutbeck Denny, at Howe in the county of Norfolk on 16 January 1501. He studied as a youth at St. Paul's School in London and then entered St. John's College at Cambridge University, where he acquired some academic polish but did not earn a degree. In 1525, Denny married Joan Champemowne, the sister of Katherine "Kat" Champemowne Ashley, the future governess of Princess Elizabeth Tudor. His union with Joan was a happy one, and the couple produced no fewer than a dozen children over the course of their 24 married years together. Sometime in the late 1520s, Denny accepted a serving position in the household of Sir Francis Bryan, one of Henry VIII's rambunctious young "henchmen" who escorted and made merry with the spirited Tudor king wherever he went. By 1531, Denny was accompanying Bryan on diplomatic missions overseas and was likely present with his master at Calais when King Henry and Anne Boleyn met there with François I of France in 1532.

By 1535, Henry VIII must have noticed Anthony Denny, for he soon hired the hardworking servant away from his friend Sir Francis Bryan to work in the privy chamber of the royal household. The king also urged Denny at this time to stand for election to Parliament from the Essex town of Ipswich. When Bryan accepted the post of chief gentleman of the royal privy chamber in 1536, Denny became the groom of the royal stool, the high-ranking valet who assisted the king when using his privy pot, or royal commode. Such a position of intimate service and trust gave Denny ready access to the king's ear, allowing him in turn to assert unrivaled influence over any personal or sovereign decision Henry might consider or need to discuss. When Sir Francis Bryan stepped down from privy chamber oversight in 1537, Anthony Denny quickly stepped up to replace him and then added keeper of the Palace of Westminster (the House of Commons' permanent assembly hall) to his résumé later the same year.

Thus clearly on the rise as a Crown servant, Denny was also a self-taught scholar and voracious reader who cultivated relationships with **Roger Ascham** and **John Cheke**, both leading intellectuals who would later tutor two of King Henry's children and heirs. The royal privy chamber gentleman was also an evangelical Protestant who was friendly with **Thomas Cromwell**, King Henry's vicegerent in spirituals (religious superintendent), and with **Thomas Cranmer**, the reform-minded archbishop of Canterbury. Denny was wise enough to conceal his true religious opinions from the conservative Tudor king (something Cromwell could not do), and he accordingly received multiple manors, dissolved abbeys, lucrative collectorships, and London townhouses as rewards from his unsuspecting sovereign. The influence he curried with Henry VIII was also for sale, as was his control of the dry stamp, a device that duplicated the royal signature and could be used to authorize grants of land, titles, and offices to the highest bidders. By the early 1540s, Denny's annual income totaled more than £750 (around $825,000 in modern American currency), and he was so important and wealthy that he was able to engage the eminent German artist **Hans Holbein** the Younger to paint his portrait.

Henry VIII's privy chamber gentleman and confidant was with the royal entourage in January 1540, when the king first met **Anne of Cleves** and then shared with Denny his profound distaste for her. More happily, he later served as a witness at the quiet wedding of King Henry and **Katherine Parr** at **Hampton Court** in July 1543. He accompanied the Tudor king on his final **French invasion in 1544–45** and, equipping and paying 200 soldiers for the expedition from his own pocket, was knighted outside the captured town of Boulogne for his service to the Crown.

Denny commissioned an elaborate new commode for King Henry late in 1546 that cost £5 and consisted of a large pewter basin topped with silk-fringed black velvet and stuffed with 31 pounds of feathers for his majesty's comfort. Sir Anthony helped draw up the last will and testament of Henry VIII with **Edward Seymour**, the Earl of Hertford; **John Dudley** Lord Lisle; and **William Paget** and was present (with Archbishop Cranmer) at his royal master's bedside during Henry's final days and hours in late January 1547. Denny became a member of young King Edward VI's privy council in the new reign and took in the teenaged Princess Elizabeth once Katherine Parr sent her away following her scandalous dalliance with **Thomas Seymour** in 1548. In January 1549, Denny contracted an unknown illness, died the following month at his home in Cheshunt in Hertfordshire, and was laid to rest in St. Mary the Virgin Church in Cheshunt village, now located in the Broxbourne district of northern London.

DISSOLUTION OF THE MONASTERIES. *See* MONASTERIES, DISSOLUTION OR SUPPRESSION OF THE (1535–40).

DUDLEY, EDMUND (1462–1510). Edmund Dudley was a lawyer, revenue collector, and government servant of King **Henry VII**. He was roundly hated by many English **nobles** and by high-ranking members of the English **clergy** for his efforts on behalf of his king to collect recognizance and benevolence payments as bonds against disloyalty or rebellion. Dudley enriched himself as he collected these monies, using his newfound wealth to acquire several homes and estates across the south and midlands of England. When Henry VIII acceded to the throne in 1509, he had Dudley (and his associate Sir **Richard Empson**) arrested and incarcerated in the **Tower of London**. While awaiting his fate there, Dudley composed his political treatise *The Tree of Commonwealth*, which offered advice to his new king on how best to rule England. Henry VIII may never have seen this little book, for he had Dudley and Empson beheaded as traitors in August 1510. Edmund Dudley was the father of **John Dudley**, Viscount Lovell and later Duke of Northumberland, and was the grandfather of Robert Dudley, Earl of Leicester and confidante of Princess **Elizabeth** Tudor, later Queen Elizabeth I.

Edmund Dudley was born in 1462 (or less probably in 1471) in Sussex, but beyond this, little else is known about his early life. He was educated at **Oxford University** and studied law at Gray's Inn in London, before he entered royal service as a member of King Henry VII's council in the 1480s. The first Tudor king employed him on several diplomatic missions, including an embassy to negotiate the Treaty of Étaples in 1492 that ended hostilities with King Charles VIII of France. He also represented his home county of Sussex in the House of Commons in **Parliament**, where he eventually became speaker of the house in 1504. Having earned King Henry's trust, Dudley was sent forth with Sir Richard Empson to collect recognizance and benevolence remittances, substantial sums that many of the great lords and prelates of the realm were required to surrender to Henry's agents to discourage rebellion and ensure their loyal obedience. Most wealthy magnates deeply resented Dudley's role in collecting these payments and developed grudges against him (and Empson) that spilled over into the next Tudor reign. When young Henry VIII succeeded his father as king in 1509, he was anxious to win widespread approval from his subjects and so had the extremely unpopular Edmund Dudley arrested, charged with treason, and clapped into the Tower of London. Dudley briefly considered a plan to escape but abandoned it when he believed a royal reprieve was in the offing. He was wrong, of course, and died on the block as a traitor with his associate Richard Empson on 17 August 1510.

Dudley wrote *The Tree of Commonwealth* while imprisoned in the tower, hoping he might win favor and perhaps a pardon from the youthful, vain, and impressionable King Henry VIII. *The Tree* declares that royal authority comes from God alone and describes Henry as a ruler "without spot or blemish of untruth." Dudley then outlined the several virtues he believed a commonwealth must possess to ensure its prosperity and security and likened those virtues to the roots of a tree, whose shade protects all. The tree's roots represent the love of God, justice, unity, truth, concord, and peace. Dudley argued that, if all the social

orders (nobility, **gentry**, townsmen, peasants) of the English realm were to cultivate and live by these virtues, then the kingdom would flourish under the rule of a righteous king and a paternal God. It is unknown if Henry VIII ever read or even saw Dudley's *Tree of Commonwealth*, but the little treatise ended up surviving both men in the form of a few manuscript and several printed editions.

DUDLEY, JOHN, EARL OF WARWICK, FIRST DUKE OF NORTHUMBERLAND (1504–53).

John Dudley belonged to an influential family who rose from obscurity to serve—or fall afoul of—every Tudor ruler from King **Henry VII** to Queen **Elizabeth I**. The son of a Crown minister whom Henry VIII had executed early in his reign, John Dudley's personal courage and athletic vigor soon won favor with the second Tudor king and earned him a privileged position at court. Having demonstrated his military prowess on foreign battlefields, Dudley was ennobled, given command of the English **navy**, and then appointed to King Henry's privy council. At the old king's death in 1547, he served as an executor of the royal will and as a member of the regency council that presided over the early reign of young King **Edward VI**. As Duke of Northumberland and the realm's lord protector, Dudley swept aside his political rivals, further reformed the Church of England, and finally devised an improbable and unsuccessful plot to place his own son on the English throne. He was arrested at the accession of Queen **Mary I** and suffered a traitor's death on Tower Hill in August 1553.

Born in London, John Dudley was the eldest son of royal revenue officer **Edmund Dudley** and his wife, Elizabeth Grey Dudley, the daughter of Lord Edward Grey of Lisle. Responsible for collecting the hated benevolence and recognizance exactions of Henry VII, the elder Dudley was arrested and beheaded in 1510 by an insecure young Henry VIII eager to win public popularity as England's new king. As a youngster, John Dudley became a ward of Sir Edward Guildford, the marshal of **Calais**, who gave his young charge extensive military training and even brought him along to France as a fortification apprentice. Dudley accompanied **Thomas Cardinal Wolsey** on several diplomatic missions abroad during the 1520s and was knighted by **Charles Brandon**, the Duke of Suffolk and King Henry's brother-in-law, when both men took part in the **French invasion of 1523–24**. Sir John married Guildford's daughter Jane in 1525, and they produced no fewer than 13 children over the course of their long union together. Dudley's prowess in **jousting tournaments** and at the archery butts soon attracted the admiration of Henry VIII, who made the athletic young man a knight of the royal body and master armorer. When Sir Edward Guildford died intestate in 1534, Dudley used his influence at court to secure most of his former guardian's inheritance for himself and his family.

By the early 1530s, Sir John had become a committed Lutheran and so allied himself with fellow religious reformers **Thomas Cromwell**, Henry VIII's chief minister and vicegerent in spirituals, and **Edward Seymour**, the king's future brother-in-law. He represented the county of Kent in **Parliament**, attended the christenings of Princess Elizabeth and Prince Edward, and led a detachment of troops against the **Pilgrimage of Grace** insurgents in 1536. The following year, a grateful king created Dudley vice admiral of the English navy, a post he eagerly accepted and in which he soon distinguished himself. In 1542, Henry elevated Dudley to the peerage as Viscount Lisle, a title that fell to him from his mother's family, and the next year, he became lord high admiral and joined the Order of the **Garter** as a companion knight. In 1544, Lisle took part in both land and sea raids against Scotland and then traveled to the Continent to fortify and defend the English-held town of Boulogne against the French. Meanwhile the energetic lord admiral completely reorganized the English fleet and directed naval operations in the Solvent when a massive French flotilla threatened the southern Hampshire coast in 1545. The ailing Henry VIII granted Viscount Lisle the Earldom of Warwick in 1546, and after the old king

breathed his last in January of the following year, Dudley agreed to serve with Edward Seymour, the soon-to-be Duke of Somerset, on the regency council of the nine-year-old King Edward VI.

The Earl of Warwick now embarked on the tumultuous six-year span that brought him great infamy and ultimately led to his inglorious end under the headsman's axe. He worked closely on the royal council at first with Somerset, the boy-king's uncle and lord protector, but the duke's unpopular **coinage** debasement, **enclosure** restrictions, and religious reforms prompted Warwick to have his political rival imprisoned in the **Tower of London** on charges of incompetence and corruption in 1549. The two men subsequently reconciled, and the duke even rejoined King Edward's council for a time, but the ambitious Warwick soon turned on the former lord protector again and this time had him executed in January 1552. By now the Duke of Northumberland and lord protector of the young king himself, John Dudley set about more radically reforming the Church of England along Calvinist lines and initiated coinage rebasement to help stabilize the realm's economy.

Northumberland's great undoing, however, proved to be the misguided royal coup he attempted to bring about in 1553. First he wed his youngest son, Guilford, to Jane Grey, a distant heir to the English throne; then he persuaded the dying Edward VI to sign over his Crown to Guilford and Jane; and finally, he proclaimed Queen Jane just days after the young king's death to insert his Dudley son into the royal succession. Northumberland's elaborate plot unraveled nine days later, when Princess Mary Tudor raised an army in East Anglia, marched on London, seized the throne, and had the now contrite and obsequious duke arrested as a traitor. Mounting the scaffold to die on the block, Northumberland proclaimed himself a true Roman Catholic and was beheaded and then buried in the chapel of Peter ad Vincula within the precincts of the Tower of London.

E

EDWARD VI (TUDOR), PRINCE OF WALES AND KING OF ENGLAND (1537–53; r. 1547–53). King Henry VIII's only legitimate son to survive beyond infancy, Edward jumped ahead of his two older half-sisters in the Tudor line of succession to inherit the English throne from his father in 1547. Young Edward never knew his mother, for his birth caused complications that killed her, so he was mostly raised and educated by King Henry's sixth wife and queen, **Katherine Parr**. She ensured that Edward grew up a zealous Protestant who loved the Christian Scriptures as much as he despised the superstition and idolatry he saw in the Church of Rome. Edward VI became king at age nine and, mostly governed during his reign by two powerful "protectors," died a few months before his 16th birthday without leaving an uncontested candidate to succeed him on the throne.

When Henry VIII became king in 1509, his first dynastic concern was to safeguard the royal claims of the House of Tudor by siring a male heir. Well aware that an unsettled path to the English throne had precipitated the 15th-century **Wars of the Roses**, King Henry was eager to avoid similar upheavals by providing a son whose regal claims could not be challenged. He thus did his best to father that all-important Tudor prince with his first two queens, **Katherine of Aragon** and **Anne Boleyn**, but over the course of nine pregnancies, both women only gave their anxious husband a pair of daughters. King Henry married again after Katherine and Anne died in 1535–36, this time taking the meek, agreeable, and presumably fecund **Jane Seymour** (she was one of eight siblings) as his third wife and queen. By spring 1537, Queen Jane was indeed pregnant, and after court astrologers assured the king that her unborn child was male, she fulfilled her promise and presented Henry with his longed-for prince at **Hampton Court** on 12 October 1537. The Tudor king was elated: He had his son christened Edward; created him Duke of Cornwall and Earl of Chester; and then ordered celebratory bonfires, Te Deum services, and artillery discharges across the land. Mother and child seemed healthy at first, but then Queen Jane developed puerperal fever 10 days after Edward's birth, and she died during the early morning of 24 October 1537. Grief-stricken over his wife's untimely demise, King Henry managed to console himself with the infant boy he knew could finally secure the Tudor royal succession for generations to come.

Contrary to popular belief, Prince Edward Tudor was not a sickly and fragile youngster but was in fact fairly robust, vigorous, and even athletic until the final years of his life. The child must have seemed slight of build next to his tall and corpulent father, but many reports from the time of Edward's youth attest to his love of sport and skill in the saddle and with the bow. He was by his own admission raised "among the women" at first, with a host of wet nurses, governesses, and other female attendants coddling and spoiling the prince at every turn. When Edward (now the Prince of **Wales**) reached the age of six, King Henry married Katherine Parr and then handed responsibility for his son's education over to her. A serious and scholarly woman, she immediately engaged Dr. Richard Cox, the noted **Cambridge University** theologian, to instruct the lad in Greek, Latin, Scripture knowledge, and Christian doctrine. Queen Katherine then reinforced Cox with **John Cheke** and **Roger Ascham**, who added modern languages, philosophy, the classics, astronomy, music, history, and geography to the prince's course of study. All three of Edward's tutors were prominent evangelicals (Protestants) and so were chosen to educate young Edward by a queen who harbored Calvinist sympathies herself. When he became king of England, Edward VI saw himself as a latter-day Josiah, a great scriptural sovereign whom God had summoned to bring religious truth and doctrinal purity to his subjects.

In addition to all his other attributes, the Prince of Wales was also highly intelligent and a competent scholar in his own right. During the years before and after his royal accession, Edward penned multiple essays on the English body politic, the lessons of Scripture, moral and ethical behavior, and even economic theory. The prince did not have friends in the conventional sense, but he did share his royal schoolroom with the privileged sons of several ranking **noble** families. The one boy with whom he developed a lasting bond was Barnaby Fitzpatrick, the son of a minor Irish lord, who studied and sported with Edward at the Tudor court and then corresponded with him from France later in their lives. Henry VIII also occasionally offered his son (as he did his two daughters) as a diplomatic pawn on the European marriage market. When the English king signed a peace treaty with Scotland in 1543, the hand of the six-year-old Prince Edward was promised to the infant Mary Stuart, later the queen of Scots. Edinburgh soon repudiated the pact, however, prompting an insulted King Henry to order **Edward Seymour**, the Earl of Hertford and young Edward's uncle, to retaliate by invading and pillaging the southern Scottish countryside.

When Henry VIII breathed his last in January 1547, Edward VI acceded to the throne under the watchful authority of a regency council that included the boy-king's uncle Edward Seymour, now the first Duke of Somerset; **John Dudley**, the Earl of Warwick and later the first Duke of Northumberland; and **Thomas Cranmer**, the archbishop of Canterbury. The story of Edward VI's brief reign was more about the struggle for power between Somerset and Northumberland than it was about anything the youthful Tudor king may have achieved on his own. Still, King Edward was well educated, a confident son of "Great Harry," and an enthusiastic religious reformer who had (at least) to be consulted and even heard (though often ignored) on all matters of state policy. Indeed, his reign produced two of the seminal features of the English Reformation in the first and second *Books of Common Prayer* and the *Forty-Two Articles of Faith* for the Anglican Church. Healthy throughout much of his life, Edward was as susceptible to consumption (tuberculosis) as were other Tudor males, and finally contracting that illness himself around the age of 14, he died on 6 July 1553 and was laid to rest in Westminster Abbey. Never married and without any recognized heirs of his own, King Edward VI left Northumberland and Henry VIII's eldest daughter, Mary, to challenge each other for control of his vacant throne.

ELIZABETH I (TUDOR), QUEEN OF ENGLAND (1533–1603; r. 1558–1603).

The daughter of Henry VIII and his second wife and queen, **Anne Boleyn**, Elizabeth Tudor spent her early life either as an acknowledged princess and heir to the throne or as a royal disappointment and an unwanted bastard. She received an excellent education, and unlike her Catholic half-sister **Mary** Tudor (later Queen Mary I), Elizabeth grew up to embrace the reformed faith of her stepmother Queen **Katherine Parr**. Anne Boleyn's controversial marriage to King Henry and her dramatic downfall and execution limited Princess Elizabeth's matrimonial prospects as an adolescent, and she famously remained unwed for the rest of her life as a "virgin queen." After King Henry reconciled with his youngest daughter, Elizabeth survived his death and the reigns of her two half-siblings to inherit the English throne herself in 1558. Over the next 44 years, Queen Elizabeth I ruled her island kingdom wisely and became one of the most beloved and successful monarchs in English history.

Mistress Anne Boleyn was already with child—the future Princess Elizabeth—when Henry VIII married her and had her crowned queen of England in 1533. With both royal parents fervently praying for a son, Queen Anne was delivered of a healthy baby girl instead on 7 September at **Greenwich Palace**. King Henry was deeply disappointed by this outcome, but he was confident Queen Anne was still young enough to give him more (male) children soon. The infant princess was christened Elizabeth (after the king's mother, **Elizabeth of York**) three days after her birth in the chapel of the Franciscan Observant Friars at Greenwich. The king then ordered his infant daughter moved to Hatfield House some 20 miles north of London, where she was placed in the nurturing care of her first governess, Lady Margaret Bryan.

Within months of her birth, little Elizabeth replaced her older half-sister Mary Tudor (**Katherine of Aragon**'s daughter) as heir to the English throne when **Parliament** passed the **Act of Succession** in March 1534. The infant princess in the meantime lived a carefree existence at Hatfield and other royal residences while Queen Anne showered her with expensive playthings and clothing. Anne Boleyn did not long remain in the king's favor, however; when Elizabeth was just 32 months old, her mother was arrested, tried, and executed as a traitorous adulterer in May 1536. Henry VIII hastily remarried **Jane Seymour**, had both his daughters declared illegitimate by another Act of Succession, and then banished "Lady" Elizabeth (as she was now to be known) from court to make room for his new queen's expected children. Her demotion from princess to bastard was so precipitous that her governess had to beg the Crown for money to replace the clothing her young charge was fast outgrowing. When Queen Jane finally presented her overjoyed husband with a healthy prince in October 1537, Lady Margaret Bryan became his governess and was replaced in Elizabeth's household by the bright and well-educated Katherine "Kat" Ashley.

As a toddler, Elizabeth was beginning to show the quick wit, shrewd intelligence, and eager curiosity that had made her mother so attractive at court in years past. Kat Ashley quickly recognized the intellectual potential of the girl in her care and began to teach her the rudiments of reading, writing, and courtly manners at an early age. As Elizabeth grew older, she often shared the same residence with her younger brother, Prince **Edward** Tudor, which exposed her to the wisdom of his learned tutor **John Cheke** at the same time. By age six, the precocious little princess was studying in a schoolroom of her own under the watchful gaze of William Grindal and later the eminent **Cambridge University** scholar **Roger Ascham**. These tutors primarily instructed her in Latin, Greek, and the ancient classics, but they brought in foreign teachers to develop her fluency in modern European languages as well. Soon a proficient linguist, Elizabeth translated Marguerite d'Angoulême's devotional work *Mirror of the Sinful Soul* from French into Latin and Italian as a gift for her stepmother Katherine Parr in 1545.

Indeed, the Lady Elizabeth (as she was still styled) was cordial with several of King Henry's later wives. She was present at Greenwich when her father met **Anne of Cleves** for the first time in January 1540, and at age eight, she developed a sisterly rapport with her cousin **Katherine Howard**. That relationship ended tragically, however, when Henry VIII's promiscuous young queen suffered the same fate in 1542 that Elizabeth's own mother had suffered some six years before. Shaken by these events, Lady Elizabeth recovered sufficiently to witness the private wedding ceremony of her father and Katherine Parr at Greenwich Palace in 1543. Of all the Tudor king's later spouses, Elizabeth was closest to this last Queen Katherine, who took charge of her stepdaughter's education and saw her brought up a committed if somewhat flexible Protestant. Katherine Parr convinced her husband to invite both his daughters back to court, whereupon he restored each of them to the royal succession in 1544. Now third in line for the English throne, Elizabeth's hand was offered to the sons of several royal houses across Europe, but these offers were never accepted thanks to the uncertain validity of her mother's union with King Henry.

When Henry VIII passed away on 28 January 1547, Elizabeth went to live in the household of his widow, who had married her former suitor and now her fourth husband, **Thomas Seymour**, just a few months after the old king's death. The ambitious Seymour developed an inappropriate interest in his wife's 15-year-old ward, and after Katherine caught them frolicking together in their bedclothes, she sent Elizabeth away to live with Sir **Anthony Denny** and his wife, Joan, at their Cheshunt and Hatfield manors. There she quietly and happily lived out the brief reign of her brother Edward VI, only to be arrested and held in the **Tower of London** in 1554 after her elder sister Mary became queen. Somehow the wily and resilient Elizabeth managed to survive this trial to claim the English throne herself just 11 years after the death of her larger-than-life father. With the launch of the Elizabethan Renaissance, her victory over the Spanish Armada, and the birth of England's overseas empire to her credit, Queen Elizabeth I truly earned the title Gloriana over the course of her lengthy reign.

ELIZABETH OF YORK, QUEEN OF ENGLAND (1465–1503).

Elizabeth of York was the daughter of King Edward IV, the queen consort of King **Henry VII**, and the mother of King Henry VIII and his three surviving royal siblings. Until her marriage to the first Tudor monarch, she was a dynastic pawn whose hand was often courted by men with regal or aristocratic ambitions of their own. By finally making the statuesque Yorkist princess his bride and queen, Henry VII legitimized his own very tenuous claim to the English throne and greatly strengthened the inherited royal claims of each of his Tudor offspring. The mother of a king of England, a Prince of Wales, and two queens of foreign kingdoms, Elizabeth of York died following the delivery of her seventh child at a relatively young age. She is widely believed today to have inspired the image of the queen on standard decks of playing cards used in casinos and at cribbage, poker, and bridge tables all over the globe.

Elizabeth of York was born the eldest of nine children to the Yorkist king Edward IV and his queen consort, Elizabeth Woodville, at **Westminster Palace** on 11 February 1465. In 1470–71, her father fled to Flanders during a short-lived Lancastrian restoration, leaving her mother to seek sanctuary for the first time with her young children—including Elizabeth of York—in Westminster Abbey. Once King Edward recovered his throne, Elizabeth began her study of classical and modern languages, history, arithmetic, music, needlework, riding, and household oversight in hopeful preparation for a royal marriage. In 1475, King Louis XI of France proposed a nuptial union between Elizabeth and Charles, the French dauphin, but the king of England suspected Louis's motives, and negotiations for the match eventually collapsed.

In April 1483, the hedonistic Edward IV died, leaving Elizabeth of York's younger 12-year-old brother Prince Edward to inherit what would soon be a very unsettled throne. Elizabeth's mother, Queen Elizabeth Woodville, believed that she and her family should retain control of the young Yorkist heir, but the brother of the deceased king, Richard of Gloucester, seized Prince Edward instead and locked him away in the **Tower of London**. When the queen sought sanctuary for a second time in Westminster Abbey, Gloucester claimed that his deceased brother had previously been betrothed (akin to being married), thus invalidating his union with Elizabeth Woodville and rendering illegitimate all their children. Gloucester soon took the throne himself as Richard III, and when his wife, Anne Neville, died early in 1485, he briefly thought to wed his niece Elizabeth of York before his councilors wisely convinced him to abandon the idea. Meanwhile, Elizabeth Woodville began negotiating with Lady **Margaret Beaufort**, the mother of exiled royal pretender Henry Tudor, to marry her daughter Elizabeth of York to Lady Margaret's son when the latter (it was hoped) succeeded in wresting the throne away from the usurper Richard III.

Henry Tudor did exactly that in August 1485, when he defeated and killed King Richard at Bosworth Field, thus clearing the way for his negotiated union with Elizabeth of York and her much stronger claim to royalty than his own. Careful to secure **Parliament**'s recognition of his own royal title first, Henry VII then married Elizabeth of York on 18 January 1486 in Westminster Abbey to unite the Houses of Lancaster and York and put an end to the destructive **Wars of the Roses**. As queen of England, Elizabeth of York was attractive but almost absurdly tall (nearly six feet in height); she was also reportedly gracious, kind, and generous, and she enjoyed dancing, gambling, hunting, and even archery. Although their marriage was initially one of dynastic exigency, the royal couple grew to love each other and appear to have been genuinely happy together. Although Queen Elizabeth lived at court in the shadow of her domineering mother-in-law, Margaret Beaufort, King Henry did seek her advice on many occasions and even renovated parts of **Greenwich Palace** to suit her decorative tastes.

Elizabeth of York's most important achievement was the brood of royal children she produced for Henry VII, which stabilized the House of Tudor and ensured a smooth succession after her husband's death. In September 1486, Queen Elizabeth presented King Henry with a male heir, **Arthur** Tudor, Prince of Wales, who was just the first of seven children to follow over the next 17 years. Prince Arthur married the Spanish princess **Katherine of Aragon** but did not live long enough to succeed his father as king. Elizabeth of York also gave birth to **Margaret** Tudor (1489), who grew up to wed the king of Scots; Henry Tudor (1491), the future Henry VIII; and **Mary** Tudor (1496), who was briefly queen of France by marriage in late 1514. Three other children were born to the royal Tudor couple (Elizabeth in 1492, Edmund in 1499, and Katherine in 1503), but none of these survived for longer than a few years at most. Henry VII arranged foreign marriages for his surviving offspring in order to win international recognition for his regime in England and to secure peace treaties with neighboring kingdoms to the north and on the Continent. After giving birth to a sickly daughter who soon died, Queen Elizabeth of York passed away herself nine days later in the Tower of London on her birthday,

11 February 1503, at the age of just 38 years. When her husband died six years later, Queen Elizabeth's remains were interred next to his in the Henry VII Lady Chapel tomb of Westminster Abbey.

ELTHAM ORDINANCES (1526). Drawn up by **Thomas Cardinal Wolsey**, this collection of regulations was intended to reform, streamline, and control the expenses of the royal household and the court establishment of King Henry VIII. The first two Tudor monarchs well knew the need to display their majesty in lavish fashion, but the royal treasury was nearly empty by the mid-1520s and had then been further depleted by the cost of King Henry's second **French invasion of 1523–24**. Although Wolsey's principal aim with the ordinances was to eliminate court waste, superfluous staff positions, and self-serving hangers-on, he also sought to reduce the number of young **noble** courtiers who surrounded and influenced the king, a political objective that ultimately failed along with the ordinances themselves.

By the start of King Henry's second decade in power, the Crown's ability to "live of its own" (operate on revenues from royal estates alone) was no longer a viable budgetary possibility. Cardinal Wolsey, always eager to limit excessive court spending, began planning financial reforms within the king's household as early as 1519 and was eventually able to draft his set of regulations at Eltham Palace in Kent in autumn 1525. The resulting ordinances were wide ranging and minutely detailed and addressed multiple fiscal abuses, such as theft from the king's privy purse, wastage of leftover banquet food, overcrowded and unwieldy royal hunting parties, and the extravagance of a bloated privy chamber staff. The duties of royal servants were carefully enumerated, expenditures on various foodstuffs were curbed, and the number of horses and dogs that each courtier was allowed to keep at Crown expense was greatly restricted. The Eltham Ordinances ordered court servants to curtail their swearing and wear clothing appropriate to their duties, while all those resident at court—from nobles to the lowest scullery boys—were expected to show the king and his family all due deference.

Wolsey completed the ordinance in January 1526 and, having bound them up in a large leather volume, convinced King Henry to approve their implementation within his household during the following spring.

In addition to financial reforms, Cardinal Wolsey cut the number of royal privy chamber attendants from 12 to 6 in order to reduce the influence that some of his principal political rivals enjoyed with the king. Such jovial and athletic men as Sir William Compton, groom of the stool; Sir Francis Bryan, soldier and diplomat; Sir **Nicholas Carew**, master of horse; and the **Boleyn** lords Thomas (father) and George (son) were all banished from the royal household. Evidently, King Henry missed the raucous company of these favorites, his fellow huntsmen, masquers, and **jousters**, for within a few months, nearly all of them had resumed their former duties in the privy chamber once again.

The rest of the Eltham Ordinances fared little better. Although some royal expenses were temporarily brought under control, household wastage and parasitic favor seekers quickly returned to drain the royal treasury further and defeat the cardinal's ambitious schemes for reform. By 1527, Wolsey's fortunes were fading thanks to his failure to secure the marriage annulment his royal master so desperately desired. Within two years, he was stripped of the lord chancellor's chain of office and was banished from King Henry's sight, thus ending the cardinal's own period of dominance at court and rendering his ordinances irrelevant in the bargain.

ELYOT, SIR THOMAS (c. 1490–1546). A philosopher, humanist, jurist, educator, diplomat, and linguist, Elyot is best known today for his work of political science entitled *The Book Named the Governor* (1531). Considered by many to be an English version of Niccolò Machiavelli's *The Prince*, this treatise offers suggestions on the objectives, training, and virtues of successful Renaissance rulers and magistrates. Elyot kept company with some of the most notable humanist scholars of his age, translated several important classical texts into English, and produced the first-ever Latin-English dictionary to assist students of the new learning, or *studia humanitatis*. In addition, Elyot was a religious conservative who generally disapproved of the **Henrician Reformation**, though he kept his views to himself and thus avoided the traitor's death suffered by his friend Sir **Thomas More**.

Thomas Elyot was born around 1490 in Wiltshire and was the only son of Sir Richard Elyot, a member of the **gentry** who served the English **judiciary** over many years as an officer of the western assizes (circuit courts) and as a justice on the Court of King's Bench. Young Thomas was educated first at home and then matriculated at the Middle Temple, one of the **Inns of Court** in London, before attending **Oxford University**, where he earned his baccalaureate degree in 1519 and an advanced degree in civil laws in 1524. Soon invited to join the inner intellectual circle of Sir Thomas More, Elyot met **Thomas Linacre** at More's Chelsea estate and learned Greek and the elements of medicine from the eminent physician and humanist scholar. While at Chelsea, he certainly met **Hans Holbein** the Younger, who sketched portraits of Elyot and his wife, Margaret, and he may also have come to know renowned humanist scholars **Desiderius Erasmus** and **John Colet** there at the same time.

When Sir Richard Elyot died in 1522, his son Thomas inherited most of his properties along with a large library of printed and manuscript books. Between 1515 and 1530, Elyot became justice of the peace for several Midland counties, and in 1525, **Thomas Cardinal Wolsey** promoted him to the office of senior clerk on King Henry VIII's royal council. When Wolsey fell from grace and died in 1530, Elyot was dismissed from the council but was knighted in compensation for the work he had performed. For the moment free of governmental duties, Sir Thomas retreated to his favorite manor house at Carlton in Cambridgeshire and there began to compose the work for which he is most famous today.

Elyot wrote *The Book Named the Governor* in English, a language he believed was as well suited for philosophical discourse as Latin or Greek, and he divided his work into three sections, or books. In the first of these, the opening chapters explore the nature of royal government and stress the absolute need for a divinely appointed monarch to rule all from the very pinnacle of the social hierarchy. The remaining 29 chapters of the first book outline an educational curriculum for would-be rulers that includes the study of Latin and Greek letters, classical texts, modern languages, music, art, history, and poetry and insists that physical exercise be part of the student's daily routine. The second and third books of Elyot's *Governor* recommend the cultivation of positive moral, religious, intellectual, and social virtues and call on aspiring rulers to practice mercy, generosity, justice, good faith, and common sense in all their dealings with their subjects. Finally advising kings to consult with the wisest scholars they could find, Sir Thomas dedicated his completed book to King Henry VIII in the hope of attracting his renewed royal favor.

Such favor came soon enough when Elyot accepted an appointment as ambassador to the court of Holy Roman Emperor **Charles V** in 1531. His charge was to gauge how King Henry's impending rejection of Queen **Katherine of Aragon** might affect Anglo-imperial relations, but because the Spanish queen was also Charles V's aunt, Elyot was understandably shunned while in Germany and returned to England early in 1532 in disgrace. Now hoping to avoid further royal service, Sir Thomas retreated once again to his Carlton estate so he could devote the rest of his life to learned pursuits. He began in 1533 by translating *The Doctrinal of Princes* by the Athenian statesman Isocrates from Greek into English and then published his *Castle of Health*, a discussion of the four bodily humors, in 1536. Based on the linguistic principles of the *studia humanitatis*, Elyot's *Latin-English Dictionary* appeared in 1538 and soon graced library shelves in grammar schools and university colleges all across the realm. In the meantime, Elyot had carefully managed to conceal from Crown authorities his opposition to the English Reformation as well as his fondness for the deceased Katherine of Aragon. Thus his 1540 *Defense of Good Women*, which ostensibly praises all virtuous ladies, is in fact a thinly disguised tribute to King Henry's first wife and queen. Elyot lived quietly enough during the years of conservative religious reaction during the 1540s and died in his bed (unlike other loyal sons of Rome) on 26 March 1546.

EMPSON, SIR RICHARD (c. 1450–1510). The governmental colleague of fellow lawyer **Edmund Dudley**, Sir Richard Empson served King **Henry VII** as a Crown agent and councilor and more famously as a ruthless royal revenue collector. Empson helped amass the enormous fortune that the first Tudor king believed necessary to remain independent of **Parliament** and secure his questionable claim to the English throne. Thoroughly despised by most English **nobles** when the old king died in 1509, young Henry VIII had both Empson and Dudley arrested in order to win the affection of the English people he now ruled. Both men endured many months of confinement in the **Tower of London** before they were convicted of high treason and then executed on the block in August 1510.

Richard Empson (occasionally spelled Emson) was born in Towcester, Northamptonshire, to Peter Empson and his wife, Elizabeth Joseph Empson, around 1450. Richard's father was reportedly a sieve or basket maker, but his apparent ownership of some properties in the vicinity of Towcester suggest he was more probably a member of the lower **gentry** or yeomanry. Nothing is known of Richard Empson's childhood or teen years, but by his early 20s he was studying law at the Middle Temple of the **Inns of Court** in London. From there he established a successful legal practice in the English Midlands, which in turn led to his appointment as justice of the peace in Northamptonshire by the mid-1470s. In 1478, he became the attorney general for the Duchy of Lancaster, a lucrative position he relinquished at the accession of Richard III but then recovered when Henry VII seized the English throne following the battle of Bosworth Field. Clearly a Woodville Yorkist—supporters of the family of Edward IV's queen, Elizabeth Woodville, against the royal ambitions of Richard III—Empson joined the entourage of the new Tudor king, as did many disaffected

Yorkists after 1485. Empson was representing his home county of Northamptonshire in the House of Commons by the late 1480s, and in 1491, Henry VII promoted him to the dignity of speaker of the House.

Four years later, Richard Empson was asked by his sovereign to join the shadowy "council learned in the law," an ad hoc committee charged with ensuring the timely collection of monies owed to the Crown. As a member of this council, Empson met Edmund Dudley, a fellow Inns of Court lawyer and a trusted royal diplomat, and together they formed a team of special revenue agents responsible only to King Henry. As such, Empson and Dudley collected recognizance and benevolence assessments, large sums of money that Henry VII demanded as surety for the good behavior of the many great landowners he still distrusted. Most of the aristocratic targets of this scheme detested Empson for the brutal efficiency he brought to his collection task, but his royal master appreciated his efforts and rewarded him with a knighthood and the office of chancellor of the Duchy of Lancaster in 1504. Still, because many of Empson and Dudley's enemies believed they were skimming large amounts of recognizance and benevolence funds to enrich themselves, resentment toward both men erupted when old Henry VII breathed his last on 21 April 1509.

The young man who acceded to the English throne the following day was an insecure teenager, who, having inherited what should have been his brother's Crown and about to marry his brother's widow, was desperate to earn the popular acclaim and love of his new subjects in the very first days of his reign. Young Henry VIII thus wasted little time having the wildly unpopular Empson and Dudley seized on largely invented conspiracy charges and consigned both men to the Tower of London to await his further pleasure. Empson was subsequently taken to Northampton Castle in early October 1509 to stand trial and, despite his spirited defense, was convicted of treason and then returned to the tower to languish in captivity for another 10 months. In an attempt to save his own life, Sir Richard's old colleague Edmund Dudley composed his obsequious *Tree of Commonwealth* to try to flatter King Henry into a pardon, a gesture that was summarily ignored. On 17 August 1510, both Empson and Dudley were led to Tower Hill, where they died under the headsman's axe before a large crowd of jeering spectators. One of the first casualties of the reign of Henry VIII, Richard Empson may not have enriched himself at Crown expense, for his will left only £300–400 worth of cash and property to his wife and three children. He was laid to rest in the Carmelite monastery of Whitefriars in the district of Farrindon outside London.

ENCLOSURE (c. 1250–1550). The practice of enclosure was principally undertaken in late-medieval and early-modern England to make more cost-effective and profitable use of agricultural land by converting common and/or arable (grain-producing) fields to pasture for grazing sheep. The term *enclosure* referred to the consolidation of multiple smaller land holdings into large single properties and their encirclement by ditches, fences, and especially hedges to exclude trespassers and prevent livestock from wandering off. Such shifts from crop cultivation to pasture were usually driven by the high value of English wool, which was widely regarded in **Flanders**, northern Italy, and other textile-producing regions as the finest in Europe. Although the majority of land enclosures in England had already taken place by the dawn of the Tudor age, Henry VIII and his successors regarded the practice as an evil perversion of the natural order and worked to limit or even outlaw it wherever and whenever they could.

Following the devastation of the medieval Black Death, many estates in England lacked a sufficient number of peasant laborers to cultivate the "corn" (grain) crops that had once dominated the English agrarian economy. Lower demand for foodstuffs after the plague dropped the prices that peasants could get for their harvested grain, which in turn reduced the amount of rental income that members of the landowning classes could collect from the lease-holding tenants who lived on and worked their estates. As a result, some of those landowners replaced labor-intensive arable farming with sheep husbandry, which required far fewer human workers (a shepherd and perhaps a dog) but promised greater financial returns from the sale of high-quality English wool, both domestically and abroad.

Throughout the medieval period, peasant farmers on England's rural manors had traditionally grown wheat, barley, oats, and rye on scattered plots spread unevenly across their lords' open fields. Once landowners discovered how profitable wool could be, however, they began to amalgamate those small plots into expansive single meadows and then surrounded them with hedges to accommodate large herds of sheep or other livestock. This process of consolidation and enclosure naturally prompted **noble** and **gentry** manor lords to push tenant corn farmers off their lands to make room for the more lucrative production of wool. To do this, landowners either refused to renew leases on peasant holdings or they inflated the heriot fines, or renewal fees, on those leases to exorbitant levels the farmers could not pay. The peasants who were thus forced to leave, most of whose ancestors had lived on and farmed the same small plots on the same estates for generations, now found themselves adrift without homes or meaningful work. Mostly reduced to accepting short-term day-labor jobs or even turning to begging or crime to survive, they came to be called "masterless men" or "vagabonds" and were regarded with scorn by their contemporaries.

Although a great deal of land enclosure occurred before **Henry VII** seized the English throne in 1485, his son Henry VIII especially disliked the practice because he believed it depopulated the countryside, increased unemployment, limited rural military recruitment, and reduced food supplies in the name of ready profits. Other Tudor luminaries tended to agree with their king. Sir **Thomas More** warned in book 1 of his *Utopia* that, if left unchecked, enclosure would destroy English agriculture and lead purposeless drifters to take up lives of theft or violent crime. Henry VIII tried to legislate against the perceived evils of enclosure in 1515 and 1536 by confiscating half the profits that enclosing landlords realized from their wool sales. Unfortunately, such

measures often proved ineffective because most offenders were able to distract or bribe the few royal inspectors sent out by the Crown to collect the fines. **Thomas Cardinal Wolsey**, remembering his roots as the son of a common butcher, actually established a commission of inquiry between 1517 and 1519 to investigate allegations of clandestine enclosure and agrarian depopulation. When Henry VIII implemented his **coinage**-debasement program, however, which drove up foreign demand for English wool once again, the corresponding surge in new enclosures only served to nullify the best efforts of king and cardinal to curtail the practice.

Despite the anxiety it may have caused in early-modern England, enclosure was gradually losing its appeal by the beginning of the reign of Henry VIII's successor **Edward VI**. Harvests were by that time somewhat diminished, which inflated grain prices, while English wool had already saturated Flemish markets, thus driving prices down and weakening the incentive to enclose land and raise sheep. **Edward Seymour**, the first Duke of Somerset and lord protector of young King Edward, so feared the ill-effects of enclosure that he established a commission of so-called commonwealth men (including **Hugh Latimer**, among others) that strictly limited new enclosures and imposed heavy taxes on the rearing of sheep. In the end, Tudor hostility to enclosure may have been unwarranted because by the time of the death of Henry VIII's daughter Queen **Elizabeth I** in 1603, only 9 percent of all the productive agricultural land in England had been enclosed.

ERASMUS, DESIDERIUS (1466–1536). This Dutch intellectual was recognized during his own lifetime—and is still regarded today—as the leading scholar of the *studia humanitatis*, or the Renaissance new learning of 16th-century Europe. Although he traveled widely and never claimed any one residence as home, he visited England four times and at one point lived there long enough to cultivate lasting friendships with several of that kingdom's most prominent scholars and churchmen. Erasmus was a prodigious letter writer, author, and translator who penned many influential treatises and who brought forth the revised Greek-to-Latin New Testament that in turn formed the basis of most future vernacular Bibles in German, English, and French. During much of his life, he was a stern and often cynical critic of the Catholic Church and its **clergy**, but he never turned his back on Rome, despite continuous pleas to do so from Martin Luther and other reformers. The spiritual piety and classical learning he blended in his work gave full expression to the idea of Christian humanism, or the application of Renaissance linguistic and analytical methods to the ancient Christian sources of religious truth.

Desiderius Erasmus was born around 1466 in Rotterdam (or possibly nearby in Gouda) and was the second illegitimate son of a priest named Roger Gerhardt and his mistress Margaretha Rutgers, the daughter of a local physician. His parents named him in honor of the early Christian martyr St. Erasmus of Formiae, and later he adopted the name Desiderius as the Latinized form of Erasmus. He attended elementary school in Gouda before enrolling in St. Lebwin's School in Deventer, a place where the Brethren of the Common Life immersed their pupils in the *devotio moderna* of classical learning, ascetic piety and selfless charity. After both his parents died, Erasmus entered an Augustinian friary in Steyn in 1487, and although he intensely disliked the regimentation of monastic life, he remained there for several years and took holy orders as a priest in 1492.

The next year, he solicited and received a papal dispensation to leave the friary (never to return) and accepted a secretarial post with Henry of Bergen, the bishop of Cambrai. Bishop Henry soon recognized his secretary's genius and sent him off in 1495 to begin an undergraduate program in the liberal arts at the University of Paris. Having been introduced to humanistic "new learning" at Deventer, Erasmus found himself stifled by the cumbersome medieval curriculum he encountered at the Sorbonne. Before long, he was skipping university lectures to conduct his own classical studies, draft his own original tracts, and tutor his fellow students in the finer points of Latin prose. After earning his baccalaureate degree from Paris, Erasmus began tutoring William

Blount, Lord Mountjoy, an English **noble** who then became the Dutch scholar's patron and invited him to his native England in 1499.

Erasmus went with his aristocratic pupil to **Oxford University**, where he made the acquaintance of such leading academics as **Thomas More**, Dr. **Thomas Linacre**, and **John Colet**. The latter convinced him to devote his life to the study of theology and urged him to learn the Greek language in preparation for such work. By 1500, he was back in Paris, where he published *Adagia* (*The Adages*), a collection of 800 ancient aphorisms, and *Enchiridion militis Christiani* (*Handbook of a Christian Soldier*), a treatise that urged believers to live piously and avoid sin. Erasmus returned briefly to England in 1505, renewed his friendships with Colet and More, and met influential bishops like **John Fisher** of Rochester, **Richard Fox** of Winchester, and **William Warham** of Canterbury. He was soon on the move again, and after touring Italy and earning his doctorate in theology at Turin University, he returned for a third time to England in 1509.

Staying on this occasion with the More family at their Chelsea estate near London, Erasmus authored his masterpiece *Moriae encomium* (*In Praise of Folly*) and dedicated it to his English host and close friend Sir Thomas More. This little work of satire featured Lady Folly, a clever solicitor who urged the Court of Humanity to condemn the pride and greed of the pope, the clergy, and the nobility of Christian Europe. In 1511, Bishop Fisher persuaded Erasmus to relocate to **Cambridge University**, where the Dutch scholar began offering informal instruction in Greek to small groups of interested students. He finally left England in 1514 for Basel and the print shop of Johann Froben, who two years later published Erasmus's *Novum instrumentum*, a sweeping revision of the New Testament with facing pages in Greek and Latin. That same year, Froben also printed an early edition of Erasmus's *Colloquia* (*The Discourses*), a series of dialogues that critically examine (and often poke fun at) many of the more absurd and even superstitious practices of his European contemporaries. After a final visit to England in 1517, Erasmus moved to Louvain University in

Flanders, where he kept busy translating the writings of such early church fathers such as Irenaeus, Cyprian, Origen, Ambrose, Augustine, and Chrysostom.

Although he often criticized the Catholic Church as passionately as had Martin Luther, Desiderius Erasmus always stopped short (as did Sir Thomas More) of rejecting Rome and its doctrines entirely out of hand. When the Dutch theologian published his defense of good-works salvation in *De libero arbitrio diatribe sive collatio* (*Sermon on Free Will*) in 1524, the German reformer replied with his *De servo arbitrio* (*On the Bondage of the Will*) the following year. Erasmus offered a lengthy and ponderous rebuttal to Luther in 1526, but largely ignored by most European readers, it brought the great debate between Catholic apologist and Protestant champion to an anticlimactic standstill. Pope **Clement VII**, Emperor **Charles V**, and even King Henry VIII of England—himself the Defender of the Faith for his own attack on Luther's teachings—all offered Erasmus their congratulations, but none offered to reward him with any patronage or financial support.

Thus often destitute in his last years, Erasmus resided in Basel and then Freiburg in southern Germany while he continued his theological and translation work and fired off letters in search of more permanent sources of income. He was understandably appalled when he learned of the execution of his friend Sir Thomas More in 1535, and with his own health steadily failing, he finally succumbed to dysentery and died during a visit to Basel on 12 July 1536. He was interred with much fanfare in the Basel Minster (cathedral), while a stone (later bronze) statue was erected to his memory and still stands in his native Rotterdam.

"EVIL" MAY DAY RIOTS (28 April–22 May 1517).

This uprising of mostly artisans, apprentices, and day laborers was aimed against the business activities—and even the very presence—of foreign merchants in the city of London. Believing that alien traders engaged in profitable commerce at the expense of their English counterparts, the May Day rioters pillaged large swaths of the capital before troops finally arrived to help restore order. Although several ringleaders were executed as traitors, hundreds more received pardons in a contrived display of royal mercy and goodwill. In the aftermath of this May Day violence, the Crown found itself uncomfortably aware that "evil" London mobs could threaten royal authority at any time and with very little provocation.

From the time of the Norman conquest in the 11th century and through the High Middle Ages, when Continental traders first came to England, Londoners had always been suspicious of foreigners, whom they saw as parasites come to snatch honest livings from hard-working English families. This xenophobia continued into the Tudor period, when repeated English insults and even attacks prompted Italian, Flemish, Baltic, Spanish, and Portuguese visitors to arm themselves and travel about the capital in large groups for safety. Spring 1517 saw Londoners in a particularly restive mood as rumors spread (falsely, it turned out) that King Henry himself was financing Florentine trade initiatives against those of their English competitors. Then during Easter week following, one Dr. Beale preached a sermon that blamed the city's resident alien population for all of London's recent economic woes. When several continental merchants were shoved into a sewage ditch on 28 April 1517, a resentful English trader named John Lincoln began planning a massive uprising on the forthcoming May Day holiday to loot the possessions and take the lives of every foreigner in town.

Thomas Cardinal Wolsey got wind of this plan, and after convincing the city's mayor to impose an overnight curfew on 30 April, he hastily fortified his residence of York Place in the Strand against the rampaging mob he expected early the next day. Sure enough, Lincoln aroused groups of apprentices and journeymen in Cheapside on May Day morning; led them to Newgate and other London prisons to free the inmates; and then swept on with his followers to plunder the foreign districts of St. Martin's-le-Grand, Cornhill, and Whitechapel. Isolated from this violence at his suburban palace in Richmond, King Henry threatened the rioters with dire punishment, and when this had little effect, he called on **Thomas Howard**, the second Duke of Norfolk, to muster his armed retainers for a march on the capital. Norfolk soon came with his son the Earl of Surrey and some 1,300 soldiers, who quickly overran the city's key strategic points and scuffled with insurgents in the streets until by nightfall all was quiet once more. Though much damage had been done to property and especially to commercial warehouses, none of the targeted foreign residents, the unruly London agitators, or Norfolk's troops had lost their lives in the rioting.

Understandably disturbed by these events, the king ordered John Lincoln and a dozen of his chief lieutenants rounded up and hanged, drawn, and quartered as traitors, while another 400 of Lincoln's followers were apprehended and imprisoned to await a similar fate. Cardinal Wolsey, however, sensing an opportunity to send a different message, convinced King Henry to stage an elaborate display of clemency instead in an effort to win back the loyalty of his subjects. Accordingly, **Westminster Palace** was draped in cloth of gold on 22 May 1517, and as King Henry, Queen **Katherine of Aragon**, and Wolsey looked on, more than 340 captive May Day rioters paraded in chains past the royal dais calling on their sovereign to show them mercy. After their initial plea was denied, Wolsey and Queen Katherine tearfully knelt before Henry and begged him to reconsider, which he finally did with an appropriately regal flourish. The pardoned prisoners immediately removed their restraints, danced and sang, and then rushed out of the palace to join other jubilant Londoners in the streets. Although royal clemency had thus been extravagantly and very publicly demonstrated, the grisly heads and quarters of the uprising's ringleaders remained on display at the city's principal gates to remind Londoners and alien residents alike of the true mature of the king's justice. *See also* THE STEELYARD (c. 1280–1598).

F

FERDINAND II OF ARAGON (1452–1516) AND ISABEL I OF CASTILE (1451–1504), KING AND QUEEN OF SPAIN (r. 1474–1516). King Ferdinand II of Aragon and Queen Isabel I of Castile, known together as "Their Most Catholic Majesties," began the process of uniting their respective realms into the single kingdom of Spain by marrying one another in 1469. Their union produced six living children; one of these was the mother of **Charles V**, the future king of Spain and Holy Roman Emperor, while another, **Katherine of Aragon**, married first Prince **Arthur** Tudor of England and then (after Arthur's death) his younger brother King Henry VIII. Although Queen Isabel died five years before Henry inherited the English Crown, her husband lived long enough to become a great rival to the second Tudor king through the early stages of his reign.

Ferdinand of Aragon was born to King Juan II of Aragon and his consort, Queen Juana Enríquez, at the Sada Palace in Sos, Aragon, on 10 March 1452. Educated to become a Renaissance prince and entrusted with military command at an early age, Ferdinand became King Juan's heir apparent when his older brother, Alfonso, died in 1461 and was then installed as the titular king of Sicily—a territory controlled by Aragon—seven years later. Meanwhile Infanta Isabel of Castile (Isabella, the diminutive form of Isabel, was never used by the future queen) was born to King Juan II of Castile and his queen, Isabel of Portugal, in the castle of Madrigal de las Altas Torres on 22 April 1451. Within three years of her birth, Isabel's father died, and her half-brother

seized the Castilian throne as Enríque IV. The new king at first recognized his half-sister as his heir and had her brought to court in 1464 so he could better control her movements and manage her marriage prospects. Brushing off proposals from the royal houses of Portugal and France, however, Isabel married Ferdinand of Aragon (one year her junior) at Valladolid in 1469 without the approval of her half-brother. Enríque was furious and disinherited Isabel in favor of his teenaged daughter Juana, dubbed "Beltraneja" because she was thought to be the true daughter of Beltrán, duque de Albuquerque. When the Castilian king died in 1474, Isabel and Ferdinand fought a succession war against the Infanta Juana and her Portuguese allies that ended victoriously for the married royal couple in 1479.

Ferdinand and Isabel formed a successful governing team and did much to assert greater central control over the institutions and magnates of their two independent but jointly ruled kingdoms. In 1478, the Catholic Majesties received authority from Pope Sixtus IV to establish their own "Holy Office of the Inquisition" in Aragon and Castile, an institution that targeted as heretics those conversos and Moriscos (nominally Christian Jews and Moors) suspected of practicing their old beliefs and rituals in secret. King Ferdinand also worked to break the autonomy of the Iberian nobility by stripping away their privileges and dismantling their castles, and he created the *santa hermandad*, or holy brotherhood, police force to ensure obedience to Crown edicts. Between 1481 and 1492, Ferdinand and Isabel completed the *reconquista* of Spain by capturing the stronghold of Granada from the last of Castile's Moorish rulers, and finally freed from the expenses of continuous warfare, they funded the voyage of Cristoforo Colombo to find a westward route to Asia across the Atlantic Ocean. In 1492, the Catholic Majesties also ordered all remaining Jews to convert to Christianity or else leave their kingdoms, a policy they imposed 10 years later on the Muslim population of Spain as well.

Niccolò Machiavelli describes King Ferdinand in *The Prince* as a consummate international puppet master who possessed the ability to bend foreign rulers to his will. Realizing that King **Henry VII** of England coveted European recognition for his shaky Tudor throne, Ferdinand and Isabel proposed a marriage alliance between their respective kingdoms in 1496. Arthur Tudor, Prince of **Wales**, was thus betrothed to Infanta Katherine of Aragon, and the two teenagers were wed by proxy at Bewdley Manor in the diocese of Hereford in May 1499. Two years later, the Spanish princess sailed to England, where she formally married the Tudor heir in London in November 1501. Within six months of their wedding, however, the Prince of Wales was dead, leaving the 17-year-old Katherine widowed and living in political limbo in an alien and foreign land. Queen Isabel herself died two years later, and because she was the hereditary ruler of Castile (Ferdinand only reigned there as her husband), their son-in-law Philip the Fair succeeded Isabel as King Felipe I of Castile in 1504. When he, too, died in 1506, Ferdinand was forced to take over as Castilian regent for his six-year-old grandson Carlos, who in 10 years would accede to the Spanish throne and then would be elected Holy Roman Emperor as Charles V in 1519.

In the meantime, the widowed Katherine of Aragon begged Henry VII to send her back to her native Spain, but the wily English king was loath to return her dowry to King Ferdinand and so betrothed her to his second son, Prince Henry, instead. When the first Tudor king died in 1509, the handsome and athletic Henry VIII used a dispensation from Pope Julius II to wed his brother's widow so he could keep possession of her dowry and maintain England's alliance with Ferdinand in Spain. In 1513, Henry VIII committed his kingdom to the Holy League, an association that joined England, Spain, the empire, and the papacy in a military pact against France. Eager to recapture the martial glory of his royal forebears and expecting assistance from his ally King Ferdinand to the south, the English king launched a massive **French invasion in 1513–14** that ultimately achieved very little and nearly bankrupted the English war chest. Part of this disappointing outcome was caused by the inertia of King Ferdinand, who delayed his own advance into France and then simply abandoned Henry VIII to fight the French on his own. King Ferdinand II of Aragon, Castile, Sicily, and New Spain in the Americas died on 23 January 1516 in the town of Madrigalejo in Extremadura, having done a great deal (with Queen Isabel) to unite the Iberian Peninsula, establish a global empire, and avoid costly and destructive wars on the European continent.

THE FIELD OF CLOTH OF GOLD (7–24 JUNE 1520).

This was a summit meeting that took place near the English-held town of **Calais** in northern France between King Henry VIII of England and King **François I** of France. The summit was the brainchild of **Thomas Cardinal Wolsey**, King Henry's chief minister at the time, who believed that a face-to-face meeting of the rival rulers could lead to a lasting friendship between them and might even result in a treaty of "universal peace" to end the seemingly perpetual warfare between their two kingdoms. The event is best remembered today for its ostentatious displays of grandeur and wealth, all carefully choreographed to demonstrate the power and majesty of both monarchs. The summit was named for the extravagant "cloth of gold" that was everywhere in evidence, from the costumes of thousands of **nobles** and courtiers who made up the English and French delegations to the textile structures of the prefabricated palaces, banquet halls, and tent quarters that made up the sprawling meeting complex. Though impressive for its glittering splendor, the Field of

Cloth of Gold failed to produce any significant diplomatic results for either side. Within a year of its conclusion, King Henry and Cardinal Wolsey had engineered a new treaty with Emperor **Charles V** that allied England with the Holy Roman Empire and left France as the odd man out.

In 1518, most of the major European powers had agreed to abide by the Treaty of London, which pledged its signatories to maintain peace among themselves in the face of a growing threat from the Ottoman Turks. By the following year, however, this pact was already disintegrating amid the age-old suspicions and renewed military maneuverings of traditional European enemies. Cardinal Wolsey, longing to avoid another costly war on the Continent, sought to shore up the crumbling alliance by arranging face-to-face meetings between his sovereign lord Henry VIII and the monarchs of England's principal European rivals Spain, France, and the Holy Roman Empire. Between 26 and 31 May 1520, the Emperor Charles V, ruler of both Spain and the empire, visited England, where he won King Henry's affections and agreed to a second meeting in six weeks' time in **Flanders**. With this imperial accord still fresh in mind, the Tudor king and his chief minister now turned their attentions to France.

With all the detailed preparations necessary to stage such a grand royal summit, Cardinal Wolsey had clearly been busy arranging this event well before King Henry's meeting with the emperor in England. The site chosen for Henry to meet with King François was an open field just inside the pale (or territory) of Calais, the French town that had been in English hands since the start of the Hundred Years' War. It was located in a narrow valley (known to the French as Val Dore) that lay halfway between the castles of Guisnes and Ardres, where each king was hoping to stay and use as his headquarters. Before the two royal principals arrived, however, thousands of workmen swarmed over the field to make ready for all the **pageants** and opulent displays to come. On the English side, a prefabricated village soon arose, whose centerpiece was a 110,000-square-foot palace constructed of brick, timber, and canvas. The English village was fully equipped with **jousting** lists, stables, kitchens, sporting fields, viewing stands, and more than 2,300 tents to accommodate the nearly 5,000 government ministers, nobles, courtiers, and servants expected to attend.

Provisioning and clothing this vast English contingent was a task that for Wolsey was even more challenging than preparing for the **French invasion of 1513–14**. King Henry's chief minister had to procure enormous quantities of livestock, fish, poultry, flour, wine, and beer to satisfy the ravening hunger and thirst of this great horde. In order to show off the English sense of fashion, Wolsey was also obliged to purchase thousands of yards of expensive fabrics, including a great many bolts of cloth of gold, a specialized textile made from silk, linen, or wool threads wrapped with thin gold strips. The French for their part were similarly supplied and caparisoned, so the overall effect of this flamboyant assembly must have been dazzling indeed to peasant onlookers and visiting ambassadors alike.

The actual meetings between Henry and François were so carefully orchestrated that neither king was seen—or could claim—to possess an advantage in splendor, majesty, or grace over the other. Amid much feasting, jousting, gift exchanges, and protestations of friendship, very little of real substance was ever discussed, and no lasting diplomatic agreements were hammered out. An unscripted wrestling match that broke out suddenly between the two athletic rulers ended when François threw Henry to the earth and left his pride (if not his body) deeply wounded. After 16 days of showy (and very expensive) public spectacle, Cardinal Wolsey officiated at a closing mass, and the two young monarchs withdrew to their respective kingdoms to eye one other suspiciously once more. Within two weeks of the summit's conclusion, King Henry met again as previously planned with the Emperor Charles at Gravelines in Flanders. There they began preparations for a joint attack on France, a campaign that the English eventually conducted mostly on their own without much imperial support in the **French invasion of 1523–24**.

FISH, SIMON (c. 1500–1531). This theological rebel lived a brief but very engaged life, crossing paths along the way with some of the great religious figures of the early Henrician age. Born and raised in obscurity, Fish rose above his humble origins to incur the wrath of **Thomas Cardinal Wolsey**, support the scriptural translation work of **William Tyndale**, and conduct a vitriolic pamphlet exchange with Sir **Thomas More**. His radically evangelical beliefs offended Henry VIII, but his criticism of the Roman regular **clergy** (monks) appealed to the Tudor king and may have provided inspiration for the **monastic** dissolution of the late 1530s. Having twice lived in exile on the Continent, Fish returned to England and was there charged with heresy by church officials in 1530. He passed away while awaiting trial and so was probably spared the horrific death of a condemned heretic at the stake.

The date and place of Simon Fish's birth, along with the names and background of his parents, are all unknown. Many scholars of the Tudor period believe he attended **Oxford University** for a time before entering Gray's Inn (at the London **Inns of Court**) to study law in 1525. Fish made the acquaintance of several reform-minded young men while in the capital, and in 1526, he took part with them in a short Christmas skit that criticized the venality of the English clergy and lambasted Cardinal Wolsey for his pride and great personal wealth. Fearing retaliation from the cardinal, Fish fled in 1527 to **Flanders**, where he joined a group of evangelical Lutherans led by William Tyndale, the scholar who by that time was busy translating the New Testament into English. The passionate young exile soaked up the reformist ideas of Tyndale and his friends and then volunteered to help smuggle copies of the translated Scriptures into England. Fish returned to London in 1528 with Tyndale's Bibles hidden in bales of wool and quickly set about distributing the books to an underground network of renegade English believers. He wisely fled to the Continent again, however, when his illegal smuggling activities aroused the suspicions of England's ecclesiastical authorities.

Eager to contribute to the cause of religious reform himself, Simon Fish composed and then published his *Supplication for the Beggars* in Antwerp in 1528. This little tract contains just 5,000 words, covers a scant 15 pages, and was priced so inexpensively it soon reached a wide reading public. Fish's *Supplication* is a scathing indictment of corrupted English priests and (especially) monks who amassed fortunes and sinned with women instead of working to alleviate the suffering of poor beggars. Recalling the 1514 **Richard Hunne** affair in London, when an unpaid burial charge had led to Hunne's mysterious prison death, Fish heaped abuse on such "invented" religious institutions as purgatory, indulgences, tithes, sacramental fees, and masses for the dead. Legend holds that reform-minded **Anne Boleyn** gave a copy of the *Supplication* to Henry VIII during their courtship in the late 1520s. Although the king would not have appreciated Fish's criticism of church doctrines and practices, he may well have embraced the *Supplication*'s claims of monastic vice and possibly used them to help justify the closure of England's monasteries in the later 1530s.

With Tyndale's New Testament and Fish's *Supplication* freely circulating in southeastern England, Bishop **Cuthbert Tunstall** of London licensed the eminent scholar Sir Thomas More to review and respond to these heretical works. Accordingly, More's reply to Fish's scurrilous little booklet, entitled the *Supplication of Souls*, appeared in print in two volumes during autumn 1529. A much longer and more complex work than Fish's brief offering, More's *Supplication of Souls* first refutes the reformer's allegations of clerical corruption and then presents a defense of purgatory and prayers for the dead. Despite his best intentions, Sir Thomas's *Supplication of Souls* was too ponderously dense and costly to attract many readers and so failed in the end to suppress Tyndale's and Fish's radical calls for reform. More's lengthy treatise did attract the attention of Archbishop **William Warham** of Canterbury, however, who had Simon Fish apprehended and charged with heresy when he returned to England again early in 1530. Languishing in prison awaiting his heresy trial in the archepiscopal court of Lambeth, Fish contracted some sort of plague and perished early in 1531.

Fish's widow went on to wed James Bainham, another zealous religious reformer, who was himself convicted of heresy and burned at the stake in Smithfield in late April 1532.

FISHER, JOHN, BISHOP OF ROCHESTER
(1469–1535). An eminent theologian, humanist, royal confessor, Catholic cardinal, and bishop of England's smallest diocese for more than 30 years, John Fisher was a devoted son of the Roman Church and a loyal supporter of Queen **Katherine of Aragon** during the political and religious upheaval of King Henry VIII's "**Great Matter.**" Fisher's steadfast refusal to countenance either the king's second marriage to **Anne Boleyn** or his break with the pope in Rome led to the bishop's arrest, trial, conviction, and execution as a traitor in June 1535. Due to his widely known reputation for piety and integrity, Fisher's death shocked many of his European contemporaries and four centuries later saw him canonized a saint by Pope Pius XI in 1935.

John Fisher was born into the family of a well-to-do mercer in the Yorkshire town of Beverley and began his formal education at the cathedral school attached to the York Minster in the 1470s. Around the age of 14, he enrolled in the Michaelhouse at **Cambridge University**, where he earned his baccalaureate degree in 1488 and his master's degree in 1491. The latter year also saw him take holy orders as a priest, and he accepted a teaching fellowship at Michaelhouse soon thereafter. With his doctorate of divinity in hand by the start of the 16th century, Lady **Margaret Beaufort**, the mother of King **Henry VII**, took Fisher on as her personal confessor and spiritual advisor. His association with her acquainted him in turn with Bishop **Richard Fox** of Winchester, King Henry's lord privy seal, who nominated Dr. Fisher in 1504 to serve as the chancellor of Cambridge University. That same year, he took his place on England's episcopal bench when an admiring and grateful Tudor king named him bishop of the tiny see of Rochester in Kent.

Already involved in academic governance as a university chancellor, Fisher now embraced the role of an active educationalist as well. His patron Lady Margaret Beaufort, intent on training the next generation of young men for the priesthood, was persuaded by Fisher to provide endowment funds to establish Christ's (1505) and then St. John's (posthumously in 1511) Colleges at Cambridge. The bishop of Rochester followed his patron's example by granting money and income-generating lands to the latter school and then bequeathed his extensive collection of books to the college in his will to form the nucleus of its library. Also eager to bring the *studia humanitatis*, or new learning of humanism, to England, Fisher invited noted humanist scholar **Desiderius Erasmus** to Cambridge in 1511 to offer informal lessons in Greek and classical texts to interested students. When the first Tudor king died in April 1509 and his mother followed him to the grave just 10 weeks later, Bishop Fisher was called on to deliver both funeral sermons.

The Lutheran Reformation opened the door for John Fisher to earn a European-wide reputation as a distinguished theologian. It has long been supposed that the bishop of Rochester, along with other scholars, such as **Thomas Cardinal Wolsey** and Sir **Thomas More**, were the principal authors behind the anti-Lutheran *Assertio septem sacramentorum*, or *Defense of the Seven Sacraments*, that won Henry VIII's title of Defender of the Faith from the pope in 1521, but such suppositions have never been proved. Fisher did, however, preach his own refutation of Lutheran teachings in the same year with his "Sermon against the Pernicious Doctrine of Martin Luther," which he delivered prior to Cardinal Wolsey's book-burning rally at Paul's Cross in London. Two years later, he renewed his assault on the German reformer with the publication of his ponderous *Assertionis Lutheranae confutatio*, or *A Refutation of Luther's Assertions*. Most famously, the bishop-turned-theologian published in 1527 his *De veritate corporis et sanguinis Christi in eucharistia*, or *On the True Body and Blood of Christ in the Eucharist*, against the sacramental doctrines of Swiss reformer Johann Oecolampadius. Clearly a zealous defender of Roman teachings, Fisher was at the same time deeply aggrieved by the corruption and worldliness he observed among the Roman clergy and especially among the prelates and officials at the papal court in Rome itself.

In 1528, Katherine of Aragon asked the bishop of Rochester to attend her as confessor and counselor, a role he took to heart the following year when he defended the Spanish queen as King Henry's "true wife" at Wolsey's and **Lorenzo Cardinal Campeggio**'s legatine court. The king was furious and briefly imprisoned Fisher and two other prelates in 1530 for encouraging the appeal of Queen Katherine's case to Rome. Soon released, however, Fisher was present in **Convocation of the Bishops** in 1531–32, when Henry VIII threatened to prosecute all of the assembled bishops for their violations of the praemunire law against appeals to Rome. Convocation submitted to this royal bullying by paying an enormous fine, surrendering its control of ecclesiastical affairs to the Crown, and acknowledging the king's supreme lordship over the English Church. Bishop Fisher could not bring himself to approve this last measure until the phrase "as far as the law of Christ allows" was added, a concession that Convocation then passed and King Henry grudgingly accepted.

The bishop of Rochester started down the path toward his own execution when he interviewed and then became an adherent of **Elizabeth Barton**, the so-called Holy Maid of Kent, who, having denounced the king's second marriage and prophesied his death, was arrested, convicted of treason, and hanged in April 1534. In addition, when **Parliament** passed the **Act of Succession** early that same spring, Fisher (along with Sir Thomas More) refused to swear the required oath to support its provisions and was duly sent to the **Tower of London**. When the new **Act of Treasons** with its "spoken words" provision became law in November 1534, Bishop Fisher's earlier offenses of association with the Holy Maid and refusal of the succession oath now turned into full charges of high treason. While still incarcerated in the tower, ongoing efforts were made to secure Fisher's oath, but when Pope **Paul III** made him a cardinal of the Roman Church in spring 1535, King Henry flew into a rage. The fate of the aging, frail bishop was now sealed; on 17 June, he was condemned

to death and went to the block within six days of his trial, while More was executed just a few weeks later. Nearly 400 years passed before another pope canonized both John Fisher and Thomas More as Catholic martyrs and saints.

FITZROY, HENRY, DUKE OF RICHMOND (1519–36).

This bastard son of King Henry VIII and his mistress **Elizabeth Blount** was groomed to succeed his father as king in the event that Henry did not sire a legitimate male heir with one of his queens. Showered with titles and estates and dangled before other European royal families as a potential marriage and alliance prospect, Fitzroy (meaning "son of the king" in Norman French) was the only acknowledged illegitimate child of Henry VIII. Fairly robust physically, he succumbed to what was probably some sort of respiratory illness at age 17, although rumors that he was poisoned by members of the **Boleyn** family still persist to this day. King Henry was deeply aggrieved by his son's death but recovered quickly once Queen **Jane Seymour** gave birth to Prince **Edward** Tudor, the future King Edward VI, in October 1537.

Henry Fitzroy was born on 15 June 1519 in the Augustinian priory of St. Lawrence at Blackmore in Essex to Elizabeth "Bessie" Blount, who had been Henry VIII's mistress since 1514. **Thomas Cardinal Wolsey** served as godfather when the child was christened some days later, and the king soon named the infant Fitzroy to eliminate any doubt about the boy's royal parentage. Soon after her son's birth, Wolsey arranged Bessie Blount's marriage to Gilbert Tailboys, a gentleman in the cardinal's household, with whom she then had a happy union and three more children during their years together. Meanwhile, young Fitzroy was cared for by his nurse, Agnes Partridge, and by his governess, Lady Margaret Bryan, and was educated by Richard Croke, an eminent classical scholar, and by John Palsgrave, who tutored the boy in music and modern languages.

In 1525, King Henry asked Wolsey to establish a more formal household for his six-year-old son, so the cardinal offered his own episcopal residence of Durham House in the

Strand in London for this purpose. Furnished with a miniature throne and a cloth-of-gold canopy of state, Fitzroy now enjoyed the trappings of a royal prince and was treated at court as if he were a legitimate heir to the English throne. The king also granted various honors to his son in 1525, naming him Earl of Nottingham, Duke of Somerset, and Duke of Richmond, the same title his grandfather **Henry VII** had borne before seizing the throne himself 40 years before. In addition, the little boy became Lord Lieutenant of Ireland, Warden of the Cinque Ports, and Lord Admiral of England, and he was knighted into the Order of the **Garter** for good measure. Favoring his bastard son over **Mary** Tudor, his legitimate daughter by Queen **Katherine of Aragon**, King Henry sent the young Duke of Richmond off to his new establishment at Pontefract Castle in Yorkshire in autumn 1525, while he "banished" Princess Mary to virtual exile on the Welsh marches at Ludlow Castle.

Meanwhile, negotiations for Richmond's hand in marriage commenced at around this time as well. During the next few years, it was proposed that he wed various French, Italian, Danish, and Portuguese princesses, but his illegitimate status was a difficult sell, and eventually none of these potential matches came to fruition. In 1528, the **sweating sickness** arrived at Pontefract, causing Richmond's household to flee for safety to several other royal estates and then to settle at Richmond Palace outside London in 1530. In 1532, the young duke accompanied his father and **Anne Boleyn**, soon to become queen of England, to **Calais**, where he was introduced to the king of France, **François I**.

By 1533, an athletic adolescent who rode, hunted, and danced energetically, Richmond married Mary Howard, the daughter of the Duke of Norfolk and the sister of his friend Henry Howard, the Earl of Surrey. The next few years saw Richmond attend sessions of **Parliament** and attempt an aborted invasion of Ireland, but by summer 1535, he was struggling with occasional bouts of illness and had developed a noticeable cough. After attending the execution of Queen Anne Boleyn in May 1536, King Henry's only living son began to experience chest pains, and combined with raging fevers and a worsening cough, he died on 22 July 1536. Given Richmond's symptoms, modern medical historians have speculated that either consumption (tuberculosis) or pneumonic plague may have carried him off. At the time of Anne Boleyn's downfall, however, the queen's enemies accused her of having bewitched the king and accused her brother **George Boleyn**, Lord Rochford, of having served both Richmond and his friend Surrey poisoned wine. Once his father's great hope for survival of the House of Tudor, the 17-year-old Duke of Richmond was initially buried in Thetford Priory and was then permanently laid to rest two years later in St. Michael's Church in Framlingham, Suffolk, among his Howard kinsmen.

FITZWILLIAM, WILLIAM, FIRST EARL OF SOUTHAMPTON, LORD PRIVY SEAL

(1490–1542). A courtier, diplomat, soldier, admiral, and Crown minister, Sir William Fitzwilliam spent most of his professional life in the service of King Henry VIII. Fitzwilliam grew up in the same household as Henry and so became one of the Tudor king's few real friends and a trusted advisor when both men reached adulthood. He took part in King Henry's **French invasions of 1513–14 and 1523–24** and participated in the downfall of three of Henry's queens. Created Earl of Southampton late in life, Fitzwilliam also briefly held other important administrative and military offices before his premature death at the age of just 52 years.

William Fitzwilliam was born in the village of Aldwark in northern Yorkshire to Thomas Fitzwilliam and Lucy Neville Fitzwilliam, the niece of Richard Neville, the "kingmaker" Earl of Warwick. Young William's father died soon after his birth, so his mother married Sir Anthony Browne, King **Henry VII**'s standard-bearer and constable of **Calais**. Because of his stepfather's royal connections, the Fitzwilliam lad was invited to live at the Tudor court and there provided companionship for Henry Tudor, the Prince of **Wales** and the future Henry VIII. The two boys became fast friends, hunted and **jousted** together, and received a princely Renaissance education. After Henry VIII became king, Fitzwilliam took part in an unsuccessful attack on Gascony in 1512 and was wounded by a crossbow bolt in an abortive naval operation the next year. Soon recovered, however, he accompanied King Henry on his first invasion of France, where he participated in the siege of Tournai, and then was knighted by the Tudor king in September 1513. Two months later and with Henry VIII in attendance, Sir William married Mabel Clifford, a lady-in-waiting to Queen **Katherine of Aragon**. Their union was to prove childless, even though Fitzwilliam for his part probably fathered at least one child out of wedlock.

In 1517, he joined Henry VIII's royal council and traveled on his first diplomatic mission to France the following year. Sir William helped prepare the flotilla under **Thomas Howard**, the Earl of Surrey (and later the third Duke of Norfolk), that ferried most of the Tudor court to Calais for the **Field of Cloth of Gold** summit in 1520. In 1521, he was appointed resident ambassador to France and, praised by **Thomas Cardinal Wolsey** for his negotiating skill, remained in Paris until illness forced his return to England. Fitzwilliam again recovered quickly to outfit and command a fleet of warships that drove off a Franco-Scottish naval force, then ravaged the northwestern coast of France during King Henry's second French invasion of 1523–24. Two years later, he accompanied an embassy to **Flanders** to negotiate an important commercial treaty with **Margaret of Austria**, the imperial regent of the Netherlands. Well pleased, Henry VIII initiated Fitzwilliam into the Order of the **Garter** and elevated him to the powerful (and lucrative) office of treasurer of the royal household in 1526.

The next few years saw Sir William appointed castellan of Calais and elected to **Parliament** as a representative knight from the county of Surrey. He came to know Wolsey well at this time and remained friendly with the cardinal, even when his influence at court began to wane in 1529. That year, Fitzwilliam accepted the chancellorship of the Duchy of Lancaster, along with the rich income it generated. Despite his wife's long service to Katherine of Aragon, he signed a petition urging

Pope **Clement VII** to annul Henry VIII's marriage to his Spanish queen in 1530. When the pontiff refused, the English king led his church away from Roman obedience, an action warmly embraced by Sir William as one of Henry's closest advisors and allies. In spring 1536, he interrogated several of the men accused of adultery with Queen **Anne Boleyn** and further supported the Crown five months later by marching with **Charles Brandon**, the Duke of Suffolk, to suppress the **Pilgrimage of Grace**. In 1537, the king rewarded his boyhood friend by elevating him to the Earldom of Southampton and promoting him to the office of lord high admiral of the royal fleet. Now ennobled, Fitzwilliam took advantage of his new social position and wealth to buy up several religious houses during the **monastic** dissolution of the later 1530s.

The Earl of Southampton's last few years proved to be among his most active. At the end of December 1539, he captained the vessel that brought **Anne of Cleves** from Calais to England to marry Henry VIII. Although Fitzwilliam praised the beauty of the German princess on this occasion, the king vigorously disagreed with him and later sent his friend to inform her of the imminent annulment of their marriage. The Cleves fiasco ultimately precipitated the fall of the king's chief minister, **Thomas Cromwell**, whom Southampton helped interrogate as an alleged traitor and heretic in summer 1540. Cromwell soon died on the block, as did Henry VIII's fifth queen, **Katherine Howard**, whose accused lovers also endured interrogation by Fitzwilliam and Crown prosecutor **Thomas Wriothesley** before their own grisly deaths in late 1541. The Earl of Southampton became lord privy seal in 1540 and then was appointed lord lieutenant of the Scottish marches, even though his health was rapidly deteriorating at the time. He was borne in a litter to Newcastle to take up his marcher lord duties but died there just three days after his arrival, on 15 October 1542. He was buried in the local church of St. Nicholas, now Newcastle's Cathedral. He left no legitimate heirs, so his Earldom of Southampton became extinct, only to be acquired a few years later by his former colleague Thomas Wriothesley.

FLANDERS (c. 1384–1547). Roughly corresponding to the modern nation of Belgium, the province of Flanders was an important trading partner with Lancastrian, Yorkist, and especially Tudor England in the 15th and 16th centuries. The foundation of cordial Anglo-Flemish relations rested in the lucrative wool trade that undergirded the commercial and manufacturing economies of both realms. Raw woolen cloth was exported from England in great quantities to the dyeing and finishing houses of Flanders, where the rough fabric was then transformed into high-quality, fashionable apparel and reexported to markets all over Europe. During much of the 15th century, the Dukes of Burgundy ruled Flanders and were often allied with the kings of England for the purposes of trade and common defense. Urbanized and prosperous Flanders eventually became an object of contention between all her powerful neighbors, prompting much diplomatic intercourse and occasional military clashes between England, France, and the Holy Roman Empire during the 16th century.

Known to the ancient world as the home of the Belgae, Flanders was originally incorporated into the Roman Empire as part of northern Gaul by Gaius Julius Caesar in the first century BC. As the Roman legions withdrew from the region in the fifth century AD, Saxon and Frisian raiders sailed into the North Sea and settled not only in southern Britain but along the Flemish coast as well. The Salic Franks, hailing from the Sala area around the mouth of the Rhine River, also occupied much of Flanders in the early-medieval period. The province remained part of the Frankish Empire through the reign of Charles the Bald, Charlemagne's grandson, who established the embryonic kingdom of France in the ninth century.

Local Flemish counts managed to win a certain measure of independence from the French during the following centuries and then acquired the districts of Hainaut, Brabant, Limburg, and Liège during the High Middle Ages. A thriving textile industry meanwhile grew up around the burgeoning trade centers of Ghent, Bruges, and Ypres, where wool and flax from neighboring regions was spun, woven, finished, dyed, and sewn into clothing for domestic consumption and for export. The Black Death, the Hundred Years' War, and various peasant uprisings in the 14th century temporarily interrupted the Flemish economic boom, but prosperity eventually returned when Duke Philip the Bold of Burgundy inherited the province in 1384.

With its new capital at Brussels, Flanders now found itself at the cultural, educational, and commercial center of the high Burgundian Renaissance during the 15th century. Under Dukes Philip the Bold, John the Fearless, and Philip the Good of Burgundy, spectacular **pageants** were produced and performed, gorgeous books of hours (daily prayer guides) were copied out and lavishly illustrated, and one of Europe's leading universities was established at Louvain in 1425. The Yorkist rulers of England became closely connected to Flanders when Margaret of York, the sister of King Edward IV, married Duke Charles the Bold of Burgundy in 1468. Two years later, King Edward fled into exile during the **Wars of the Roses** and, seeking his sister's protection in Flanders, then accepted money and troops from his brother-in-law for a return to England in 1471 to reclaim his throne. When Duke Charles died at the Battle of Nancy in January 1477, King Louis XI of France seized the Burgundian territories in central Europe, but the province of Flanders fell instead via marriage alliance to the Habsburg ruler Frederick III, the Holy Roman Emperor.

Emperor **Maximilian I** succeeded Frederick in 1493 and ruled the 17 counties of the Netherlands (including the southern 10 that comprised Flanders) as part of his vast continental empire. In 1496, he concluded the Treaty of Intercursus Magnus with King **Henry VII** of England to reinvigorate the Anglo-Flemish wool trade and discourage the sheltering of hostile political refugees. **Charles V**, Maximilian's grandson and eventual imperial successor, was born in Ghent in Flanders in 1500. When the lad's father, Philip the Fair, died six years later, the emperor appointed his daughter **Margaret of Austria** to rule the Low Countries as regent of the Netherlands in 1507. She received and almost immediately turned down a proposal of marriage from the widowed Henry VII, but she renewed the Intercursus Magnus Treaty with England in 1508 and took in **Anne Boleyn** (the future queen) as a teenaged lady-in-waiting five years later. Charles V soon wrested control of Flanders from his aunt, inherited the crown of Spain in 1516, and then was elected Holy Roman Emperor in 1519. After his own accession to the English throne, Henry VIII attempted to wed his sister **Mary** Tudor and later his daughter **Mary** Tudor to the young emperor, but these diplomatic overtures ultimately came to nothing. King Henry did host Charles V in England twice and met with his imperial counterpart at Gravelines in Flanders in July 1520 to plan a joint invasion of France, as well.

Long considered the finest in Europe, English wool was exported in ever-increasing volume from London, Ipswich, Lynn, and Hull to Flanders during the long reign of the second Tudor king. English middlemen known as clothiers collected raw wool and distributed it to peasant cottages to be spun into thread and woven into large sheets of broadcloth. The clothiers then paid for and retrieved the broadcloths and in turn sold them to commodity merchants responsible for exporting them overseas. This wool trade flowed through the agency of three commercial enterprises that included the Staple, the Hanseatic League, and the Merchant Adventurers of London. The Staple (more formally the Company of Merchants of the Staple of England) was an association of traders who, beginning in 1314, pooled their resources, shipped their woolens to Flanders, and then rented warehouses in Antwerp and Bruges to store their cloth during sale negotiations. The Hanseatic League was a commercial consortium in the Baltic region, Scandinavia, northern Germany, and Flanders that maintained the **Steelyard** compound in London and facilitated the exchange of English woolens and other commodities within its trading network. The Merchant Adventurers of London, chartered in 1486 by Henry VII, was a proprietary company whose operations were funded by investors and coordinated by a board of directors. Thus was English wool shipped and sold to textile manufacturers

in Flanders during the reign of Henry VIII, a brisk and profitable business that flourished and even expanded through the reigns of King Henry's Tudor successors and beyond.

FLODDEN, BATTLE OF (9 SEPTEMBER 1513). Recognized today as the last truly medieval battle on British soil, this clash between English and Scottish forces also involved the largest number of combatants (approximately 56,000 on both sides) during the Tudor era. Significantly, King **James IV** of Scotland lost his life at Flodden, leaving his widowed queen, Henry VIII's sister **Margaret** Tudor, to serve as regent and protector for their infant son and heir, **James V**. The victorious English commander at Flodden was **Thomas Howard**, the Earl of Surrey, who, having defended the realm while King Henry was waging war in France, was created second Duke of Norfolk by a grateful monarch five months after the battle.

The roots of Scotland's enmity toward the English ran deep, dating to the late 13th century with the Scottish wars of independence under William Wallace and King Robert the Bruce. Needing support against their southern foes, Scotland's rulers entered into the "Auld Alliance" with France, a mutual defense pact that was still in force by the start of the 16th century. Thus, when the young, brash, and bellicose King Henry VIII launched his **French invasion** in the summer of 1513, King **Louis XII** appealed to his ally King James IV of Scotland for help. Despite attempts by Henry VIII's elder sister Queen Margaret to dissuade him, the Scottish king sent his most powerful warship, *Great Michael*, to bolster King Louis's fleet and began organizing his own invasion of northern England to help divert English forces away from the French campaign.

During July and August 1513, the king of Scots assembled nearly 30,000 men and 17 artillery pieces in Berwickshire across the River Tweed from English Northumberland. King James's objective was to capture Norham Castle, the frontier English fortress that had withstood his last assault and siege in 1497. Meanwhile, King Henry, having anticipated a Scottish incursion before leaving for France, had appointed Queen **Katherine of Aragon** as regent and the 70-year-old Thomas Howard, Earl of Surrey, as lord lieutenant of the north to defend the kingdom in case of attack from the Scots. Surrey began raising his own army during the summer of 1513, and marching to Pontefract Castle in Yorkshire with a goodly force, he then called up additional local levies to augment his numbers. When he received word that the Scots had indeed crossed the frontier on 25 August, Surrey hurried north with his 26,000 men to intercept the invaders.

Once in England, King James's troops quickly captured Norham Castle and then took up a strong defensive position atop a ridge known as Flodden Hill. When Surrey arrived with his troops on 4 September, the two sides traded challenges and threats for several days, but neither would commit to a pitched battle. Suddenly, Surrey forced King James's hand on 9 September by marching his force around Flodden Hill to occupy the slopes of nearby Branxton Hill, thus blocking the Scots' route of retreat to the north. After absorbing several deadly volleys of arrows from Surrey's archers, the agitated Scots formed up into five schiltrons (phalanxes) of tightly packed pikemen and lurched toward the English lines. The uneven ground and drenching rain scattered their ranks, however, exposing them to lethal thrusts from the English bills, or halberds, which were spear-axes atop eight-foot oaken poles. The English infantry hacked their confused enemies to pieces, and when the brutal slaughter finally ended near sunset, about a third of the Scottish host lay dead or dying on the blood-soaked field. Among them, riddled with arrows and gashed by multiple halberds, was the battered and naked body of King James IV of Scotland. His courageous but foolhardy insistence on leading his troops into battle himself, and his resulting death at age 40, placed a child on the Scottish throne and established Henry VIII and England as the dominant political power in the British Isles for the next three decades and beyond.

FOX, RICHARD, BISHOP OF WINCHESTER, LORD PRIVY SEAL (c. 1447–1528). An influential prelate, statesman, diplomat, and educationalist during the reigns of **Henry VII**

and his son Henry VIII, Bishop Fox served both the Roman Church and the English Crown with tireless energy, devotion, and efficiency for more than 40 years. Considered by some to have been an early architect of the Tudor age, Fox authored many renovation and construction projects on cathedrals, colleges, and even fortifications during his lifetime. He was also an architect in a figurative sense, building the careers of important Tudor personalities and laying the foundation of future ruling dynasties in Britain as well. Bishop Fox's greatest achievement was perhaps his endowment of an academic chair in the Greek language at **Oxford University**, a daring innovation that ultimately opened the door to a full flowering of the English Renaissance.

Richard Fox was born into a family of yeoman farmers in the village of Ropsley, just east of Grantham in Lincolnshire, between 1446 and 1448. Although little is known about his early life, it is likely (given his later educational achievements) that he attended a local grammar school—probably in nearby Boston—before entering Magdalen College at Oxford in his late teens. At some point, Fox may have fled a plague outbreak in Oxford to study briefly at **Cambridge University**, but there exists no direct evidence to substantiate this claim. Ordained to holy orders in 1477, Fox studied at Louvain University in **Flanders** and then at the University of Paris, where he earned his doctorate in canon laws in the early 1480s. The next few years saw him return to England, where he acquired several ecclesiastical benefices (church livings) in the dioceses of Lincoln, Salisbury, and London. When King Richard III suspected him of treachery and deprived him of these holdings, however, Fox escaped to France, where he joined the entourage of Henry Tudor, the Earl of Richmond and the pretender to the English throne.

Richmond immediately appointed Dr. Fox his personal secretary and sent him off to Paris to negotiate with the French government for troops to support his planned invasion of Britain. After landing in **Wales**, the Earl of Richmond and his army defeated and killed Richard III in 1485 at Bosworth Field, a victory that saw Henry Tudor proclaimed king of England on the battlefield as Richard Fox looked on. He continued as the new king's personal secretary until 1487, when Henry VII elevated Fox to the episcopal dignity of Exeter and appointed him keeper of the privy seal, an office he would retain for the next 30 years. The new bishop of Exeter never visited his diocese, and he did not travel to Bath and Wells when that bishopric came to him in 1492, but he did appoint very able suffragans (substitute bishops), chancellors, and vicars general who performed his episcopal duties in both sees in his place. In 1491–92, King Henry ordered his lord privy seal to organize troops and supplies for an invasion of France. When Charles VIII offered to pay the Tudor king and his army to withdraw, it was Richard Fox who then negotiated the Treaty of Étaples that ended the conflict and brought 750,000 gold crowns into the English treasury.

Soon translated again to the palatine diocese of Durham as its prince bishop (viceroy in the north), Richard Fox now lived in his see for the first time and almost immediately began renovating the great hall and kitchens of his new residence at Durham Castle. Henry VII needed a trustworthy Crown official to watch over the volatile Scottish frontier and keep the king's peace in the remote northern shires, a role for which Prince Bishop Fox was ideally suited. After first hammering out the Intercursus Magnus Treaty that restored commercial relations with Flanders in 1496, Fox returned to his diocese and fortified Norham Castle in time to fend off a Scottish assault led by King **James IV** in 1497. During his time in Durham, he also became a mentor and patron to **Thomas Wolsey** and **John Fisher**, whom he employed as secretaries and chaplains in his household and later commended to the service of the Tudor royal family. When several episcopal deaths left a few southern dioceses vacant in 1501, Henry VII rewarded his dutiful lord privy seal with a translation to the wealthy See of Winchester, where the king could more readily utilize Richard Fox as a Crown minister and advisor.

Before he could even take up residence in Winchester, Bishop Fox escorted **Katherine of Aragon** from her arrival port of Plymouth to London in autumn 1501 for her wedding with **Arthur** Tudor, Henry VII's son and heir. During these early years in his new diocese, Fox assisted **Edmund Dudley** and **Richard Empson** in collecting the king's extortionate benevolence and recognizance payments that helped ensure the good behavior and loyalty of the English **nobility**. On the diplomatic front, he negotiated the treaty and subsequent marriage of James IV of Scots and Princess **Margaret** Tudor in 1502, and he petitioned the pope in 1504 to canonize the saintly King Henry VI (1422–71) of England, though on this occasion without success. As a prelate, Bishop Fox "visited" Magdalen College at Oxford to clean up corruption there in 1507, and enthused by this return to academia, he stayed on to revise the collegiate statutes of Balliol College as well. When his patron and benefactor Henry VII died in April 1509, Fox helped settle the dead king's will and then joined the royal council of his teenaged successor, Henry VIII.

Ever a man of peace, the lord privy seal recoiled when his bellicose young master ordered him to assist Thomas Wolsey in organizing a planned **French invasion in 1513–14**. The bishop of Winchester reluctantly complied with the king's wishes and then accompanied Henry and his army of 40,000 men across the English Channel to **Calais** to open the conflict. When the campaign bogged down in the winter of 1513–14, Fox negotiated peace terms and then arranged the Treaty of London that sent Princess **Mary** Tudor to Paris to wed the aged King **Louis XII**. By this time, Bishop Fox was well into his mid-60s and was growing weary of his many administrative and diplomatic duties, so in April 1516, he resigned the privy seal to devote the rest of his life to his episcopal duties and neglected cure of souls. Now a full-time prelate for the first time, Fox undertook clerical and monastic reforms, suppressed an outbreak of **Lollard** heresy, and translated the Benedictine rule into English for the nuns of his diocese. He also renovated the eastern gable, altar screen, and ceiling bosses in Winchester Cathedral and installed his private chapel retreat along its south aisle that, later known as Fox's Study, was also to serve as his final resting place.

Perhaps the crowning achievement of Richard Fox's life and career was his foundation of Corpus Christi College at Oxford University in 1516–17. Long interested in higher education, Bishop Fox wished to emulate his predecessors in Winchester and establish his own collegiate foundation to train young men for the Roman priesthood. After purchasing land in Oxford in 1511 and beginning construction two years later, Fox named his school Corpus Christi to honor the eucharistic body of Christ, composed statutes for its governance, and then opened its doors in 1517 to 20 fellows (faculty members), 20 scholars (scholarship students), and a small number of commoners (paying students) soon to follow. Although informal instruction in Greek had taken place in Oxford before, Bishop Fox knew that the Greek language (used by the breakaway Eastern Orthodox Church) was officially banned as heretical at the university. Despite such opposition, Fox was determined to offer open instruction in Greek at Corpus Christi, for he believed the *studia humanitatis* (the new learning) in England would be hollow and incomplete without it. He therefore endowed three academic chairs at CCC in Latin, theology, and Greek and, drawing support from such humanist scholars as **Desiderius Erasmus**, Sir **Thomas More**, and even King Henry VIII, initiated a whole new trend in English higher education that quickly spread to other Oxford colleges and to Cambridge University as well.

Richard Fox went totally blind between 1518 and 1522 and died at age 80 in his residence of St. Cross outside Winchester on 5 October 1528. He was buried beneath his private chapel in Winchester Cathedral in a tomb that is still marked today by his skeletal effigy. *See also* CONVOCATION OF BISHOPS (c. AD 690–).

FRANCE. *See* FRANÇOIS I, KING OF FRANCE (1494–1547; r. 1515–47); LOUIS XII, KING OF FRANCE (1462–1515; r. 1498–1515).

FRANÇOIS I, KING OF FRANCE (1494–1547; r. 1515–47). Often credited with establishing the European Renaissance in France,

King François I was the first of five French monarchs to hail from the Angoulême branch of the House of Valois. He spent much of his 32-year reign fighting wars in Italy against his great nemesis **Charles V**, the Holy Roman Emperor and king of Spain. As a result of those interminable conflicts, François entered into surprising alliances with the Ottoman Turks and with the Protestant princes of Germany in order to counterbalance the imperial forces arrayed against him in Europe. He was also allied at times with King Henry VIII of England, but they, too, clashed on several occasions and generally remained at odds through most of their nearly contemporary reigns. Jealous of Spain's colonies in the New World, François sent explorers across the Atlantic to lay the foundations of a French colonial empire in North America. He passed away just two months after Henry VIII, leaving Henri II and his formidable spouse, Catherine de' Medici, to lead France through the coming decades of the turbulent 16th century.

François Valois d'Orléans was born on 12 September 1494 in the north Gascon town of Cognac to Charles Valois d'Orléans, count d'Angoulême, and his wife, Louise of Savoy. Though members of the ruling Valois family, Count Charles and his son were not expected to inherit the French throne because other family branches and claimants stood ahead of them in the royal line of succession. When Count Charles d'Angoulême died in 1496 and then King Charles VIII followed him to an early grave two years later, four-year-old François suddenly became the heir apparent of his first cousin (once removed) Louis Valois duc d'Orléans, who acceded to the French throne as **Louis XII** in 1498.

King Louis saw his youthful kinsman educated in the style of a Valois prince, bringing in such renowned tutors as Christopher de Longueil from **Flanders** to teach him ancient languages, the classics, Scripture knowledge, philosophy, mathematics, history, Italian, and Spanish. François also mastered court etiquette, dancing, and several musical instruments, and athletic and tall for his age, he learned the knightly skills of riding, hunting, hawking, **jousting**, and wrestling as well. He came to love the *studia humanitatis*, or the new learning, of the Renaissance and remained fascinated with literature, poetry, painting, sculpture, architecture, music, and science for the rest of his life.

After marrying Louis XII's daughter Claude in 1514, François acceded to the French throne at the age of 20 years when his frail and sickly royal cousin breathed his last on New Year's Day in 1515. The dead king's third wife, Queen **Mary** Tudor, Henry VIII's 18-year-old sister, survived Louis to wed her former suitor **Charles Brandon**, the Duke of Suffolk, while **Anne Boleyn**, King Henry's future wife, arrived from Flanders at this time to serve Queen Claude as a lady-in-waiting. Like many of his contemporary rulers, François was eager to win military glory, and leading an army into Italy in September 1515, he routed a force of Swiss mercenaries at Marignano and then occupied the Duchy of Milan. Pope **Leo X**, fearful that the French might soon threaten Rome, handed control of the church in France to François I with the Concordat of Bologna in 1516. When **Maximilian I** of the Holy Roman Empire died in 1519, François offered himself as a possible successor, but **Margaret of Austria**, the old emperor's daughter, bribed the seven imperial electors to choose her nephew Charles V instead. Disappointed by this outcome, the French king courted an alliance with King Henry VIII against the emperor and personally met with the Tudor king at the **Field of Cloth of Gold** outside the English-held town of **Calais** in June 1520. Unfortunately, the summit collapsed when François bested King Henry in a wrestling match, a humiliation that drove the embarrassed English king to conclude an alliance with Emperor Charles instead. The two having agreed to invade France, Henry VIII ordered a large English force under the Duke of Suffolk across the channel in the **French invasion of 1523–24** to ravage the French countryside. When the emperor failed to support his English allies with imperial troops, however, Suffolk withdrew again to Calais, and the short war was over.

Now relieved of the English menace from the west, François led another invasion of Italy in autumn 1524, but his forces were crushed by Spanish troops outside Pavia in late February 1525, and the French king himself was wounded and taken prisoner. He was removed to Madrid, where he languished in close but comfortable captivity in a fortress for almost a year, until he was compelled to sign the Treaty of Madrid early in 1526. By its terms, François surrendered Lombardy, Burgundy, and his claims on Flanders to the emperor; he also agreed to send two of his sons to Spain as hostages and promised to marry Charles's sister Eleanor of Portugal, all in return for his freedom. Charles V took the French king at his word and released him, but when François returned to Paris, he renounced the treaty he felt he had been coerced to sign. Seeking vengeance, François convinced the Ottoman Turks to attack the imperial province of Hungary, then formed the Cognac League with England, the Swiss, and four Italian city-states to wage another war against the emperor in Italy. This conflict exhausted both sides and led to the 1529 Treaty of Cambrai, by which François abandoned his Milanese claims, recovered Burgundy, and (as a widower since 1524) finally married Charles's sister Eleanor in 1530.

Over the next six years, the king of France was content to remain at home and at peace while he devoted himself to cultural pursuits both in Paris and across his realm. He dismantled the Louvre fortress and replaced it with an opulent palace and royal residence, and he built a luxurious "hunting lodge" château at Chambord on the Loire River that soon became one of his favorite haunts. King François built a workshop and villa for Leonardo da Vinci at Amboise early in his reign and later invited Benvenuto Cellini, the eccentric Italian sculptor and goldsmith, to work for him in France as well. François also founded the Imprimerie Nationale (royal printing office) and the Collège de France in Paris to nurture the intellectual Renaissance he had helped sponsor in his kingdom. And with Spain and Portugal growing rich from their overseas empires, the king of France sent Jacques Cartier and other adventurers forth to explore and establish fledgling French colonies in North America and Asia.

Ever the warrior, François I could not long resist the temptation to renew military operations against his old enemy Emperor Charles V. In 1536, he formally joined forces with the Ottoman Turks, an arrangement that shocked most Europeans because it allied "His Most Christian Majesty" (François) with the leading power in the Muslim world. The next round of land and seaborne engagements that soon followed came to nothing, however, as had most of the Franco-imperial wars of the past. Undaunted, the French king then signed a pact in 1542 with another strange bedfellow, the Schmalkaldic princes of Germany, who were evangelical Protestants and thus (in theory) religious adversaries of the Catholic François. As Charles V's Protestant subjects harassed him in his German territories, a new war broke out in 1543 between the French king and the emperor in Flanders that soon spread once again to Italy.

Meanwhile, with François thus distracted, Henry VIII seized his last chance to press home his claim to the French throne and invaded northern France for the final time in the **French invasion of 1544–45**. The English managed to capture Boulogne, but when the ailing and obese King Henry withdrew his forces, François retaliated by sending an invasion fleet of his own to attack southern England the following year. After sinking Henry's prized warship *Mary Rose*, the French forces also withdrew, leaving Franco-English relations in a strained state of glowering hostility. These last conflicts exhausted and nearly bankrupted both rival kings, and with François suffering from crippling gout and advanced venereal disease, he followed Henry VIII of England to his grave at the age of 52 years on 31 March 1547. King François was laid to rest beside the remains of Queen Claude and his mother, Louise of Savoy, in the abbey church of St. Denis in northern Paris, where the tombs were later vandalized during the upheavals of the French Revolution.

FRENCH INVASION OF 1513–14 (JUNE 1513–SUMMER 1514).

Hoping to achieve the same kind of military glory as had his predecessor and namesake Henry V, young King Henry VIII joined the Holy League alliance with other continental powers to secure support for his own invasion and conquest of France. The English king assembled a vast army and fleet and accompanied these forces to northern France in summer 1513, but the conflict itself was short lived and only yielded two captured towns and a quick skirmish victory over some French cavalry. Though his gains in the war were small, King Henry's campaign expenses were heavy, and he squandered most of the large patrimony left him by his father at his death in 1509.

Just as Henry VIII acceded to the English throne, the alliance of Cambrai was combining papal, Venetian, Spanish, and imperial forces to drive the French out of northern Italy. Disagreements among the victors over the spoils of war, however, led Venice to defect to the French, prompting the remaining Cambrai signatories to add a new partner to bolster their alliance. That new partner was England, previously considered a marginal player in European geopolitics but now, as a traditional enemy of France, a natural opponent of further French aggression. Representatives of the Cambrai powers and England met in **Flanders** in April 1513 to forge a new alliance called the Holy League, an association that committed all four parties to a massive invasion of their common French enemy in the very near future.

For his part, King Henry VIII was eager to attack France in what he saw as an extension of the Hundred Years' War, when his ancestors Edward III and Henry V had won great military fame but England had later lost nearly all her territories on the Continent. Believing that imperial and Spanish troops were amassing to support his own, the English king ordered his chief minister, **Thomas Wolsey**, and his lord privy seal, Bishop **Richard Fox** of Winchester, to assemble what was then the largest invasion force in English history in late spring 1513. Twelve bronze cannons called "the apostles," along with suits of armor, bow staves, barrels of beer and gunpowder, tents, wagons, horses, foodstuffs, and countless other supplies were brought together along the Sussex and Kentish coasts to equip an army of more than 40,000 soldiers. At the end of June 1513, King Henry sailed on his flagship *Henry Grace à Dieu* with his expeditionary force to the English-held port of **Calais**, where he landed and organized his troops before launching his incursion into France.

On 21 July 1513, the English army lumbered out of Calais, requiring 10 days before it could reach the town of Thérouanne, the agreed-upon early objective of the campaign, just 40 miles distant. There Emperor **Maximilian I** met the English army with a token imperial force, and following a three-week siege, King Henry claimed the town as his first (if relatively insignificant) prize of the war. In the midst of the siege, a squadron of French cavalry came upon the English king and a detachment of his mounted bodyguards in a meadow outside Thérouanne. When the outnumbered French fled, King Henry gave chase with his men and managed to kill or capture a few of the enemy's stragglers. This little action, more a skirmish than a full-fledged engagement, was later dubbed the Battle of the Spurs by the glory-hungry Tudor king. After besieging and taking the episcopal city of Tournai in late September, King Henry feasted and **jousted** until the approaching winter ended the campaigning season, whereupon he took his leave of the emperor and made his way back to England.

Meanwhile, with King Henry away in France, the king of Scots, **James IV**, had invaded northern England but had been defeated and killed by the army of **Thomas Howard**, the Earl of Surrey, at the Battle of **Flodden** on 9 September 1513. This good news was tempered, however, by reports that King **Ferdinand** of Spain had recently backed out of the Holy League, thus leaving England practically alone in the field against France. Well aware by now of the drastically depleted royal treasury, Wolsey and Fox pressured the king (who was still keen to fight on) to seek détente with King **Louis XII** of France in spring 1514. By the Treaty of London that emerged over the following summer, the rulers of France and England agreed to forego further military action against one another. King Louis also (grudgingly) promised to pay off an old debt to England from 40 years before, while Henry

pledged the hand of his teenaged sister **Mary Tudor** in marriage to the aged French monarch to seal the terms of the pact. Although Mary and Louis were duly wed in October 1514, the pretty Tudor princess was soon freed by the old king's death to marry her childhood sweetheart **Charles Brandon**, the Duke of Suffolk, in May 1515. Henry VIII went on to invade France two more times in the **French invasions of 1523–24** and **1544–45**, but neither campaign produced any tangible results for England or for her Tudor king.

FRENCH INVASION OF 1523–24 (SEPTEMBER 1523–AUGUST 1524). Still entertaining dreams of a French crown and an overseas empire, Henry VIII believed a second invasion of France might succeed in ways his first such campaign had not just 10 years earlier. In the early 1520s, the Holy Roman Emperor **Charles V** persuaded King Henry to take part in a coordinated assault against their mutual enemy King **François I** of France. This time Henry did not lead the invasion himself but instead appointed **Charles Brandon**, the Duke of Suffolk, to command the expedition. Suffolk's army arrived in France in 1523 and at first struck hard toward Paris, but the emperor's promised support never materialized, and then inclement weather caused rampant illness among the English troops. Suffolk eventually withdrew his men to the French coast and thence to England, leaving Charles to battle later with King François on his own and dashing Henry VIII's lust for military glory a second time.

In 1520, King Henry embarked on a duplicitous game of international statecraft by meeting in person with both Emperor Charles V and King François I over a span of just seven weeks. After hosting the emperor in late May in England and then joining François at the **Field of Cloth of Gold** summit in June, the English king quickly hurried off to Gravelines in **Flanders** to consult with Charles a second time. Clearly favoring an imperial alliance over détente with France, Henry invited the emperor back to England in summer 1522 to finalize arrangements for a joint French invasion the following year. They ostensibly agreed that Charles's armies should cross into southern France from Italy and Spain while English forces descended on Paris from their northern base at **Calais**. Despite these bold plans, the English king privately thought he might limit and even delay English military operations entirely for another year until 1524. When the powerful French lord Charles III, duc de Bourbon, led an uprising against King François in late spring 1523, however, Henry VIII rediscovered his martial spirit, changed his mind, and began readying a sizable army in Kent for immediate deployment to France.

On this occasion, the Tudor king suppressed his ego and offered command of the expedition to his brother-in-law Charles Brandon, first Duke of Suffolk, Henry's best friend and fellow comrade in arms during the **French invasion of 1513–14**. What Suffolk lacked in military leadership experience he more than made up for in organizing skill, enthusiasm, and personal courage. In September 1523, he arrived in Calais at the head of 10,000 well-equipped men, and following new orders from London to bypass enemy towns and fortresses, he set off to cross the Somme River and march straight for Paris. Along the way, Suffolk hoped to receive additional troops and supplies from **Margaret of Austria**, the emperor's aunt and regent in the Netherlands, while he planned to rendezvous with the rebellious duc de Bourbon once he reached the outskirts of the French capital. Meanwhile, the English army moved quickly, covering 75 miles in three weeks, crossing the Somme, and standing just 50 miles away from Paris by the end of October 1523.

Just as victory seemed within his grasp, however, Suffolk's good fortune evaporated, and his steady advance across northern France ground to a sudden halt. Emperor Charles had indeed launched a double-pronged attack in the south as promised, but his armies ran into determined French resistance and failed to provide the diversion Suffolk had been expecting. In addition, Margaret of Austria became so distracted by insurrections in the Netherlands that she forgot about her commitment to support Suffolk's invasion. Bourbon's revolt in the meantime completely collapsed when most of

his mercenary soldiers deserted him, forcing his retreat to Italy and freeing King François to reinforce his capital city. These military disasters were compounded by the unexpected onslaught in northern France of unseasonably cold, wet, and destructive storms. This freakish weather system turned Suffolk's position into a quagmire, afflicted much of his host with sickness, and caused many of his men to flee back to the shelter of Calais. Suffolk allowed them to go, and at Christmas 1523, he finally returned to the Tudor court himself to explain to his irate royal master exactly what had gone wrong in France.

Despite the failures of 1523, Charles V was still eager to renew the war against King François and urged Henry VIII to make common cause with him by invading France again in the new year. At first the English king agreed to do just that but then cooled to the idea when informed that his royal treasury was nearly empty. After consulting with his lord chancellor, **Thomas Cardinal Wolsey**, Henry announced his intention to launch another French incursion but only when and if the emperor and the duc de Bourbon had already struck the first blows successfully. During spring 1524, King Henry played his allies off against each other and his enemy, assembling an even larger invasion force under Suffolk while simultaneously engaging in peace talks with French envoys in London and Calais. A few months later, Bourbon actually did attack southern France and was poised to capture Marseilles, but by then, neither the emperor's troops nor Suffolk's English army were prepared to move or fight. Eventually, Bourbon abandoned his offensive and crept back to Milan, thus ending the war against King François and postponing Henry VIII's active designs on the French throne for the next 20 years.

FRENCH INVASION OF 1544–45 (JULY 1544–JULY 1545). Having attempted twice before to conquer France without much success, King Henry VIII decided to chase his dream of military glory one last time and launched a third French invasion late in his reign. The English king believed the time was right for such a campaign because the Scottish frontier was finally secure following the death of King **James V** of Scots, while his nemesis King **François I** was again distracted by his interminable wars with the Holy Roman Emperor **Charles V**. Much like his earlier **French invasions of 1513–14** and **1523–24**, King Henry's final thrust into northern France squandered vast sums of treasure but achieved very few military or territorial gains. In the end, the physical exertions required to command his own armies in the field probably hastened the death of the corpulent and sickly Tudor king just 30 months after his return from France in autumn 1544.

By the start of 1542, the formerly vigorous and lighthearted Henry VIII was very likely suffering from the kind of deep depression he had rarely known over the course of his privileged life. The robust health, athleticism, and physical grace of his youth had given way in his later years to extreme obesity, painful gout, and a grossly ulcerated leg, all afflictions that constantly reminded the aging king that his death was not far off. Then, too, the resurgent joy and boyish affection Henry had felt for his fifth wife and queen, the pretty teenager **Katherine Howard**, had turned to bitter disappointment once her many infidelities prompted him to order her execution in February 1542.

The end of that year brought better news from the far north, however, when the ever-present threat of Scottish invasion vanished with a victory over the Scots at Solway Moss and the subsequent death of their king a few weeks later. Then, following the renewal of hostilities between France and the empire in 1543, Charles V invited Henry to join him in an alliance against King François and offered to return the French province of Gascony to the English king in return for his military assistance. Seeing a last-chance opportunity to demonstrate his martial prowess, Henry VIII gladly accepted the emperor's proposal and enthusiastically began planning for his final French campaign.

Though doubtless relieved by Henry's rejuvenated mood, the members of the royal privy council were alarmed when their bloated and infirm king announced his intention to lead the English army into France himself. His advisors only dropped their objections when Henry promised to share command with his old friend **Charles Brandon**, the Duke of Suffolk, and with **Thomas Howard**, the third Duke of Norfolk and the uncle of the king's recently executed fifth queen. English and imperial envoys signed a pact in spring 1544 that committed Henry VIII to invade France from **Calais** along the Somme River Valley toward Paris, while the emperor promised an attack from the east to rendezvous with the English in the French capital. After taking delivery on a new suit of armor that could accommodate his 54-inch waist and amassing some 40,000 troops with vast quantities of food, horses, weapons, beer, and other supplies on the southern English coast, the bellicose Henry VIII finally felt ready by summer 1544 to claim the military renown in France that had twice eluded him in years past.

Before crossing into France himself, however, the Tudor king ordered the Duke of Norfolk to launch a preliminary strike on the town of Montreuil some 40 miles south of Calais. Norfolk dutifully set off in early July 1544 with 10,000 men, but torrential rains, lack of supplies, and stiff resistance from the town's defenders halted his advance and forced him to dig in for a siege. King Henry meanwhile arrived in Calais with the Duke of Suffolk and the main invasion force of 30,000 soldiers a few weeks later. Choosing to ignore Norfolk's plight, Henry and Suffolk instead marched on Boulogne and there began their own siege of that fortified hilltop town in late July. The king's force hammered away at Boulogne with more than 100 artillery pieces until a mining operation breached the town's walls and its defenders surrendered to the English in mid-September 1544. When the emperor broke off his own invasion from the east and made a separate peace with France, Henry VIII went back to England in (feigned) triumph a few weeks later. He left Suffolk and Norfolk (now returned from Montreuil) to stand guard over his single prize of Boulogne, a town that had cost the royal treasury a staggering £2 million to conquer.

After a French assault to retake Boulogne failed late in 1544, King François vowed to take the war to his enemy's homeland to compel an English withdrawal from his own realm once and for all. King Henry took these threats seriously and, recalling Suffolk and Norfolk from France, fortified England's coasts and commandeered scores of merchant ships to strengthen his royal **navy**. When a major French invasion fleet appeared in the Solent Strait off the Hampshire shoreline on 19 July 1545, the English king looked on with pride as his great warship *Mary Rose*, all 700 tons and 90 guns of her, sailed out from Portsmouth to do battle with the advancing enemy. A sudden maneuver and an unexpected wind gust toppled the *Mary Rose*, however, causing the great vessel to sink before a horrified King Henry, with the loss of some 350 sailors and marines. Despite this embarrassing setback, the French never pressed their invasion of England home, and so Henry VIII's third and final war with France came to an ignominious end. After Henry's death in 1547, the English garrison abandoned Boulogne three years later, and the French were permitted to regain formal possession of the town by treaty in 1554.

FRITH (OR FRYTH), JOHN (1503–33). A prominent English scholar, clergyman, and reformer, Frith preached and wrote against many Catholic doctrines and was burned at the stake as a heretic just before England broke away from the Roman Church during the **Henrician Reformation**. Frith kept in close contact through his adult years with **William Tyndale**, the eminent Bible translator, even though the two men may never have met in person. This courageous reformer also knew such important English prelates as **Stephen Gardiner** and **Thomas Cranmer**, both of whom tried to persuade their friend to renounce his heterodox beliefs and thus save himself from the flames. This he steadfastly refused to do, and so Frith gave his life in defense of religious views that, ironically, were eventually adopted as orthodox doctrines by the Protestant Church of England.

John Frith was born into the family of Richard Frith, an innkeeper, in the village of Westerham in Kent. His education commenced at a grammar school in nearby Sevenoaks and continued at prestigious Eton College, before he was admitted as a scholar (undergraduate student) to Queen's and then King's Colleges at **Cambridge University**. While studying there, Frith was tutored by Stephen Gardiner, the future bishop of Winchester, and he certainly met **Thomas Bilney** and possibly William Tyndale during his student days at Cambridge as well. Bilney, Tyndale, **Robert Barnes**, and even the conservative Gardiner were at that time meeting regularly with other theologians at the White Horse Inn to discuss the daring new ideas of Martin Luther, and it may be that young Frith joined those conversations from time to time. Having earned his collegiate degree in 1525, he made his way to **Oxford University**, where **Thomas Cardinal Wolsey**, aware of Frith's scholarly reputation, installed him as a junior canon (cleric) at his new Cardinal College foundation.

It was not long, however, before Frith began preaching in Oxford some of the reformed Lutheran teachings he had picked up in Cambridge, and as a result, he soon found himself arrested and locked away in a dark cellar. Wolsey freed him on condition that he not leave the environs of Oxford, but instead, he fled in 1528 to Antwerp and then to Marburg University in Germany. There he met a large group of Lutheran and Zwinglian reformers, married and had children, and published several translations of others' works along with his own *Disputation of Purgatory* in 1529. In 1530, he returned briefly to England but quickly left for the Continent once more after surviving some rough treatment in the stocks at Reading.

When Frith came back to England for good in 1532, he was arrested in Essex on charges of heresy and was imprisoned in the **Tower of London** by order of **Thomas More**, Henry VIII's former lord chancellor. Still not yet 30 years of age, the zealous evangelical cleric particularly aimed his reformist barbs at two of the fundamental doctrines of the Roman Church: the existence of purgatory and transubstantiation of the elements in the communion service. During his incarceration, More and his brother-in-law John Rastell authored tracts denouncing

Frith's views and had them delivered to the reformer in the tower. Frith quickly responded with his *Answer to Sir Thomas More* and *The Bulwark against John Rastell*, but by committing his reformist ideas to writing, he now provided his Catholic enemies with clear evidence of what they regarded as his heresy. A panel of bishops (including Gardiner, Cranmer, and **John Stokesley** of London), along with such Crown officials as Lord Chancellor **Thomas Audley** and **Charles Brandon**, Duke of Suffolk, questioned Frith closely in the tower before transferring him first to Croydon in Surrey and then to Newgate Prison back in London. There he formally stood trial for heresy before his episcopal accusers and, condemned to death, was taken to Smithfield on 4 July 1533 for his execution. Bound back to back at the stake with one Andrew Hewet, a tailor's apprentice, Frith met his end bravely and was heard to utter the words "Lord forgive them" as he expired in the flames. His death as a Protestant martyr was recorded in John Foxe's *Acts and Monuments* 30 years later, while his views on the sacrament of the Lord's Supper were eventually adopted by the Church of England in Archbishop Cranmer's 1552 *Book of Common Prayer*.

G

GARDINER, STEPHEN, BISHOP OF WIN-
CHESTER (c. 1490–1555). Known to contemporaries and later to posterity as "Wily
Winchester," Stephen Gardiner was a theologian and prelate who walked a fine line between
competing religious factions during the turbulent **Henrician Reformation** and beyond. As an
early reformer, he studied Lutheran doctrines
and championed Henry VIII's royal supremacy,
but later he launched a conservative religious
reaction during King Henry's final years and
then served the Catholic queen **Mary I** toward
the end of his own lifetime. Gardiner is most
notoriously associated today with the burning
deaths of nearly 300 Protestant "Marian martyrs" in the 1550s, often leaving his successful
career as a diplomat and trusted royal advisor
largely forgotten. Despite the dangers he navi-
gated throughout much of his life, Gardiner
was fortunate to die in his bed and so avoided
the more violent end often suffered by many of
his contemporaries.

Stephen Gardiner was born sometime between 1483and 1497 (the date is uncertain)
in the town of Bury St. Edmunds in Suffolk.
His parentage is also obscure, though it seems
likely his father was one William Gardiner, a
prosperous East Anglian cloth merchant.
Educated as a youth in Paris, Gardiner reputedly met **Desiderius Erasmus** there before returning to England in 1511. In that year, he
entered Trinity Hall at **Cambridge University**
to study Greek and read the ancient classics.
Gardiner earned baccalaureate and master's
degrees at Trinity and then taught for a time
(his students included **Thomas Wriothesley**

and **William Paget**), before adding a doctorate
in canon and civil law to his résumé during the
early 1520s.

In 1523, Gardiner began meeting with other
scholars, like **Thomas Bilney, Hugh Latimer,
Robert Barnes,** and **William Tyndale** (among
others) at the White Horse Inn in Cambridge to
discuss the revolutionary ideas of the German
monk and reformer Martin Luther. Despite his
keeping such company, he came to the notice
of **Thomas Cardinal Wolsey,** Henry VIII's chief
minister, who recognized Gardiner's intellectual potential and took him into his household
as a secretary in 1524. Service to Wolsey at
that time usually translated to diplomatic missions abroad, and so Gardiner soon found
himself in France, Italy, and the empire negotiating with representatives of Europe's major
powers. In 1528–29, he twice visited Rome,
where he tried without success to convince
Pope **Clement VII** to annul Henry VIII's marriage to Queen **Katherine of Aragon.** When he
returned to England, he found that Wolsey had
fallen from the Tudor king's favor, but Gardiner
continued to enjoy Henry's trust and accepted
the post of royal secretary later in 1529. After
the death of the "Great Cardinal" the following
year, King Henry rewarded Gardiner with Wolsey's former diocese of Winchester, England's
wealthiest, with a beneficed income of nearly
£4,000 per annum.

Despite these honored promotions and his
earlier efforts to help dissolve the king's first
marriage, Bishop Gardiner nevertheless opposed his royal master's campaign to overturn the authority of the pope in England. He

also stood firm against King Henry's attempt to control the English **clergy** through the Supplication against the Ordinaries [*see* SUBMISSION OF THE CLERGY AND SUPPLICATION AGAINST THE ORDINARIES (1531–32)] and helped compose the bishops' *Answer to the Supplication* rebuttal in 1532. Even so, the bishop of Winchester was present at Dunstable in May 1533, when Archbishop **Thomas Cranmer** of Canterbury annulled Henry VIII's marriage to Queen Katherine, and he carried the train of the new queen **Anne Boleyn** at her coronation the following month. Such flip-flopping between support of the Roman clergy on the one hand and acceptance of King Henry's remarriage to Queen Anne on the other surely earned Gardiner his "Wily Winchester" moniker during these years. When Henry VIII demanded episcopal acknowledgment of his supremacy over the English Church, Bishop Gardiner finally abandoned the pope and published his famous *De vera obedientia* (*On True Obedience*) in 1535. This tract argues that all English believers owed religious allegiance to the king of England, who after all had been chosen to rule both his kingdom and his church by God. Having demonstrated his loyalty in this way, Stephen Gardiner retained Henry's goodwill for the remainder of the Tudor king's reign.

The essentially conservative but often changeable Bishop Gardiner kept a low profile when England's vicegerent in spirituals (chief religious officer) **Thomas Cromwell** worked to introduce Lutheran doctrines into the English Church between 1535 and 1539. When Cromwell pushed King Henry too far with this policy, however, Gardiner saw his chance to reverse the course of Reformation and bring back to England several elements of the "old church" once again. At the king's behest, the bishop of Winchester outlined several key Catholic doctrines in his **Six Articles of Faith** in spring 1539. Renamed the Act Abolishing Diversity of Opinions but called the "Whip with Six Strings" by its evangelical opponents, Gardiner's articles were approved by Henry VIII and passed into law by **Parliament** a few months later. This statute inaugurated a religious backlash in the English Church that was

soon reinforced by the 1543 King's Book and its revival of Rome's seven sacraments. Gardiner and some of his conservative court cronies even accused Henry VIII's reform-minded sixth queen, **Katherine Parr**, of heresy in 1546, but she threw herself on the king's mercy, and her ailing and worn-out husband eventually granted her a pardon.

When King Henry died in January 1547, the bishop of Winchester's experiment in religious retrenchment came to an abrupt end. After young **Edward VI** and Lord Protector **Edward Seymour**, the Duke of Somerset, repealed the Act of Six Articles early in the new reign, Gardiner was deprived of his diocese and imprisoned in the Fleet and the **Tower of London** for the next five years. Queen Mary released the aging prelate at her accession in 1553, restored him to his See of Winchester, and then appointed him lord chancellor of England the following year. Although Gardiner had once worked against Mary's mother, Katherine of Aragon, and was actively opposed to the new queen's marriage with Prince Philip of Spain, he served Henry VIII's daughter loyally as a royal councilor and held his tongue as hundreds of Protestant heretics were burned at the stake. Stephen Gardiner did not live to witness the last of these horrific atrocities, for he contracted a fever late in 1555 and died the following February in Westminster near London. He was buried in Winchester Cathedral, where his grisly skeletal effigy can still be seen today behind a grate of iron bars along the church's northern aisle.

GARTER, ORDER OR KNIGHTS OF THE

(1348–). The Most Noble Order of the Garter was a medieval and early-modern society of chivalrous knights that still exists today as one of Britain's highest civil and military honors. Founded by King Edward III in the 14th century, the Order of the Garter was an English version of similar knightly associations in other kingdoms, such as the Order of the Golden Fleece in the Holy Roman Empire, the Order of the Band in Castile, and the Order of the Thistle in Scotland. Many distinguished individuals throughout English history have been inducted into the order as Garter knights, including several women and a number of foreign princes and dignitaries. Some of the best-known personalities of the Tudor age were proud members of the Order of the Garter, including the first two Tudor kings, along with their heirs, the Princes of **Wales**.

Tradition holds that King Edward III (r. 1327–77) founded the Most Noble Order of the Garter in 1348 following his earliest victories over the French in the Hundred Years' War at Crécy (1346) and **Calais** (1347). Although the exact date of the order's foundation is uncertain, the robes of Garter knights were first issued in 1348, and the order's original statutes were first drawn up in the same year. Some historians believe that King Edward, himself the image of a gallant knight, by creating the order, wished to revive the values of courage, honor, and chivalry exhibited by the knights of the Round Table in the Arthurian legends. The presence of the garter in the order's name and symbolism supposedly derives from a dancing mishap; when Edward III's dance partner dropped her blue garter from beneath her skirts to the floor, the courteous king retrieved it and wore it on his own leg to divert ridicule from his embarrassed lady. As he donned the garter himself, Edward is said to have scolded the mocking onlookers with the French words *Honi soit qui mal y pense,* or Shame to him who evil thinks, a phrase that was soon adopted as the motto of the Order of the Garter.

The English Knights of the Garter have never numbered more than 24 members at a time, although the king of England and the Prince of Wales have always been automatically included as "royal knights companion" to swell the full number of knights to 26. Each English Garter knight held the dignity of "knight companion," but over time, foreign rulers or magnates have also been accepted into the order as "extra knights." The Order of the Garter boasted five officers that included the prelate (always the bishop of Winchester), chancellor, registrar, Garter king of arms (master of heraldry), and gentleman usher. The insignia of the order was (and still is) a blue belt or garter that, trimmed in gold and bearing the society's motto, encircles the cross of St. George, the patron saint of the Garter

knights. The order met for religious services at Windsor Castle in the Chapel of St. George, where each member knight had an assigned choir stall containing his banner, helmet, and coat of arms. It was in this very chapel that King Henry VIII was laid to rest (next to his beloved third queen, **Jane Seymour**) following his death in January 1547.

No fewer than 18 knights companion accepted membership in the Order of the Garter during the reigns of the first two Tudor kings, along with four Princes of Wales, two "ladies of the Garter" (the daughters of Henry VIII), and four foreign monarchs as extra knights. The Princes of Wales and/or Tudor heirs included **Arthur**, son of **Henry VII**; Henry VIII himself as Duke of York before he became king; **Henry Fitzroy**, the illegitimate son of Henry VIII; and Prince **Edward** Tudor, Henry VIII's heir and the future Edward VI. The extra knights included Holy Roman Emperors **Maximilian I** and **Charles V** as well as King **James V** of Scotland and King **François I** of France. Some of the most familiar names among the **noble** Garter knights included **Edward Stafford**, third Duke of Buckingham; **Thomas Howard**, third Duke of Norfolk; **Charles Brandon**, first Duke of Suffolk; **Thomas Boleyn**, Earl of Wiltshire and father of Queen **Anne Boleyn**; **Edward Seymour**, Earl of Hertford, later first Duke of Somerset, and the brother of Queen Jane Seymour; and **Thomas Cromwell**, lord privy seal and later Earl of Essex. Over the centuries, 36 knights of the Garter were executed for treason, with no fewer than 6 dying on the block during the reign of Henry VIII.

GENTRY (c. 800–). Gentry families in Tudor England belonged to a socially and economically privileged class of landowners who today would be recognized by most readers as members of an "upper middle class." Individuals who identified themselves as gentry in Tudor times were those who realized enough rental income from their estates to free themselves from the need to earn a living with their hands. Unlike English **nobles** or "peers of the realm," patriarchs of gentry families generally could not inherit titles from their forebears but rather earned or purchased them (if they possessed any titles at all) during their lifetimes. Also unlike members of the nobility, the heads of gentry households were liable to assessed taxation in the form of **parliamentary** subsidies on percentages of their income. For this reason, members of the gentry met in the House of Commons in Parliament, where they regularly voted to approve subsidy measures (tax levies) on themselves and their fellow gentry landowners. This control over Crown revenue collection was quietly transforming the gentry class into a rising political and economic power bloc in England by the time Henry VIII became king in 1509.

The origins of the gentry class in England stretch back to the early Middle Ages, when armored and mounted knights first became the most dominant figures on feudal battlefields. Although medieval folk regarded knighthood as the lowest tier of nobility, the title of knight (and the right of address as sir) could not be acquired by birth but rather was bestowed upon worthy recipients by kings or ranking nobles. Gradually, knights accumulated their own estates and so emerged in later centuries as gentrified "almost nobles" who possessed wealth and social status but not hereditary titles. Certain younger sons of noble families also ended up as "gentlemen" because, barred from their father's titles by the laws of primogeniture, they often hired out as "freelance" warriors in return for landed compensation. In addition, some squires (formerly knights' assistants) acquired enough wealth and property in their own rights to join the ranks of the gentry and usually brought the honorific title of esquire with them when they did.

Over time, other social and professional groups earned sufficient income and purchased enough land to identify themselves as members of the gentry as well. As England's population recovered following the Black Death, successful merchants and lawyers from growing urban centers tried to buy up country manors as secure investments for the future. Substantial yeoman or "franklin" farmers, those who owned their farmsteads outright, often expanded their landed holdings when they could for the same reason. During the first half of Henry VIII's reign, the amount of productive acreage available for purchase in England was relatively limited. Once the king and his chief minister, **Thomas Cromwell**, began selling off properties from the suppressed **monasteries**, however, the English gentry quickly took advantage and snapped up as much available land as they could afford. Estates and manors also came onto the market when cash-poor peers liquidated some of their holdings or when a rebellious lord was attainted of treason and his confiscated properties were offered for sale.

Always aspiring to nobility themselves, the heads of gentry households often enlarged their estates so extensively they came to rival those of the barons and viscounts whose social status they hoped to adopt for themselves. Some ambitious gentry landowners acquired noble rank and even titles by offering cash incentives in return for marriage into the families of their "betters." Others still were able to purchase family crests from the College of Arms, the royal agency whose heralds regulated and validated the sale and display of coats of arms among the various tiers of nobility. Occasionally low-born but talented commoners, such as **Thomas Cardinal Wolsey** or Thomas Cromwell, could also rise to gentry status (and even ascend to the peerage) on the strength of their indispensable service to the Crown. So eager were some gentlemen for noble recognition, they adorned themselves and their families with expensive clothing and accessories that were officially limited by sumptuary laws to members of the aristocracy alone. Though much more restricted than in our own age, upward social mobility in Tudor times was certainly more achievable than it ever had been in centuries past.

During the long reign of Henry VIII, the group making up the gentry class in England never comprised more than 2–4 percent of the overall population. Many gentry landowners became efficient managers of their estates—something most nobles felt was socially beneath them—by investing their excess revenues in the latest agricultural techniques and exploiting such landed resources as coal, timber, minerals, and metallic ores for profit. The sons of gentry families also enjoyed access to the universities of **Oxford** and **Cambridge**, where they studied the liberal arts and the classics, or to the **Inns of Court** in London, where they acquired expertise in the law. The education these young men received in turn prepared them for careers as diplomats, Crown ministers, sheriffs, legal solicitors, justices of the peace, and military officers, to name just a few.

Perhaps the greatest professional opportunity that awaited some of these privileged gentlemen was membership in the House of Commons in Parliament, where statute (standing) laws were introduced, debated, and passed on for ratification by the House of Lords and the king. Because the English peerage had been exempt from royal taxation since the Middle Ages, it fell to the gentry members of Commons to raise Crown revenues by approving percentage subsidy levies on their own annual incomes. These two great legislative powers—the passage of kingdom-wide laws and control over the royal purse strings—helped the Tudor-era gentry gradually bypass the old nobility to become the dominant political and economic class of the future in England. *See also* ENCLOSURE (c. 1250–1550).

GREAT BIBLE (1539). Informally called the Great Bible because of its large size but also known as the Coverdale or Whitchurch Bible, this complete translation of the Old and New Testaments into English was the first edition fully approved (not declared illegal) by the Crown for use in the Church of England. Based largely on the banned New Testament translation produced by **William Tyndale** in exile in the 1520s but also drawn from editions in other languages, the final authorized version of 1539 was completed and first offered for publication by Miles Coverdale, an evangelical reformer and later bishop of Exeter. When King Henry VIII and his chief minister, **Thomas Cromwell**, ordered that copies of the Great Bible be made available in every parish church in England, they formalized the transition from a largely ceremonial and ritualized Roman Church to the more cerebral and Scripture-based worship service of the Church of England.

During the Middle Ages, leaders of the Roman Church prohibited the translation of the Bible into common European languages because they feared misinterpretation of the word of God by untrained layfolk. Despite this ban, the founder of the great Waldensian heresy, Waldo of Lyons, had a monk translate the Bible into French for his own use and that of his followers in the late 12th century. Two hundred years later, the **Oxford University** professor John Wyclif, founder of the heretical **Lollard** movement, began rendering the Scriptures into English, and following his death in 1384, his students continued the work and soon established Bible-translation and -copy centers in various locations across England. Most lay believers could not read but were eager to hear the word of God read to them, while a literate few memorized scriptural passages so they could recite them to crowds of enthusiastic listeners. Ecclesiastical authorities declared possession of Bibles in English to be heresy and destroyed all the illicit volumes they could seize. The fact that more than 200 Lollard Bibles still survive today, however, bears witness to the huge numbers that must have been produced during the late-medieval and early-Tudor periods.

The next serious attempt to translate the Scriptures into English was undertaken by William Tyndale, a Gloucestershire man and Oxford graduate who was convinced by the early 1520s that believers in England had a right to read or hear the word of God in their own tongue. In 1524, he traveled to Germany, where he began his translation project, and despite some Catholic hostility, he managed to complete an English New Testament, printed it in Worms, and then had it smuggled back into his homeland hidden in bales of woolen cloth. **Thomas Cardinal Wolsey**, Henry VIII's chief minister at the time, and Sir **Thomas More**, a noted humanist and conservative Catholic apologist, were both incensed that Tyndale's Bible had somehow entered England without their authorization and had as many copies as possible rounded up and burned. Tyndale responded with several vitriolic polemics, including *The Obedience of a Christian Man* (1528), a denunciation of the Roman clergy and a call for universal lay access to vernacular Scripture. After translating the first five books of the Old Testament into English in 1530, Tyndale was betrayed to the Catholic Inquisition in **Flanders** five years later, convicted of heresy, and then burned at the stake in October 1536.

By this time, however, Wolsey and More were dead, and King Henry's new chief minister was Thomas Cromwell, an evangelical sympathizer and the new vicegerent in spirituals (Crown's religious director), who was wholly committed to the publication of a Bible in English. After Cromwell prompted **Convocation of Bishops** to request the publication of an official English translation of Scripture, he persuaded Henry VIII to discard his earlier opposition and grant the necessary authorization in 1534. Master Cromwell then searched for a qualified scholar to undertake the work and finally settled on Miles Coverdale, a priest-turned-reformer who had been living in exile with Tyndale and had assisted him with his translation of the Pentateuch in 1530. Coverdale eagerly took on the commission, but essentially a Latinist who knew little Greek or Hebrew, he drew very heavily on the earlier English New Testament of his friend Tyndale. Then, translating Latin and German passages from revised editions of the Old Testament by **Desiderius Erasmus**, Martin Luther, and others, Coverdale was able to produce a complete Bible in English by 1535.

Meanwhile, a theologian from Cambridge, John Rogers, had been hard at work on his own version of the English Scriptures, but his so-called Matthew Bible (Rogers's pseudonym) was so rife with harsh criticism of the old Roman faith that many conservative English bishops rejected it as too radical. Not wanting competing editions, Cromwell ordered Coverdale, who had returned to England in 1537, to edit the two Bible translations into a single, seamless, and more elegant revision and ready the text for publication. Coverdale completed his editing work in due course and then traveled to Paris, where he engaged the master printer François Regnault to reproduce thousands of copies of his oversized English Bible. When the Catholic Inquisition once again intervened, however, Cromwell had Regnault's entire print operation purchased and turned over to London printers Richard Grafton and Edward Whitchurch, who then published the first complete edition of the Great Bible in April 1539.

This first legal Bible in English was a magnificent achievement, not only on a scriptural and literary level, but also from the standpoint of the bookmaker's craft. **Hans Holbein** the Younger designed the exquisitely engraved frontispiece that featured an omnipotent God looking down on an enthroned Henry VIII, who then handed Great Bibles to both Cromwell and Archbishop **Thomas Cranmer** of Canterbury and thence to the English people. The text was produced in clear black-print type, and the entire volume was dedicated to King Henry as the benign sovereign who had finally brought the word of God to all his subjects. Some 2,500 copies of the Great Bible rolled off the presses in April 1539, and after six more editions were ordered by the Crown, some 9,000 copies overall were in circulation by the end of 1541. Most of those Bibles found their way onto tables in parish churches across England, purchased and placed there by order of Convocation so that parishioners could freely read from the Holy Book for themselves. Along with the dissolution of the **monasteries** and the **Act of Supremacy**, the publication of the Great Bible was one of the key achievements of the **Henrician Reformation** because it provided lay access to Scripture in England the same way reformed churches across the rest of Europe had already done. Miles Coverdale eventually became bishop of Exeter in 1551 and died in his bed 17 years later, but his coeditor, John Rogers, producer of the Matthew Bible, was burned at the stake as a heretic in February 1555 by order of Queen **Mary I**.

THE GREAT MATTER (c. 1526–33). This term refers to the marital crisis brought about by Henry VIII to cast aside his first wife and queen, **Katherine of Aragon**, in order to marry another in her place. King Henry had hoped for a son to succeed him since his accession and marriage to Queen Katherine in 1509, but she failed to provide his long-awaited male heir before reaching the end of her child-bearing years. At the same time, the philandering king met and became infatuated with a darkly attractive lady at court, **Anne Boleyn**, the younger sister of one of Henry's earlier mistresses. It gradually dawned on Henry that, if he could free himself from his infertile Spanish queen and take the much younger Anne as his spouse instead, he might yet sire the son and heir he believed necessary to ensure the Tudor line of succession. Accordingly, King Henry exhausted every means at his disposal to achieve these ends, but the drawn-out struggle it ultimately required cost him his brilliant chief minister, good relations with the Roman Church, and the loyalty of many of his subjects.

Henry VIII and Katherine of Aragon were quite happy together for the first 16 years of their marriage, regularly enjoying each other's company at banquets, **pageants**, **jousts**, and even while riding with the hunt. The king appointed his Spanish consort regent to rule in his place whenever he was away on campaign, and she repaid his trust bountifully with her quick intelligence, attention to detail, and steady leadership. Queen Katherine was pregnant six times between 1510 and 1518, but only one child, Princess **Mary** Tudor, survived to adulthood, thus leaving the English king with no son to succeed him. Henry meanwhile was acutely aware of the weakness of his father's and his own claim to the throne and believed that the long-term stability of the Tudor regime in England depended on the birth and survival of a healthy male heir. As Katherine of Aragon approached and then passed her 40th year, the chance that she might still conceive and bear an infant prince for her royal husband became ever more remote.

By 1524, Henry VIII's affair with **Mary Boleyn**, the lascivious daughter of courtier Sir **Thomas Boleyn**, was nearing its end. At around the same time, Mary's younger sister Anne, just returned from France in 1522, reluctantly parted ways with her beau Lord **Henry Percy** after his father, the intimidating Earl of Northumberland, had threatened to exclude the lad from his inheritance. Anne possessed

a lively personality, an alluring French accent, sparkling dark eyes, and a thick head of ebony-black hair that drew the attention of all who encountered her or even looked her way. Now free of Mary Boleyn and increasingly disappointed with Queen Katherine, Henry VIII was soon enchanted with the coquettish 21-year-old who showed off the latest fashions and sophisticated manners of her nine-year stay on the Continent. Although the king first courted Anne Boleyn as a potential new mistress, she was well aware of how he had used and discarded her sister Mary and so flirted with Henry but refused to sleep with him until he might make her his wife. Enflamed by desire and realizing that a younger spouse could provide his longed-for male heir, King Henry began to explore the possibility of voiding his union with Queen Katherine to enter a second marriage with Anne.

In summer 1527, Henry VIII's lord chancellor, **Thomas Cardinal Wolsey**, traveled to Rome to convince Pope **Clement VII** to annul his royal master's first marriage. Because Katherine had originally been wed to the king's deceased brother **Arthur**, a papal dispensation had been procured to allow Henry to marry his brother's widow based on Deuteronomy 25:5, which urged men to "take in" their dead brother's wives. When Wolsey arrived in Rome, he was prepared to argue Leviticus 20:21, which condemned marriages between men and their brother's widows as cursed, a warning that seemed applicable to England's royal couple because they had no male heir. However, the pontiff was at that moment the prisoner of Holy Roman Emperor **Charles V**, whose unpaid and unruly troops had carried out a sack of **Rome** in May 1527. Because the emperor was the nephew of Katherine of Aragon, he refused to permit Pope Clement to grant Wolsey's annulment petition, thus sending the disappointed cardinal back to England empty handed.

Still determined to free himself from his Spanish queen, King Henry was initially delighted when the pontiff was released from imperial custody and soon sent his representative **Lorenzo Cardinal Campeggio** to London to hear the annulment case in person with Wolsey. The two cardinals conducted interviews, gathered evidence, and convened the trial in summer 1529, but Queen Katherine begged her husband to reconcile with her and then (as was her Christian right) threatened to appeal her case to papal arbitration in Rome. Campeggio accordingly adjourned the trial and left England, while Wolsey fell from royal favor, was exiled, and died. An angry King Henry was thus left no closer to the annulment he sought or the remarriage with Anne Boleyn he so ardently desired.

By 1530, Henry VIII believed he might never satisfactorily solve his Great Matter (as his subjects euphemistically called it), but he did banish Katherine of Aragon from court and installed Mistress Boleyn in the old queen's quarters at **Whitehall Palace** in her stead. Meanwhile, one of Wolsey's former secretaries, **Thomas Cromwell**, a rising star on the Tudor royal council, stepped forward with a new plan to bypass the pope and yet still achieve King Henry's marriage annulment. Between 1531 and 1533, Cromwell initiated a campaign to sever relations with Rome and thus free the English Church to make its own ruling on the king's Great Matter. First, he persuaded the House of Commons to pass a statute denouncing the corruption of the Roman clergy, and then he bullied the Southern **Convocation of Bishops** into granting significant ecclesiastical authority in England to King Henry. In January 1533, Cromwell had **Parliament** pass the **Act in Restraint of Appeals** to transfer jurisdiction over religious matters from the pope to the archbishop of Canterbury and then urged the king to appoint the reformist scholar **Thomas Cranmer** to that vacant archepiscopal post just two months later. Three months after that, in May 1533, Cranmer issued the marriage annulment that had eluded Henry VIII for the past seven years. Now finally free of Katherine of Aragon, the king closed out the Great Matter by formally making Anne Boleyn his new wife and queen in June 1533.

Although Henry VIII had thus accomplished the replacement of his first queen with a second, none of the positive results he hoped would emerge from the lengthy annulment process ever came to fruition. Anne Boleyn only produced one living child, a daughter named **Elizabeth**, and so the king was thwarted (for the time being) in his quest for a male heir after all. His great love for Anne quickly faded as well, and he ordered her execution as soon as allegations of her infidelity surfaced in 1536. Cardinal Wolsey, perhaps the most able minister of King Henry's entire reign, was also a casualty of the Great Matter, as was England's affiliation with the Roman Church, which was lost when Thomas Cromwell engineered the royal supremacy of the Church of England in 1534. That separation from Rome in turn unsettled many English believers, some of whom died as martyrs for their faith (Sir **Thomas More**, Bishop **John Fisher**, the **Carthusian** monks), while others rose in revolt during the **Pilgrimage of Grace** in 1536–37. Henry VIII finally did father his longed-for son with his third queen, **Jane Seymour**, but the Great Matter greatly disturbed the political, social, and religious fabric of England and had lasting effects for many centuries to come.

GREENWICH PALACE (1433–1660). This royal palace was one of the favorite residences of the kings and queens of the early-Tudor period. Located five miles downstream from London on the bank of the Thames River, Greenwich provided easy access to the capital but was distant enough to serve as a quiet refuge from the city's incessant bustle and filth. King Henry VIII was born at Greenwich, as were both of his legitimate daughters, and he married two of his queens there as well. One of the two queens he had executed for adulterous treason was arrested at Greenwich Palace and taken from there to await her fate in the **Tower of London**. Located next to the monastery of the Franciscan Observant Friars, Greenwich was an ideal place to birth and then christen royal infants, and it was attractive to the more pious members of the Tudor household as a spiritual sanctuary and retreat. The palace was seldom used during the Stuart era, fell into ruin, and was finally torn down to make way for the Royal Navy College that occupies the site today.

The origins of Greenwich Palace can be traced back to the time of the early Lancastrian rulers of England, when Duke Humphrey of Gloucester, the brother of King Henry V, acquired a manor house on the lower Thames River at Greenwich in 1417. In 1433, the duke added 200 acres to the property, renamed it Belle Court, and then constructed a fortified tower on the site that came to be known as Greenwich Castle. In 1447, Duke Humphrey fell from royal favor, and when he died under mysterious circumstances, Queen Margaret of Anjou took possession of his Thames-side estate and renamed it Palace of Placentia, or Pleasant House. In 1478, the Yorkist king Edward IV founded an Observant Franciscan friary adjacent to the palace, an addition that soon made the place especially suitable for royal marriages and baptisms. The first Tudor king, **Henry VII**, renovated Placentia by encasing its façade in Renaissance-style red brick and installing fountains and gardens in the park and then renaming the property simply Greenwich Palace to reflect its geographic location.

Prince Henry Tudor, the second son of Henry VII and his consort, **Elizabeth of York**, was the only one of their four surviving children to draw his first breath and receive the sacrament of baptism at Greenwich Palace. Because most of the royal family's attention was focused on Prince **Arthur** Tudor, the heir to the throne, little Prince Henry spent his early years at Greenwich under the watchful eye of his paternal grandmother, Lady **Margaret Beaufort**, who directed the lad's education and otherwise saw to his every need. The Greenwich Palace he knew as a youth featured a five-story residential tower that, flanked by a chapel and a massive kitchen, occupied the central position of several encircling open-air courtyards. We know less about the palace's interior except that it boasted a sprawling great hall, was decorated with painted roof timbers, and housed a cluster of administrative Crown offices. As Henry grew older, he visited other palaces at Richmond and **Westminster**, and as king, he acquired and stayed at **Hampton Court** and **Whitehall** as well, but Greenwich remained his favorite, and he spent more time there during his long reign than at any other royal residence. On 11 June 1509, Archbishop **William Warham** of Canterbury quietly married King Henry VIII to **Katherine of Aragon**, his brother's widow, in the queen's closet (private boudoir) of Greenwich Palace.

Queen Katherine was a devout daughter of the Roman Church and chose to hear mass in the friary and palace chapels at Greenwich whenever she was in residence there. Ever interested in expanding his **navy**, Henry VIII built new dockyard facilities at nearby Deptford and Woolwich and then moored several of his most powerful warships there to protect London from foreign invasion. He enlarged Greenwich Palace itself, added a new banqueting hall, and constructed stables and iron forges to produce mail and weapons for his armed forces. King Henry also installed an impressively large tiltyard at Greenwich, where he and his more athletic court minions could practice and then compete in knightly **jousts** before crowds of cheering spectators. In February 1516, Queen Katherine gave birth at Greenwich to Princess **Mary** Tudor, the only child she and Henry produced together who survived to adulthood. At Christmas 1516, the English king hosted a lavish **pageant** and masked ball at Greenwich that later became the stuff of legend around the Tudor court and at royal capitals all across Europe.

Once Henry VIII had replaced Queen Katherine with **Anne Boleyn**, Greenwich took center stage again when the new queen gave birth to Princess **Elizabeth** Tudor at the Thames-side palace in September 1533. Some 30 months later, King Henry suffered a serious injury in a jousting tournament at Greenwich and lay in a coma for hours before he awoke to the great relief of the entire Tudor court. Already disenchanted with Queen Anne by then, Henry had her arrested at Greenwich Palace early in May 1536 after hearing of her alleged affairs with several courtiers and (improbably) even her own brother **George Boleyn**. Following Anne Boleyn's execution and Queen **Jane Seymour**'s tragic death in childbirth, Henry VIII married the unattractive **Anne of Cleves** at Greenwich Palace in January 1540 but had their union annulled just six months later. Then, when English and Scottish diplomats agreed to a peace treaty at Greenwich in July 1543, King Henry ordered a punitive raid against Scotland after Edinburgh insulted him by renouncing the pact early the next year.

King Henry continued to visit Greenwich from time to time through the end of his reign, and his three Tudor successors did likewise, but once the Stuart kings inherited the throne, they ignored the palace, and it fell into disrepair by the time of the English Civil War. King Charles II had the entire Greenwich complex demolished in 1660 to clear the way for a new palace, but the site remained vacant until William III built the Royal Navy College (today's Old Royal Navy College) there in 1694.

GREY, THOMAS, SECOND MARQUIS (MARQUESS) OF DORSET (1477–1530).

A wealthy **nobleman** who was renowned in his own day as a skilled **jouster**, Thomas Grey boasted Yorkist ancestors and himself produced a grandchild who later sat (briefly) on the English throne. As one of the ranking magnates of early-16th-century England, the Marquis of Dorset commanded English troops on campaign, attended important Tudor court functions, and represented Henry VIII on a number of embassies to France. Although he suffered imprisonment at the hands of the first Tudor king and carried on lengthy feuds with local landowners in the Midlands, Dorset nonetheless managed to retain the good opinion of Henry VIII through much of his later life. Dorset's health declined following a bout of the **sweating sickness**, which eventually led to his premature death at the age of just 53 years.

Thomas Grey drew his first breath at one of his family's estates near the village of Astley in Warwickshire on 22 June 1477. His father and namesake, Thomas Grey, the first Marquis of Dorset, was the eldest son of Elizabeth Woodville, the queen consort of King Edward IV and the grandmother of Henry VIII. Young Thomas's mother was Cecily Bonville, the daughter and heiress of William Bonville, Lord Harington of Aldingham. The first marquis supported the rebellion of Henry Stafford, the Duke of Buckingham, against Richard III and so fled with his family to Brittany to join the entourage of Henry Tudor in exile following the duke's capture and execution in 1483. When Henry Tudor seized the English throne as **Henry VII**

two years later, the elder Grey at first became a prominent member of the new king's royal council. Implicated in the Lambert Simnel affair of 1487, however, he lost King Henry's trust and ended up languishing in prison for the next seven years. His son Thomas meanwhile seems to have attended the Magdalen College School in Oxford around this time and may have received tuition there from a bright student two years his senior named **Thomas Wolsey**.

Young Thomas Grey was invited to reside at the Tudor court by his relative **Elizabeth of York**, King Henry's queen, where he soon acquired the gentlemanly and military skills appropriate to his aristocratic rank. During his time with the royal family, Grey attended the christening of Prince Henry, and he participated in the wedding ceremony (and celebratory joust) of Prince **Arthur** Tudor and his Spanish bride, **Katherine of Aragon**, in 1501. In that same year, he accepted membership in the Order of the **Garter**, and when his father died a few months later, the youthful Sir Thomas inherited a good deal of his father's extensive land holdings along with his title. Grey continued to acquire additional manors, offices, and wardships as the new second Marquis of Dorset and was even present at a meeting between the Tudor king and his "guest" Prince Philip of Castile at Windsor Castle in 1506. Like his father, the first marquis before him, however, son Thomas Grey was rumored in 1507 to be plotting against the ever-suspicious Henry VII. As a result, he endured confinement in the **Tower of London** and afterward in a **Calais** prison until the old king's heir and successor, Henry VIII, pardoned him two years later.

During the first years of the new reign, Dorset reclaimed his former place at court and soon earned a glowing reputation for his prowess with the warhorse and the lance in the Tudor tiltyard. In 1512, the bellicose Henry VIII decided to conquer Gascony in southwestern France and appointed Dorset as commander of the expedition, but expected military assistance from King **Ferdinand** of Spain never materialized, and the invasion force limped back to England in disgrace. Undeterred by this failure, King Henry insisted that Dorset accompany him on his **French invasion of 1513–14**; there they both took part in the siege of Tournai and the cavalry skirmish that later came to be known as the Battle of the Spurs. The Tudor king then nominated the marquis to escort Princess **Mary** Tudor to France in 1514 to marry King **Louis XII** as part of the treaty that ended the recent Anglo-French war. He took part in the wedding ceremony in Paris as King Henry's representative and distinguished himself in the opulent jousting tourneys that followed. In 1516, Henry granted Dorset the office of lieutenant of the Garter, and in 1518, he helped negotiate and then signed the Treaty of London—also known as the Treaty of Universal Peace—that sought (but ultimately failed) to end hostile relations between Europe's major powers. Dorset also traveled with most of the Tudor court to the **Field of Cloth of Gold** summit meeting between Henry VIII and King **François I** near Calais in 1520 and helped fête Emperor **Charles V** when he visited England two years later.

Having contracted but then recovered from the "sweate" in 1517, Thomas Grey never enjoyed robust health again through the remainder of his relatively short life. Henry VIII believed Dorset fit enough to command troops on his **French invasion of 1523–24**, but Cardinal Wolsey disagreed and quickly managed to divert the appointment to another candidate. Instead, the ailing marquis traveled north to advise **Thomas Howard**, the Earl of Surrey, on his defense of the ever-restive Scottish marches. Dorset also entered into a long quarrel during these years with Sir Richard Sacheverell and Lord George Hastings over conflicting land claims in Leicestershire. This dispute became so acrimonious that Wolsey had to demand substantial monetary sureties from each of the squabbling parties in order to defuse the situation and maintain the peace. Nearing the end of his life, Dorset supported King Henry's attempt to annul his marriage with Katherine of Aragon in 1529 by declaring under oath that the Spanish queen and Prince Arthur had in fact consummated their own union in 1501. Having married twice himself and sired eight children by his second wife,

Margaret Wotton Grey, the second Marquis of Dorset passed away on 10 October 1530 and was laid to rest in the parish church near his birthplace in Astley, Warwickshire. His eldest son, Henry Grey, succeeded to his title and estates and, married to Frances Brandon Grey, became the Duke of Suffolk and then the father of Lady Jane Grey, the teenager who would later wear the Crown of England for nine days in 1553.

GROCYN, WILLIAM (c. 1446–1519). Recognized today as one of the leading early-modern scholars of the *studia humanitatis* in England, William Grocyn began teaching lessons in Greek letters at **Oxford University** before that language officially became an accepted part of the collegiate curriculum in the early 16th century. Grocyn belonged to a scholarly circle that included **Thomas Linacre**, **John Colet**, Sir **Thomas More**, and the famous Dutch humanist **Desiderius Erasmus**. During his lifetime, he traveled and studied in Italy, he tutored and was later rewarded by a future archbishop, and he participated in a debate before an English king. Although almost none of his presumed written work is extant, William Grocyn still holds a prominent place as one of the signature founders of the English Renaissance, an intellectual movement that richly informed the education of young Prince Henry Tudor—later Henry VIII—as an adolescent prior to his royal accession in 1509.

William Grocyn was born into the family of a prosperous lease-holding farmer around 1446 in the village of Colerne, near Bath in Somersetshire. Little is known of his early life, but in 1463, he entered Winchester College and then two years later matriculated at New College, Oxford, where in 1467 he accepted a position as a teaching fellow. During his years at New College, Grocyn tutored **William Warham**, the future archbishop of Canterbury, who in 1481 appointed his former instructor to his first church living at Newton Longueville in Buckinghamshire. The same year, Grocyn left his fellowship at New College to become a reader in divinity at Magdalen College, also at Oxford, a position he then further legitimized by entering into holy orders as a priest. In

1483, he took part in a theological disputation before Bishop William Waynfleet of Winchester and King Richard III, who rewarded the 37-year-old scholar with a haunch of venison and a purse full of coins. After resigning his readership at Magdalen in 1488, the restless Oxford don set off for Italy to visit the sites of antiquity and study the Greek language.

Having arrived in Florence, the queen city of the Italian Renaissance, William Grocyn engaged the eminent humanist Angelo Poliziano as his principal tutor and then began studying Greek with Demetrius Chalcondyles, the Athenian scholar who had by then been teaching in Italy for more than 40 years. While in Florence Grocyn met Thomas Linacre, a fellow Chalcondyles pupil, and soon the two men became friends and took to studying their Greek lessons together. It was also at this time that both Englishmen made the acquaintance of Aldous Manutius, the renowned Venetian printer. When Grocyn returned to Oxford in the early 1490s, he moved into rooms at Exeter College, where he offered informal lectures in Greek to interested students and faculty fellows. This was a somewhat risky enterprise in late-15th-century England because Greek was the language of the Eastern Orthodox Church, which was still considered heretical (after its medieval break with Rome) by many conservative scholars at Oxford. During the later 1490s, Grocyn met and developed lasting relationships with John Colet and Thomas More, and after his chance encounter with Desiderius Erasmus in 1497, the Oxford don welcomed the Dutch humanist into his circle of scholarly friends as well.

While William Grocyn continued to teach unofficial lessons in Greek letters and literature at Oxford, his former student William Warham, after 1503 the archbishop of Canterbury, granted him multiple church livings that soon yielded a relatively lucrative income. When John Colet became dean of St. Paul's Cathedral in London in 1505, Grocyn probably followed him to the capital because, after that date, he is known to have preached multiple sermons there at the behest of his friend. Aside from these pastoral duties, Grocyn also undertook an intensive study of the *Ecclesiastical Hierarchy of Dionysius*, a mystical work by an obscure ancient theologian that the displaced Oxford scholar eventually exposed as a forgery. The only piece of Grocyn's own writing that still survives today is a letter he penned to Aldous Manutius in 1499, in which he thanked the Venetian printer for hosting his friend Thomas Linacre and then insisted that the works of Aristotle were superior to those of Plato as fit subjects for publication.

Toward the end of his life, both Thomas More and Desiderius Erasmus credited Grocyn with introducing the *studia humanitatis* to Oxford University. His informal lessons in Greek challenged conservative hostility toward the language, an attitude that only softened when Bishop **Richard Fox** of Winchester endowed a chair in Greek studies at Corpus Christi College in Oxford in 1516. William Grocyn suffered a stroke that left him paralyzed in 1518; he passed away the following year and was buried in his parsonage of All Saints collegiate church in Maidstone, Kent.

H

HALL, EDWARD (1496–1547). A contemporary of historian **Polydore Vergil**, Edward Hall was a lawyer, member of **Parliament**, and historian himself whose firsthand account of the reign of King Henry VIII ranks among the most reliable and most elegantly written of any work of Tudor history we possess today. His magisterial account of England's past, known by most modern scholars simply as Hall's *Chronicle*, begins with the accession of Henry IV in 1399–1400 and covers events through the end of King Henry VIII's reign. Hall's *Chronicle* is best remembered today as a principal source for many of the history plays of William Shakespeare.

Edward Hall was born in the parish of St. Mildred in London and was the son of John Hall, a prosperous grocer and merchant of the Staple who had moved to the capital from Shropshire in the early 1490s. Young Edward attended Eton College and then entered King's College at **Cambridge University**, where he earned his baccalaureate degree in 1518. It was around this time that Edward Hall began taking copious notes on the political events that swirled around him, perhaps inspired by the son of a well-known chronicler who was apprenticed to his father in 1518. By 1521, Edward was already a student at Gray's Inn, one of the **Inns of Court** law schools in London, after which he pursued a career as a practicing attorney. Although it is possible that he first entered the House of Commons in 1523, Hall later represented the towns of Wenlock and Bridgnorth in Shropshire in four different parliamentary sessions between 1529

and 1545. In 1535, he was appointed under-sheriff of London, an office he held until his death a dozen years later.

It is unknown exactly when or how long it took Edward Hall to compose his history of England, a work he formally titled *The Union of the Two Noble and Illustre Famelies of Lancastre and York*. It fell, however, to Richard Grafton, the same printer who produced the **Great Bible** translation in the late 1530s, to publish Hall's book in 1548 following the historian's death one year earlier. In writing his magnum opus, Hall relied heavily on the *Anglicae historiae* of Polydore Vergil and Sir **Thomas More**'s *History of King Richard III* for most of the historical background predating his own life. He then drew on his own personal notes to describe the events and personalities of Henry VIII's reign, but when he inexplicably left off the work in 1532, Richard Grafton used those same notes to complete Hall's English history to the year of the Tudor king's death in 1547.

A common theme that runs through Hall's *Chronicle*, as it came to be known, is his hatred of **Thomas Cardinal Wolsey**, King Henry's lord chancellor, who for Hall represented the worst greed, hedonism, and power lust of the Roman clergy in England. However, Hall enthusiastically champions the publication of vernacular Scripture in English, and he roundly condemns those who had authored the burning deaths of religious reformers **Robert Barnes** and **Thomas Bilney** as heretics. The pages of his *Chronicle* also exhibit unwavering support for the House of Tudor and for King Henry VIII in particular, whom Hall considered the savior of England for restoring peace and order after the destructive **Wars of the Roses**.

According to his will, Edward Hall never married and so had no issue to whom he might leave his worldly goods at his death. He died sometime prior to May 1547, when his will passed probate, leaving all his printed books to his brother William and his manuscript copies of his history to his publisher Richard Grafton. Hall's *Chronicle* was an instant success and required the production of a second 1550 edition to keep up with demand. After Queen **Mary I** ordered the book burned for denouncing the Roman Church in 1555, Queen **Elizabeth I** had a new revised edition issued just 10 years later. Raphael Holinshed, the great Elizabethan historian, relied heavily on Hall's work for much of his own *Chronicle of England, Scotland and Ireland*, a work that also informed William Shakespeare as he composed most of his history plays.

HAMPTON COURT PALACE (1515–). Today one of Britain's most famous and frequently visited royal palaces, Hampton Court was originally constructed in magnificent fashion to serve as the principal residence, audience hall, and entertainment venue of **Thomas Cardinal Wolsey**, Henry VIII's early chief minister and lord chancellor. Combining elements of both medieval and early-modern architectural styles and embellished with multiple decorative features, Wolsey's palace was meant to impress diplomats and dignitaries and so reflected his passion for ostentatious display. When Cardinal Wolsey fell from royal favor in 1529, King Henry acquired Hampton Court and thoroughly renovated the complex to suit his own tastes and needs. In October 1537, his son and heir, **Edward VI**, was born in the palace, but tragically his third queen and wife, **Jane Seymour**, died there just 12 days later. A little more than four years after these events, the king's fifth queen, **Katherine Howard**, was arrested at Hampton Court, from whence she was taken to her eventual execution within the precincts of the **Tower of London**.

By the time Thomas Wolsey had become a royal councilor and the archbishop of York in 1514, he had realized that a sumptuous palace of his own was now required to show off his newfound status, wealth, and power. Always fearful of contagious disease, Wolsey was determined to choose as healthy a site as possible for his new château and finally settled on a location some 12 miles upstream from London on the north bank of the Thames River. There his grand new mansion would have access to the clear, pure waters of the nearby Coombe Springs, thus avoiding use of the Thames for any purpose other than barge transportation to and from the capital. Wolsey purchased an old manor house and chapel on his chosen site that had once belonged to the Knights of St. John Hospitaller, and by the time he had become King Henry's lord chancellor and a cardinal of the Roman Church in 1515, construction on his palatial new residence was well underway. An elaborate cistern and piping system was first installed to convey fresh spring water to the place, and then thousands of bricks, huge vats of lime, many tons of stone, entire forests of lumber, and great quantities of other essential materials were stockpiled at the building site. The initial phase of construction was complete by 1517, when Wolsey and his household moved in, but additional wings, outbuildings, and decorative features were regularly added over the next dozen years.

Overall, the early footprint of Hampton Court covered nearly eight acres and contained approximately 1,000 rooms. Of these, 280 were separate double lodgings, or two-room suites, the larger chamber to accommodate the distinguished guest himself and the smaller to house his attendants. When visitors first arrived at Hampton Court, they passed through the First or Base Court to the Great Gatehouse, an imposing brick-and-stone structure that was surmounted by an ornate mullioned window and featured faux crenellations along its adjoining curtain walls. Proceeding through the gatehouse, visitors found themselves standing in the Interior or Clock Court, an enclosed quadrangle measuring 167 feet by 142 feet that provided access on three sides to long, windowed galleries and thence to guest apartments. The fourth side of the

Clock Court rose to three stories and, flanked by two octagonal brick towers, displayed a magnificent central clock positioned some 80 feet above the gothic gate that then led visitors into two smaller courtyards with access to additional galleries, guest chambers, chapels, and offices. Wolsey's armorial crest (with cardinal's hat) was carved in stone just above the Clock Court gate and featured his motto, *Dominus michi adjutor*, meaning the Lord my Helper.

The architect who supervised construction of Hampton Court, Henry Redmayne, skillfully combined high-gothic, Tudor, and Renaissance building styles to erect a unique collection of structures never before seen in early-modern England. Pointed gothic archways led into the various courtyards and galleries, while Tudor brickwork—newly rediscovered from Roman times—covered the exterior façades of the curtain walls and towers and spiraled upward on the roof in multiple groupings of column-like chimneys. To add a classical touch to his palace, Wolsey commissioned an Italian sculptor to create several terracotta medallions bearing busts of Roman emperors to adorn the turrets and walls that enclosed his sprawling courts. To the north side of the Clock Court stood Wolsey's Great Hall, the place where the lord chancellor feasted and entertained King Henry VIII with masked galliards, allegorical **pageants**, and comic mummeries. Detached from his Great Hall were Wolsey's audience chamber and private (or privy) rooms, all exquisitely paneled in oak and draped in tapestries depicting classical scenes of Roman gods, statesmen, and mythic figures. A formal garden with sculpted shrubs and beds of medicinal and culinary herbs occupied the space between the Great Gatehouse and the Thames, though this was uprooted and replanted by several later royal owners of Hampton Court.

When Cardinal Wolsey failed in 1529 to secure Henry VIII's longed-for "divorce" from **Katherine of Aragon**, the disappointed king exiled his former chief minister and then occupied Hampton Court himself the following year with his paramour **Anne Boleyn**. King Henry immediately began renovating the palace to meet the needs of his huge royal household, enlarging the already-expansive kitchens to include butteries, bakehouses, larders, pantries, and wine cellars. He had most traces of Wolsey's former ownership replaced with his own royal arms and badges, and he installed fanciful carvings of such heraldic beasts as lions, dragons, deer, leopards, and unicorns on palace gables, fountains, and ceiling bosses. Rehiring Henry Redmayne to carry out this work, the king ordered Wolsey's Great Hall demolished to make way for his own much grander Great Hall that, when completed in 1535, measured 105 feet by 40 feet by 60 feet in height and boasted an ornate hammer-beam ceiling. A royal library was built, and tennis courts were installed on the grounds, and in 1540, Henry replaced Wolsey's impressive first clock with an astronomical device that displayed the time, date, month of the year, phases of the moon, and even the point of high tide at London Bridge. After Henry VIII's death in 1547, Hampton Court remained in royal hands and underwent additional renovations in the late-Stuart and early-Georgian periods to emerge as the palace we know and visit today.

Hampton Court witnessed several important episodes during the reign of Henry VIII that involved the birth and death of some well-known members of the Tudor royal family. Following the execution of Queen Anne Boleyn in May 1536, King Henry quickly married Jane Seymour, who was soon with child and entered into her prebirth confinement at Hampton Court during the autumn of 1537. There Queen Jane endured nearly 60 hours of painful labor before presenting her overjoyed husband with the healthy male heir he had long desired. The prince—later Edward VI—was christened in the King's Chapel at Hampton Court within three days of his birth, but the boy's mother contracted a puerperal fever on 23 October 1537 and, delirious through the night, died early the next day. She lay in state in the presence chamber of Hampton Court until her burial in in the Chapel of St. George at Windsor Castle on 12 November 1537. Four years later, the king's fifth wife, Katherine Howard, was arrested at Hampton Court for having engaged in multiple adulterous affairs with various courtiers. The promiscuous queen was conveyed from the sprawling royal palace to the Tower of London, where she was convicted of treason and beheaded in February 1542.

HANSEATIC LEAGUE. *See* THE STEELYARD (c. 1280–1598).

HENRICIAN REFORMATION (1531–47). Perhaps the most significant series of events in Tudor history, this religious revolution saw the overthrow of the Roman Church and its replacement by the new Church of England with Henry VIII at its head. Unlike other Protestant movements on the Continent, the Henrician Reformation had its roots in Henry's marital problems but then took a more Lutheran turn under the Tudor king's reform-minded religious lieutenants. The English people were surprisingly ready for the reformation of their church and, despite resistance from a few key individuals and one full-scale popular uprising, generally accepted the Crown's religious changes with at least resignation or indifference but also with great enthusiasm. Doctrinally conservative himself, King Henry eventually reversed the course of his English Reformation and restored most Roman teachings and rituals during the final seven years of his reign.

The ground for religious change in England was well prepared during the first three decades of the 16th century. The 1510s and 1520s, saw a resurgence of **Lollardy**, the late-medieval English heresy that attacked the papacy and many of the beliefs and practices of the Roman Church. A group of academics also began meeting in the White Horse Inn near **Cambridge University** to discuss the revolutionary teachings of the German reformer Martin Luther, whose 1521 excommunication by the pope had condemned him as a heretic in England, as well. Alongside Lollardy and Lutheranism, the kingdom's layfolk were increasingly suspicious of and hostile to the ecclesiastical establishment of Rome. Many common English believers resented the apathy, laziness, greed, and corruption of their **clergy**, while members of the **nobility** and

gentry longed to acquire the vast landed estates of church prelates and **monasteries** for themselves. Although Pope **Leo X** had granted the title Defender of the Faith to Henry VIII, the people he ruled were by the late 1520s quite fed up with the ceremonies, doctrines, and especially the leadership of the Roman Church.

The spark that really ignited the Henrician Reformation was King Henry's "**Great Matter**," his campaign to annul his first marriage so that he might be free to marry again. By the mid-1520s, Henry's first queen, **Katherine of Aragon**, had failed to give him a male heir, and having by then reached the age of 40, the chances of her doing so were rapidly deteriorating. Desperate for a son and lately infatuated with the younger **Anne Boleyn**, the Tudor king sought an annulment of his union with his Spanish consort from Pope **Clement VII** so he might wed Mistress Boleyn and with her sire a son. At first the pope refused, then sent his legate to England to hear Henry VIII's arguments for annulment, but Queen Katherine derailed the trial by threatening to appeal her case to Clement himself in Rome. With little hope of a papal resolution in sight, the English king began casting about for an alternate way to free himself from his first marriage.

One such course of action initially involved asserting greater royal control over the Roman Church in England. In 1531, King Henry received a petition from the House of Commons (the Supplication against the Ordinaries) asking him to clean up clerical corruption. He responded by fining his bishops, then ordered them to acknowledge him as "supreme lord of the English Church as far as the law of Christ allows." The prelates balked at first but eventually capitulated in the 1532 **Submission of the Clergy**, a declaration that handed unprecedented religious authority in England to Henry VIII. The king soon needed such enhanced church control, for his longtime mistress Anne Boleyn announced she was pregnant in January 1533. King Henry quickly legitimized her unborn child by secretly marrying her, then appointed **Thomas Cranmer** his new archbishop of Canterbury, and finally had **Parliament** pass the **Act in Restraint of Appeals** to cut off further judicial recourse to the pope. Archbishop Cranmer duly annulled Henry's marriage to Queen Katherine in May 1533, which allowed the king and his second consort to wed more formally and publicly a few weeks later. Much to King Henry's great disappointment, Queen Anne presented him with a daughter—not the son he had long desired—the following September.

With papal power thus greatly weakened, the time had come to sever the realm's final ties to Rome and establish an independent ecclesiastical authority in England. Henry VIII's new chief minister, **Thomas Cromwell**, a master of administrative efficiency and control, pushed three new statutes through a compliant Parliament to achieve those ends in 1534. Early that year, the **Act of Succession** settled future claims to the English throne on the children of King Henry and Queen Anne and further stripped the pope of religious authority by demoting him to the humble rank of "bishop of Rome." The **Act of Supremacy** the following November made Henry VIII the "Supreme Head of the Church of England," vested in him the power to "amend" doctrinal "errors," and ordered all English believers to acknowledge the king's ecclesiastical leadership with an oath. The **Act of Treasons** that rapidly followed added traitorous words as capital crimes, thus granting vicious punitive powers to the Crown to enforce the new religious settlement.

Remarkably, most of King Henry's subjects accepted his royal supremacy over the English Church and swore the required oath without serious complaint or opposition. A group of **Carthusian** monks from London refused to renounce their allegiance to the pope, however, and were duly arrested, tried, convicted, and executed as traitors in 1535. A similar fate befell Bishop **John Fisher** of Rochester and Sir **Thomas More**, King Henry's former lord chancellor, during the summer of the same year. Fisher openly refused to swear the oath and died on the block in June 1535; the evasive More did not refuse but simply said nothing to avoid the treason charge, a ruse that ultimately failed and led to his own decapitation one month later. In addition, a great uprising broke out in Lincolnshire and Yorkshire in 1536 to protest certain social and economic injustices along with many of the religious changes of the English Reformation. Some 40,000 insurgents joined this so-called **Pilgrimage of Grace**, but King Henry sent the Dukes of Suffolk and Norfolk north with armies to scatter the rebels and put their ringleaders to death. On the whole, however, such instances of religious disaffection among the English were few. Of the 900 or so individuals whom Thomas Cromwell interrogated for resisting the supremacy oath, only 329 met a traitor's death, while the rest were either exonerated or pardoned.

In fact, the Church of England under the theologically conservative Henry VIII was initially only Protestant in its rejection of the Roman pontiff. The retention of "old church" teachings and practices began to change only when King Henry made Thomas Cromwell his vicegerent in spirituals, in effect the chief manager of religious affairs in England. Long an ardent but secretive Lutheran himself, Cromwell reconciled his royal master's remaining Catholic sensibilities with his own reformist program in the **Ten Articles of Faith** he persuaded the English bishops to pass in **Convocation of Bishops** in 1536. He then set about the gradual closure of England's monasteries in an effort to reduce clerical corruption and at the same time replenish the royal treasury by selling off monastic possessions and estates. Finally, Cromwell brought a major component of the Lutheran Reformation to England in 1539 by authorizing (with King Henry's permission) the vernacular translation, publication, and distribution of the **Great Bible** throughout the realm. The vicegerent himself fell from royal favor when he arranged a distasteful marriage for the king, a misstep that, coupled with his overly zealous religious reforms, finally led to his own execution as a traitor and heretic in July 1540.

The remaining years of King Henry's reign saw Cromwell replaced at the center of Crown governance by such closet Catholics as Bishop **Stephen Gardiner** of Winchester and **Thomas Howard**, the third Duke of Norfolk. These men supported their king's traditional religious views and, persuading him to sponsor the **Act of Six Articles** through Parliament in 1539, inaugurated a theological reaction in England that restored much "old-church" belief and ceremony but not the pope, monasteries, or Latin Bible. Thus did the Church of England remain until the old king's death, when his son and heir, **Edward VI**, introduced more radically Calvinist doctrines and a scripturally based service to the church he inherited. Edward's half-sister and successor Queen **Mary I** tried to return the English Church to Roman obedience and burned hundreds of her subjects as heretics in the attempt before her half-sister **Elizabeth I** finally settled on the fully reformed Church of England that largely survives to this day.

HENRY VII, KING OF ENGLAND (1457–1509; r. 1485–1509).

The founder of the Tudor dynasty and father of King Henry VIII, Henry VII made good on a very thin claim to the throne of England by defeating and killing his principal rival in battle. His major accomplishment as king was the peace and prosperity he brought to his realm after three decades of sporadic conflict during the bloody **Wars of the Roses**. King Henry amassed a huge royal fortune by tightly controlling Crown expenses and revenues, extorting money from foreign princes, and holding financial sureties from restive **nobles** against their good behavior. He also improved royal administration by appointing talented men to key Crown posts and used the English **judiciary** effectively to control his enemies and reward his supporters. Having wed a daughter of the House of York to unite rival royal factions, he then secured international recognition for his regime by marrying three of his children to the offspring of prestigious European ruling houses. After he died, his progeny governed England for 94 more years to become the most famous ruling dynasty in British history.

Henry Tudor (also spelled Tuddur, Tydier, Tyddor, or Tythier by contemporaries) was born in Pembroke Castle in **Wales** on 28 January 1457. His father, Edmund Tudor, the Earl of Richmond, was the son of Sir Owen Tudor, a Welsh adventurer who had attracted and then married Katherine de Valois, the dowager queen of the Lancastrian King Henry V. Henry Tudor's mother was the formidable **Margaret Beaufort**, the daughter of an illegitimate line of descent from John of Gaunt, the Duke of Lancaster and third son of King Edward III. Henry Tudor thus possessed two very tenuous and distant claims to the English throne; from his father, he inherited French royal blood but not English, while through his mother, he claimed questionable (bastardized) Plantagenet ancestry. **Parliament** legitimized the Beaufort family in the early 15th century on condition that their descendants never lay claim to the English Crown. In any case, little thought was given to Henry Tudor's kingly aspirations at his birth because there were so many potential royal claimants ahead of him in the line of succession.

Edmund Tudor died on campaign in Wales a few months before Henry was born. Because the infant's mother delivered him at the age of just 14 years, she was never able to conceive again, so Henry grew up an only child. When the Yorkist King Edward IV seized the English throne in 1461, he confiscated the extensive Beaufort land holdings and placed little Henry Tudor in wardship with his loyal client Lord William Herbert of Raglan. The Lancastrians briefly returned to power in 1470–71, which allowed Lady Margaret to recover custody of her son. Fearing for his life, however, she almost immediately sent him off to the safety of Brittany and France in the care of his exiled uncle Jasper Tudor. Young Henry grew to adulthood overseas, and as older royal claimants died in battle or on the block, he gradually ascended the line of succession until by 1483 he represented the last hope of the Lancastrian cause.

That year, the Yorkist King Edward IV died and was replaced by his brother Richard of Gloucester, who acceded to the English throne as Richard III following the mysterious disappearance of his two nephews in the **Tower of London**. Because the new king was very unpopular—especially in the south of England—Margaret Beaufort saw an opportunity for her son to overthrow Richard and claim the Crown for himself. She helped finance the Duke of Buckingham's rebellion against King Richard in autumn 1483, but the uprising was soon crushed, and Henry Tudor was forced to return to exile in France. His next chance came two years later, when his mother and the French king provided him with a small mercenary army. After sailing to and landing in England, the 27-year-old Tudor heir defeated and killed King Richard in battle at Bosworth Field in August 1485 to become the seventh king named Henry in English history.

Because his claim to the throne was so weak, the new king quickly strengthened his grip on power by marrying **Elizabeth of York**, his defeated enemy's niece, in order to pass along Yorkist as well as Tudor blood to their future offspring. Flimsy royal claims often inspire revolts, however, and it was not long before King Henry faced an uprising from one Lambert Simnel, the son of an Irish baker who claimed to be a long-lost Yorkist heir. Henry VII defeated Simnel's supporters at the Battle of Stoke in 1487 but then turned to confront another threat to his throne from a second foreign pretender named Perkin Warbeck. Warbeck attempted two landings in England but was captured by the Tudor king and then executed. While dealing with these challenges, King Henry appointed intelligent and well-educated men to serve on his royal council and advise him on all policy matters, both foreign and domestic. He named John Morton his archbishop of Canterbury in 1486, and he made **Richard Fox** his lord privy seal and promoted him through three other episcopal dioceses to wealthy Winchester in 1501. The Tudor king also established the court of Star Chamber (so named for the starry ceiling of its meeting hall) to try cases involving noble dissidents, and he used **Parliament** (as a high court) to attaint 138 vanquished Yorkist adherents of treason and confiscate their properties.

Clearly convinced that wealthy kings are also powerful kings, Henry VII set about enriching himself from the start to the finish of his reign. He more efficiently exploited Crown demesne lands for profit, and he tightened the imposition of wardship dues, import tariffs, and inheritance fees to maximize the flow of funds into his royal coffers. King Henry also levied benevolence and recognizance surcharges (sums of money held hostage) on potentially rebellious English lords to control them and employed ruthless lawyers **Edmund**

Dudley and **Richard Empson** as his royal collection agents. Following the example of his Yorkist predecessor Edward IV, the Tudor king invaded France in 1492 and then accepted £160,000 from the French king Charles VIII to withdraw his forces back to England. Henry VII was thus able to build up an astonishing £200,000 in Crown revenues to pass along to his son and successor Henry VIII by the end of his reign.

Perhaps most importantly, the strategic marriages King Henry arranged for three of his children resulted in foreign alliances that in turn ensured the future survival of his Tudor dynasty. He married off his eldest daughter, **Margaret** Tudor to **James IV** of Scotland in 1503, a union that eventually produced the line of Stuart monarchs in Great Britain in the 17th century. Henry also wed his eldest son, **Arthur** Tudor, to **Katherine of Aragon** in 1501, but when the sickly lad died just 19 months later, the wily Tudor king arranged for the Spanish princess to marry his younger son Prince Henry in Arthur's place. Henry VII thus won recognition and support for his shaky English throne while avoiding costly foreign wars and legitimizing his own questionable family lineage in the process. A religious man, his final will and testament ordered that 10,000 masses be said for the repose of his soul. Henry VII coughed fitfully from consumption (tuberculosis) during his final months and finally died of a fatal stroke at Richmond Palace near London on 21 April 1509. He was laid to rest in his own chapel in Westminster Abbey, where his mother, Lady Margaret Beaufort, was soon buried near him just a few months later.

HOLBEIN, HANS, THE YOUNGER (1497–1543).

A renowned portrait painter and miniaturist, Hans Holbein the Younger was a German-born artist whose career mostly flourished first in Basel and then, from 1532 until his death, in London. He is best known as the official portraitist of the Henrician court. Holbein's larger-than-life renderings of King Henry VIII, his family, and several of his ministers and advisors are the most frequently recalled images today of the major personalities of the Tudor age.

Hans Holbein the Younger was born in Augsburg; he was the son of artist Hans Holbein the Elder, whose family also counted the painter Ambrosius Holbein and the printmaker Hans Burgkmair among its members. Hans the Younger began his artistic training in his father's workshop but soon relocated in his late teens to the workshop of one Hans Herbst in Basel. There the younger Holbein met and developed a friendship with the Dutch humanist **Desiderius Erasmus**, who would later provide introductory references when the German artist visited England. Thanks to Basel's thriving printing industry at this time—Erasmus's New Testament translation and Sebastian Brandt's *Ship of Fools* were both published there—Holbein was able to secure one of his most important early commissions, a series of 41 miniature woodcuts illustrating the moralistic picture book *The Dance of Death*. He also traveled in these early years to nearby Lucerne to decorate the home of a wealthy patron and to northern Italy, where he studied the work of Renaissance masters Leonardo da Vinci and Andrea Mantegna.

After returning to Basel in 1519, Holbein joined the painters' guild and then married the widow Elsbeth Schmid. The growing climate of religious reform in the city, however, soon convinced him that demand for the kind of religious and portrait art he depended on for commissions was beginning to evaporate. In 1526, he visited England for the first time and was there introduced to the humanist and statesman Sir **Thomas More** by letters he bore from More's good friend Erasmus. During his 18 months in England, Holbein executed portraits of More and his family, Archbishop **William Warham** of Canterbury, Nicholas Kratzer of **Oxford University**, and several others. He returned to Basel in 1528 but left Switzerland for good five years later to take up permanent residence and establish a new workshop in the as-yet-unreformed city of London.

Holbein's first commissions in his adopted country came from the German merchants of the Hanseatic League, who hired him to paint their portraits while living as ex-patriots at their London headquarters of the **Steelyard**. In 1533, he created one of his best-known works, *The Ambassadors*, a double portrait of French emissaries to both the courts of Henry VIII and Pope **Clement VII**. After completing a likeness of King Henry's chief minister, **Thomas Cromwell**, Holbein painted Queen **Jane Seymour** in 1536 and was rewarded with a lucrative appointment as the new royal court artist. The following year, Holbein executed a group fresco depicting King Henry and Queen Jane, along with the king's parents, **Henry VII** and **Elizabeth of York**, on the walls of the presence chamber in **Whitehall Palace**. His full-figured, grandiosely regal portrait of Henry VIII himself, along with his perhaps overly flattering image of **Anne of Cleves** (King Henry was horrified when he met her in person!), remain two of the most famous pictures Holbein the Younger ever produced. To this day, King Henry VIII and many of the Tudor luminaries associated with his reign are best remembered through Holbein's work. The transplanted German artist died, possibly of the plague or the **sweating sickness**, in London in 1543.

HOLY ROMAN EMPIRE. *See* CHARLES V, HOLY ROMAN EMPEROR (1500–1558; r. 1519–1556; a.k.a., CARLOS I, KING OF SPAIN, r. 1516–1556); MAXIMILIAN I, HOLY ROMAN EMPEROR (1459–1519; r. 1493–1519).

HOWARD, KATHERINE, QUEEN OF ENGLAND (c. 1521–42). King Henry VIII's fifth wife and queen, this young woman provided her aging and sickly husband with 15 months of marital happiness before her adulterous affairs provoked his anger and sent her to an early death on the block. Queen Katherine was naïve and foolish enough to ignore the consequences of her extramarital liaisons, but her lax and probably abusive upbringing and the political ambitions of her Howard relatives can also be blamed for her lustful later behavior and untimely end. The adultery Queen Katherine almost certainly committed could have clouded the validity of the Tudor succession had she conceived and borne a prince, so ultimately her execution as a traitor was a forgone conclusion once her husband became aware of her ill-advised transgressions.

Katherine Howard was a younger daughter of Lord Edmund Howard, a granddaughter of **Thomas Howard**, the second Duke of Norfolk, and a niece of **Thomas Howard**, the third Duke of Norfolk as well. Lord Edmund sired 10 children by his wife, Joyce Culpepper, who was distantly related to one of Katherine's later lovers. Due to her father's straitened circumstances, Katherine was sent off around the age of eight to live in the well-appointed household of her step-grandmother Agnes Howard, the widow of the second Duke of Norfolk, who presided over a bustling establishment at her Horsham estate in East Anglia. Although the dowager duchess had been entrusted with the care of several young ladies in this manner, she seems to have allowed them great freedom to admit and entertain practically any visitors—male or female—they wished. Katherine very likely suffered sexual abuse at age 14 at the hands of her music teacher, one Henry Mannox, who then carried on with her for about a year. The gentlemen Francis Dereham subsequently began a relationship with the teenaged Howard girl as well, that may have led to their secret betrothal sometime in 1538. By the time she turned 18 and was called on to attend the Tudor court, the precocious young Katherine was involved with her third paramour, **Thomas Culpepper**, a distant cousin and a gentleman of King Henry's privy chamber.

When Katherine Howard arrived at **Hampton Court** in early 1540, she became a personal servant to **Anne of Cleves**, Henry VIII's fourth wife and queen. The fact that the king found his German wife wholly unappealing and had consequently never consummated their union left Henry unfulfilled and his roving eye eager to wander anew. He probably first noticed Katherine soon after her arrival at court and, beguiled by her lively and flirtatious youth, began to pay serious attention to her just months into his fourth marriage. The king showered Katherine with gifts, leading many observers to assume she was merely his latest mistress. When Henry had **Convocation of Bishops** dissolve his union with Queen Anne, however, he promptly wed the diminutive Howard girl at Oatlands Palace just a few weeks later.

At first, King Henry was delighted with his new queen; he constantly embraced and caressed her (even in public), and courtiers reported that his health, energy, and spirits were all substantially improved. For her part, Katherine played the role of dutiful royal wife and, perhaps following the example of her predecessor Queen **Jane Seymour**, catered to Henry's every need and desire. A grateful king rewarded his young bride with lands from the estate of his recently executed chief minister, **Thomas Cromwell**, and granted her an enormous allowance of £4,600 per year to spend as she pleased.

The luster began to fade from their marital bliss, however, when the old king, now nearing 50 years of age; grossly overweight; and afflicted with gout, leg ulcers, and various other ailments, became seriously ill in spring 1541 and refused to see Queen Katherine or admit her to his bed. Thus neglected and much out of her depth as a frivolous adolescent in a dangerous political world, Henry's fifth queen now reverted to old habits and sought out some of her former male companions. With the clandestine cooperation of **Jane Boleyn**, Lady Rochford, the widow of Queen **Anne Boleyn**'s brother **George Boleyn**, Queen Katherine Howard began secretly entertaining the handsome Thomas Culpepper in her bedchamber, and by summer 1541, she had also hired her old paramour Francis Dereham as her private secretary. While Henry VIII had by now recovered somewhat from his illness, the queen's surreptitious trysts with her former (and likely present) lovers continued through the following autumn yet somehow remained hidden from her elderly, ailing husband.

In the meantime, the Howard family and especially the third Duke of Norfolk, had profited much from their young niece's royal marriage. They seemed too distracted by their own success to grasp how Katherine's reckless indiscretions might threaten their own good fortunes and newly elevated status. Still ignorant of these affairs, King Henry ordered that a special mass be said on All Saints' Day 1541 in thanksgiving for the happiness he had found with his pretty young consort. All the while, however, rumors of the queen's risqué behavior had been circulating at court, which in turn prompted an investigation by Archbishop **Thomas Cranmer** and Lord Chancellor **Thomas Audley**, both enemies of the Howards. Witnesses who had lived with and known Katherine at Horsham were questioned, and they quickly named Dereham and Culpepper as former and very likely current lovers of the queen. It then fell to Cranmer to share this devastating information with Henry, which he did by slipping the king a brief note the day after the All Saints' Day mass of thanksgiving.

Events soon spiraled out of control for the blithely promiscuous Queen Katherine, but at first, she seemed unaware of the real dangers she now faced as a suspected royal adulterer. When Dereham and Culpepper were apprehended and racked in the **Tower of London**, they each confessed to having had intercourse with Katherine during their early years together, but both tried to deny any inappropriate relations with her during her marriage with the king. The Duke of Norfolk discretely retreated to one of his country estates, but his stepmother Agnes, the Dowager Duchess of Norfolk, and Jane Boleyn, Lady Rochford, were both arrested for their failure to report the queen's old and current affairs to Crown authorities. Katherine herself was confined to her rooms at Hampton Court until she, too, confessed tearfully to her crimes and was then moved to Syon Abbey to await her fate. Dereham and Culpepper were both executed on 10 December 1541, while Agnes Howard was eventually released six months later. Queen Katherine Howard was convicted of treason by a **parliamentary** act of attainder in early February 1542 and, now confined in the tower herself, requested that the headsman's block be delivered to her chamber so she might practice the placement of her head for the day of her execution. On 13 February, Queen Katherine was beheaded, along with Lady Rochford, at the same spot on Tower Green where Anne Boleyn had suffered a similar fate six years earlier. King Henry was despondent that the springtime love he had briefly enjoyed during his autumn years had come to such an unhappy and tragic end, and he appears never to have experienced much

joy following Katherine's death over the final five years that remained to him.

HOWARD, THOMAS, SECOND DUKE OF NORFOLK (1443–1524).

This important English nobleman served not only the Yorkist kings Edward IV and Richard III but the first two Tudor monarchs **Henry VII** and Henry VIII as well. Norfolk was adept at sidestepping disaster when the factions he backed in the **Wars of the Roses**, and in his personal feud with **Thomas Cardinal Wolsey**, ended up on the losing side. He is best known during King Henry VIII's reign for leading the English army to victory over the Scots at **Flodden** in 1513 and for presiding at the 1521 treason trial of his close friend the Duke of Buckingham. His son **Thomas Howard**, third Duke of Norfolk, was the uncle of **Anne Boleyn** and **Katherine Howard**, two of Henry VIII's wives and queens.

Thomas Howard was born to Katherine and Sir John Howard (later the first Duke of Norfolk) in 1443 in the village of Stoke-by-Nayland in Suffolk and received his early education at Thetford Grammar School in Cambridgeshire. Like his father, Thomas grew up to support the House of York during the Wars of the Roses and entered royal service as one of King Edward IV's men-at-arms in the 1460s. In 1470–71, he fought to help King Edward win back his throne against his brother the Duke of Clarence, the Earl of Warwick, and their Lancastrian allies and was badly wounded (but survived) at the Battle of Barnet. Howard married the wealthy widow Elizabeth Tilney Bourchier in 1472, was named an esquire of the king's body in 1473, and accepted a knighthood from King Edward in 1478 before his royal patron died five years later.

When Edward's youngest brother seized the throne in 1483 as King Richard III, both Sir John and Sir Thomas Howard so enthusiastically supported him that some historians have linked them to the murders of the two Yorkist princes in the **Tower of London**. The Howards also rode with King Richard when he suppressed the revolt of the Duke of Buckingham in October 1483. Whatever form their service to the new Yorkist ruler took, King Richard was grateful enough to elevate Sir John to the

Duchy of Norfolk and granted the Earldom of Surrey to his son Thomas. Both Howards fought for Richard III against Henry Tudor at Bosworth Field in August 1485, where the first Duke of Norfolk was killed and his son the Earl of Surrey was wounded, captured, and imprisoned in the tower by the victorious King Henry VII.

Surrey languished in captivity until 1489, when King Henry released him and restored his title but not his estates. Gradually earning the trust of the first Tudor ruler and eventually regaining his lands, Surrey put down two revolts and then repelled a Scottish invasion in 1497 as the newly appointed lord lieutenant of the north. In 1501, Henry VII named Surrey a member of his royal council and granted to him the lucrative office of lord treasurer. Surrey joined **William Warham** and **Richard Fox**, bishop of Winchester, on their mission to negotiate the marriage of **Katherine of Aragon** to Prince **Arthur**, and in 1503, he escorted Princess **Margaret** Tudor to Scotland to marry King **James IV**. As the end of his life approached, Henry VII named Surrey one of the executors of his will, a final display of trust in a man who had once been his Yorkist enemy.

When King Henry VIII acceded to the English throne in 1509, he immediately bestowed the office of earl marshal (royal military commander) on the 66-year-old Surrey and added him to his royal council to benefit from his extensive experience. Away on his first **French invasion of 1513–14**, the king left Surrey behind to defend the kingdom during the regency of Queen Katherine. When a large Scottish army crossed the northern frontier that autumn, a slightly smaller English force led by the earl marshal routed the invaders and killed King James IV at the Battle of Flodden in Northumberland. A grateful King Henry created Thomas Howard the second Duke of Norfolk the following February, passed the Earldom of Surrey on to his son, and ordered the Howard arms adorned with the Scottish lion rampant to commemorate England's great northern victory the previous year.

All this success, however, was tarnished during the final years of Norfolk's life by his intense loathing for and ongoing feud with King Henry's chief minister, Thomas Cardinal Wolsey. As the scion of a great English aristocratic family, the duke resented Wolsey's meteoric rise from common-born obscurity to enormous wealth and great power as England's lord chancellor. Norfolk was part of the delegation that negotiated the peace terms with France after King Henry's invasion bogged down in 1514, but he objected to the marriage of Princess **Mary** Tudor to the aged French King **Louis XII** as part of the treaty and balked when ordered by Wolsey to escort her across the English Channel for the wedding. After successfully suppressing the **"evil" May Day riots** in London in 1517, Henry VIII commanded Norfolk to preside over the 1521 trial of his good friend **Edward Stafford**, the third Duke of Buckingham, who had unwisely belittled Cardinal Wolsey and had been charged with treason as a result. Eyewitnesses reported that "tears streamed down his face" as Norfolk pronounced the sentence of death upon his friend, although this bitter pill was made somewhat easier to swallow when Buckingham's estates were awarded to Norfolk for his loyal service. Thomas Howard, second Duke of Norfolk, breathed his last on 21 May 1524, leaving his title and lands to his namesake and eldest son, Thomas.

HOWARD, THOMAS, THIRD DUKE OF NORFOLK (1473–1554). A powerful magnate and key servant of the Crown under Henry VIII, this son of **Thomas Howard**, second Duke of Norfolk, was the uncle of both **Anne Boleyn** and **Katherine Howard**, the ill-fated queens of King Henry VIII. A religious conservative, Norfolk opposed the evangelical changes wrought by **Thomas Cromwell** and **Thomas Cranmer**, archbishop of Canterbury, during the **Henrician Reformation**. Along with **Stephen Gardiner**, bishop of Winchester, Norfolk helped implement a conservative religious backlash during the last years of King Henry's reign, and attempted (without success) to bring charges of heresy in 1546 against **Katherine Parr**, Henry VIII's sixth and last queen. Accused of treason himself and awaiting execution in the **Tower of London**, Norfolk won a last-moment reprieve when the old king died just before the sentence could be carried out.

This younger Thomas Howard was the eldest son of his namesake, the second Duke of Norfolk, and his first wife, Elizabeth Tilney, the widow of Sir Humphrey Bourchier. Little is known of Howard's early life, but by the 1490s, he was earning a reputation as an able soldier. He fought under the command of his father, the Earl of Surrey, against a Scottish invasion in 1497 and was subsequently knighted by the elder Howard on the battlefield as a reward for his bravery. When Henry VIII became king, Sir Thomas rose quickly in his service; the new Tudor made him a knight in the Order of the **Garter** in 1509; bestowed the title lord admiral on him in 1510; and, after fighting at his father's side against the Scots at the Battle of **Flodden**, elevated him to the royal council and to the Earldom of Surrey in 1514. In the meantime, his first wife, Anne of York, had passed away, leaving him free in 1513 to wed Elizabeth Stafford, a daughter of the prominent Stafford and Percy families. Although honors and important missions continued to come Surrey's way during these years, he still toiled mostly in his father's shadow. They both escorted Princess **Mary** Tudor to France in 1514 for her wedding and put down the **"evil" May Day riots** in London in 1517. As his father aged and Surrey finally began directing his own affairs, however, the successes of his earlier career under Henry VIII started to elude him. He was unable to pacify warring Irish factions as lord deputy of Ireland between 1520 and 1521, and he authorized a few raids and an ill-fated blockade of the Breton coast during King Henry's second **French invasion of 1523–24**. After his father's death in May 1524, the younger Thomas Howard (already 51 himself) became the third Duke of Norfolk and claimed the office of lord treasurer as well, both dignities that made him one of the wealthiest and most powerful men in England.

Having inherited the senior Howard's titles, offices, and lands, the new Duke of Norfolk also took up his father's dispute with **Thomas Cardinal Wolsey**, the Tudor king's chief minister and lord chancellor. Part of Norfolk's hatred of Wolsey sprang from the cardinal's campaign

in 1521 to discredit and execute Howard's father-in-law, **Edward Stafford**, the third Duke of Buckingham. Wolsey also reassigned such offices as earl marshal and lord admiral, once held by Howards, to his own favorites or to other clients of the House of Tudor. Exasperated, an indignant Norfolk finally isolated himself on his estates between 1525 and 1528 to avoid Henry's pushy chief minister. When his niece Anne Boleyn (the daughter of his sister Elizabeth Howard Boleyn) caught the roving eye of the king, however, the duke returned to court to bask in the glow of royal favor once more.

When Wolsey failed to secure the papal marriage annulment King Henry needed to set aside his first queen, **Katherine of Aragon**, the cardinal's fall from grace and death in 1529–30 opened the door for Norfolk and his Boleyn allies to take his place. The duke quickly took over leadership of the royal council, acquired multiple new properties, and reclaimed his father's old office of earl marshal by the time King Henry had "divorced" Queen Katherine and married Anne Boleyn in 1533.

Thomas Howard's reign at the pinnacle of the Tudor regime only lasted as long as Henry's love for Queen Anne, which was already beginning to fade by 1535. When Anne was accused of treasonous infidelity, her uncle was forced to preside at her trial, pronounce the sentence of death against her, and attend her execution in May 1536. Norfolk briefly managed to regain Henry VIII's favor when he suppressed the **Pilgrimage of Grace** revolt between 1536 and 1537. A religious conservative, however, Norfolk also found himself at odds during these years with the archbishop of Canterbury, Thomas Cranmer, and the ascendant Thomas Cromwell, King Henry's new chief minister and his vicegerent in spirituals. These men had been busy between 1536 and 1539 introducing Lutheran-style changes into the Church of England, reforms that disturbed the Duke of Norfolk and his ally Stephen Gardiner, the bishop of Winchester. In response, Norfolk and Gardiner authored and then persuaded the House of Commons to pass the **Act of Six Articles** in 1539, which restored many Roman Catholic doctrines on the sacraments and salvation to the English Church. Cromwell sealed his own fate when he arranged Henry VIII's marriage with **Anne of Cleves**, a woman the Tudor king found so unappealing he had their union annulled only six months later. Cromwell was attainted of treason by the House of Lords for this egregious misstep and died on the block in July 1540.

The Duke of Norfolk and the bishop of Winchester now presided over a conservative religious reaction that largely restored the teachings and ceremonies of the Roman Church to England but did not bring back the pope, the **monasteries**, or the old Latin Bible. Norfolk fell further from grace when another of his nieces, Katherine Howard, was briefly married to King Henry but was (like Queen Anne) beheaded for treasonous adultery in 1542. Henry VIII's sixth and final wife, Queen Katherine Parr, favored the evangelical faith of the continental reformers, but when Norfolk and Gardiner tried to bring charges of heresy against her, she threw herself on the mercy of her royal husband, and he chose to forgive her.

Though hardly guilty of such charges himself, Norfolk was accused of treason in late 1546 when his son Henry Howard, the Earl of Surrey, allegedly emblazoned the royal insignia on his own family arms. Surrey was executed in mid-January 1547, leaving his father to await the same fate in the Tower of London. Before the elder Howard's sentence could be carried out, however, King Henry VIII died on 28 January 1547, thus sparing Norfolk's life with the customary pardon of royal succession. The old duke remained in the tower during the reign of King Henry's son **Edward VI**, was released with the 1553 accession of Catholic Queen **Mary I**, but then died the following year at his estate of Kenninghall Manor at age 81.

HUNNE, RICHARD (c. 1480–1514). This prosperous London artisan challenged the greed of the **clergy** and the power of church courts in England during the early years of Henry VIII's reign. When Hunne became embroiled in a legal dispute with his parish priest, the ecclesiastical authorities arrested and locked him away in prison, where he was later found hanged in his cell. Because many believed he had been murdered, the Hunne affair turned into a cause célèbre that inspired protests against the Roman Church across the capital. In the end, this episode gave voice to the deep-seated anticlericalism that then gripped many English believers and indirectly led to a resurgence of the **Lollard** heresy and (eventually) to general acceptance of a complete break with Rome during the **Henrician Reformation**.

Almost nothing is known of Richard Hunne's early life except that he was a successful tailor and merchant, earned an income of some £600 per annum, and lived with his family along Bridge Street in the parish of St. Mary Malfellow in London. He also was probably a closet Lollard, one who deeply resented clerical corruption and who longed to read the Scriptures in English translation as well. In 1511, Hunne put his newborn child out to nurse in nearby Whitechapel, but the baby suddenly died at the tender age of just five weeks. The parson of Malfellow, Thomas Dryffeld, duly performed the infant's burial and then (as was customary) demanded the deceased child's fancy linen christening gown as his funeral fee. When the grief-stricken Hunne refused to hand over the garment, Dryffeld waited over a year before bringing suit against the recalcitrant tailor in the consistory court of Richard Fitzjames, the bishop of London, whose clerical judges naturally found for the unpaid priest. Now more outraged than ever, Hunne countersued Dryffeld early in 1513 in the Court of King's Bench for violating the 14th-century statute of praemunire, which set limits on the jurisdiction of all church institutions in England.

As tensions mounted and with Hunne's case stalled in the royal court, Bishop Fitzjames ordered his vicar general, William Horsey, to ransack the tailor's home for incriminating evidence of heretical Lollard beliefs. After the search turned up a Wycliffite Bible in English, the bishop had Hunne arrested, interrogated, and finally jailed on 2 December 1514 in the so-called Lollard's Tower (later named for Hunne) within the precincts of Old St. Paul's Cathedral in London. There the accused heretic languished until an assistant jailer discovered Hunne's limp body hanging from a cell beam by his own belt, just two days after his incarceration in the prison. Embarrassed, Bishop Fitzjames announced that the deceased tailor had committed suicide, although most Londoners—as well as a coroner's jury assembled to investigate the matter—placed blame for the crime on either William Horsey or the prison's chief jailer, Charles Joseph. In an attempt to sidestep the growing scandal, Fitzjames had a public sermon preached against the "sinful" Hunne, pronounced him guilty of doctrinal "error," and then had his remains exhumed and burned as an unrepentant heretic five days before Christmas.

The assumed cover-up of Hunne's murder, along with the ill treatment of his body and family (his children were disinherited), only enflamed public indignation further and forced King Henry VIII to call out his yeoman guards to keep the peace in the capital. Horsey and Joseph were both indicted for murder in spring 1515, but protected by Bishop Fitzjames, they claimed benefit of clergy, which allowed them to avoid a trial in a royal or municipal court. The Hunne affair was not soon forgotten in London and the south of England, awakening new interest in heretical Lollard ideas that eventually became open hostility toward the Roman Church itself. Thanks in part to Richard Hunne and the ecclesiastical misconduct he exposed, far more English believers were willing to accept King Henry's break with Rome when it finally came in the 1530s.

I

INNS OF COURT (c. 1150–). Although the name suggests hostelries or taverns, these four London institutions were essentially colleges of law that educated clerks and attorneys for legal careers or Crown service during the late-medieval and Tudor periods. They differed from **Oxford** and **Cambridge Universities** in that they offered courses in English common law that were taught in "legal French," while the universities granted degrees in civil or canon law and taught those courses in Latin. Many prominent Tudor personalities, such as **Edmund Dudley**, **Thomas Audley**, **Richard Rich**, **Thomas Wriothesley**, and (most notably) Sir **Thomas More**, studied English law at the Inns of Court, training that ultimately prepared them to serve the Tudor government as diplomats, lawyers, members of **Parliament**, and royal ministers.

The origins of the Inns of Court in London are difficult to pin down, though they likely got their start in the 12th century as true inns or hostels where barristers (certified lawyers) could stay while arguing cases in the royal courts of Westminster. Members of the **clergy** originally taught law courses in London, until a 13th-century papal bull prohibited priests from offering legal instruction outside the confines of the universities. Lay barristers then took over law courses and taught them in "legal French," a strange holdover from the days of William the Conqueror, when all military, diplomatic, and especially legal matters were addressed in the language of the occupying Normans.

By the turn of the 16th century, the four Inns of Court in London included Gray's Inn, Lincoln's Inn, the Inner Temple, and the Middle Temple. Each of these schools took in the most promising students from preparatory institutions known as the Inns of Chancery. Much of what we know about the early-Tudor-era inns comes to us from Sir John Fortescue, whose 1470 *De laudibus legum anglie* (*Concerning the Glories of English Law*) describes the nature of the four law colleges themselves, along with the curriculum and style of instruction offered by each of them. Fees to study at the inns were expensive, Fortescue tells us, thus limiting the number of students who could attend all four schools to around 400 in any given year.

New pupils, called apprentices (typically around 16 years of age), first learned music, history, Scripture, virtuous behavior, and good manners at the Inns of Chancery, lessons intended to support and enhance potential careers in law and government later in life. At the Inns of Court, early education in English law began with the study of parliamentary statutes, the legal French language, and selected precedent cases. Tuition continued with reading and discussion—in simulated or moot courts—of more complicated legal principles and procedures as contained in a vast set of "Year Book" case records. Law students also attended the morning hearings or pleadings of the several courts in Westminster Hall that comprised the English **judicial** system and debated what they had heard in their moot sessions when they returned to the inns. A complete legal education lasted from four to eight years, depending on the ability of the pupil, who was then called to the bar (from the Latin *barrae*, or bench) to be examined by a group of senior governors of the inns called masters of the bench or benchers. If he passed this examination, the successful candidate was admitted to the bar and became a full-fledged member or barrister of the Inn of Court he had attended.

Lincoln's Inn was established in 1422 according to the so-called black books of benchers' meeting minutes, although tradition holds that Henry de Lacey, the third Earl of Lincoln, built a residence and school for lawyers next to **Westminster Palace** in the late 13th century. Sir Thomas More was educated at Lincoln's Inn and, as Henry VIII's lord chancellor between 1529 and 1532, was easily its most prestigious barrister during the early-Tudor age. The Inner and Middle Temples were located on the banks of the Thames River at the site of the headquarters of the Knights Templar (hence their names), a **monastic** crusading order, and were originally intended as residences for lawyers serving the legal needs of the knights themselves. When the Templars were dissolved in 1314, the Knights of St. John acquired the properties, and when Henry VIII closed England's monasteries in the late 1530s, the Inner and Middle Temples emerged as independent law schools governed by their own councils of benchers. Gray's Inn was likely founded as early as 1370 on the site of Lord Reynold de Gray's townhouse in London, although there is no written record of its existence prior to 1437. Eventually acquired by the **Carthusian** monks of Sheen Priory, Gray's Inn also became an independent school of law when King Henry completed his dissolution of the **monasteries** in 1539. Although the preparatory Inns of Chancery have all disappeared, the Inns of Court survive today and represent one of the most distinguished groups of law schools to be found anywhere in the world.

IRELAND (c. 1487–1547). When Henry VIII became king of England, he also inherited the title Lord of Ireland from his father and their Plantagenet ancestors. The island country was strategically important to the second Tudor king, and he contemplated its complete conquest, its colonization by English settlers, and the exploitation of its landed resources from time to time during his reign. As he courted **Anne Boleyn** and tried to make her his second queen, Henry granted the wealthy Irish Lordship of Ormond to her father, **Thomas Boleyn**. Following the defeat of the "Silken Thomas" revolt in 1534–35 and acceptance of the Henrician supremacy by several Irish bishops a few years later, King Henry tried to dissolve the **monasteries** in Ireland but could not succeed to the extent he did in England. By the time of his death in 1547, Henry VIII had proclaimed himself king of Ireland, not just its lord, a title he then passed on to his royal children and to his Stuart and even Georgian successors.

Before the arrival of Anglo-Norman interlopers from England in the 12th century, Ireland supported an ethnically diverse population of indigenous inhabitants, later Celtic settlers, and early-medieval Norse colonists. Ireland was by the 11th century divided up among several petty chieftains who routinely fought one another for the right to exercise limited sovereignty or high kingship over all the others. In the 1160s, one of those Irish kings recruited a force of knights in neighboring England to help fight his rivals, but many of those Anglo-Norman recruits remained in Ireland or returned after a few years to claim lands for themselves near Dublin and Wexford.

Significantly, more English immigrants arrived in Ireland over the ensuing centuries to carve out additional estates and build castles and towns, and over time, they intermarried with the resident Irish and adopted their culture. When King Richard II (1377–1400) raised "wild Irish" troops to help recover his lost throne in 1399, their presence in England aroused great hostility, and most of his warriors deserted him. A century later, **Henry VII**, the first Tudor king, faced and defeated an attempted coup d'état in 1487 led by the imposter Lambert Simnel, whose campaign to seize the English throne was based in Ireland. Now concerned about potential threats from his Irish "back door," King Henry sent Sir Edward Poynings to pacify the island and then enlisted the powerful eighth Earl of Kildare, Gerald Mór FitzGerald, to rule Ireland as his regal lord deputy.

Henry VIII acceded to the English throne in 1509, and he confirmed Kildare's appointment the following year, but when the old earl died in 1513, the office of Irish lord deputy passed without incident to his son Gerald Óg FitzGerald, the ninth Earl of Kildare. The new Tudor king soon became suspicious of the younger Kildare and, summoning him to London and holding him there under house arrest, sent **Thomas Howard**, the Earl of Surrey and later the third Duke of Norfolk to Dublin with 1,100 soldiers in 1520 to serve as an English lord deputy of Ireland. Because Surrey was unable to bend all the Irish chieftains to his will, King Henry recalled him in 1522 and sent Kildare back two years later to resume his former office. Around the same time, the English king was falling in love with Anne Boleyn, and wishing to elevate her father to the Irish peerage, he forced the Earl of Ormond, Piers Butler, to surrender his title to Boleyn in 1529 and accept the lesser dignity of Earl of Ossory in its place.

With the new Earl of Ormond representing his interests in Ireland and again suspicious of the powerful Earl of Kildare, Henry VIII ordered the latter to England in 1534, where the Tudor king had him locked away in the **Tower of London**. Before he left Ireland, Kildare appointed his impetuous young son Thomas FitzGerald, Lord Offaly, to serve as a stand-in lord deputy during his absence. Offaly, known to contemporaries as "Silken Thomas" for his extravagant style of dress, heard a rumor in June 1534 that his father had been executed in the tower. This distressing news prompted him to renounce his allegiance to Henry VIII and take possession of most of the land area (the Pale) around Dublin. Few native Irishmen rallied to his cause, however, and after his castle at Maynooth was sacked by the English in March 1535, Lord Offaly surrendered himself to the mercy of King Henry seven months later. No mercy was shown to the rebel lord, for he suffered a grisly traitor's death at Tyburn with five of his compatriots in February 1537.

In the meantime, Henry VIII's efforts to annul his first marriage in order to wed Mistress Boleyn, euphemistically known to his subjects as the **"Great Matter,"** had caused the king to split away from Rome and declare himself the supreme head of the Church of England. Eager to extend his new religious establishment to Ireland, King Henry appointed an English archbishop of Dublin, George Brown, when the Irish incumbent John Allen died in 1536. The new primate of Dublin convinced most of the other Irish bishops in 1537 to accept Henry VIII's supremacy over the Irish Church as well, and then led efforts to shutter Ireland's 400 monasteries. This last measure faced stiff resistance from native Irish believers, and in the end, only half the religious houses were closed and parceled out as bribes to secure oaths of loyalty to the English Crown. In 1541, King Henry finally discarded the title Lord of Ireland and replaced it with king to reflect his elevated status as the island's true sovereign and the ruling head of its church.

ISABEL OF CASTILE. *See* FERDINAND OF ARAGON (1452–1516) AND ISABEL I OF CASTILE (1451–1504), KING AND QUEEN OF SPAIN (r. 1474–1516).

J

JAMES IV, KING OF SCOTLAND (1473–1513; r. 1488–1513). This ill-fated Scottish ruler led his kingdom from remote obscurity to a position of geopolitical relevance, both in the British Isles and on the Continent, during the early-Tudor age. King James patronized the "new learning" of the Renaissance, added to Scotland's military assets, and reduced the power of the restive Scottish lairds (**nobles**) and the semiautonomous clans they ruled. When he married **Margaret** Tudor, the daughter of **Henry VII** and sister of Henry VIII, he forged a relationship with his southern neighbor that eventually saw his Stuart great-grandson inherit the English throne when the House of Tudor failed in 1603. James IV also renewed the "Auld (Old) Alliance" with France that brought his realm back into conflict with England, resulting in his untimely death at the Battle of **Flodden** in September 1513.

Prince James Stuart (alternately Stewart) was born the eldest son of King James III (r. 1460–88) and his queen, Margaret of Denmark, at Stirling Castle on the edge of the Scottish Highlands on 17 March 1473. The Danish queen supervised the upbringing of Prince James and his two younger brothers at Stirling and at Holyrood Palace in Edinburgh, where the boys studied the latest ideas of Renaissance humanism from Italy and the Continent. When an English army threatened Scotland and captured the border town of Berwick in 1482, many of the kingdom's most powerful lairds rebelled against the autocratic James III and briefly placed him under house arrest. Six years later, another group of barons rose up against the unpopular Stuart king and, proclaiming the 15-year-old Prince James their true sovereign lord, defeated and killed his father at the Battle of Sauchieburn on 11 June 1488. The new king of Scots felt guilty for his part in his father's overthrow and death, however, and was slow to declare his majority and take up the reins of power for himself. Instead, he was content with hunting, his mistresses, and his books and allowed the Earl of Angus and the bishop of Aberdeen to rule in his name, until he finally asserted himself and seized control of the government at age 22 in 1495.

The young man who now ruled as King James IV of Scots was an enthusiastic proponent of the *studia humanitatis*, with a goodly command of six European languages and a keen interest in history, literature, the law, and science. James IV founded colleges at St. Andrew's and Aberdeen Universities, established the Royal College of Surgeons in Edinburgh, and even tried his own hand at dentistry and some simple surgical procedures. Fascinated by the sea and the military prospects it offered, the Scottish king built up his navy by installing dry-dock facilities at Newhaven and ordering construction of the *Great Michael*, reputedly the largest warship afloat at that time. He was also a ready student of gunnery who commissioned the casting of dozens of new artillery pieces for his army and who brought his grandfather's gigantic Mons Meg cannon back into service in the late 1490s. Thus stoutly armed, King James took up the cause of Perkin Warbeck, the Flemish royal imposter, and twice invaded his southern neighbor in support of the pretender's claim to the English throne. On the second such incursion, the king of Scots laid siege to the frontier stronghold of Norham Castle in August 1497 but was forced to withdraw when **Richard Fox**, the prince bishop of Durham, anticipated the attack and fortified the place to withstand the big Scottish guns.

In addition to his military interests, James IV was a legal reformer who repealed obsolete statutes, appointed more responsible judges, and brought clan courts more strictly under royal control. He patronized the work of such Scottish poets as William Dunbar, Walter Kennedy, and Robert Henryson, and he set up his kingdom's first printing press in Edinburgh in 1507. Outwardly pious, the king often voiced his desire to go on pilgrimage or lead a crusade, but he never fulfilled any of these ambitions. And while he wore a self-mortifying iron cilice on the anniversary of his father's death each year, he cynically appointed his teenaged bastard son to the vacant archbishopric of St. Andrew in 1497. Curiously, King James isolated two infant boys with a mute nurse to determine if language is inborn or learned, and he was obsessed with alchemical recipes and experiments he hoped might transform base metals into gold.

Perhaps most notably, James IV was a skilled diplomat who negotiated treaties of support and friendship with England and France, his two most powerful neighbors in Britain and on the Continent. Working with Richard Fox, now the bishop of Winchester, King James signed a Treaty of Perpetual Peace with the English in 1502 to reduce the seemingly endless conflicts that constantly plagued their mutual border. After James agreed to seal the treaty by marrying Margaret Tudor, the teenaged daughter of King Henry VII of England, the two young royals were duly wed in a lavish ceremony at Holyrood Abbey in Edinburgh on 8 August 1503. A few years later, the king of Scots also convinced the French king **Louis XII** to renew their "Auld Alliance," a mutual defense pact that obligated each monarch to aid the other in case of attack by a third party.

That attack came when King Henry VIII launched his **French invasion of 1513–14,**

leaving James IV with a difficult choice: either honor the peace with England or support his "auld" ally King Louis. Ignoring the pleas of his English queen, James mobilized some 30,000 troops and 17 artillery pieces and crossed into Northumbria in August 1513 to divert English forces away from King Henry's French campaign. **Thomas Howard**, the Earl of Surrey and future second Duke of Norfolk, met the northern invaders with 26,000 men of his own at a place called Flodden Field on 9 September. The English attacked with longbows and their deadly halberd pikes, leaving thousands of Scottish warriors dead or dying on the blood-soaked field when darkness fell and the fighting finally stopped. Amid the carnage lay the broken and naked corpse of King James IV of Scots, a casualty of his heroic but foolhardy decision to command his troops in the battle himself. Following the devastating defeat at Flodden, James's widow and some of the kingdom's ranking lairds were left to rule an enfeebled Scotland as regents for the dead king's child successor, **James V**. Rumors have persisted that James IV somehow survived the slaughter at Flodden and lived on for three more years in a dungeon at Roxburgh Castle, but the evidence that supports this claim is overwhelmingly circumstantial in nature.

JAMES V, KING OF SCOTLAND (1512–42; r. 1513–42).

This short-lived Scottish king was the nephew of Henry VIII of England, the father of Mary Queen of Scots, and the grandfather of James VI of Scots, who eventually inherited the Crown of England from King Henry's daughter **Elizabeth I** in 1603. Acceding to the Scottish throne as an infant, James V grew up amid a tug of war between pro-French and pro-English **noble** factions to declare his majority and seize control of the Scottish government himself at the age of 15 years. King James effectively suppressed the unruly frontier bandits along his southern border, remained a loyal though self-serving son of the Roman Church, and extended Scotland's "Auld (Old) Alliance" with France by twice marrying French princesses. Relations with his Tudor uncle gradually deteriorated in the early 1540s, leading to an English invasion, a Scottish counterattack, and a complete rout of James's army at Solway Moss. The king of Scots suffered an emotional breakdown in the wake of this devastating defeat and died one week after the birth of his daughter Mary in mid-December 1542.

James Stuart was born to King **James IV** of Scots and his consort, Queen **Margaret**, the older sister of King Henry VIII of England, at Linlithgow Palace in West Lothian, Scotland, on 10 April 1512. Little James never came to know his father, for the king of Scots was killed in battle at **Flodden** in September 1513, leaving his infant son—now King James V— and the boy's English mother to exercise what royal authority they could over a shattered Scottish kingdom. Just more than a year after her first husband's death, the dowager queen impulsively (and many thought indecently) married Archibald Douglas, the third Earl of Angus. This sudden turn of events brought John Stuart, a cousin of the dead king and the second Duke of Albany, back from his estates in France to snatch away the regency over young King James for himself.

Meanwhile, during his early years, the boy-king of Scots split time between the royal residences of Stirling, Linlithgow, and Holyrood in Edinburgh, where he acquired a kingly education under the tutelage of the noted diplomat, humanist, and poet Sir David Lyndsay. As he grew older, his mother and her second husband (who favored improved relations with England) competed with the pro-French Duke of Albany for control of the youthful Scottish king. When Albany finally retired permanently to France and the dowager queen obtained a papal divorce from Angus to remarry again, King James declared his majority in 1528 and took personal control of his dominions for the first time.

Now determined to assert his independence as Scotland's king, James V forced his stepfather, Angus, into exile in England and had several members of the earl's family arrested and executed. In 1529, he led a punitive raid into the southwestern marcher (frontier) country, where he met and then suddenly hanged one of the most powerful border lords,

Johnnie Armstrong, in a ruthless demonstration of his royal authority. King James also kept a close watch on royal finances, tightening collection of customs dues and demanding the maximum possible rent revenues from his many estates. Despite pressure from England, James remained true to the Roman Church and actively persecuted Lutherans and later members of the Church of England as heretics. When Pope **Clement VII** granted him the right to appoint his own bishops, the cynical king of Scots installed a few of his bastard sons in selected Scottish dioceses and then siphoned off their episcopal incomes to help replenish his royal treasury.

King James V also possessed a somewhat more humane quality that at times seemed to balance the crueler and more self-aggrandizing aspects of his character. For instance, he enjoyed disguising himself as a farmer and wandering among the common folk of his realm, an activity that earned him a reputation as the "poor man's king" from contemporaries and later historians alike. James reportedly wrote poetry and played the lute with some skill and employed Scottish, French, and Italian musicians to play at royal **pageants**, masques, and balls. He extensively renovated palaces like Linlithgow, Falkland, Stirling, and Holyrood, incorporating the latest Renaissance designs and furnishing each residence with rich tapestries inherited from his father. In 1536–37, the king of Scots traveled to Paris to wed Princess Madeleine Valois, the daughter of King **François I**, but the girl suffered from consumption (tuberculosis) and died within weeks of her arrival in Scotland. Anxious to maintain the "Auld Alliance" with France, the Scottish king next married Marie de Guise, the daughter of the duc de Guise and the recent widow of the duc d'Orléans, both close relatives of the French king. Queen Marie bore James V two sons— both of whom died in infancy—before giving birth to their daughter, Mary, soon to become queen of Scots upon the death of her father one week later.

Thus confirmed in his "Auld Alliance" with France, and by 1540, styling himself Lord of Ireland, King James seemed hell-bent on provoking his uncle Henry VIII, who hated the French and had recently taken the title king of the Irish for himself. The English king also demanded that James break with the Roman Church and, when the king of Scots refused, proposed a meeting between the two monarchs in York in September 1541 to discuss the matter. King Henry traveled to York at the appointed time, but his Scottish counterpart did not show up, further enraging the Tudor ruler and prompting him to begin planning a large-scale invasion of Scotland within the year. A sizable English force under border warden Sir Robert Bowes and the exiled Earl of Angus mustered in summer 1542 along the Scottish marches, but when these troops crossed into Scotland at Hadden Rig on 24 August, they were repulsed with heavy losses by an army of Scottish clansmen under the command of the Earl of Huntly.

King James was now the aggrieved party and tried to raise a retaliatory invasion force of his own, but his heavy-handed treatment of many of his border subjects served to limit the number of recruits willing to answer his call to arms. Undaunted, Robert Lord Maxwell and Sir Oliver Sinclair (a favorite of King James) led what troops they could gather across the Solway River in late November 1542. Maxwell and Sinclair quarreled, however, and their small force met with disaster when more than 2,000 of their soldiers were slaughtered by English defenders or drowned in the Solway while trying to flee. King James was ill and was not present at the battle, but when he heard the news of the great defeat at Solway Moss, he suffered some sort of nervous collapse. Having lost the will to live at this point, James V of Scotland died of reported melancholy on 14 December 1542, just seven days after the birth of his baby daughter, Mary, the future queen of Scots. The Scottish king drew his last breath at Falkland Palace, but his remains were interred at Holyrood Abbey in Edinburgh next to the tomb of his first wife, Madeleine Valois.

JOUSTING TOURNAMENTS (1066–1600 AND BEYOND). Originally a friendly martial contest between medieval warriors, the joust

later came to symbolize the knightly code of chivalry and offered participants the opportunity to show off their courage, horsemanship, and skill with an assortment of weapons before an admiring audience. The sport was enthusiastically pursued from the medieval period to the 16th century and beyond, well past the time when gunpowder weapons had rendered protective armor on real battlefields mostly obsolete. Jousting was one of King Henry VIII's favorite pastimes; he presided over and took part in many such warlike demonstrations over the course of his reign, and as a muscular, vigorous, and fearless athlete (especially during his younger years), the Tudor monarch often prevailed in these contests against all comers. The sport could also be very dangerous, however, and courtiers worried about King Henry's safety on more than one occasion. When a serious tiltyard accident left him unconscious for several hours in 1536, he woke up angry and fearful and never entered the lists as a jousting knight again.

The sport of jousting probably first came to England with the Norman invaders of King William I in the mid-11th century. The word *joust* derives from the Latin *iuxtere* and thence from the French *joster*, meaning to meet or to cross. Jousts, or mock combats between two heavily armored, mounted knights, were originally warm-up events to the main spectacle of the tournament, the mêlée, a free-for-all battle staged between two groups of warriors on foot. Gradually, the jousting portion of the tourney began to overshadow the mêlée as the featured event by the late 13th century because the mounted combatants were often famous knights or high-ranking **nobles** who drew larger and more prestigious crowds of spectators to their individualized contests. Sometimes elimination events called round tables were conducted in which knights who were victorious in early rounds moved on to face other victors until just one champion remained on the field. Jousting success could win much fame and, perhaps on occasion, the hand of an aristocratic maiden, but cash prizes were also offered, and many a brave knight made his fortune besting his opponents in the jousting tiltyard.

Jousting tourneys took place in open spaces known as lists, fields that were cordoned off from spectator areas with ropes or low walls. The principal mode of combat in jousts involved mounting a powerful warhorse, or destrier, and clad in a protective suit of armor and helm, the knight then charged his opponent at full speed with leveled lance to unhorse or otherwise disable him in an action known as tilting. Some jousts also featured three rounds of fighting using different weapons in each round. Early tournament participants wore chainmail armor with solid round helmets, but by 1400, knights entered the lists completely covered by a suit of plate armor called harness and were armed not only with several lances but cudgels, swords, and axes as well. Because the object of the joust was not to kill or maim but to unhorse or incapacitate, blunt weapons were most often employed, and score was kept by counting the number of wooden lances that one knight shattered against the shields and armor of his opponents.

From the earliest days of jousting contests, the fighters who took part in them were thought to embody the values of chivalry, the Christian code of conduct that required chevaliers, or mounted knights, to protect the weak and battle their adversaries fairly and with honor. With the emergence of vernacular tales and the wandering troubadours who put them to verse and song, the courageous knight winning great jousting victories in the tiltyards of Europe became the featured hero of the chansons de geste and chivalric romances that entertained noble audiences from the late 12th century onward.

King Henry VIII was obsessed with the joust and held many tournaments during his reign, including one major jousting event each year on the anniversary of his accession as king. Because Henry also loved ostentatious display, he often combined jousting tourneys with **pageants** that, set on rolling stages or floats, featured mock settings, fabricated buildings, costumed performers, and much chivalric symbolism. King Henry thus opened a celebratory jousting event in 1511 with a splendid pageant and then ran dozens of courses

(charges) and broke nearly 20 lances while wearing an original silver-and-gold-trimmed armor specially made for the occasion. His royal councilors and his queens were often greatly concerned lest the king be gravely or even fatally injured in these violent clashes, as once occurred in 1524, when Henry almost lost an eye while jousting with his close friend **Charles Brandon**, the Duke of Suffolk.

The Tudor king's most serious jousting accident occurred on 24 January 1536, when, at age 44 and overweight, he crashed heavily to earth following a lance strike and was then trapped beneath his huge, armored warhorse. King Henry was unconscious for two hours and seemed as if he might be dead, but he did eventually recover to the great relief of tournament officials and royal councilors alike. The injuries the king suffered very likely aggravated his badly ulcerated leg, however, and may well have caused a brain injury that in turn profoundly affected the royal personality. Once genial, generous, and even sentimental at times, Henry VIII awoke from his tiltyard fall a distrustful and vindictive man whose famous temper was even more sudden and explosive than before. Within five days of the accident, Queen **Anne Boleyn** miscarried a male fetus aged about 16 weeks, an event that, coupled with the king's tempestuous new disposition, marked the beginning of the end for his second wife and queen.

JUDICIARY (1178–1600 AND BEYOND). The English judicial system under King Henry VIII was an archaic and confusing collection of courts. whose powers and jurisdictions often overlapped and in some cases even cancelled each other out. Established for the most part in the Middle Ages, the basic common law courts were over time augmented by mobile circuit tribunals and then by shire courts presided over by justices of the peace. King **Henry VII** also transformed his royal council into a high court of sorts, while **Parliament** was frequently called on as well, to attaint traitors and confiscate their estates to the Crown. In addition, the Tudor kings could appoint special commissions to raise troops or try rebel leaders in times of crisis, while rural districts maintained manor courts to rule on landholding, inheritance, and field-rotation issues. Finally, such royal ministers as **Thomas Cardinal Wolsey** and **Thomas Cromwell** created new courts to provide speedier justice to commoners and receive diverted ecclesiastical revenues during the reign of Henry VIII.

The fundamental royal courts of England operated on the principle of common law, which drew on earlier legal precedents to inform and decide later comparable cases. The Courts of King's Bench and Common Pleas can be traced back to the reign of King Henry II and were originally presided over by the king himself or by judges he appointed from his Curia Regis, or royal council. King's Bench primarily heard criminal cases, while Common Pleas dealt with civil disputes involving property or land ownership. The Court of the Exchequer, also a late-12th-century arm of the Curia Regis, was a financial committee charged with revenue collection oversight and the prosecution of tax dodgers. The Court of Chancery came into being during the 14th century as an appellate court that could overturn harsh King's Bench or Common Pleas decisions and also try petitions brought against the Crown itself. Because common law courts at **Westminster** were difficult and expensive to access, medieval assize (sitting) judges from King's Bench, Common Pleas, and the Exchequer rode out from London twice each year to bring royal justice to the countryside. These biannual assizes used juries to resolve cases and summoned men of good character to serve on them with calls to "hear and determine," or oyer and terminer.

Another level of the judiciary existed in rural counties across England and **Wales** in the form of quarter-session courts. As their name implies, these tribunals came together every three months and tended to adjudicate less-serious offenses than those tried by the royal courts or the assizes. First appointed by King Edward III in the early 14th century, justices of the peace were originally local law enforcement officers, but by the 16th century, they presided over quarter sessions as well. Justices were usually men of wealth and influence in their respective shires, and often

calling juries to help determine trial verdicts, they sometimes heard and decided cases less formally in the comfort of their own homes. Quarter sessions were busy courts that were responsible by the end of Henry VIII's reign for upholding the letter and intent of nearly 200 parliamentary statutes. Quarter sessions handled a far greater volume of business than any other legal institution in the realm and were for that reason the courts to which most of King Henry's subjects had most frequent recourse. Typical cases that came before quarter-session courts involved assault and battery, drunken or disorderly conduct, the poaching of game, and the regulation of alehouses, to name just a few.

When military crises or social unrest erupted in Tudor England, the Crown frequently invoked special judicial commissions to deal swiftly and often savagely with the troubles at hand. Threats of war or foreign invasion prompted Henry VIII to form commissions of array (armament) in the counties to raise mercenary companies, feudal levies, provisions, stores, and weaponry for the coming fight. Following popular rebellions, as in the **Pilgrimage of Grace** of 1536–37, the Tudor king also authorized field commissions to try and publicly execute insurgent leaders to help defuse the violence and end the revolt. In addition, Parliament had long served as a high court of justice for members of the **nobility** or for individuals whose misdeeds fell outside the proscriptions of the medieval **Act of Treasons**. In such instances, the House of Lords had the power to attaint these offenders as traitors, which then allowed the Crown to seize their belongings and estates. As added judicial insurance, King Henry VII deputized members of his royal council to pass judgment on high-ranking magnates in his Court of Star Chamber, a Westminster Palace meeting room so named for the painted constellations on its ceiling.

The Tudor regime of Henry VIII was also active in creating its own legal institutions and so left its mark on the judiciary of early-modern England. Thomas Cardinal Wolsey, a man of humble origins himself, was well aware that the English common law courts of his time were corrupt and outside the bribed financial reach of the ordinary plaintiff. In the 1520s, he founded (or perhaps took over and enlarged) the Court of Requests as a "poor man's court" to make quick, inexpensive, and fair justice available to all of King Henry's subjects. Wolsey's successor, Thomas Cromwell, widely regarded as the author of a "revolution in government," established four new courts that operated more as financial repositories than as tribunals of justice. His Courts of Wardship and General Survey took in revenues from Crown feudal concessions and land rents, while the Court of First Fruits and Tenths held episcopal tax receipts following England's 1534 break with the Roman Church. Lastly, Cromwell set up the Court of Augmentations to receive the vast treasure realized from the sale of religious houses during the dissolution of the **monasteries** in the late 1530s. Each of these "banking" courts helped organize Crown financial holdings and featured its own judicial machinery to help enforce revenue collection.

K

KATHERINE OF ARAGON, QUEEN OF ENGLAND (1485–1536). The first wife and queen of Henry VIII, this daughter of Iberian royalty originally married into the House of Tudor as part of a treaty between England and the emergent kingdom of Spain. Queen Katherine was unable to bear a male heir to succeed King Henry, however, which led to his estrangement from her and his amorous pursuit of a court lady named **Anne Boleyn**. The English king ultimately sought to annul his marriage with Katherine in order to wed the younger Boleyn woman and, with her, father the son he had always desired, a series of events that euphemistically came to be known as the king's "**Great Matter**." Queen Katherine was duly cast aside, and Henry married for a second time, but his actions only severed his kingdom from the Roman Church and never did produce his coveted male heir. Katherine of Aragon, relegated after 1533 to the lesser title of dowager princess, lived out her ill-fated life in relative penury and declining health until she died as an exile from court in the English countryside at the age of just 50 years.

Katherine of Aragon was born the youngest surviving child of **Ferdinand and Isabel**, king and queen of Spain, in the archepiscopal palace of Alcalá de Henares outside Madrid on 16 December 1485. As a descendant of the English king Edward III and his son John of Gaunt, Duke of Lancaster, Princess Katherine was a distant relative of both the royal Houses of York and Tudor. Ferdinand and Isabel were constantly on the move, so young Katherine grew up in a variety of palaces, castles, and religious houses and always traveled to each location with a supporting cast of nursemaids, governesses, and tutors. Exposed from infancy to a heavy dose of Roman Catholicism, Katherine also received instruction in Latin, French, history, mathematics, philosophy, theology, and classical literature. In addition, she developed expertise at a young age in the practical royal arts of riding, hunting, music, dancing, and needlework. Katherine, though diminutive as an adult, was a pretty girl who was blessed with a fair complexion, lively blue eyes, and strawberry-blond hair. When she was six, her parents conquered the last Moorish stronghold in southeastern Spain, Granada (pomegranate in translation), a victory that later inspired Katherine to adopt the seedy fruit as her personal insignia.

In 1489, King Ferdinand began negotiations to marry his youngest daughter to the son and heir of **Henry VII** of England, **Arthur**, while both royal children were still just toddlers. The first Tudor king was anxious to legitimize his regime by marrying his children into prestigious ruling families across Europe, while the Spanish monarchs needed allies in their struggle against threatened incursions from France. The resulting Treaty of Medina del Campo initially promised the hand of Katherine to the English prince; in 1497, their betrothal was formalized, and two years later, they entered into marriage, albeit through substitute proxies. Katherine of Aragon finally arrived in England in person early in October 1501, and escorted to London by Crown dignitaries, she married her Tudor fiancé in a sumptuous wedding at

St. Paul's Cathedral some five weeks later. As befitted the Prince of **Wales**, Arthur traveled with his new bride to the Welsh border and took up residence with her at Ludlow Castle. There they lived happily enough for several months, despite Katherine's later claim that their marriage was never properly consummated or thus legally validated. They both fell seriously ill in March 1502, and although his Spanish spouse soon recovered, the teenaged Arthur died on 2 April either from the dreaded **sweating sickness** or more probably from consumption, now known as tuberculosis.

The death of her husband left Katherine of Aragon a youthful dowager princess (widow of the prince), but still new to English ways and weather, she began to beg her father-in-law to send her back to her parents in Spain. The Tudor king was loath to comply, however, for he stood to forfeit the rich wedding dowry King Ferdinand had provided if her request to leave England were granted. When Henry VII's queen consort, **Elizabeth of York**, passed away in 1503, he briefly considered marrying his son's widow himself, but strenuous objections from Spain quickly put a stop to the idea. Instead, King Henry decided to betroth Katherine to his next son, Henry, the new Prince of Wales, who was by this time just 11 years of age and not yet ready for matrimony.

A few years later, in 1505, Prince Henry himself actually recoiled briefly from the idea of marrying his sister-in-law. His objections on this occasion may have been coached by his scheming father, who wished to keep King Ferdinand diplomatically off-balance. For his part, Henry probably believed that marriage to Katherine might violate canon law, for at that time the church condemned unions between men and their sisters-in-law as incestuous. When the young prince finally overcame his concerns, his father applied for and obtained a papal dispensation of incest (based on Deuteronomy 25:5) to allow his surviving son to take as his wife the widow of his deceased son. When Henry VIII became king in April 1509, he married Katherine of Aragon in a private chapel near **Greenwich Palace** and then shared a lavish coronation ceremony with her in Westminster Abbey two months later.

Though separated in age by six years, Henry and Katherine became close friends and even grew to love each other over the course of their early marriage together. The young king trusted his Spanish consort so completely that he left her to rule England in his place as regent while he was abroad leading his **French invasion of 1513–14**. Queen Katherine justified his trust on this occasion by keeping her husband informed of developments at home and by sending an army north under **Thomas Howard**, the Earl of Surrey and later the second Duke of Norfolk, to defeat a Scottish invasion at **Flodden** in September 1513.

A devoted daughter of the Church of Rome, Katherine of Aragon was widely known for her frequent visits to English **shrines** at Walsingham, Oxford, and Glastonbury. She also spent long hours praying each day for the health of her Spanish and English relations; for the success of King Henry's policies and campaigns; and for the conception, healthy pregnancy, and safe delivery of the many children she hoped to give her husband and the kingdom.

Queen Katherine was pregnant six times between 1510 and 1518, but only one child, a princess, survived to adulthood. The queen was first with child soon after her royal wedding and coronation, but the infant girl was stillborn at the end of January 1510. The following May, Katherine was pregnant again, and this time a prince was born, christened, and actually lived for 52 days before he, too, expired from some sort of abdominal ailment in February 1511. Two years later, the Spanish queen was again with child, but the pregnancy coincided with her regency during Henry's French invasion, and she delivered another stillborn child just one week after the great English victory over the Scots at Flodden. After a fourth pregnancy resulted in yet another stillbirth early in 1515, Queen Katherine finally delivered a healthy baby daughter, **Mary** Tudor, on 18 February 1516. Following a miscarriage in 1517, a final pregnancy in 1518 produced a living baby girl, but the child was sickly and passed away within a few hours of her birth.

Katherine of Aragon had thus failed in her most important duty as queen: to provide a male heir to follow her husband on the English throne and carry on the Tudor line of succession. As his Spanish consort neared her 40th year without any new pregnancies, King Henry began to despair of ever having the son and heir he believed was essential to avoid a repeat of the bloody **Wars of the Roses** in the previous century. Ever the lusty philanderer, the king had been enjoying the favors of several mistresses for years—and had even sired children by a few of them—before his roving eye fell on one of Queen Katherine's ladies, a 21-year-old with a French accent and flirtatious style named Anne Boleyn. By 1525–26, Henry was in hot pursuit of Mistress Boleyn, but she refused to share her bed with the king until such time as he might marry her. Thus frustrated, Henry VIII embarked on his "Great Matter" to set aside his first queen in order to marry the younger Anne and with her produce his longed-for male heir.

Accordingly, the English king sent his lord chancellor, **Thomas Cardinal Wolsey**, off to Rome in 1527 to obtain a papal annulment of his marriage to Queen Katherine. The cardinal's pleas were ignored by Pope **Clement VII**, however, who was at that moment the virtual prisoner of Emperor **Charles V**, the nephew of Katherine of Aragon. The pontiff understandably refused Wolsey's petition for the moment and sent him home empty handed, but when Clement obtained his release the next year, he changed his mind and sent his representative **Lorenzo Cardinal Campeggio** to preside with Wolsey over an annulment trial at the Blackfriars monastery outside London in 1529. King Henry and other Crown officials argued that his union with Katherine was null and void because, by Leviticus 20:21, marriages with the widow of one's brother were cursed and barren. Defiantly, Queen Katherine countered with plans to appeal her case to Pope Clement in Rome, which prompted Campeggio to adjourn the court and plunged her short-tempered husband into an uncontrollable rage.

Having thus failed to obtain his desired annulment, Henry VIII became vindictive and turned Queen Katherine out of her rooms at his newly renovated **Whitehall Palace** and installed Anne Boleyn there in her place. Katherine was banished to a modest manor house in Hertfordshire during 1531–32, while her increasingly impatient husband searched for alternate ways to solve his matrimonial difficulties. In quick succession, King Henry had **Parliament** cut off appeals to Rome, appointed **Thomas Cranmer** his new archbishop of Canterbury, had Cranmer annul his union with Katherine, and then made Anne Boleyn his second wife and queen—all during the first half of 1533.

Insisting that her marriage with Prince Arthur had never been consummated, which made her King Henry's true wife and queen all along, Katherine of Aragon was nonetheless demoted to the status of dowager princess, endured ever-worsening living arrangements, and was denied permission to see her only surviving daughter, Mary, ever again. Supported from afar by Sir **Thomas More** and Bishop **John Fisher** of Rochester, her only regular visitor during her last years was the imperial ambassador **Eustace Chapuys**, who secretly carried her letters to family members and other correspondents on the Continent. Transferred to Kimbolton Hall in Huntingdonshire early in 1535, the dowager princess donned rough clothing, fasted on a daily basis, and generally adopted the devotional lifestyle of a cloistered nun. Katherine of Aragon died at Kimbolton on 7 January 1536 and was laid to rest three weeks later in nearby Peterborough Cathedral.

L

LATIMER, HUGH, BISHOP OF WORCESTER
(c. 1488–1555). Hugh Latimer was a passionate preacher and religious reformer who
briefly served the English Church as bishop
of Worcester before his resignation in a crisis
of conscience in 1539. A lifelong member of
the **Cambridge University** community, Latimer
began his clerical career as a committed son
of the Roman Church but eventually embraced
the doctrines of the German reformer Martin
Luther instead. He was an active supporter of
Henry VIII's efforts to annul his first marriage,
yet he often infuriated the king with his radical
criticism of the **clergy** and teachings of Rome.
Hugh Latimer enjoyed wide popularity as an
inspirational preacher under **Edward VI**, but
his evangelical zeal finally led to his arrest and
death at the stake as a heretic during the reign
of the Catholic Queen **Mary I** in October 1555.

Hugh Latimer was born in the village of
Thurcaston near Leicester sometime between
1485 and 1492. His father (name unknown)
was a well-to-do yeoman farmer who employed six laborers, owned more than 100
sheep, and produced £4 worth of arable crops
from his land each year. Young Hugh began his
schooling at the tender age of four and then
enrolled in Clare College at Cambridge University in 1506. There he earned a fellowship
in 1510, took a master's degree in 1514, and
then entered holy orders as a Catholic priest
the next year. In 1524, he completed the bach-
elor of divinity degree by arguing his thesis
disputation against the evangelical teachings
of Martin Luther's protégé Philip Melanchthon.
Describing himself at the time as an "obstinate

papist," Latimer agreed after his disputation
to hear the sacramental confession of the diminutive Cambridge reformer **Thomas Bilney**.
Alone together in the confessional, Bilney apparently persuaded Latimer to reject papal
authority and Catholic doctrines and adopt in
their place the Scripture-based program of the
Lutherans. Thereafter, Latimer became a regular member of the reformist group that met at
the White Horse Inn in Cambridge during the
mid-1520s to discuss the latest theological innovations then trickling into England from the
Continent.

By this time, Latimer was acquiring a
reputation for the passion and provocative
language of his sermons, both rhetorical qualities that in turn attracted the disapproving notice of England's ecclesiastical authorities. In
1525, Bishop Nicholas West of Ely attended
Latimer's service in the Cambridge University
chapel and, shocked by his reformist zeal,
tried to silence the fiery preacher. Latimer
simply took his evangelical beliefs on the road,
delivering sermons on the corruption of the
Roman clergy and the need for English Scriptures whenever the opportunity presented itself. Soon **Thomas Cardinal Wolsey** got wind
of his activities and summoned him to London
late in 1527 to answer for his Lutheran "errors." When Latimer disingenuously denied
any connection to the German reformer or
his doctrines, the cardinal released him with
a warning but also authorized him to continue
preaching in any diocese he wished.

The following year—the same in which
Wolsey himself fell from royal favor—Hugh

Latimer delivered a cynical sermon comparing Christian pursuit of heavenly salvation to an allegorical card game. He won Henry VIII's goodwill, however, by championing the king's attempts to set aside Queen **Katherine of Aragon** in order to wed **Anne Boleyn** in her place. King Henry rewarded the controversial cleric in 1530 by inviting him to preach a sermon before the royal court and by granting him a lucrative rectory in the parish of West Kington in Wiltshire. Latimer managed to retain the king's favor over the next few years despite the scandalous homilies he delivered on the sins of the Blessed Virgin, the falsehood of saints, and the fictional existence of purgatory. In 1533, he was obliged to appear before Bishop **John Stokesley** of London, who forced him to submit to a series of disciplinary injunctions. Still, King Henry continued to patronize Latimer by having him preach several Lenten services in 1534 and then by creating him bishop of Worcester the following year.

During the later 1530s, Hugh Latimer's activities became ever more incendiary. He challenged his fellow prelates in **Convocation of Bishops** to surrender their episcopal wealth to the poor, and he habitually discredited human good works as a legitimate way to attain the Christian afterlife. When the **Pilgrimage of Grace** uprising broke out in Yorkshire and Lincolnshire in 1536–37, the angry Catholic rebels demanded that Latimer be handed over to them as a Protestant enemy of the people. In his diocese, the bishop of Worcester insisted that every parish acquire a copy of the Scriptures in English and ordered his clergy to withhold communion from parishioners who could not recite the Lord's Prayer in English. In 1538, he helped investigate the **shrine** of the Holy Blood of Hailes, a relic purporting to be the preserved blood of Christ that Latimer later exposed as a mere blob of yellowed gum or beeswax.

When Henry VIII restored many Catholic doctrines with the **Act of Six Articles** in 1539, Latimer could not bring himself to support the new religious settlement and resigned his episcopal see in protest. He languished in the household custody of Bishop Richard Sampson of Chichester for a year, then was barred from further preaching in London or in the diocese of Worcester following his release in 1541. Latimer wisely kept a low profile over the next several years but was again arrested as a suspected heretic in the **Anne Askew** affair in 1546 and was imprisoned in the **Tower of London**. The controversial preacher gained his freedom once more, however, when old King Henry died and was succeeded on the throne by his fiercely evangelical son King Edward VI in January 1547.

During the new reign, Hugh Latimer refused to reoccupy his old diocese of Worcester and instead accepted a position as chaplain to Katherine Brandon, the widowed Duchess of Suffolk. He remained active on the preaching circuit as well, delivering sermons on England's lazy and corrupted bishops and on the duty of wealthy magnates to distribute alms to the poor. Leading by example, Latimer became an outspoken member of the so-called commonwealth men between 1547 and 1549. This group of political, economic, and religious reformers worked with **Edward Seymour**, the first Duke of Somerset and royal lord protector, to curtail the destructive practice of **enclosure** that evicted thousands of tenant farmers from their lands each year. Upon the accession of Queen Mary, an ardent daughter of the Roman Church, Latimer was arrested and put on trial in Oxford as a heretic along with fellow reformers Nicholas Ridley, bishop of London, and **Thomas Cranmer**, the archbishop of Canterbury. All three were eventually found guilty, and on 16 October 1555, Latimer and Ridley died together in the flames near Balliol College in Oxford. Their remains were later interred beneath their (and Cranmer's) statues atop the tall neogothic Martyrs' Monument that still stands at the intersection of St. Giles, Magdalen, and Beaumont Streets near the entrance to Balliol College in Oxford.

LEO X, POPE (1475–1521; r. 1513–21).
Born Giovanni de' Medici, the second son of the great Florentine ruler Lorenzo the Magnificent, this Renaissance pope was famous for his extravagant lifestyle, his diplomatic duplicity, his patronage of the arts, and his irresponsible management of papal finances. Martin Luther

touched off the Protestant Reformation during his pontificate, but Leo took little notice at first and then only belatedly reacted with papal censures that were largely ignored. When King Henry VIII condemned Luther's teachings in his *Assertio septem sacramentorum*, or *Defense of the Seven Sacraments*, Pope Leo conferred upon him the honor of *Defensor Fidei*, or Defender of the Faith, a title still claimed by British monarchs today.

Giovanni de' Medici was born on 11 December 1475 to Lorenzo de' Medici, dubbed Il Magnifico for his patronage of art and scholarship in Florence, and his consort, Clarice Orsini, the daughter of a family of cardinals and past popes. As the second son of a great Renaissance magnate, Giovanni acquired an excellent humanist education in classical languages and texts, but he was groomed for service in the church because he stood to inherit no property of his own from his family. He was tonsured (entered into holy orders) at the tender age of 7, was named a cardinal deacon at age 13, and became a cardinal priest at 17. When the Medici were driven from Florence in 1494, young Giovanni spent the next six years traveling in Germany, France, and **Flanders** and then arrived in Rome to accept minor positions in the papal administrations of Alexander VI and Julius II. During these early years in the Eternal City, the precocious Cardinal de' Medici learned to appreciate the wonders of Renaissance painting and sculpture, and he began to test the treacherous waters of international diplomacy and papal court politics as well. In 1512, he helped engineer a Medici return to power in Florence, and now the ranking head of his family, Giovanni assumed effective control over his native city for what remained of his short life.

Pope Julius II died early in 1513 but not before pronouncing a ban on the use of bribes in conclave to win election to the throne of St. Peter. Instead promising to reward his supporters *after* the election, Giovanni de' Medici was duly chosen as the next pontiff and enthroned as Leo X in mid-March 1513. Upon his election, the exuberant new bishop of Rome is said to have exclaimed, "Now that God has given us the Papacy, let us enjoy it!" Leo was fond of feasting and hunting, both activities he pursued passionately but without regard to cost, while his craving to own some of the great masterworks of the Italian Renaissance drove him close to bankruptcy. In addition, the new pontiff inherited membership in the Holy League military alliance from his predecessor, obliging him to spend vast sums defending Italy from France and underwriting King Henry VIII's **French invasion of 1513–14**. When the Medici pope launched his own campaign to conquer Urbino for his nephew Lorenzo in 1516, he emptied what remained in the papal *camera* (treasury) and then borrowed heavily to prevent collapse of his regime.

Desperate at this point to replenish his coffers, Leo X turned a 1517 assassination plot to his own financial advantage by offering pardons to the chief conspirators in return for the payment of enormous fines. He then created 31 new cardinals, all of whom compensated the pope handsomely for the right to wear their crimson hats. Meanwhile, Leo also authorized the sale of a new indulgence (a payment for sin remission) in parts of northern Germany on condition that half the proceeds be remitted to the papacy to help fund construction of the opulent new Basilica of St. Peter in Rome.

It was this last revenue-raising measure that prompted the German monk Martin Luther, a university theologian in Wittenberg, to compose his *95 Theses*, or arguments against indulgence sales, a tract he posted locally in 1517 but soon had printed and distributed all across northern Europe. Perhaps distracted by his profligate lifestyle and political concerns in Florence and the Papal States, Pope Leo at first dismissed Luther's protest as the ranting of a drunken Saxon priest. In 1518, however, he finally took action by ordering Luther's monastic superior, along with the ruler of Saxony, to silence the upstart professor. When both these censorship efforts failed, the irate pope condemned 41 of Luther's teachings as heresy and excommunicated him with the 1520 papal bull *Exsurge domine*. In response, Luther simply burned the bull of excommunication and then published his doctrine of *solafideism*, or salvation by faith alone, in his comprehensive work *On the Freedom of a Christian*.

With little more than a year left to live, the Medici pope was irritated by Luther's religious revolt but seemed not to grasp the full enormity of what it truly meant for Christendom. He was nonetheless pleased when King Henry VIII of England produced his *Assertio septem sacramentorum* in April 1521 to uphold the teachings of the Roman Church against Lutheran dissent. Although the English king claimed full credit for the *Assertio*, it is possible that some of England's finest religious minds—**Thomas Cardinal Wolsey**, Sir **Thomas More**, and Bishop **John Fisher** of Rochester— also had a hand in its composition. In October 1521, Pope Leo named King Henry *Defensor Fidei*, a title granting the same level of papal favor to England's Tudor ruler as already enjoyed by the "Most Catholic" and "Most Christian" majesties of Spain and France. Following a particularly raucous banquet on the evening of 30 November 1521, Pope Leo complained of a chill (perhaps from malaria) and died the next day, leaving his cousin Giulio Cardinal de' Medici to succeed him as Pope **Clement VII** just two years later.

LINACRE, THOMAS (c. 1460–1524). A noted humanist, medical practitioner, and cleric, Thomas Linacre served as schoolmaster to two royal Tudor heirs and attended King Henry VIII himself as his personal physician. Linacre counted among his friends some of the leading classical scholars of his day and did much to preserve and disseminate ancient medical knowledge by translating Greek texts into more accessible Latin. In addition to the king of England, Linacre treated famous men of learning, Crown ministers, and high-ranking prelates of the church as his patients. Perhaps his greatest achievement was his foundation of the Royal College of Physicians in 1518, an institution that has survived to oversee medical licensure in Britain for the past five centuries.

Little is known of Thomas Linacre's family or early life. His place of birth was probably Canterbury, where in his youth he apparently attended Christ Church Grammar School as a pupil of headmaster William Sellyng. Linacre studied at **Oxford University** in his early 20s and then accepted a fellowship (a junior faculty

position) at All Souls College in 1484. While at Oxford, he made the acquaintance of **William Grocyn**, a scholar of the "new learning" of humanism, who took Linacre on as a student and taught him the rudiments of the ancient Greek language. In 1485, Linacre traveled with Sellyng to Italy and, having parted ways with his mentor in Bologna, made his way to Florence. There he met and studied with the sons of Lorenzo de' Medici and also engaged the linguist, poet, and philologist Angelo Poliziano to instruct him further in Greek.

Around 1490, Linacre was resident in Rome when he first developed an interest in the medical arts, a discipline to which he devoted much of his intellectual energy for the rest of his life. Next, in Venice, he befriended Aldus Manutius, the founder of Italy's first and most prominent printing operation. Linacre and Manutius collaborated on an Aldine edition of the Greek works of Aristotle in 1496 and then published the Englishman's translation of Proclus's astronomical treatise *De sphaera* the following year. Meanwhile, Linacre had been studying the physician's craft at the University of Padua, and after earning his doctorate in medicine there in 1497, he returned to England, where the Oxford medical faculty quickly conferred their own MD upon him in 1499.

Around the turn of the 16th century, Dr. Linacre came to know **Thomas More**, the future lord chancellor, whom the repatriated physician now took on as his own student of Greek letters. At the same time, he was introduced to and then joined the scholarly circle of the priest and educationalist **John Colet**, a group that also included the great Dutch humanist **Desiderius Erasmus**, who was then resident in England. In 1500, Linacre was appointed schoolmaster to **Arthur** Tudor, the son and heir of King **Henry VII**, but with the prince's death two years later, the physician's teaching duties came to an abrupt end. Dr. Linacre instead became a full-time medical practitioner, and as his reputation grew, he accumulated an impressive list of patients, such as More, Colet, Erasmus, Archbishop **William Warham**, Bishop **Richard Fox** of Winchester, and the future cardinal **Thomas Wolsey**. When these influential men praised his medical expertise, King Henry VIII invited Linacre to become his personal physician in 1509, a post he accepted and did not relinquish until his own death 15 years later.

Although the salary he commanded as a royal doctor was only £50 per year, Linacre was ordained a priest in 1511 and then collected a number of beneficed church livings that eventually made him quite wealthy. With the king and his other illustrious patients requiring only occasional medical attention, Linacre turned to more intellectual pursuits and published the first of his translations of Galen's works, *De sanitate tuenda*, in 1515. His most important contribution to Renaissance scholarship was *De emendata structura Latini sermonis*, or *On the Correct Construction of the Latin Language*, a six-volume classical grammar guide that appeared near the end of Linacre's life in 1523. That year saw the aging humanist and physician once again hired as a royal schoolmaster, this time to Princess **Mary** Tudor, King Henry's daughter by his first marriage with **Katherine of Aragon**. Linacre's tutelage of the seven-year-old princess was cut short, however, when he died from calculus, or kidney stone complications, at age 64 in 1524.

LOLLARDY (1382–c. 1530). The word *Lollardy* was used by orthodox Christian detractors to describe a movement of religious dissidents, or heretics, who originally embraced the teachings of Oxford theologian John Wyclif. Because Wyclif was bitterly critical of the **clergy**, sacraments, institutions, and wealth of the Roman Church, his Lollard followers appeared over the course of the 15th and early 16th centuries to represent a significant threat to that church and to the Crown authorities allied with it. Never comprising more than a tiny minority of English believers, the Lollards survived church and Crown persecution for more than 150 years in small cells in parts of southern and central England, helping to prepare the way for and then blending into the Church of England in the wake of the **Henrician Reformation**.

John Wyclif (1330–84), a native of Yorkshire, studied at Balliol, Merton, and Queen's Colleges at **Oxford University** before earning his doctorate in divinity there in 1372. While teaching theology at Oxford, he entered the service of John of Gaunt, Duke of Lancaster, as a secretary and polemicist. In 1376, Wyclif authored *De civili dominio*, a treatise that condemned clerical corruption and called for the disendowment of church property. There followed a series of inflammatory tracts, such as *De veritate sacre scripture*, *De ecclesia*, and *De eucharistia*, which respectively taught the need for vernacular Scriptures, the doctrine of predestined salvation, and a more rational understanding of the transubstantiated eucharist. Twice investigated for heresy in 1377 and 1382, Wyclif was never arrested or jailed, but the pope condemned most of his teachings, and his books were banned from both English universities. He was forced to leave his faculty post at Oxford and retired to his small parish living at Luttersworth in Leicestershire, where he died following a stroke in 1384.

Had Wyclif's radical ideas not spilled forth from the walls of Oxford University, they would never have attracted much notice outside the English academic community. But spill forth from the university they did, mostly disseminated and preached in public by former Wyclif students Nicholas Hereford, Philip Repington, and John Aston. Their message of religious reform reached primarily yeoman-, peasant-, and artisan-class audiences across England, helping to satisfy a spiritual thirst among common folk whose anticlericalism was increasingly turning them away from the established church.

Early Wycliffite disciples were known to their enemies as Lollards, a term that perhaps meant mumblers of prayers but also may have derived from the Latin for weed (*lolia*) or from the Dutch for idler (*loller*). Most Lollards held that priests were tricksters, images and statues were idols, the sacraments were nonsense, tithes only enriched the clergy, and the pope in Rome was the Anti-Christ. Lollard leaders demanded that the church distribute its wealth among the poor and called for translations of Scripture into the vernacular English language. Dr. Wyclif and his disciples had begun translating the "vulgate" Latin Bible as early as 1380, and with complete English editions available in manuscript form by 1392, copy centers on the estates of Sir Thomas Latimer, Sir John Clanvow, and other Lollard knights reproduced hundreds of these vernacular Bibles (more than 200 are still extant today) for public consumption. The English Scriptures were read aloud in conventicles, or schoolhouse assemblies, to illiterate layfolk, who then memorized whole chapters of Holy Writ to share with their families and neighbors.

Tiny, scattered cells of Lollards were almost invisible to the rest of society until they were connected with two uprisings against the established Crown and church authorities. The first of these, the Peasants' Revolt of 1381, was led in part by a priest named John Ball, whose calls for the distribution of church wealth among the poor reminded many of Wyclif's *De civili dominio*. The other rebellion—really little more than an ill-attended rally—was organized in 1414 by Sir John Oldcastle, an avowed Lollard who intended to overthrow the monarchy and replace it with a "people's republic" of sorts. Both uprisings were suppressed and their leaders executed, but each so frightened the authorities that **Parliament** passed an act entitled *De Heretico Comburendo*, or Concerning the Burning of Heretics, to punish at the stake those individuals convicted of heresy in episcopal courts. Over the course of the next century, some 400 Lollards were investigated and tried as heretics in England, and although most "abjured" or recanted their "errors" and endured a harsh penance, around 70 suffered a martyr's death rather than submit to the Roman Church they despised.

By the late 15th century, the number of heresy trials and executions had declined, but a resurgence of Lollard activity after the turn of the 16th century led to fresh persecutions in dioceses like Winchester, London, Coventry, and Canterbury. In 1514, the murder (and cover-up by church authorities) of an alleged London Lollard named **Richard Hunne** aroused widespread popular indignation, and royal intervention was necessary to prevent an anticlerical riot in the capital. Three years later, Martin Luther launched the Protestant Reformation in Germany with doctrines that closely resembled those of England's 14th-century heresiarch John Wyclif. Some English believers seemed quite taken with the breakaway Lutheran sect, prepared as they were by the anticlerical sentiments behind the Hunne affair and by the long-term existence of Lollardy across the realm. In addition, such learned academics as **Thomas Bilney**, **Robert Barnes**, and **William Tyndale** were already gathering at the White Horse Inn in Cambridge during the early 1520s to discuss Lutheran ideas, whose origins could be traced back to the Lollard movement. Thus, when King Henry VIII led his island kingdom away from the Roman orbit in the 1530s, the latent influences of Lollardy had already long been at work helping to shape the theological foundations of the new Church of England. *See also* GREAT BIBLE (1539).

LONDON, TOWER OF. *See* TOWER OF LONDON (1066–).

LOUIS XII, KING OF FRANCE (1462–1515; r. 1498–1515). A popular but relatively short-lived Valois monarch, King Louis XII was an active player in European geopolitics and did his best to expand French territorial interests into both **Flanders** and Italy. He is best remembered in English history for bearing the brunt of Henry VIII's first **French invasion of 1513–14** and for his subsequent but very brief marriage to King Henry's favorite younger sister **Mary** Tudor at the end of his life. Louis XII was alternately hostile and then friendly toward England, a common approach to conflict and diplomacy across Renaissance Europe that the prematurely aged French king passed on to his successor, **François I**, when Louis died at the fairly young age of 52 years.

Louis Valois was born in the Loire Valley at Blois to Charles duc d'Orléans and his consort duchess, Marie de Clèves, on 27 June 1462. Louis's great-grandfather was King Charles V, the third in the line of Valois kings of France, while his grandfather, Louis duc d'Orléans, was a younger son of King Charles who perished by the hand of an assassin in 1407. Early in Louis's life, his father died, thus passing the ducal title of Orléans on to his three-year-old son and heir in 1465. In adolescence, Louis was wed to Princess Jeanne, the daughter of King Louis XI, in an arranged match that did not particularly please either of the youthful parties involved. When his cousin Charles VIII acceded to the French throne in 1483, Louis d'Orléans briefly rebelled to press his own royal claims forward and was captured and imprisoned for a time. He soon regained his cousin's favor, however, and fought as an officer in King Charles's Italian invasion force in 1494. When the 28-year-old French monarch struck his head on a doorpost in his Amboise château and died without issue, the duc d'Orléans accepted the French crown to become the eighth Valois king of France as Louis XII in 1498.

One of the new ruler's first acts was to obtain an annulment of his marriage to Queen Jeanne from Pope Alexander VI, who then issued (in return for a hefty cash payment) a dispensation for King Louis to wed his cousin's widow Anne of Brittany, a union designed to keep the Duchy of Brittany in Valois hands. King Louis then invaded Italy as his regal cousin had done several years earlier, but his attempts to conquer the Duchy of Milan and the kingdom of Naples were soon thwarted by the combined forces of Emperor **Maximilian I** and King **Ferdinand of Aragon**. In the meantime, Louis and his second queen had produced a daughter, Claude, whom they betrothed to Louis's adolescent nephew and presumptive heir **François** duc d'Angoulême in 1506. After France joined with Pope Julius II, Spain, and the Holy Roman Empire against Venice in the League of Cambrai in 1508, the treaty signatories quickly fell out, and within three years Louis's old allies had sided with Venice against him. In 1512, Henry VIII of England threw in his lot with the enemies of France to form the so-called Holy League, but King Louis was able to reduce the threat of this hostile alliance by negotiating separate peace agreements with Venice and Spain in 1513.

Determined to recapture the martial glory of his royal English forebears, however, Henry VIII could not be so easily deterred from aggressive action against France, and in summer 1513, he crossed the channel with a huge army totaling more than 40,000 men. Launching their assault from the English-held port of **Calais**, the invaders managed to capture the towns of Thérouanne and Tournai, while King Henry won a small cavalry skirmish known as the Battle of the Spurs. The approach of winter put an end to the campaigning season in late autumn 1513, and both sides having lost their appetites for war by the following spring, a treaty of peace was hammered out in London in summer 1514. According to the terms of this pact, the French king agreed to pay off an old debt to the English Crown in return for an end to the military conflict. In addition, the recently widowed King Louis demanded the hand of King Henry's younger sister Mary Tudor in marriage. The treaty was duly signed, and Princess Mary reluctantly sailed off to France to wed a man who was by then some 34 years her senior.

At the time of their wedding in early October 1514, King Louis of France had been in poor health for several years. He suffered from an advanced case of syphilis, the so-called French disease, and experienced painful episodes of gout; most of his teeth had also rotted away, and he slobbered and drooled uncontrollably. His third wife and queen, Mary Tudor, was a pretty 18-year-old who had bravely agreed to marry Louis and thus fulfill the terms of the London Treaty, if upon her decrepit husband's death she could marry whomever she wished. Despite his gallant efforts to please and even satisfy his lovely young bride, King Louis breathed his last on 1 January 1515, thus freeing Queen Mary to wed her childhood sweetheart **Charles Brandon**, the newly created Duke of Suffolk. Louis XII was succeeded on the French throne by his nephew François I, a robust and promiscuous 21-year-old who would in time become Henry VIII's great rival and nemesis.

M

MARGARET (TUDOR), QUEEN OF SCOT-
LAND, COUNTESS OF ANGUS AND
METHVEN (1489–1541). The daughter of
Henry VII and sister of Henry VIII, Margaret Tudor's fortunes were closely aligned with those
of Scotland following her youthful marriage to
King James IV of Scots in 1503. After her royal
husband died in battle 10 years later, Margaret
served intermittently as regent for her young
son but was often brushed aside by competing
Scottish factions intent on playing off their
French allies against the English. She married
twice more—each time to adulterous Scottish
lairds (nobles)—and produced a line of succession that ultimately acceded to both the
Scottish and English thrones. Never comfortable with her adopted country or its ways, Margaret nevertheless died in Scotland near Perth
at the relatively young age of just 51 years.

Margaret Tudor was born the eldest
daughter and second child of Henry VII and his
consort, Elizabeth of York, on 29 November
1489 at Westminster Palace outside London.
The infant was named for her paternal grandmother, Lady Margaret Beaufort, the Countess
of Richmond, who stood as godmother to the
baby girl at her christening within a few days
of her birth. Princess Margaret learned to read,
write, and play several musical instruments,
but she was not a scholar and never acquired
any fluency in foreign languages or the classics. When his daughter was just six years of
age, Henry VII offered her hand in marriage to
King James IV of Scots but made the match
conditional on the expulsion of the royal imposter Perkin Warbeck from the Scottish court.

This demand was not met, and the negotiations for Margaret's hand broke off, but they
soon revived with Warbeck's capture and execution by the English a few years later. With
that obstacle removed, Henry VII approached
James IV once more in 1502 and concluded
a Treaty of Perpetual Peace with Scotland, a
pact that included the delayed marriage of
Margaret Tudor and the king of Scots to seal
its terms. Thus, some 18 months after a brief
proxy ceremony near London, the English
princess traveled north to wed King James in
person at Holyrood Abbey in Edinburgh on 8
August 1503.

Aggrieved by the recent deaths of her
brother Arthur Tudor and her mother, Queen
Elizabeth of York, the new queen of Scots
sought solace by throwing herself into her
many royal duties at the Scottish court. Queen
Margaret, who was just 13 years old on her
wedding day, accompanied her new husband
on a progress across central Scotland to tour
the royal residences of Linlithgow and Stirling
Castle in autumn 1503. She cannot have been
pleased by the presence of some of James's
mistresses and seven of his royal bastards in
those homes, but if she objected in any way or
flashed her Tudor temper, no record of such
behavior survives. Despite his many infidelities, James IV was in fact an attentive and
generous husband to his queen, showering
her with jewels and expensive gowns and
even naming his great warship *Margaret* in her
honor when he launched the vessel in 1508.
Margaret's first pregnancy did not occur until
three years into her marriage, and after her

first three children died in infancy, the queen of Scots finally produced a male heir named James in 1512.

Over the course of many centuries, Scotland had maintained close ties with France in a relationship popularly known in both kingdoms as the "Auld (Old) Alliance." Once she was married to the king of Scots, however, Margaret Tudor gently nudged her husband toward more amicable relations with her father in England and tried to promote the "perpetual peace" that both rulers had agreed to uphold in 1502. When Henry VII passed away in April 1509, his brash and bellicose son Henry VIII came to the English throne and almost immediately began planning a **French invasion** to relive the past military glories of his royal ancestors. Queen Margaret desperately pleaded with her husband to remain neutral in the coming fight, but the English king's massive assault on France in summer 1513 prompted King James to support his "auld" ally and launch his own attack on England a few months later. With Henry VIII away on campaign, a large English army under Earl **Thomas Howard** of Surrey (later the second Duke of Norfolk) marched swiftly to counter the Scottish advance in Northumbria. In the fierce battle that followed at **Flodden**, the king of Scots and thousands of his troops fell and died on the bloody battlefield, a devastating defeat that left Queen Margaret and her 17-month-old infant son, James—now King **James V**—to somehow rule the Scottish kingdom themselves.

Because Margaret had been appointed regent for the baby-king of Scots by her deceased husband's will, she embraced her new authority and initially enjoyed some success in reducing tensions between the kingdom's competing noble factions. Her regency came to an abrupt end, however, when the still-young dowager queen suddenly took as her second spouse the sixth Earl of Angus, Archibald Douglas, a little over a year after her first husband's death. This rash and overhasty act motivated John Stuart, James IV's cousin and the second Duke of Albany, to return to Scotland from France in order to seize the reins of power as regent for himself.

After Albany besieged her in Stirling Castle in August 1515, Margaret managed to escape to England, where her younger brother Henry VIII sheltered her for the next few years. Margaret quietly returned to Scotland in 1518 to find her unfaithful second husband living with his former mistress and freely spending what was left of her royal dowry. Incensed, Margaret joined forces with her former enemy Albany just long enough to drive the worthless Angus from court, then turned against Albany as well to reclaim her ruling regency over the child-king of Scots. Thus did control of James V pass between Margaret, Albany, and occasionally even to Angus over the next 9 years, until the lad finally declared his majority at age 15 and asserted control over the Scottish government for himself. By then, the queen dowager had lost patience with her feckless second husband and, securing a divorce from Pope **Clement VII**, almost immediately entered into a new union with Henry Stuart, Lord Methven, a distant cousin of her deceased first spouse, King James IV.

Although the youthful Scottish king now ruled his dominions in his own right, his mother and the Earl of Methven continued to serve as his principal advisors. Always eager to bring Scotland and England closer together, the dowager queen attempted to arrange a summit between her son and her brother Henry VIII in 1536, but young James and the Tudor king were both too distracted by other concerns to agree to meet in person. Meanwhile, Margaret's third husband proved to be more of a scoundrel than even Angus had been, but her petition for another papal divorce was this time blocked by her son, the king.

When James V married Marie de Guise in 1538, his mother welcomed the new French queen, and the two women became fast friends and formidable political allies at court together. Just six weeks short of her 52nd birthday, Queen Margaret of Scotland contracted some sort of palsy and died at Methven Castle outside Perth on 18 October 1541. She was laid to rest in a **Carthusian monastery** that later was dismantled during the Scottish Reformation under John Knox in the late 1550s. Her great-grandson James VI of Scotland went on to inherit the throne of England following the reign of Henry VIII's childless daughter **Elizabeth I** in 1603.

MARGARET OF AUSTRIA, DUCHESS OF SAVOY AND REGENT OF THE NETHERLANDS (1480–1530).

The daughter of Holy Roman Emperor **Maximilian I** and the aunt of his successor **Charles V**, Margaret ruled as regent of the Netherlands for both emperors during the period 1507–15 and again from 1517 until her death in 1530. She became, as many royal women did during Tudor times, a marriage pawn in a high-stakes game of European diplomacy that saw her married and widowed twice before her 25th birthday. Margaret was an active and reasonably successful regent in the Netherlands (or Low Countries) who negotiated treaties, pacified her often-unruly subjects, and manipulated the election that placed her nephew Charles Habsburg on the imperial throne. Remarkably, Margaret's position as regent allowed her to exercise real political, military, and diplomatic power in a "man's world," a rare achievement for a woman at a time when most of her female peers were relegated to roles as mere consorts, alliance "bait," and royal mothers.

Margaret was born in Brussels early in 1480 to Maximilian of Austria, the future Holy Roman Emperor and ruler of the Netherlands, and his wife, Mary of Burgundy, the daughter of Duke Charles the Bold of Burgundy and the stepdaughter of Margaret of York, the sister of King Edward IV of England. In 1482, Maximilian signed the Treaty of Arras promising his daughter's hand in marriage to the 11-year-old French dauphin, Charles Valois, and so she traveled to Paris the following year to be raised and educated as a future queen of France. Although the couple grew fond of each other over the years, the young King Charles VIII set Margaret aside in 1491 so he could marry Anne of Brittany and annex her strategically important duchy to his kingdom. Margaret returned briefly to Cambrai in **Flanders** two years later, but in 1496, her father betrothed her to Prince Juan of Asturias, the heir of King **Ferdinand of Aragon** and Queen Isabel of Castile, and she found herself on the move again, this time to Spain.

Margaret and Juan were wed in 1497, but when her sickly Spanish spouse died six months later and her pregnancy failed, the dejected widow returned home to the city of Ghent in Flanders once more. In 1500, she stood as godmother to her newborn nephew Charles Habsburg, the heir of her brother Philip the Fair and his Spanish bride, Juana la Loca ("the Mad"), Ferdinand and Isabel's eldest daughter. In 1501, Margaret married Philibert, Duke of Savoy, but once again the unlucky Flemish princess (her father was now emperor) lost her husband after a few short years, and she spiraled into a state of deep depression. Once she recovered, Margaret swore an oath never to marry again, a vow that freed her from future marital and childbirth duties to devote herself full-time to the governance of her own sovereign state in the Low Countries.

After filling in as Savoy's interim regent for her deceased husband, Margaret was ready for the call to power when her brother Philip the Fair also died in 1506, leaving her as the obvious candidate to replace him as governor of the Netherlands. Emperor Maximilian made his daughter's appointment to that position official in 1507 and entrusted her with the guardianship of her young nephew and godson Charles, who was now heir to the Spanish throne following the death of his father. Margaret took up residence in the glittering palace of Mechelen in the town of Malines in Flanders, where she commissioned construction of several ornate Renaissance buildings and patronized some of the most important artists and musicians in western Europe. One of her first acts as imperial regent was to turn down an offer of marriage from King **Henry VII** of England, who, himself a widower since 1503, had hoped to strengthen commercial relations between their two countries by marrying Margaret. She did, however, renew the 1496 Intercursus Magnus Treaty in 1508 to rekindle the lucrative wool trade between Flanders and England, and she deflected a potential French invasion in the same year by joining Venice and the papacy in a mutual defense pact known as the Holy League. It may have been in 1513 that a young **Anne Boleyn**, the future queen of England, came to attend Margaret as a lady-in-waiting for two years before moving on to the service of Queen Claude in Paris.

When her nephew declared his majority and assumed personal rule over the Low Countries in 1515, Margaret temporarily stepped aside but was soon reinstated two years later when the teenaged Charles (now king of Spain) realized how much he missed her outstanding administrative and diplomatic talents. She repaid his trust by pressuring and then bribing the seven imperial electors to choose Charles as the next Holy Roman Emperor upon the death of her father, Maximilian, in 1519. During the 1520s, Margaret also managed to put down a revolt in Guelders, ordered Lutheran reformers burned at the stake as heretics, and ended the war between Emperor Charles and his enemies by negotiating a separate peace with France. In 1530, at the age of 50, Margaret injured her leg at Methelen, and when it became gangrenous, she died before the infected limb could be amputated. Mary of Hungary (or Austria), daughter of Philip the Fair and thus Margaret's niece, reluctantly succeeded her aunt as regent of the Netherlands until her own death in 1558.

MARY (TUDOR), QUEEN OF FRANCE, DUCHESS OF SUFFOLK (1496–1533).
Mary Rose, as she came to be known, was King Henry VIII's younger—and favorite—sister and played a significant role during her early life as a diplomatic pawn on the royal matrimonial market of Europe. Promised or betrothed to various princes as a child, she finally married the King of France as required by the treaty that ended her brother's first **French invasion of 1513–14**. Following this brief union, the teenaged queen then married her childhood sweetheart and bore him four children before her untimely death at age 37. The daughter, sister, and wife of kings, Mary was also the grandmother of Lady Jane Grey, who became queen of England for just nine days in July 1553.

Mary Tudor was born the second daughter and fourth child of **Henry VII** and his consort, **Elizabeth of York**, at Richmond Palace, just west of London, on 28 March 1496. During her infancy and early childhood, Mary (along with her older sister **Margaret** Tudor) shuffled incessantly between several different royal residences in the vicinity of London, where both girls grew up under the watchful eye of their paternal grandmother, **Margaret Beaufort**, the Countess of Richmond. The Tudor sisters flourished in the care of their governess, Lady Elizabeth Denton, and were educated by **John Skelton**, the humanist scholar and poet, and by **Jane Popincourt**, the French tutor who later may have became an early lover of their brother Prince Henry. Princess Mary bloomed into an exceptionally beautiful young lady by her midteens, winning high praise for her porcelain complexion, strawberry-blond hair, and dazzling green eyes from all who met her. She was energetic and gregarious, loved music and dancing, and possessed a refined sense of fashion that rivaled the haute couture of the royal French court in Paris. Prince Henry came to dote on his younger sister throughout their childhood together, nicknaming her Mary Rose, partly as a tribute to her flower-like beauty, but partly also to reflect the rose insignia of their common Tudor heritage.

The pretty little princess became an early player on the high stage of European politics when her father, Henry VII, first entertained an offer for her hand from Ludovico Sforza, the swarthy Duke of Milan, who sought Mary as a bride for his infant son in 1498. When her older brother **Arthur**, Prince of **Wales**, married the Spanish princess **Katherine of Aragon** in 1501, the prestige of the House of Tudor soared, and Mary was then promised to Katherine's nephew Charles of Castile, the future Emperor **Charles V**. Under the manipulative hand of his grandfather, the Holy Roman Emperor **Maximilian I**, however, this arrangement was set aside but then renewed once the youthful Charles became Maximilian's heir in 1506. He and Mary became formally engaged via proxy in an elegant ceremony at **Greenwich Palace** in 1508, a betrothal that Henry VII helped along by providing a rich dowry of 250,000 crowns (about £60,000 in Tudor currency) to assuage the greed of the ever-insolvent Maximilian.

After the old English king breathed his last the following year, his successor, Henry

VIII, delayed the nuptials of his favorite sister and her imperial fiancé so long that Emperor Maximilian finally broke off their engagement himself in frustration. Temporarily unpromised in marriage, Mary Rose began to appear at her brother's royal court, dancing and playing parts in **pageants** that attracted the admiring attention of male and female observers alike.

Meanwhile Maximilian, now past his grandson's snubbed English betrothal, approached Henry VIII and persuaded him to take part in a joint Anglo-imperial invasion of France in summer 1513. The bellicose Tudor king eagerly assembled an enormous army for the purpose, crossed the channel and then personally led his troops into the northern French countryside. The ensuing campaign achieved little, but by the Treaty of London that ended the hostilities the next year, the French King **Louis XII** agreed to pay off an old debt to the English Crown in return for the hand of King Henry's younger sister in marriage. At the time, King Louis was a toothless, slobbering, and syphilitic 52-year-old, clearly someone the attractive Tudor princess would rather not have married. She agreed to fulfill the terms of the treaty for her brother, however, if he promised her a free hand in choosing her next husband after Louis's death. Having won this concession from Henry, Mary Tudor set sail for France in late September 1514 and was duly wed to her repulsive new husband two weeks later.

Following a wedding night that was probably far less romantic than it was strange and awkward, the French king treated his 18-year-old queen courteously enough over the next few months and provided her with every luxury she desired. Apparently frustrated, the neglected old man soon sent Mary's English ladies-in-waiting away within weeks of their wedding because he felt they formed a barrier between himself and his lovely young bride. At the same time, Mary's real love interest, **Charles Brandon**, the newly created Duke of Suffolk and King Henry's closest friend, had recently arrived in France on a diplomatic mission for the English Crown. Mary Rose and the dashing young duke had secretly fallen deeply in love before leaving the English court, and

now, with the diseased old French king nearing the end of his days, they agreed to marry once the Tudor queen of France was free to do so. Happily for her, King Louis died on 1 January 1515, and hoping to avoid another hastily arranged state marriage, the two young lovers secretly wed some 10 weeks later and then made plans to return to England.

Henry VIII was at first furious that his friend and sister had married without his consent, but his anger soon abated when the couple paid an enormous fine of £24,000 and returned most of Mary's French dowry in order to regain the king's affections. Mary and Suffolk officially married again at Greenwich Palace on 13 May 1515, and over the next four years, the couple produced three of their four children. When King Henry's first wife and queen, Katherine of Aragon, gave birth to a daughter in February 1516, Mary's brother had sufficiently forgiven her to christen the infant Princess **Mary** Tudor in his favorite sister's honor. Now restored to royal favor, the Duke and Duchess of Suffolk attended the extravagant **Field of Cloth of Gold** summit meeting with King **François I** of France near **Calais** in 1520. Several years later, when her royal brother became infatuated with **Anne Boleyn**, Mary threw her support behind the neglected Katherine of Aragon and openly opposed the king's growing resolve to set his first queen aside.

It is widely believed today that Henry VIII named his great warship *Mary Rose* after his favorite younger sister, but it is far likelier that the devout Tudor king actually named it for the Blessed Virgin Mary, the mother of Jesus. The Duchess of Suffolk survived a bout of the **sweating sickness** in 1528, but she had never enjoyed robust health, and following her recovery, she entered a physical decline that continued over the next several years. Mary Rose died of complications from the sweating sickness (or perhaps from angina, cancer, or tuberculosis—the exact cause of death is not clear) on 26 June 1533 at the youthful age of 37. She was buried in the abbey church of Bury St. Edmunds in Suffolk, but her remains were translated five years later to nearby St. Mary's Church when Henry VIII closed England's **monasteries**. Her two sons both died as children, but her eldest daughter, Frances, grew up to marry Henry Grey, the future Duke of Suffolk. The Greys in turn raised two daughters of their own, one of whom was destined to become the future "nine-day queen" Lady Jane Grey.

MARY I (TUDOR), PRINCESS AND QUEEN OF ENGLAND (1516–58; r. 1553–58).

The only surviving child of King Henry VIII and Queen **Katherine of Aragon**, Mary Tudor was a political pawn during the first 30 years of her life whose marriage eligibility (with its accompanying English alliance) was repeatedly dangled before a number of potential royal suitors. She was also caught up in the shifting winds of Henry VIII's matrimonial difficulties and in the tensions between the Roman Church and her father's **Henrician Reformation** of the Church of England. The second of King Henry's three legitimate children to accede to the English throne, Queen Mary I was the kingdom's first queen regnant, if one disqualifies Lady Jane Grey. In attempting to return her subjects to the Roman faith, she earned the epithet Bloody Mary by ordering the burning deaths of nearly 300 Protestants as religious heretics.

Princess Mary was born on 18 February 1516 at **Greenwich Palace** and was the only live birth of Queen Katherine's six pregnancies to survive to adulthood. Her mother entrusted care of the infant Mary to **Margaret Pole**, the Countess of Salisbury, and later engaged the eminent humanist and physician **Thomas Linacre** to tutor her daughter in languages, music, history, and the classics. Queen Katherine also employed the great Spanish humanist Juan Luis Vives to compose a pedagogical treatise entitled *De institutione feminae Christianae*, or *On the Instruction of a Christian Woman*, which he sent to the Tudor court in 1520 to guide the education of the young princess. Her life as a potential marriage prospect and political pawn began early when Mary was promised to the newborn dauphin of France in 1518. The negotiations to arrange this match broke down, however, as did other attempts to conclude matrimonial alliances with her cousins Emperor **Charles V** and King **James V** of Scots over the next few years. At the age

of nine years, the Tudor princess was installed at Ludlow Castle on the Welsh marches with her own small court to represent her father's regime as an informal "Princess of **Wales**" in 1525.

The life of the child princess began to change dramatically with the onset of King Henry's "**Great Matter**," his campaign to annul his marriage with Mary's mother so he might wed **Anne Boleyn** and with her sire a son and heir. Princess Mary returned from Ludlow to the environs of London in 1528, but she rarely had contact with either of her parents, and in 1531, she was cut off from her mother completely and never saw her again. When Henry VIII married Anne Boleyn in 1533 and Archbishop **Thomas Cranmer** formally annulled the king's first marriage, Katherine of Aragon was relegated to the status of dowager princess (widow of King Henry's deceased brother **Arthur**, Prince of Wales), while Mary was declared illegitimate and was barred from the throne by the **Act of Succession**. Queen Anne's daughter, **Elizabeth**, was born in September 1533, which prompted the king to dismiss Mary's former court attendants and send her to live in the household of the newborn princess at Hatfield House. There "Lady Mary" would not accept Anne Boleyn as queen or her half-sister as royal heir, and when Henry VIII renounced Rome and the pope in 1534, she refused to acknowledge her father's supremacy over the English Church as well. Mary was kept from her mother when Katherine fell ill and died early in 1536, plunging the former princess into a state of anxiety and depression that only lifted with the news of Anne Boleyn's execution just five months later.

Mary's fortunes began to change after her father married **Jane Seymour**, his third wife and queen. One of Mary's few friends during the short reign of Anne Boleyn had been **Eustace Chapuys**, the imperial ambassador to the Tudor court; this devout Catholic and former advocate for the deceased Queen Katherine now worked with the new Queen Jane to reconcile King Henry to his estranged eldest daughter. On condition that she accept her mother's marriage annulment and her father's lordship over the English Church, Mary was invited back to court in time to celebrate Christmas at the end of 1536. The king also restored Mary's small estate and moved her between various royal residences, such as **Hampton Court**, Richmond, Hatfield, and Hunsdon. In October 1537, she served as godmother to Queen Jane's son, **Edward**, and as a royal mourner at the funeral of the prince's mother that soon followed. Distantly associated with several plots against the Crown, the royal favor that Mary now enjoyed probably saved her from sharing the executioner's scaffold with the likes of **Thomas Cromwell**, King Henry's disgraced chief minister, and the Countess of Salisbury, Margaret Pole, the mother of religious exile **Reginald Pole** and Mary's former governess.

Mary lived comfortably during the final years of her father's reign, even using the modest allowance he provided to enjoy gambling at cards, one of her favorite pastimes. In 1544, King Henry restored both his daughters to the royal line of succession behind the primary claim of their half-brother Edward. Now in her late 20s, Princess Mary also served as royal hostess at the Tudor court in 1542–43 while her father was briefly unmarried. His sixth and final wife, **Katherine Parr**, instituted a reformed educational program for the two youngest royal children, but the adult Mary remained aloof from the queen's Protestant influences and secretly heard Roman mass and received the Catholic sacraments in her own private quarters. When Henry VIII died in 1547, Princess Mary's life of ease and security died with him, as her half-brother Edward VI attempted to complete the fully evangelical Reformation their father had only halfheartedly begun. To avoid the Protestant bullying of Edward's royal council, Mary withdrew to her own household in East Anglia, where she remained out of touch with court politics until she seized the throne herself at her brother's death in July 1553. As queen regnant in her own right, Mary I wed an unpopular foreign prince and, in an attempt to restore the Roman faith in England, earned the disparaging moniker Bloody Mary for her campaign to put hundreds of Protestant heretics to death at the stake.

MARY ROSE **WARSHIP.** *See* NAVY OF HENRY VIII (c. 1485–1547).

MAXIMILIAN I, HOLY ROMAN EMPEROR (1459–1519; r. 1493–1519). As patriarch of the ruling House of Habsburg, Emperor Maximilian pursued policies that helped propel his family to a position of dynastic dominance in early-modern Europe. He consolidated the Habsburg home territories in Austria, married into control of Burgundy and **Flanders**, acquired sovereignty over Hungary and Bohemia, and inserted his own descendants into the Spanish royal succession. The emperor was so often at war with France that he twice entered into alliances with the Tudor kings of England to safeguard profitable trade relations between their two countries and to secure English military assistance against their common French foe. His grandson **Charles V** succeeded him as Holy Roman Emperor, while his younger grandson Ferdinand and his great-grandson Philip II, respectively, inherited the imperial and Spanish crowns later in the 16th century.

Maximilian was born on 22 March 1459 in the imperial Austrian capital of Weiner Neustadt and grew up the only surviving son of Emperor Frederick III and his consort, Eleanor of Portugal. He received an excellent Renaissance education in Latin and the ancient classics and also became proficient in the more modern languages of French, Flemish, and German. Young Maximilian was (unlike his obese father) muscular and athletic; enjoyed hunting, **jousting**, and swordplay; and regarded himself as one of Europe's last chivalrous knights. He was born the Archduke of Austria, and at age 18, he wed Mary of Burgundy to seize power in that wealthy duchy as well. His wife died after only five years of marriage but not before giving him two children who survived to adulthood. Their son was Philip the Fair, soon to marry into the Spanish royal family, and their daughter was **Margaret of Austria**, the future Habsburg regent in the Netherlands.

In 1486, Emperor Frederick III had his son crowned king of the Germans (or Romans) in Aachen, an honorific title traditionally bestowed on the presumptive heir to the imperial throne. Still a young man, Maximilian reasserted his family's claim to eastern Austria and then pressured the king of Hungary, Vladislav II, to name him heir to both his own realm and neighboring Bohemia as well. Maximilian fought wars against the Swiss cantons and the advancing Ottoman Turks in the Balkans, and he contested the claims of Charles VIII of France to suzerainty over several territories in Italy. He briefly promised marriage by proxy to Anne of Brittany in 1490, but when the French king claimed her for himself, he married Bianca Maria Sforza instead to forge an alliance with her uncle Ludovico Sforza in Milan. Frederick III breathed his last in 1493, and so Maximilian became the Holy Roman Emperor elect, a title he would have to wait another 15 years for the pope to confirm from Rome.

When trade relations with England became strained in the mid-1490s, the new Habsburg emperor sent emissaries to London to hammer out the Intercursus Magnus Treaty with the Tudor government of King **Henry VII**. This pact restored high-quality English wool exports to Flanders, reduced restrictions on North Sea fishing, and prevented either signatory from sheltering the enemies or rebels of the other. In addition to his own dynastic unions, Emperor Maximilian married his son Philip the Fair to Princess Juana of Castile and his daughter Margaret of Austria to Prince Juan of Asturias—both heirs to the dual kingdoms of Spain—in 1496–97. Margaret's sickly husband passed away within six months of their wedding, but Philip and his Spanish bride produced two healthy sons, Charles and Ferdinand, before Philip died suddenly from a fever in 1506. The following year, Maximilian appointed his widowed daughter Margaret his imperial regent in the Netherlands (Low Countries), an office she ably executed (with one brief interruption) over the next 23 years.

Still suspicious of the French, the emperor signed the Treaty of Cambrai in 1508 to help the Papal States, Spain, and Venice defend Italy from further territorial incursions by King **Louis XII**. When the Venetians changed sides, Maximilian and his allies recruited Henry VIII of England in spring 1513 to join a new Holy League against France and then sent officers to London to formulate a combined military strategy for an upcoming **French invasion of 1513–14**. King Henry crossed the English Channel with a massive army in summer 1513, but Maximilian met him at the siege of Thérouanne with only a token imperial force of his own. The English king hosted the emperor in a cloth of gold tent on 13 August, and Maximilian was at Henry's side during the Battle of the Spurs cavalry skirmish three days later. Realizing that further conflict in France was futile, however, the emperor made his own separate peace with King Louis, left Henry VIII in the field by himself, and then withdrew his small invasion force into Burgundy.

During his lifetime, Maximilian was an enthusiastic patron of painting, sculpture, scholarship, and music, and he actively supported and corresponded with the great German artist Albrecht Dürer. The emperor himself authored several treatises, including *Geheimes Jagdbuch*, or *Personal Hunt Book*, a hunting manual; *Weisskunig*, or *White King*, an allegorical account of his early reign; *Freydal*, a recreation of his youthful jousting victories; and *Der Weisen Köninge Stammbaum*, a Habsburg family history. When King **Ferdinand of Aragon** died, Maximilian's grandson Charles inherited the combined crowns of Spain as Carlos I in 1516. Maximilian himself, strangely traveling with an empty coffin during his last years, passed away at age 60 in Wels, Austria, and was laid to rest in an elaborate tomb in the Habsburg capital of Weiner Neustadt. Carlos I of Spain then succeeded his grandfather on the imperial throne in 1519 and ruled both the German and Spanish Empires until his abdication in 1556.

MAY DAY RIOTS. *See* "EVIL" MAY DAY RIOTS (28 APRIL–22 MAY 1517).

MONASTERIES, DISSOLUTION OR SUPPRESSION OF THE (1535–40). Following the **Act of Supremacy** and the Church of England's break with Rome in 1534 and urged on by his chief religious officer, **Thomas Cromwell**, King Henry VIII ordered all the monastic institutions throughout his dominions closed and their lands, buildings, and valuables confiscated to the Crown. The Tudor king based this policy partly on his belief that most English monastic communities were parasitic and corrupt and partly on his desperate need to replenish his depleted royal coffers with income from monastic assets. The dissolution of the monasteries had a profound effect on the English people, many of whom had family connections to the religious houses or were employed by them as tenant farmers and herdsmen, day laborers, servants, or artisan craftsmen. When the smaller monasteries were first shuttered in 1536, the angry common-born folk of Yorkshire and Lincolnshire arose in the **Pilgrimage of Grace**, a popular insurrection that saw hundreds slain and much property destroyed before order was finally restored in 1537.

From the sixth and seventh centuries AD, when Christianity first made its tentative re-entry into the British Isles, and then through the High Middle Ages, monastic houses of regular **clergy** (from the Latin *regula*, lives ordered by a rule) had been a dominant feature of the English religious landscape. Varying in the number of inmates each housed, from fewer than 10 to many hundreds, these monastic communities were self-sufficient economic enterprises that grew their own crops; tended their own livestock; manufactured their own candles, tools, and clothing; and copied books by hand (manuscripts) to store and read in their cloistered libraries. Abbots or abbesses (from the Aramaic *abbas*, or father) governed the lives of the regular clergy in their care and, although they expected unquestioned obedience from them, tended to order the affairs of their religious houses with a benign and paternal hand. Monks and nuns prayed the divine offices at seven designated times each day, they dined and undertook manual labor together, and they lived more or less austere lifestyles depending on the order to which they belonged. At the time of Henry VIII's early reign, England boasted some 800 monasteries in all, a number that included at least one house from among many orders of Benedictines; Cluniacs; Observantines; **Carthusians**; Cistercians; Brigittines; the mendicant "begging" orders (by then mostly university professors); and the remaining military orders, such as the Knights of St. John.

By the turn of the 16th century, a considerable anticlerical sentiment had taken hold of the minds and hearts of lay believers across England. Many thought that English regular clerics were lazy, promiscuous, and worldly, while their monasteries charged admission fees to worship at the holy **shrines** they housed, and most owned vast tracts of valuable agricultural and grazing land as well. Members of the **noble** and **gentry** classes in England were envious of the church's enormous property holdings and hoped someday to acquire some of that land for themselves and their heirs. Thus, when the Crown took its initial steps to suppress the kingdom's religious houses in the mid-1530s, few of the more privileged elements of English society at the time thought to object to or oppose the policy.

Once he was supreme head of the English Church, King Henry made Chief Minister Thomas Cromwell his vicegerent in spirituals, an office that granted him oversight of all religious affairs and gave him authority even over the archbishop of Canterbury. After selling his revenue-starved sovereign on the idea of a monastic dissolution, Cromwell sent forth his agents Richard Layton, Thomas Legh, John Tregonwell, and others to investigate monastic vices and then ordered them to submit their reports to the House of Commons in **Parliament**. Meanwhile, the vicegerent also dispatched assessment teams to determine the monetary worth of England's religious houses and had those values recorded in a great monastic ledger called the *Valor ecclesiasticus*, or *Value of the Church*. In March 1536, Parliament passed the first Act of Suppression, which authorized closure of all monastic institutions with smaller resident populations and less income than £200 per year.

When some 240 smaller monasteries were duly closed over the next few years, the Crown quickly moved to seize their lands, herds, buildings, and other possessions. Another 67 houses applied for—and paid fines or fees to obtain—closure exemptions in order to remain open at least for the time being. As fines were collected and many confiscated properties were leased out or sold off, Cromwell created a Court of Augmentations to account for and stockpile the new revenues now flowing into his hands. The monks and nuns who were turned out of the suppressed religious houses were offered a choice of either returning to lay society (abbots or priors with pensions) or transferring to one of the larger houses of their order. The shuttering of the smaller monasteries was not well received in the more staunchly Catholic north of England, where some 30,000 layfolk rose in the Pilgrimage of Grace rebellion in autumn 1536. King Henry sent **Thomas Howard**, third Duke of Norfolk, to intercept the insurgents, and offering amnesty if most pilgrims returned to their homes, he arrested the ringleaders and dragged them off to London to die as traitors.

When (at Cromwell's urging) Parliament passed a second Act of Suppression in 1538, the remaining larger monasteries were systematically closed over the next two years. Considerable pressure was brought to bear on the heads of these houses, who eventually complied with surrender orders to avoid punishment as rebels and traitors or to please the king and his vicegerent in the hope of winning future royal favor. This time, all those leaving the religious life (there could be no more transfers) were offered a subsistence pension. By the time the last religious house, Waltham Abbey, closed its doors in March 1540, the ancient institution of monasticism no longer existed in Henry VIII's England. Overall, the dissolution netted the Crown the staggering sum of £1.8 million, an amount equivalent to more than $1 trillion in today's American currency.

MORE, MARGARET ROPER. *See* ROPER, MARGARET MORE (1505–44).

MORE, SIR THOMAS, LORD CHANCELLOR OF ENGLAND (1478–1535). Thanks to the Robert Bolt play *A Man for All Seasons* and the 1966 Academy Award–winning Best Picture of the same name, Sir Thomas More is one of the most familiar of all the colorful figures who graced the early-Tudor world of King Henry VIII. A family man, lawyer, humanist, philosopher, historian, diplomat, and statesman, More is best known for his invention and description of an idealized society in his 1516 *Utopia*. He is also remembered for his refusal to acknowledge King Henry's break with the Roman Church, a stance that ultimately cost him his life but earned him a sainthood four centuries later. More was a complicated man, admired by many for his incorruptibility and integrity as a government official yet feared by many religious reformers for his doctrinal intransigence and zealous hostility toward those he deemed heretics. More was also one of the few men of his era to school one of his daughters, **Margaret More Roper**, in the "new learning" of humanism, an education that prepared her later to become a prominent Renaissance scholar in her own right.

Thomas More was born in February 1478 in London to Sir John More, a lawyer and later a judge in the Court of King's Bench, and his first wife, Agnes Graunger More. As his family's eldest son, Thomas attended prestigious St. Anthony's School in Threadneedle Street for a few years before entering the household of John Cardinal Morton, archbishop of Canterbury, to serve as a pageboy. Morton was so impressed with young More's intellect and wit that he sponsored the lad's attendance at **Oxford University**, where he studied with **William Grocyn** and **Thomas Linacre** and was introduced by them to the *studia humanitatis*, or new learning of humanist letters. More returned to the capital in 1494 to matriculate at Lincoln's Inn, one of London's emergent **Inns of Court** law schools, and was called to the bar (became an attorney) in 1501. During this time, he lived for several years in a **Carthusian monastery**, where he tested a possible religious vocation and acquired the habits of prayer, fasting, and self-mortification that followed him the rest of his life. These years in London also saw him make the acquaintance of **John Colet**, the humanist priest, scholar, and founder of an innovative cathedral school at St. Paul's. Having decided against formal ordination as a cleric himself, More first married Jane Colt (who bore him four children) and then Alice Middleton after his first wife died in 1511.

Still only 26 years of age, Thomas More entered **Parliament** in 1504, but his political career got off to a rocky start when he vigorously opposed King **Henry VII**'s 20 percent income tax to fund his daughter **Margaret** Tudor's wedding to the king of Scots. Furious, King Henry ordered Thomas's father, Sir John More, confined in the **Tower of London** until a fine of £100 could be paid to free him. Son Thomas fared better, however, once the old king was gone and his precocious and energetic young heir had succeeded him as King Henry VIII in 1509. The new Tudor ruler took an instant liking to More, whose career trajectory now soared, as royal favor brought him more prestigious appointments and greater wealth. As an officer of the English **judiciary** in London between 1510 and 1518, he earned a reputation for honesty and fairness, while in 1515, More accompanied an embassy to **Flanders** to help negotiate a trade agreement for London's wool merchants. He had in the meantime also met and grown close to **Desiderius Erasmus**, the eminent Dutch humanist, who in 1509 dedicated his *Moraiae encomium* (*In Praise of Folly*) to his learned friend and who stayed for extended periods with the More family whenever he visited England.

More joined Henry VIII's royal council in 1518, attended the **Field of Cloth of Gold** summit in France in 1520, received a knighthood from an admiring king in 1521, and was elected speaker of the House of Commons in 1523. Having previously lived in the Bucklersbury and Bishopsgate neighborhoods of the capital, More purchased land and built a spacious manor house for his family in Chelsea outside London in the mid-1520s. There he established a schoolroom and hired tutors for his children, including his favorite daughter, Margaret, or Meg, who excelled in her studies of Latin and Greek and grew up to become an accomplished humanist scholar herself.

Already a rising political star, Sir Thomas was also earning a name for himself in European intellectual circles for his scholarly writings at the same time. In 1513, he published his *History of King Richard III*, a thinly veiled defense of the Tudor monarchy that presents the last Yorkist ruler as a deformed murderer. In 1516, More published an initial Latin edition of *Utopia*, a small philosophical treatise

that he dedicated to Erasmus and divided into two books, or parts. In the opening book, a fictional Portuguese traveler named Raphael Hythloday manages to convince Thomas More himself that philosophers have a duty to serve kings as royal ministers. In the second and much better-known book, Hythloday describes a mythical island he had visited in the Atlantic that featured happy inhabitants and idealized institutions of society and government. *Utopia* proved so successful that further Latin editions were published in Flanders, Basel, Paris, and Florence between 1517 and 1519, though it was not until 1551 that a first English translation became available in London.

A loyal son of the Roman Church, Sir Thomas More devoted much of the rest of his body of written work to repudiating the ideas of evangelical reformers—such as Martin Luther—whom he regarded as heretics. In 1521, Henry VIII published his **Assertio septem sacramentorum**, or the *Defense of the Seven Sacraments against Martin Luther*, a tract that **Thomas Cardinal Wolsey**, Bishop **John Fisher** of Rochester, and Thomas More may have authored or at least edited for him. When Luther published his caustic reply to King Henry's *Assertio*, More angrily rebutted the German reformer with his own *Responsio ad Lutherum* in 1523 and followed this up five years later with his *Dialogue Concerning Heresies* in English. In 1529, Sir Thomas answered reformer **Simon Fish**'s critique of the Roman clergy with his *Supplication of Souls*, and two years later, More responded to Bible translator **William Tyndale**'s attack on his own 1528 *Dialogue* by publishing the *Confutation of Tyndale's Answer*. All the while, many contemporaries believed that the pious More wore a hair shirt and fasted daily, and it was widely rumored that his abhorrence of heresy sometimes led reformers to imprisonment at Chelsea or even to death at the stake.

Meanwhile, the political career of Sir Thomas More was still on the rise, though the prominent place he would soon occupy at the Tudor court was destined to end in a precipitous fall. After returning from an embassy to France to help negotiate the Treaty of Cambrai, More was appointed lord chancellor of

England by King Henry in October 1529 after Cardinal Wolsey had himself fallen from royal favor. As chancellor, More pressed Parliament to censure heretical books, and he investigated the seditious rantings of one **Elizabeth Barton**, known by many as the Holy Maid of Kent, whose alleged prophecies of King Henry's death were beginning to cause public relations problems for the Crown. At the same time, More was becoming ever more disturbed by the king's growing impatience to be rid of his first queen, **Katherine of Aragon**, so that he might marry **Anne Boleyn** in her stead. King Henry further alienated More when he demanded that the Southern **Convocation of Bishops** acknowledge him as supreme lord of the English Church, the so-called **Submission of the Clergy** that the prelates only accepted after adding the phrase "as far as the law of Christ allows." Chancellor More, incensed by this royal grab at papal and episcopal authority, surrendered the great seal and resigned his office in protest on 16 May 1532.

Once again a private citizen, Thomas More now attempted to return quietly to his family and his books at his Chelsea estate. The king and his new chief minister, **Thomas Cromwell**, knew, however, that the coming break with Rome could not win popular support in England without the acquiescence—if not the full approval—of the honest, forthright ex-chancellor. After Archbishop **Thomas Cranmer** set aside Queen Katherine, King Henry formally married Anne Boleyn in summer 1533 and then had Cromwell push the **Act of Succession** through Parliament the following spring. This statute settled the royal line of succession on the heirs of Henry and Queen Anne,

asserted that the "bishop of Rome" had overstepped his authority in England, and then demanded an oath from all the king's subjects to uphold these new realities or suffer the penalty for treason. When Cromwell's agents summoned More to London to secure his oath, the shrewd old lawyer did not vocally refuse to swear it; he simply remained silent except to protest his unwavering loyalty to King Henry as his sovereign lord.

Sir Thomas More soon found himself incarcerated, as his father had once been, in the Tower of London by mid-April 1534. At first, he was held in relatively comfortable quarters, and supplied with some of his books and writing materials, he kept busy penning many letters (especially to his daughter Meg), along with several devotional works, such as the *Treatise on the Passion* and *Dialogue of Comfort against Tribulation*. Cromwell and selected members of the royal council interrogated Sir Thomas four times in May and June 1535, a period during which several Carthusian monks and even the aged Bishop John Fisher went to their deaths as traitors. All the while, More continued to sidestep the Succession and (since November 1534) the **Act of Supremacy** oaths with his steadfast silence. In mid-June, however, **Richard Rich**, Cromwell's agent, claimed he heard the ex-chancellor openly deny the royal supremacy while they talked together in More's cell. Three weeks later, Sir Thomas was tried and convicted of treason at Westminster Hall and was then taken to Tower Hill to die on the block on 6 July 1535. Some 400 years passed before Pope Pius XI canonized both Thomas More and John Fisher as Catholic martyrs and saints.

N

NAVY OF HENRY VIII (c. 1485–1547). King Henry VIII is often honored today as the "father of the Royal Navy," but two other English rulers, Alfred the Great of Wessex (r. 871–99) and Henry VIII's father, **Henry VII** (r. 1485–1509), are sometimes accorded that dignity as well. Although the second Tudor king's navy never played a significant role in any of his many military campaigns, he was keenly interested in the design, construction, armament, and navigational techniques of his warships, and he presided over the largest naval build-up in English history through to the 16th century. Many innovations in seaborne fighting tactics and weaponry were also pioneered under Henry VIII, most of which became standard features of naval warfare for centuries to come. One of the great disasters of the last years of King Henry's reign was the loss of his prized warship *Mary Rose*, an impressive vessel that was reportedly so top-heavy with soldiers and guns that it capsized and sank to the floor of Portsmouth Harbor in 1545 just as it sailed forth to engage a hostile French naval squadron.

It may be impossible to pinpoint the birth of the Royal Navy exactly, but many historians credit King Alfred of Wessex with having constructed the first fleet of longships that, copied from Viking designs, fended off the seaborne attacks of those marauding Scandinavians in the ninth century AD. When King Henry VII seized the English throne in 1485, he inherited the seven vessels that had comprised the navy of his defeated Yorkist enemy King Richard III. Partly because the Yorkist navy had failed to prevent his own invasion, the first Tudor king allowed his fleet to drop to only five ships by the end of his reign, though he did refurbish most of them and added the four-masted carrack *Sweepstake* to his royal flotilla in 1495. Henry VII built England's first dry-dock facility at Portsmouth, and he created the office of clerk of the king's ships, both accomplishments for which he is occasionally also recognized as the founder of the Royal Navy.

When the exuberant young Henry VIII succeeded his father as king in 1509, he was determined to transform his realm into a first-rate sea power, and just five years into his reign, he had expanded his navy to include two dozen vessels. Some of those he commissioned and had built in England; others he purchased from Hanseatic and Italian owners and then refitted for service in the Tudor fleet. In 1514, he ordered construction of the giant *Henry Grace à Dieu*, or *Great Harry*, a 180-foot-long ship of the line that displaced more than 1,000 tons; carried a crew of 900 sailors and marines; and featured towering bow and stern "castles" for boarding enemy vessels. As the English king's flagship, the *Henry Grace à Dieu* was armed with 21 heavy bronze culverins, 130 lighter iron cannons, and around 70 swivel guns. Many of the heavier pieces were mounted below decks in the waist of the ship and were designed to fire through closable gun ports.

Along with the *Great Harry*, the Tudor king counted several caravels (smaller ships displacing 80–100 tons), row barges (ocean-worthy oared galleys), and carracks (three- or four-masted vessels displacing 200–600 tons each) among the ships in his navy. To support this force, he built his own dry-dock facilities (with storage warehouses) on the Thames River at Deptford and Woolwich, both located close to **Greenwich Palace** so Henry could pay frequent inspection visits. During the 1530s, the king commissioned the construction of 4 new warships and had 5 completely refurbished, while the 1540s saw 13 larger new vessels built in England and another 8 added to the fleet as purchases or captured prizes. By the end of his reign in 1547, King Henry boasted a combat-ready navy of close to 50 ships of all sizes and descriptions.

Thanks to efforts to raise and restore her in 1982, the best known of all Henry VIII's many warships today is the *Mary Rose*, a large carrack that sank in Portsmouth Harbor in summer 1545 on its way to engage an invading French fleet in the Solent Strait. Two popular myths about the *Mary Rose*—that she was named for King Henry's sister **Mary** Tudor and that she sank on her maiden voyage—are either unsupported by the evidence or completely false. It is likely that the ship was named for the Virgin Mary and not the Tudor princess, while the *Mary Rose* was first constructed early in Henry's reign and saw action in several of his wars before being rebuilt in 1536 and then famously sinking in 1545. Originally a carrack-style, four-masted vessel of some 450 tons' displacement, the *Mary Rose* initially carried a crew of more than 700 and boasted 78 guns of various sizes when launched at Portsmouth in 1511.

The ship was first deployed during King Henry's **French invasion of 1513–14** but then saw lighter duty clearing the English Channel of pirates prior to the **Field of Cloth of Gold** summit in 1520. Once again in action during the king's second **French invasion of 1523–24**, the *Mary Rose* was kept in ordinary (reserve) until she was completely overhauled and refitted in 1536. When the newly modernized vessel emerged from dry dock, she displaced more than 700 tons; bristled with more than 90 guns; but carried a complement of only 420 men, the smaller number due to increased firepower over boarding marines and the use of block, tackle, and pulley devices to simplify sail and rigging management.

With England at war with France once again late in Henry's reign, the *Mary Rose* sailed forth on 19 July 1545 to intercept a major French invasion force that had entered the Solent Strait between the Isle of Wight and the Hampshire coast. With King Henry watching from shore and with gun ports open for battle, the great Tudor warship abruptly came about to fire a broadside volley, then awkwardly listed to starboard and took on water following the sudden maneuver and an ill-timed gust of wind. With heavy guns, a galley brick oven, and a 360-gallon boiling cauldron all crashing across its decks, the *Mary Rose* foundered and sank in Portsmouth Harbor in full view of the horrified king, with a loss of more than 350 lives. The submerged vessel lay on the floor of the harbor until fishermen rediscovered her there in 1836. Then in 1982, with Prince Charles of **Wales** overseeing the project, engineers with the *Mary Rose* Trust raised the remaining hull of the sunken vessel and moved it to a special restoration facility called the Portsmouth Historic Dockyard. There the ship was sprayed with freshwater and polyethylene glycol preservatives for 34 years before the timbers of the hull were allowed to dry out. Today modern visitors can view the restored *Mary Rose* through windows in an airtight chamber and can tour the adjoining museum to learn more about this pride and joy of the Tudor navy.

NOBLES OR NOBILITY (c. 800–1600 AND BEYOND). Members of the nobility were also known as nobles, aristocrats, magnates, lords, barons, peers of the realm, or any combination of these in England from Anglo-Saxon times to the Tudor age and beyond. Nobles comprised the highest social order in the kingdom because they owned great tracts of land known as manors or estates, which in turn generated wealth through the production of foodstuffs, timber, wool, minerals, and metallic ores. Wealthy nobles were the warriors of society because only they could afford the armor, weapons, and specially trained warhorses necessary to engage in knightly combat. Membership in the ranks of the nobility was usually a matter of birth, though later in Tudor and

Stuart times, titles could be earned through loyal service to the Crown or purchased by upwardly mobile members of the **gentry**.

Noble families were usually identified by colorful heraldic symbols displayed on coats of arms (ceremonial shields), some of which dated back many centuries and proudly showed off the aristocratic pedigree of the families who owned and displayed them. Noble status also came with such privileges as guaranteed seats in the House of Lords, exemptions from **parliamentary** taxation, judgment in criminal trials by other nobles or peers, and feudal rights over peasants who lived on and cultivated noble estates.

The term *nobility* has its roots in the Latin verb *nobilito*, to make known or famous, and was originally applied to members of the patrician class in ancient Rome who governed the state in the Senate and who owned wide estates, or *latifundia*, that produced wealth and enriched their families. Following the collapse of the western Roman Empire in the fifth century AD, warriors or royal officers were rewarded for their service with grants of land and so augmented the patricians as Europe's earliest nobles. Gradually, the feudal system evolved in which noble landowners granted smaller properties called fiefs to vassals (those who served) in return for their military support or, if they were peasants, their agricultural labor. Over many centuries, various noble titles emerged that ranked individuals and their families by the extent of their land holdings and by the wealth that those lands generated. Thus, the title of duke (from the Latin *duco*, to lead) was the highest rank and was usually held by very wealthy relatives of the royal family; then came marquis (French for border lord); earl (from the Saxon *ealderman*, or senior advisor); barons; viscounts; and so forth. These titles were almost always hereditary and, in order to avoid splitting up estates between multiple heirs, were passed on (with their lands) through the system of primogeniture to the eldest son only. Younger sons stood to inherit little or nothing from this arrangement and were forced to pursue other livelihoods, either in the church or as mercenary freelance warriors for hire.

As medieval social elites, nobles were expected to protect their vassals and defend Christian society because they were trained in the arts of battle and because they alone could afford the expensive armor and horses that knightly warfare required. Gradually, however, the military role of the English nobility began to fade in the later Middle Ages, as kings and great magnates drew more heavily on paid professional troops and less on traditional feudal levies to fill the ranks of their armies. By the late 14th century, a system known as bastard feudalism had evolved that, based more on monetary exchanges than on oaths of protection and service, changed the character of the English nobility forever. Wealthy barons now became patrons who attracted the service of adherents, called retainers or clients, with grants of land, paid positions in their households, minor titles, privileges, purses of coins, or even advantageous marriages. The group of a noble's retainers—known collectively as his affinity—wore the patron's livery (his coat of arms or insignia on a badge) to identify its members as his men, and they signed indentures or contracts that paid them a wage in return for specified duties performed. This bastard feudal system enabled nobles to keep household staffs and small standing armies at the ready and greatly contributed to the endemic violence that plagued England during the **Wars of the Roses** in the latter half of the 15th century.

By the dawn of the Tudor age, nobles were more useful to the monarchy as government ministers, diplomats, and judges than they were as military commanders, though some of the more prominent peers of the realm continued to serve the Crown in this way. Accordingly, many more sons of noble families began to pursue higher education to prepare themselves for these new administrative roles and enrolled at **Oxford** and **Cambridge Universities** and at the **Inns of Court** law schools in London. There those students acquired the classical training of the new learning, or *studia humanitatis*, a curriculum that sent them forth to grace Tudor society as the sophisticated and elegant new nobility of the European Renaissance.

NORRIS, SIR HENRY (c. 1482/96–1536).
This influential courtier and wealthy member of the landed **gentry** became the friend and confidant of Henry VIII and served him as a gentleman of the royal privy chamber and groom of the stool as well. He knew and was friendly with **Thomas Cardinal Wolsey**, the great Crown minister, yet he aligned himself with Wolsey's enemies, the **Boleyn** family and their supporters, once King Henry took Mistress **Anne Boleyn** as his second wife and queen in 1533. When she fell from royal favor and was charged with traitorous infidelity three years later, Sir Henry Norris found himself caught up in the scandal as one of her alleged lovers. He was convicted of treason with four other men and died under the headsman's axe in London just two days before Anne Boleyn met a similar fate herself.

Today the parentage and possible date of the birth of Henry Norris (alternately Norreys) are subject to some confusion and doubt. Many modern scholars believe he was the second son of Sir Edward Norris of Tattendon Castle in Berkshire and his wife, Frideswide Lovell Norris, the daughter of a family of minor **nobility** from Northamptonshire. Because Sir Edward died in 1487, an earlier birth date of 1482 for son Henry fits this version of his parentage well. However, some historians believe he was the second son of Sir Edward Norris's younger brother Richard, in which case Henry could have been born much later, perhaps in 1496. A 17th-century heraldic register offers evidence, though, that Richard Norris only sired a single daughter named Anne. Because she inherited property from her father in 1522 that ordinarily would have gone to a son, it seems likely that Henry Norris was indeed Sir Edward's child (not Richard's) and that he drew his first breath around 1482. In any case, little more is known about Henry Norris's early life with any certainty, but we can guess from his later years that he probably was groomed as a youth for a career of service at the Tudor court.

In fact, Norris was already resident in the royal household of **Henry VII** by the time the old king died and his teenaged son Henry VIII succeeded him in April 1509. Gregarious and physically robust, Norris quickly became one of young Henry's "henchmen," a group of rowdy courtiers who accompanied and romped about with the high-spirited king wherever he went. In 1515, the second Tudor ruler granted a royal park in Berkshire to Norris who, following receipt of many other such properties over the years, managed to amass an impressive income of nearly £1,240 per annum by the time he reached the age of 50. In 1517, Norris was serving Henry VIII as a gentleman of the privy chamber (bedroom), a position that gave him daily access to the royal ear and made him a trusted confidant of the Tudor king. After Henry VIII knighted him in 1519, Norris accompanied thousands of English courtiers to France for the **Field of Cloth of Gold** summit meeting with **François I** in 1520. Six years later, he accepted the singularly important post of groom of the stool (toilet) to become the chief body servant and thus master of all King Henry's personal attendants.

The trajectory of the life and career of Sir Henry Norris might well have continued its swift ascent had Henry VIII's "**Great Matter**," his attempt to set aside one wife and queen for another, not intervened to change his fortunes forever. Ever on cordial terms with Cardinal Wolsey, Norris managed to sidestep the lord chancellor's precipitous fall from grace in 1529–30 to remain a privileged servant and trusted friend of the Tudor king. At the same time, Sir Henry seemed to sense that the ambitious Boleyn family would soon become preeminent at court, so he threw his support behind the campaign of their determined daughter Anne to become King Henry's next spouse and queen consort. In January 1533, Norris was one of only three witnesses at the secret wedding of Henry VIII and Anne Boleyn at **Whitehall Palace**, and when Sir **Thomas More** was arrested and imprisoned in the **Tower of London** a few years later, Sir Henry acquired several of the former lord chancellor's confiscated estates.

The fairy-tale reign of Anne Boleyn as queen of England did not last very long, for she failed to give King Henry his coveted male heir, she harbored heterodox religious views, and she demanded that her philandering husband remain faithful to her alone. When Queen Anne miscarried a grossly deformed male fetus early in 1536, the unhappy king refused to claim the "monster" as his own and then ordered his chief minister, **Thomas Cromwell**, to discover the identity of the unborn child's true father. Cromwell had six men—among them Anne's Flemish minstrel Mark Smeaton, her brother **George Boleyn**, the court poet **Thomas Wyatt**, and Sir Henry Norris—arrested and interrogated as suspected lovers of the queen in spring 1536.

Only Smeaton confessed (probably under torture) to the charges, while Norris and the others stoutly maintained their innocence and delivered passionate speeches in their own defense. Sir Henry was specifically accused of having slept with Queen Anne on dates and in places where the two of them could not have met, leading most modern historians to conclude that the allegations against Norris were entirely baseless. At their trial on 12 May 1536, however, all the accused, save Wyatt (who was imprisoned and later released), were condemned to the horrific hanging, drawing, and quartering deaths of traitors. After the sentences of the convicted knights (but not Smeaton) were commuted to the quicker and more humane form of beheading, Norris and the others gave short speeches and then died bravely on Tower Hill on 17 May 1536 before a large crowd of cheering onlookers. Queen Anne Boleyn died by the hand of a French swordsman, and her brother George met his end on an English block just two days later.

O

ORDER OF THE GARTER. *See* GARTER, ORDER OF THE.

OXFORD UNIVERSITY (c. 1167–). England's oldest institution of higher learning, Oxford University was the educational training ground for a number of influential Tudor-era personalities. Once they rose to prominence, a number of these religious, government, and intellectual leaders went on to found their own collegiate institutions in Oxford. Along with **Cambridge University**, Oxford served as the English port of entry for the *studia humanitatis*, the new learning of humanism, which until the reign of Henry VIII had largely been excluded from the lecture halls of both universities. Proud of his own humanistic education, King Henry actively supported the introduction of the new learning into England and insisted that Oxford University incorporate the study of classical languages and ancient authors into its undergraduate curriculum.

The exact origin of higher education in Oxford is difficult to pin down, but it seems there was some sort of instruction in Latin and rudimentary theology going on at several schools in the city as early as 1096. Students, called scholars, were soon coming to Oxford to hear lectures from secular priests, called masters, by the 1130s. These scholars found lodgings in the homes of local townsmen and often gathered in single-building communities according to their place of origin or their subject of study. The foundation date of Oxford University is usually given as 1167, when King Henry II banned further student migration to Paris, which in turn led to a sharp rise in the academic population of Oxford. In 1190, the first foreign student from Holland enrolled at Oxford to help establish the school's scholarly reputation abroad. By 1214, Oxford had its first collegiate ordinances and its first chancellor, and in 1231, King Henry III issued a charter to form the various residence halls of Oxford into a *universitas*, or corporation of learning. During this period of rapid growth, friction developed between residents of the "town" and scholars of the "gown," and after violent street clashes led to killings on both sides, a group of academics left Oxford to found their own educational institution at Cambridge in 1209.

Secular priests had mostly served as teaching masters in Oxford during the school's early years, but by the mid-13th century, highly educated members of the Dominican and Franciscan orders were taking over most of the faculty positions at the university. They founded their own *collegia*, or colleges, with lecture halls, chapels, libraries, dormitories, and dining refectories all located within the same quadrangle-style compounds. Each of these semiautonomous institutions drew up its own set of statutes to govern the daily routines, courses of study, and personal behaviors of the resident student scholars. The statutes also established rules of governance and instruction at the colleges by providing for the appointment of headmasters or presidents, deans, bursars (treasurers), and professors or fellows. Only St. Edmund's Hall (founded c. 1225) survives today from the oldest times of in-town student lodgings. Some of the more prominent Oxford colleges from the Middle Ages included University (founded c. 1249), Balliol (1263), Merton (1264), Exeter (1314), Oriel (1326), and New (1379). The foundations of Lincoln (1427), All Souls (1437), Magdalen (1458), and Brasenose (1509) Colleges followed in the early-modern period.

The first Oxford school established during the reign of Henry VIII was that of Corpus Christi College, which Bishop **Richard Fox** of Winchester founded near Merton and Oriel Colleges in 1517. In the foundation statutes he drew up for his college, Bishop Fox refers to its community of 20 fellows and 20 scholars (plus administrators, chapel officials, and servants) as an *alvearium*, or beehive, a place he hoped would reflect the constant activity level of diligent worker bees. Fox also established three endowed lectureships in classical Latin texts, theological exegesis, and ancient Greek letters at Corpus Christi. The last of these was truly revolutionary, for the study of Greek had long been officially banned at Oxford as the heretical language of the breakaway Eastern Orthodox Church. In fact, Greek studies had only recently made a tentative and informal appearance in England under Bishop **John Fisher** of Rochester and the eminent Dutch humanist **Desiderius Erasmus**. It remained, however, for Bishop Fox to endow his lectureship in that language in 1517 at Corpus Christi, thus granting official recognition to one of the defining ancient tongues of the European Renaissance. When King Henry VIII defended Fox's Greek lectureship in 1518 from the criticism of conservative Oxford dons, the

new learning had at last triumphed in England and would soon spread to other Oxford and Cambridge colleges.

The other great Oxford institution to rise during the reign of Henry VIII was initially named Cardinal College by its founder, **Thomas Cardinal Wolsey**. Inspired by his mentor Bishop Fox, the "Great Cardinal" acquired the property of St. Frideswide's priory (adjacent to Corpus Christi College) and began to build Cardinal College there in 1524–25. Wolsey also endowed a chair in Greek studies at his new school and borrowed heavily from the Corpus faculty to deliver its earliest lectures. Like most everything he planned or built, the scale of Wolsey's college would have been magnificent if he had lived long enough to see the project finished. Henry VIII's lord chancellor fell from royal favor and then died in 1530, however, leaving his school in Oxford only 70 percent complete. The king soon took over Wolsey's collegiate foundation and, approaching his own end in 1546, renamed it Christ Church but otherwise did little to improve its unfinished structure. After the building fabric was finally completed under the Stuarts, Christ Church took its place as Oxford University's largest and wealthiest college.

Some of the most important Tudor-era figures to either attend or graduate from Oxford University included Bishop Fox and Cardinal Wolsey themselves, along with humanist and theologian **John Colet**, scriptural scholar **William Tyndale**, humanist and statesman Sir **Thomas More**, archbishop of Canterbury **William Warham**, and future archbishop of Canterbury **Reginald Cardinal Pole**.

P

PACE, RICHARD (1482–1536). Richard Pace was an ordained priest, an active humanist scholar, and a trusted Crown ambassador who ably represented English interests at various European courts over the course of his relatively brief career. Associated in the early-Tudor period with two English archbishops, Pace entered the service of Henry VIII and his lord chancellor, **Thomas Cardinal Wolsey**, during the second decade of the 16th century. He was involved in negotiations with the Swiss, promoted King Henry's bid to become Holy Roman Emperor, preached at an opulent Anglo-French summit, and twice paid generous but unsuccessful bribes to see Wolsey elected pope. A noted Latin and Greek linguist, Pace befriended **Desiderius Erasmus** and authored both learned and satirical works of his own between his many diplomatic missions abroad. His health, never robust, deteriorated sharply in the later 1520s, and confined to a cloistered monastery with some sort of mental infirmity, he died prematurely in southern England at the age of just 54 years.

Richard Pace was the eldest son of John Pace (alternately Pacey, Percy, or John of Hampshire) and grew up with a younger brother named John somewhere (unknown) in late-medieval Hampshire. As a youth, he attended the prestigious Winchester College grammar school and there attracted the notice of Thomas Langton, the bishop of Winchester, as a promising student of music. The bishop sponsored Pace's further education at Queen's College in Oxford University; hired the lad as his amanuensis and then sent him off for additional study to Italy, where he met and came to know Erasmus around the turn of the 16th century. Langton became archbishop of Canterbury early in 1501 but soon died of the plague, thus ending his financial support of Pace and obliging the young English scholar to return to a teaching post at his Queen's College alma mater. Pace entered the priesthood and then accepted employment in the household of Christopher Cardinal Bainbridge, the archbishop of York. The two men took up residence at the papal court in Rome, but after Bainbridge was assassinated in 1514, Pace threw himself into the search for those who had perpetrated the crime. Clearly impressed by the English priest's loyalty to his deceased patron, Pope **Leo X** sent Pace home and commended him to the service of Henry VIII as a secretary and royal ambassador.

Richard Pace's diplomatic career began in October 1515, when Cardinal Wolsey ordered him abroad to secure Swiss support for an imperial attack against the French in northern Italy. The English envoy spent much treasure and offered many promises, but the Swiss, still shaken from recent military defeats, simply refused to get involved in another foreign war. Upon his return to England, Pace refocused his attention on more scholarly pursuits over the next two years. He first published his earlier composition entitled *Julius exclusus de coelis* (*Julius Excluded from Heaven*), a satirical portrait of the sinful Pope Julius II begging St. Peter for admission to paradise. *De fructu qui ex doctrina percipitur* (*He Who Gathers Fruit from Instruction*), in which Pace praised the virtues of a liberal education, was composed during this time in England and published in Basel in 1517. As was true of most English clerics of his day, Richard Pace also collected a number of lucrative church livings, and he occasionally delivered sermons as well during breaks from his ambassadorial duties.

When the Holy Roman Emperor **Maximilian I** died in January 1519, Pace went off to Germany and tried to convince the imperial electors to vote for his own royal master, Henry VIII, as Maximilian's successor. The electors proved unwilling to comply, so King Henry ordered his emissary to try to block the election of his closest rivals in favor of a more obscure and less threatening candidate. Pace's failure to achieve even this more modest goal left him physically and mentally drained, causing him to contract a severe fever in Germany that struck him again following his return to England. His health did not improve when, at the **Field of Cloth of Gold** summit with Henry VIII in France, he preached an emotionally exhausting series of sermons in late June 1520 on the blessings of European peace.

Pace was allowed to rest for more than a year at the English court, but the death of Pope Leo X late in 1521 once again called him to action as a foreign diplomat. This time, he traveled to Venice to persuade (and bribe) the many cardinals living there to elect Cardinal Wolsey as Christendom's next pontiff. The Venetian prelates gladly accepted English gold but ignored Wolsey and cast their ballots instead for a pious Dutchman who then became Pope Adrian VI. Pace remained in Italy, and when Pope Adrian died just 15 months later, the English ambassador headed to Rome to try to influence a second papal conclave in Wolsey's favor. The mostly Italian prelates once again bypassed the English cardinal and elected **Clement VII**, thus finally ending Wolsey's papal ambitions and leaving Richard Pace financially adrift in Europe to fend for himself.

By the mid-1520s, Pace's lifetime of punishing travel, debilitating illness, and repeated diplomatic failures were beginning to take their toll on a man more suited to intellectual scholarship than to the stresses of international affairs. Perhaps because of his failed attempts on the Roman papacy, Cardinal Wolsey turned on Richard Pace around this time and did his best to keep him occupied abroad and away from the English court. When the doge of Venice urged King Henry's government to bring the sickly Pace home in 1525, the ailing emissary was finally recalled and never left his native England again. As his mental dexterity slipped away, Pace hired assistants to help with ecclesiastical tasks in his various clerical livings, and in 1527, he entered Syon Abbey outside London for his own care and safety. Rumors that Wolsey imprisoned Pace in the **Tower of London** for two years or that he endured abuse at the hands of several enemies appear to be unfounded. Reportedly suffering from imbecility (probably advancing dementia or Alzheimer's disease), Richard Pace lingered until 1536 and finally passed away somewhere in the New Forest area of southern Hampshire. He was laid to rest in the churchyard of St. Dunstan and All Saints' parish in Stepney, Surrey, now located in a southern district of greater London.

PAGEANTS (1485–1547). King Henry VIII loved court spectacles, festivals, and pageants because they served to distract him from more tiresome kingly duties while showing off his performing abilities and royal magnificence at the same time. With Crown governance in the capable hands of talented ministers like **Thomas Cardinal Wolsey** and **Thomas Cromwell**, King Henry felt free to present and even take part in elaborately staged skits that reflected his sense of whimsy and his devotion to the ideals of chivalric romance. Partially inspired by the festive tableaux performed at the 15th-century Burgundian court, most Henrician pageants featured mythical, allegorical, and classical themes. They frequently offered subtle lessons in morality and noble virtue as well and were designed with sudden twists and surprise revelations to delight their Tudor audiences. Such extravagant entertainments greatly strained (and drained) the royal coffers, but foreign ambassadors fortunate enough to behold Henry VIII's court spectacles almost always returned home with admiring tales of the English king's generosity and grandeur.

The majority of the pageants that took place during King Henry's reign were performed between 1509 and 1530 under the creative direction of William Cornish, the choirmaster of the Chapel Royal. Cornish (and later various masters of the revels) and his staff were responsible for designing and building the elaborate large-scale sets in great halls or atop wooden platforms equipped with wheels for ease of movement. Some pageant stages were immense and, furnished with lush landscapes, miniature castles, and enchanted forests, could accommodate a dozen or more actors. The master of revels also had to invent the pageant's central theme, design and make the costumes, and even arrange the seating and lights—all with (often unsolicited) guidance from the show's principal performers. The exorbitantly expensive costumes were opulently crafted from the finest silks, satins, brocades, and cloth of gold. Possessed of a fertile imagination and some musical ability himself, Henry VIII sometimes developed the plots, wrote the scripts, and even composed the music for the entertainments he sponsored. Pageants enacted scenes of faux battles, adventurous hunts, mythical trysts, and noble courtships and frequently involved the masking or disguising of actors, who revealed their true identities at the end of the performance.

King Henry especially enjoyed participating in such playful deceptions and reveled in his audience's (often feigned) inability to identify him in a company of masked look-alikes. **George Cavendish**, Cardinal Wolsey's secretary, described one such performance that took place at the palace of **Hampton Court** in the late 1520s. Always willing to show off his own wealth and munificence, the "Great Cardinal" had just finished hosting a sumptuous banquet, when a company of mysterious French **nobles** suddenly arrived on a Thames riverboat at the palace's water gate. Ushered into the great hall, the maskers saluted Wolsey and his guests, then produced cups filled with coins to play at mumchance (a dice game) for the amusement of all. Possibly prompted by a signal from one of the visitors, the cardinal asked if any of the French "strangers" were noble enough to replace him at the head of the banquet table. When Wolsey guessed that perhaps a large, bearded fellow might indeed be so noble, the chosen visitor showed himself to be a courtier who resembled Henry VIII a good deal. Laughing heartily, the king then

removed his own mask and revealed his true identity to the assembled onlookers, who were "astonished" and "rejoiced" at the sight of their bemused sovereign lord.

Perhaps the best known of King Henry's many pageants occurred three days after Shrove Tuesday (today's Fat Tuesday), on 4 March 1522, at Cardinal Wolsey's London residence of York Place, later **Whitehall Palace**. Shrove (meaning forgiveness) Tuesday was traditionally the day that preceded Ash Wednesday, thus marking the start of the Lenten season. On this occasion, the Tudor court had also gathered to fête a group of imperial ambassadors who had just concluded a military alliance between Henry VIII and the Emperor **Charles V**. Following an appropriately lavish feast, Wolsey and his guests strolled into an adjoining chamber that was brightly festooned with rich wall hangings, dozens of torches, and three large banners bearing images of lovelorn human hearts. At one end of the hall stood an elaborate stage set featuring a prefabricated green castle (dubbed the Château Vert) with three large towers that protected eight noble ladies. Clad in white satin trimmed with gold, each lady was a prominent member of the Tudor court and represented such allegorical virtues as Beauty (**Mary** Tudor, the king's sister); Kindness (**Mary Boleyn**, Henry's mistress); and Perseverance (**Anne Boleyn**, the future queen). Below the castle's towers stood another eight ladies, similarly dressed but sporting threatening identities like Danger, Jealously, Scorn, and Unkindness.

The pageant's action began when eight lords with names like Honesty (played by Henry VIII himself), Loyalty, Gentleness, and Nobility arrived on the set wearing cloth-of-gold caps and blue satin cloaks. These gallant knights asked the virtuous ladies to admit them to the Château Vert, but the evil women at the base of the fortress prevented their approach. Following a noisy discharge of cannons from outside the performance hall, the lords rushed forward and exchanged volleys of tarts, fruit, and rose water with the castle's wicked female defenders. When the Château Vert was finally taken, the victorious knights invited the rescued ladies down from their towers to take part in an elaborately choreographed dance. All the players then removed their masks to reveal their true identities to the admiring onlookers, who eagerly repaired to the banquet hall once again to continue their feast. So typical of most Henrician pageants, this gaudy performance allowed the Tudor king to impress the visiting emissaries, display his acting and dancing skills, and demonstrate his devotion to the ideals of knightly chivalry, human virtue, and romantic love. Henry VIII took great pleasure in sponsoring, staging, and acting in these fanciful productions and clearly believed their propaganda value far outweighed their considerable drain on his financial resources.

PAGET, SIR WILLIAM, FIRST BARON PAGET OF BEAUDESERT (1506–63).

William Paget was a prominent courtier and government officer who traveled widely as a foreign diplomat and served ably in Henry VIII's later privy council. A man of humble origins, Paget received a first-class education and used the contacts he made at school to advance his career in the service of the Crown. He actively encouraged King Henry to replace his first queen with **Anne Boleyn** in order to sire a male heir and secure the Tudor succession. Paget allied himself with the Church of England Reform Party in the 1540s and positioned himself to play a significant role in the new reign when old Henry VIII died in 1547. Under **Edward VI**, Paget was ennobled and became chancellor of the Duchy of Lancaster, but he also suffered a brief period of imprisonment in the **Tower of London** in 1551–52. Involved peripherally in the Lady Jane Grey affair, Paget was pardoned by and then served Queen **Mary I** as lord privy seal between 1556 and 1558. He retired from that office at Mary's death and passed away himself of unknown causes a few years later.

William Paget was born in Wednesbury in Staffordshire to a working-class couple named Anne and John Paget (or sometimes Pachett). William's father was a wool shearer and sergeant at arms for the sheriff of London. Young Paget was first educated at St. Paul's School in the capital, the well-known institution of Christian humanist learning founded by the reformist scholar **John Colet** in 1510. At St. Paul's, he met and cultivated friendships with **Anthony Denny**, **Thomas Audley**, and **Thomas Wriothesley**, all of whom went on to serve Henry VIII and may have helped engineer Paget's rise to prominence as well. At age 16, Paget entered Trinity Hall at **Cambridge University**, where he was sponsored by the **Boleyn** family and studied under **Stephen Gardiner**, the future bishop of Winchester, privy councilor, and (eventually) lord chancellor of England. Gardiner sent his young protégé off for additional education to the University of Paris, then recalled and employed him as a household secretary beginning in 1527. The following year, Paget contracted the dreaded **sweating sickness**, but he recovered sufficiently to win election to the House of Commons for the borough of Lichfield in 1529. In 1530, he married Anne Preston, a woman four years his junior, who gave her husband six daughters and three sons over the course of their 27 years of wedded life together.

William Paget's career as a foreign ambassador also began in 1530, when Gardiner dispatched him to Paris a second time to research the validity of Henry VIII's first marriage to his brother's widow, **Katherine of Aragon**. During the euphemistic "**Great Matter**," King Henry's campaign to set aside his Spanish queen for Mistress Boleyn, Paget supported the case for annulment and in so doing remained loyal to his former Boleyn patrons. He soon found himself employed on frequent diplomatic missions to Germany to treat with representatives of the Holy Roman Emperor, the elector of Saxony, and the Protestant princes of the Schmalkaldic League. In 1534, Paget was appointed clerk of the signet (a miniature royal seal), received a knighthood a few years later, and then acquired several religious houses and their lands during the dissolution of the **monasteries**. He also survived the precipitous fall of Anne Boleyn and her family to become the personal secretary of King Henry's next two queens, **Jane Seymour** and **Anne of Cleves**.

Following the scandal and execution of Henry's fifth consort, **Katherine Howard**, Paget traveled to France in 1542 to explain the queen's sudden demise to the French court.

He earned promotion to a seat on the privy council upon his return, and also granted the post of secretary for foreign affairs, he now became one of Henry VIII's closest advisors. A few years later, the Tudor king sent Paget off to coordinate joint military operations with Emperor **Charles** V for their upcoming **French invasion of 1544–45**. Soon sensing a political shift at court, Paget quietly allied himself with **Edward Seymour** and **John Dudley**, the respective Earls of Hertford and Warwick, when those religiously reform-minded privy councilors weaned the king's favor away from the more conservative Bishop Gardiner and Duke **Thomas Howard** of Norfolk. In January 1547, a dying King Henry named Paget to the governing council he established to oversee the minority rule of his young son and heir, Prince Edward.

At the start of the new reign, Paget actively supported the regime and policies of Edward Seymour, now the Duke of Somerset and lord protector of England. Seymour duly rewarded his loyalty with a knighthood in the Order of the **Garter**, chancellorship of the Duchy of Lancaster, and elevation to the peerage as the Baron of Beaudesert in Staffordshire. When the lord protector's enemies at court accused him of plotting against them, however, Paget's close association with Somerset led to his own incarceration in the Tower of London in autumn 1551. The largely unfounded conspiracy charges against him were soon replaced, however, by far more credible allegations of Crown revenue skimming. Heavily fined and stripped of several government offices, Paget was released from prison in spring 1552 and was eventually pardoned and restored to the royal council by King Edward himself.

He was among the Crown officials who pledged allegiance to Queen Jane Grey in July 1553, but when Mary seized the throne, she forgave her contrite councilor and then appointed him lord privy seal in 1556. Paget served Queen Mary in this capacity until the accession of Queen **Elizabeth** I, when declining health (perhaps resulting from his tower confinement) obliged him to retire from public affairs. He died on 9 June 1563 at his manor house in West Drayton, Middlesex, and was buried in the parish church there. Later, some of his many children paid for construction of a funerary monument to his memory in Lichfield Cathedral in his native Staffordshire.

PAPACY. *See* CLEMENT VII, POPE (1478–1534; r. 1523–34); LEO X, POPE (1475–1521; r. 1513–21); PAUL III, POPE (1468–1549; r. 1534–49); ROME, SACK OF (MAY 1527).

PARLIAMENT (c. 1264–). For many centuries, Parliament served as the principal legislative organ of government for the kingdom of England and later for Great Britain and the United Kingdom in more modern times. Although its origins stretch back to the Anglo-Saxon period and then to the Magna Carta in the High Middle Ages, Parliament (and most especially the House of Commons) came of age during the reign of King Henry VIII in the 16th century. **Thomas Cromwell**, King Henry's second chief minister, skillfully manipulated the membership, legislative preambles, and statute laws of the House of Commons in the 1530s to secure popular support for the **Henrician Reformation**, the revolutionary break from the Roman Church that parliamentary support helped legitimize in the eyes of most English believers.

As many constitutional historians agree, Parliament's earliest roots date back to the witenagemot or witan, the council of wise men, who offered governing and military advice to the Anglo-Saxon kings of England from the seventh century onward. These assemblies were not in any way democratic or even geographically representative because they included only the thegns or **noble** war leaders each king could trust the most. Following the conquest of England by Duke William of Normandy in the 11th century, the old Saxon witan was replaced by the Norman Curia Regis, the royal council, a body of the ruler's most trusted noble lieutenants along with some high-ranking prelates of the church. The Curia Regis existed, as had the witan, to assist the sovereign with its wise counsels, but the Norman and later Plantagenet kings of England were not necessarily bound to follow or even hear its advice. When King John failed to defend English lands in France, extorted treasure from his barons and bishops, and abused his royal privileges, the nobles rose up and forced him to sign Magna Carta, the Great Charter, in June 1215. This document guaranteed the feudal rights of England's temporal and spiritual lords, limited the king's ability to overreach his royal powers, and called for a "common council of the kingdom" to advise the ruler on important political, military, and fiscal matters.

King John did not long survive his signing of Magna Carta, passing the Crown of England on to his nine-year-old son Henry III in 1216. The new Plantagenet ruler soon violated the terms of Magna Carta himself when he enriched his French relatives with English estates and titles and when he demanded money from his landed subjects to fund an ill-advised and financially ruinous conquest of Sicily. These reckless policies prompted many of England's great magnates to issue the Provisions of Oxford in 1258, which ordered King Henry to honor the dictates of the Great Charter his father had signed some 43 years earlier. When the English king ignored the provisions, the ensuing impasse inspired a second great revolt in 1264 under the leadership of Simon de Montfort, the Earl of Leicester. After Earl Simon and his allies defeated Henry's army and incarcerated him in Windsor Castle, the rebels established a parliament, or speaking body, of barons to rule the kingdom in the royal prisoner's place. Henry III's son Prince Edward raised an army in 1265 and in turn routed the rebels (and killed Simon de Montfort) at Evesham, but he never forgot the lessons of his father's overthrow and began calling regular parliamentary meetings when he became king in 1272.

Parliament's structure and authority began to evolve over the next few centuries, expanding from its original advisory role to include the powers of lawmaking and taxation. Because the English nobility (as represented in the House of Lords) had always been exempt from direct Crown taxation, King Edward wisely called wealthier members of the **gentry** and merchant classes to meet in a House of Commons so he could ask them to tax themselves (measures called subsidies) at fractional rates of their annual incomes. The Commons were at first quite willing to grant English kings the subsidies they requested, but eventually they petitioned their rulers to enact favorable laws to protect their agrarian and mercantile interests in return. These petitions came to be known as parliamentary bills, and when both houses accepted them and the king attached to them his great seal (or the lord chancellor did so for him), the resulting act of Parliament became a statute (standing) law that superseded all other manorial or common (precedent) laws in the land.

The numbers and qualifications of men who attended sessions of Parliament also changed during the late-medieval and early-modern periods. From the earliest meetings of the speaking body in the 13th century, all holders of hereditary noble titles were known as peers of the realm and enjoyed automatic invitations to join other magnates in the House of Lords. The members of the House of Commons, known later simply as MPs (members of Parliament), typically included two representatives (usually knights) from each county or shire and four representatives from each of the kingdom's boroughs or royally chartered towns. The MPs were most often appointed to serve in Parliament by important leaders in the shires and boroughs, ensuring that the House of Commons was at least geographically—if not democratically—representative of the English body politic. By the time of the first two Tudor monarchs, aspiring MPs studied law at the **Inns of Court** in London or acquired some learning at **Oxford** and **Cambridge Universities** before embarking on their parliamentary careers.

When Henry VIII acceded to the English throne in 1509, the importance of Parliament within the Tudor regime rested on its ability to cooperate with the king and provide a sense of popular support for his policies. Although Parliament's power to grant royal subsidy requests remained vital, such measures were soon overshadowed by the need for new statute laws to address the various matrimonial, religious, and succession crises that arose during King Henry's reign. In the early

1530s, Parliament passed the Supplication against the Ordinaries [*see* SUBMISSION OF THE CLERGY AND SUPPLICATION AGAINST THE ORDINARIES (1531–32)], a legislative act that asked the Crown to clean up clerical corruption and then handed considerable authority over the English Church to the king. Learning from these examples, the king's new chief minister, Thomas Cromwell, began to pack the Commons with his own supporters, and he attached persuasive preambles to the statutes they passed to encourage readier acceptance by the English public.

Thus, when King Henry's "**Great Matter**" (his campaign to set aside Queen **Katherine of Aragon** to marry **Anne Boleyn**) led inevitably to the Church of England's separation from Rome, Cromwell and his royal master were poised to use parliamentary statutes to help them achieve their ends. The **Act in Restraint of Appeals** was passed in spring 1533 to prohibit legal appeals to the pope, and after the king had replaced Queen Katherine with Queen Anne, the **Act of Succession** in spring 1534 named the children of Henry and his new consort as heirs to the English throne. The following November saw Parliament pass the **Act of Supremacy**, a briefly worded statute that appointed King Henry the "supreme head of the Church of England." Later the same month, Parliament obliged the king and Cromwell by passing the **Act of Treasons**, which counted spoken words as a traitorous offense for the first time in English law. With passage of the **Act of Six Articles** in 1539, King Henry sought to overturn Cromwell's previous attempts to reform the English Church by restoring some of the old Roman doctrines and practices. Parliament had thus become an instrument of state, religious, and dynastic policy and was destined to remain so during the reigns of the next three Tudor monarchs.

PARR, KATHERINE, QUEEN OF ENGLAND

(1512–48). Henry VIII's sixth and last queen consort and the third named Katherine, this demure, well-educated, and pious woman was herself married four times and was one of only two of Henry's wives to survive him. Queen Katherine Parr was a disciple of Europe's "new

learning" and, as the author of a devotional work herself, brought King Henry's son and youngest daughter up in the reformed evangelical faith of the mid-16th century. Although she often shared her more progressive theological views with her royal husband, a religiously conservative faction at court plotted to destroy Queen Katherine but in the end failed to turn King Henry against her. She was the perfect wife for the old Tudor king in his final years, for, having previously cared for a dying husband, Henry VIII's last queen was able to ease his own suffering and anxiety as he neared the end of his life. After he died, Katherine wed her earlier suitor **Thomas Seymour**, the brother of Henry's third queen, **Jane Seymour**, but her first late-in-life pregnancy ended in a difficult birth and the queen dowager's premature death at the age of just 36 years.

Katherine Parr was born the eldest child of Sir Thomas Parr, the Lord of Kendal Castle in the northern county of Westmorland, and Lady Maud Greene Parr, the daughter of a prominent **gentry** family from Northamptonshire. Katherine's father was knighted by young Henry VIII during his coronation celebrations in 1509, while her mother was lady-in-waiting to Queen **Katherine of Aragon** and so presumably named her first-born daughter after her royal Spanish mistress. When Sir Thomas Parr died in 1517, Lady Maud was left to raise Katherine and her two siblings and saw them soundly educated in modern European languages, Latin, Greek, the classics, and theology. After negotiations to marry Katherine off in 1524 broke down, her hand was given instead to the young but sickly Sir Edward Borough (alternately Burgh) in 1529. Her first husband soon died, releasing Katherine to wed the 40-something John Neville, third Baron Latimer, in summer 1534. Lord Latimer was involved in the great **Pilgrimage of Grace** rebellion of 1536, but his relationship with the insurgents was ill defined, and he was allowed to return peacefully to his family after the uprising was suppressed. When his health declined a few years later, his dedicated wife gently nursed him until he, too, breathed his last in March 1542.

Thus twice widowed by age 30, Lady Katherine Latimer made her way to the royal Tudor court, where she met and fell in love with the charming but disingenuous Sir Thomas Seymour, the brother of Henry VIII's third queen and of **Edward Seymour**, the first Earl of Hertford. Just as the couple agreed to marry in 1543, King Henry recovered from the distasteful debacle of his previous marriage and began to search for yet another wife to comfort him as he aged. His eye fell upon Katherine Parr, and aware of her attachment to Seymour, Henry sent him off on a diplomatic mission and then married her himself on 12 July 1543 at **Hampton Court**. The king was by this time suffering from debilitating obesity, painful gout, and oozing leg ulcers, so Katherine seemed the perfect choice to nurse him through these maladies and (educated as she was) provide stimulating companionship at the same time. As had happened in the past, the new queen's family also benefitted from her union with Henry: her brother William Parr received **Thomas Cromwell**'s forfeited Earldom of Essex, and her sister Anne and stepdaughter Margaret Neville became her ladies-in-waiting.

Queen Katherine quickly proved a resourceful and clear-headed helpmate to Henry, who trusted her and soon named her regent to rule England in his place when he led his final **French invasion in 1544–45**. Katherine also managed to reconcile her Tudor husband to the daughters he had sired with his first two queens, both of whom had been declared illegitimate but who now reclaimed their positions as princesses and royal heirs. When the king asked Katherine to supervise the education of his two youngest children, the future **Edward VI** and **Elizabeth I**, she hired the reformist **John Cheke** in 1544 to teach them Greek and Latin and introduce them to the great poets, orators, and historians of the ancient world. A competent scholar herself, Henry's sixth queen authored her *Lamentations of a Sinner* in the mid-1540s. This little treatise expressed Katherine's views on religious devotion, sinfulness, and prophecy; was humbly self-deprecating in tone; and vilified the Roman Church as corrupt, venal, and worldly.

Such evangelical (Protestant) opinions as these served to attract the hostility of a conservative faction at court, men whose Catholic leanings committed them to achieving the earliest possible downfall of King Henry's forward-thinking queen. The leaders of this group included **Thomas Howard**, third Duke of Norfolk; **Stephen Gardiner**, bishop of Winchester; **Edmund Bonner**, bishop of London; and **Thomas Wriothesley**, lord chancellor of England. In July 1546, they tried to convince Henry VIII, himself religiously conservative despite his break with Rome, to arrest Queen Katherine as a theologically deviant heretic. While the king hesitated, they had the radical reformer **Anne Askew** tortured in the **Tower of London** to reveal any contact she might have had with the queen, but brave Mistress Askew remained silent and went to her death at the stake as a heretic herself. Forewarned of the plots against her, Katherine threw herself on her husband's mercy (and ego) and swore that he alone was her beacon of religious truth. Thus mollified and probably weary of condemning his wives to death, King Henry curtly dismissed Wriothesley when the lord chancellor arrived at Hampton Court with guards to arrest his now contrite and submissive queen.

Henry VIII died on 28 January 1547, and generous to his widow in his will, he nonetheless bypassed her to appoint his former brother-in-law Edward Seymour, now the first Duke of Somerset, as lord protector over the boy-king Edward VI. Meanwhile, Somerset's brother Thomas Seymour, recently ennobled and then promoted to the rank of lord high admiral, began to court his former sweetheart again, and soon the pair were betrothed. They married in May 1547—just a few months after King Henry was laid to rest in Windsor Castle— and by the start of the new year, Katherine was with child for the first time in her life. As her pregnancy progressed, her flirtatious husband took an unhealthy interest in Lady Elizabeth Tudor, the teenaged royal princess who was Katherine's stepdaughter and ward and who was now resident in their home. When Katherine caught Seymour romping about with the pretty young princess in her bedchamber, she had the girl sent away to avoid any hint of scandal. The dowager queen gave birth to a daughter early in September 1548, but the trauma of her first pregnancy so late in life had taken its toll, and both mother and infant passed away a few days later. Katherine Parr, King Henry VIII's sixth and final queen consort, was buried following a funeral service in English in St. Mary's Chapel on the grounds of Sudeley Castle in Gloucestershire.

PAUL III, POPE (1468–1549; r. 1534–49).

Born Alessandro Farnese, this Renaissance pope is best known today for initiating the Catholic (or Counter) Reformation, an ecclesiastical "housecleaning" that addressed corruption in the Roman Church and helped slow the spread of Protestantism across Europe. Pope Paul rose in typical fashion in the service of earlier popes and amassed many lucrative church livings along the way, until he finally won election to the chair of St. Peter himself at age 67. A patron of the arts and of the *studia humanitatis*, or new learning of humanism, Paul hired some of Italy's greatest architects, painters, and sculptors to beautify St. Peter's Basilica at the Vatican. Despite enriching his own family at church expense, Paul III appointed many able men to the college of cardinals and made possible the foundation of the Roman College (today the Pontifical Gregorian University) two years after his death. He put a great deal of pressure on Henry VIII to return England to the Church of Rome, but his actions merely angered the English king and ultimately did little to alter the course of the **Henrician Reformation**.

Alessandro Farnese was born in Canino outside Rome to Pierluigi Farnese, the scion of a family of former popes and condottieri (mercenary) captains, and his wife, Giovannella Gaetani, who herself numbered popes among her ancestors as well. Alessandro received a first-rate education in ancient languages and the classics, studying first in Rome and Pisa and then moving to Florence, where he became friends with Giovanni de' Medici, the future Pope **Leo X**. In 1493, he returned to Rome, where he became a papal treasurer and cardinal deacon despite the fact that he had not yet been ordained into holy orders. He advanced quickly in the papal administration of Alexander VI partly because of his own

talents but partly also because the pope had taken his beautiful sister Giulia as his mistress. This useful connection, plus Farnese's own promiscuous lifestyle (he fathered four illegitimate children) inspired his clerical colleagues in Rome to call him "Cardinal Petticoat." Between 1496 and 1509, Popes Alexander and Julius II appointed him bishop of Corneto, Montefiascone, and Parma, all before he finally accepted ordination as a priest in 1519.

When the Medici pontiff **Clement VII** died in 1534, the three dozen cardinals who attended the subsequent conclave in Rome unanimously elected Farnese to succeed him as Paul III. Truly devoted to humanist learning, the new pope donated many valuable manuscripts to the Vatican library and commissioned Michelangelo Buonarroti to complete his *Last Judgment* fresco in the Sistine Chapel. Just like his predecessor and friend Leo X, Paul enjoyed the hunt, banquets, and masques, but he avoided entangling the papacy in foreign wars because the Protestant Reformation had left his *camera* (papal treasury) chronically short of funds. Paul III was as nepotistic as any of his fellow 16th-century pontiffs, adding his two grandsons (aged 16 and 14) to the college of cardinals and then bestowing profitable church offices upon them both. He partially redeemed himself, however, by awarding cardinal's hats to such able men as Gian Pietro Carafa (the future Pope Paul IV); Marcello Cervini (Marcellus II); and Gasparo Contarini, the Venetian diplomat and theologian.

Determined to deal with the English break from Rome, Paul III tried to persuade the religiously conservative Henry VIII to reconsider his schismatic policies and return once again to papal obedience. In spring 1535, Paul made saintly Bishop **John Fisher** a cardinal of the Roman Church in an attempt to dissuade the English king from putting the aged prelate to death as a traitor. This gesture only enraged the volatile Henry further, however, and he went ahead with Fisher's execution anyway just a few months later. Pope Paul also awarded a cardinal's hat to the conservative English theologian **Reginald Pole**, who was by the mid-1530s living in exile in Italy to protest King Henry's proclaimed supremacy over the Church of England. Pole authored a plan to reduce corruption in the Roman Church in 1537 that Paul III eventually used to shape his own reform movement eight years later. Although Clement VII had already excommunicated Henry VIII in 1534, Pope Paul renewed the damning censure in 1538 and then placed England under interdict, which in effect excommunicated all the English king's subjects as well. Because many in England were glad that papal authority in their realm had been undone, the pope's punitive measures on this occasion were largely ignored.

Well aware that his own Roman Church was in dire need of amendment, Pope Paul III undertook what became the signature achievement of his pontificate when he launched the Catholic Reformation in the 1540s. Having watched millions of European believers flock to the more cerebral and Scripture-based faith of the Protestants, the pope sanctioned the creation of a new order of highly educated priests, the Society of Jesus (or the Jesuits), to try to preach the defectors back into the Roman fold. More ominously, Paul established the Congregation of the Roman Inquisition in 1542, an ecclesiastical tribunal designed to identify, interrogate, and punish Italian evangelicals as heretics. The most important component of the Catholic Reformation got underway in December 1545, when Paul III called the first session of the Council of Trent to order with 84 cardinals, archbishops, bishops, theologians, and canon lawyers in attendance. Under the pope's watchful eye, the assembled churchmen introduced measures to clean up clerical abuses, worked to curb the political and worldly interests of the church, and discussed controversial doctrines that had driven many believers into the arms of the Protestants. Well before the Council of Trent ended (it continued to meet until 1563), however, Pope Paul III died of a fever on 10 November 1549 and was buried in the same Roman Basilica of St. Peter he had done so much to rebuild and decorate.

PERCY, HENRY ALGERNON, SIXTH EARL OF NORTHUMBERLAND (1502–37). The son and heir of the fifth Earl of Northumberland

of the same name, this ill-fated lord fell into a romantic relationship with **Anne Boleyn** just before Henry VIII first noticed and became infatuated with his future wife and queen himself. Urged on by King Henry's lord chancellor, the elder Northumberland threatened his son with disinheritance if he did not renounce his attachment to Mistress Boleyn. Young Percy grudgingly obeyed his father and then accepted an arranged match with the daughter of another prominent **noble** house. This marriage was an unhappy one, and forced to play a role in the treason trial of his former sweetheart Queen Anne Boleyn, he passed away in a sickly, bitter, and depressed state before his 36th birthday.

Henry Algernon Percy was born in 1502 into the family of Henry Algernon Percy Sr., the fifth Earl of Northumberland since 1489 and the master of vast estates across the north of England. Young Henry's mother was Katherine Spencer Percy, a descendant of Edmund Beaufort, sixth Duke of Somerset, who was himself an ancestor of King Edward III. Around 1514, the Earl of Northumberland sent his son to serve as a page in the household of **Thomas Wolsey**, King Henry's lord chancellor and a soon-to-be cardinal of the Roman Church. Because Wolsey and the Percy family had previously clashed over competing interests in the northern counties, the lord chancellor disliked young Lord Percy and treated him with the same disdain normally reserved for low-born servants. Percy did acquire some learning and social graces under Wolsey's watchful eye, however, and often accompanied his haughty master on his visits to court to confer with the Tudor king.

Henry Percy was still a ward in Cardinal Wolsey's establishment when Anne Boleyn arrived back in England in the winter of 1521–22 following several years' service as a lady-in-waiting to Queen Claude of France. Quickly assigned the same position in the household of Queen **Katherine of Aragon**, it is likely that the vivacious and darkly attractive Mistress Boleyn first made Lord Percy's acquaintance when Wolsey and his staff returned to court sometime in the spring of 1522. Over the next year, Henry Percy and Anne Boleyn fell quite deeply in love, to the extent that they certainly entertained an expectation of future marriage but perhaps even entered into a legally binding prenuptial contract as well. Cardinal Wolsey was alarmed when he got wind of their relationship, for he saw each of the young lovers more advantageously married into other more prominent noble families. Having secured the support of King Henry, who at this time was still involved in his affair with Anne's sister **Mary Boleyn**, Wolsey summoned Lord Percy's father, the fifth Earl of Northumberland, to London in summer 1523 to talk some sense into his lovelorn son.

The intimidating older earl quickly ordered his boy to break off the "understanding" he had with Mistress Boleyn, but young Henry boldly stood his ground and insisted that a marriage with Anne might also yield an alliance with her powerful and wealthy **Howard** relatives. Not to be convinced, Northumberland now threatened to disinherit his son if he did not reject Lady Anne forthwith, an ultimatum the defeated and tearful Lord Percy could no longer resist. Northumberland quickly betrothed his son to Mary Talbot, the daughter of George Talbot, fourth Earl of Shrewsbury, and the two were quietly wed in 1525 following the resolution of certain legal and inheritance issues. Meanwhile, King Henry's roving eye had finally fallen on Anne Boleyn, and so their famous romance was free to commence in 1525–26 with the inconvenient Lord Percy now safely married off to another woman.

Mary and Henry Percy were very unhappy together, and it was soon clear that the couple would not have any children, nor in fact could they suffer each other's company for very much longer. When the old Earl of Northumberland died in 1527, Henry inherited his title and estates as the sixth earl and was later that year appointed warden of the eastern and middle marches on the Scottish frontier. It was the new Earl of Northumberland who intercepted Cardinal Wolsey at Cawood Castle in southern Yorkshire in 1530 and ordered his former master back to London to stand trial on charges of high treason. In 1531, Northumberland was grateful to accept membership in the Order of the **Garter**. However, in an effort to end their unhappy marriage, his estranged wife accused him in 1532 of having made a precontract of marriage with Anne Boleyn, a charge he strenuously denied twice with sacred oaths.

Henry Percy's final years were also not his happiest. By the early 1530s, he was seriously ill with the ague, a recurring fever and stomach disorder that, possibly exacerbated by acute depression, often restricted the still-youthful earl to his bed. In spring 1536, with Henry VIII now seeking an end to his own union with Queen Anne Boleyn, Crown agents interviewed Northumberland about his alleged premarriage contract with his former lover, but once again, he denied that any such arrangement had ever existed. Despite his deteriorating condition, the sickly earl was called to London in May 1536 to attend the treason trial of Queen Anne, where he wept and then collapsed after the court pronounced the sentence of death upon her. Northumberland was too ill to take part in the **Pilgrimage of Grace** uprising in autumn 1536, but when his younger brothers Thomas and Ingram joined the rebels, they were both arrested and Thomas was executed as one of the movement's ringleaders. Well aware of his approaching end, Northumberland drew up a will that spitefully left all his properties to King Henry and not to the members of his own family. The sixth Earl of Northumberland succumbed to his lingering ailments on 29 June 1537 at the young age of 35 and was buried in the parish church of Hackney, north of London.

PILGRIMAGE OF GRACE (1536–37). This uprising involved some 40,000 insurgents and represented the most serious challenge to Henry VIII and his government during the entire course of the Tudor king's reign. Originally caused by popular economic, social, and religious grievances against the Crown, the so-called pilgrimage erupted in two separate incidents in Lincolnshire and Yorkshire in autumn 1536 but then spread to the far north of England by early 1537. King Henry dispatched two peers of the realm to deal with the insurrection and, having ordered them to show no mercy to the rebel leaders, observed from afar as peace was deceitfully and ruthlessly restored following five months of restive upheaval.

Discontent over Crown religious policies had been brewing in the more rural shires of the kingdom for a few years before the pilgrimage took place, but a particularly bad harvest in the late summer and autumn of 1536 provided the spark that ultimately ignited the massive uprising. The primary religious concern of the rebels was the plan of **Thomas Cromwell**, King Henry's chief minister and vicegerent in spirituals, to close **monasteries** and convents that had long been part of the social and economic fabric of northern England. Cromwell's plan disturbed many of the common folk of the region, who largely remained loyal to the Roman Church and whose family members often included monks and nuns or lay workers at some of the larger religious houses. Cromwell's **Ten Articles of Faith** had meanwhile begun to take effect in the northern shires as well, pressing reformed doctrines and rituals onto conservative English believers who had no wish to accept them. Coupled with the recently failed harvest, which was driving up grain prices, and the ongoing **enclosure** of common lands, which was forcing peasant families off their farms, the working people of Lincolnshire and Yorkshire began by late summer 1536 to view rebellion as the only way to relieve their frustrations and hunger.

As rumors swirled that Cromwell intended to tax baptisms, weddings, and funerals, two Crown agents were lynched in the Lincolnshire town of Louth on 1 October 1536. Within a few days of that incident, a mob of some 10,000 farmers, artisans, and clerics gathered in the city of Lincoln under the command of several gentlemen and minor lords. Furious, King Henry sent a scolding letter north to explain that **Parliament**, and not he, had ordered the monasteries closed, adding that swift and terrible punishment would follow if the rebels did not obey their sovereign and disperse. When Henry ordered **Charles Brandon**, the first Duke of Suffolk, to march on Lincoln with a sizeable royal army, the unruly crowd lost its nerve and began to melt away. Still, when Suffolk arrived, he had 46 of the Lincolnshire insurgents

executed on the spot and took another dozen of the ringleaders to London, where they were hanged, drawn, and quartered as traitors. The first phase of the revolt thus ended before it had achieved much of anything, but a second, more serious uprising was meanwhile set to erupt in the neighboring county of Yorkshire.

The charismatic individual (with only one eye!) who emerged to lead this new rebellion was Robert Aske, the younger son of a **gentry** knight who had studied at the **Inns of Court** in London before returning to the north of England to practice law. Inspired by the earlier revolt to his south, Aske occupied the city of York with some 10,000 followers, just as the Duke of Suffolk was putting an end to the troubles in Lincoln. Aske styled his incipient uprising the "Pilgrimage of Grace," transforming the primarily economic and social protest into a religious crusade with a symbolic "five wounds of Christ" banner leading the way. Welcoming reinforcements—some with weapons and arrayed in armor—Aske led his "army" of nearly 40,000 into south Yorkshire to Pontefract Castle, where he persuaded Lord **Thomas Darcy** to make common cause with the rebels. The two leaders then issued 24 articles of grievance that called for the restoration of Roman doctrines, a halt to the monastic closings, the replacement of certain royal councilors, and the return of enclosed farmland to evicted peasants.

A truly exasperated King Henry reacted with predictable anger to this latest insurrection, sending **Thomas Howard**, the third Duke of Norfolk, north with some 8,000 troops to negotiate with Aske but really to suppress the rebellion by any means possible. When the two sides met near Doncaster in late October 1536, Norfolk offered a truce and general pardon if the Pilgrims would nominate two of their number to return with him to London to confer with the king. These representatives were duly sent off to the capital, where King Henry had them lavishly entertained and feasted, and then returned them to Aske and Darcy with assurances that all the rebels' demands would be met. Aske himself journeyed to London in mid-December and was similarly fêted by his sovereign, but when the lawyer-turned-revolutionary traveled north again, he found all the royal promises unfulfilled and most of his followers back in their homes for the winter.

At this point, Aske desperately called on the king to keep his word and, failing that, tried to reassemble his rebellious host, but both pleas were ignored and ultimately failed. When spontaneous and mostly leaderless uprisings broke out in Westmoreland, Cumberland, and the East Riding of Yorkshire in the first months of 1537, the Duke of Norfolk had little difficulty defeating them all and then pursued and arrested the latest ringleaders of the Pilgrimage of Grace, among them the now-demoralized Robert Aske himself. In all, 178 insurgents were executed, including Lord Darcy, who was convicted of treason and beheaded in London, and Robert Aske, the inspirational leader of the rebellion, who suffered the ultimate penalty as a traitor on market day in York the following July.

PLANTAGENET, ARTHUR, VISCOUNT LISLE

(c. 1462–1542). As an illegitimate son of King Edward IV, Arthur Plantagenet was related to many members of the ruling Houses of York and Tudor. The half-brother of Queen **Elizabeth of York**, he was uncle to the four royal children of King **Henry VII**—including Henry VIII himself—and was a great-uncle to the last three monarchs of the Tudor dynasty. Many of his Yorkist relations were exiled or executed by the first two Tudor kings as rival royal claimants, but Arthur Plantagenet sidestepped such dangers to become Henry VIII's trusted advisor, lord deputy of **Calais**, vice admiral of England, and a knight of the Order of the **Garter**. Accused of conspiracy to commit treason near the end of his life, Lord Lisle was imprisoned in the **Tower of London** and died there in March 1542 at the approximate age of 80 years. His vast correspondence with other magnates, Crown officials, and family members (the Lisle Letters) was confiscated at the time of his arrest and survives intact today to provide a unique glimpse into the social and political world of Tudor England.

Arthur Plantagenet was born between 1461 and 1464 in the English-held port of Calais in France. He was the acknowledged bastard son of King Edward IV (r. 1461–83), the patriarch of the House of York who seized the English throne from the Lancastrians during the early stages of the **Wars of the Roses**. The identity of Plantagenet's mother is uncertain, but two likely candidates are Elizabeth Lucy, the presumed mother of several of Edward IV's illegitimate children, and Elizabeth Shore, the Yorkist king's long-term mistress. One other possibility is the "wanton wench" Elizabeth Wayte, who might have been Plantagenet's mother because he was reportedly known during his childhood as Arthur Wayte. Because his royal parentage was no secret, young Arthur grew up at King Edward's court but then vanished from the historical record at his father's death in 1483. He resurfaced in 1501 in the household of his half-sister Elizabeth of York, by then the queen consort of the first Tudor king Henry VII. Following her death in 1503, Plantagenet stayed on at the royal court and then became an esquire of the king's body (personal attendant) at his nephew Henry VIII's accession in 1509.

Uncle and nephew grew to be quite close over the ensuing years, despite a nearly three-decade difference in their ages, prompting the youthful King Henry to appoint Plantagenet to the offices of high sheriff in Hampshire and vice admiral of England in 1514. Around that same time, Plantagenet married Elizabeth Grey, the widow of the executed **Edmund Dudley**, who brought most of the confiscated Dudley estates to the marriage as well. In 1520, Arthur Plantagenet attended the **Field of Cloth of Gold** summit meeting between King Henry and King **François I** outside Calais and soon accepted the office of warden of the Cinque Ports (naval commander) from his nephew as well. In 1523, Henry created his uncle Viscount Lisle, a title that descended to him through his wife, while the following year, the king inducted him into the Order of the Garter as a knight companion. When his first wife, Elizabeth, died in 1528, Lord Lisle married Honor Grenville, a vivacious 30-year-old widow from Cornwall, who then accompanied her new husband, King Henry, and **Anne Boleyn** to a second meeting with the French king in Calais in 1532. Nearly drowned in a shipwreck on his way home from that gathering, Lisle's royal nephew made him lord deputy of Calais and sent him back overseas to take command of that strategic French town in 1533.

Resident in Calais over the next seven years, Lord Lisle fell deeply into debt; had trouble controlling the town's garrison; was dominated by his second wife; and clashed with Roman Church loyalists, who resisted the ongoing **Henrician Reformation**. His correspondence during these years, now known generally by scholars as the Lisle Letters, demonstrate his overall integrity and diligence as Calais's governor, but his readiness to appease enemies and reward favor seekers undermined King Henry's trust in him back in London. When Crown authorities accused several members of the Plantagenet family in 1540 of conspiring to return Calais to the French, Lord Lisle was implicated in the plot and was himself arrested and taken to the Tower of London. Treason convictions and executions of some of his relations soon followed, but the evidence against Lisle was circumstantial, and he managed to avoid a grisly death under the headsman's axe. Still, he endured nearly two more years in the tower until, told he would soon be freed, he suffered a fatal heart attack, died on 3 March 1542, and was buried in the Chapel of Peter ad Vincula within the precincts of the tower.

POLE, MARGARET, COUNTESS OF SALISBURY (1473–1541).

Margaret Pole was a prominent descendant of the royal House of York and one of the few women of her age to join the English peerage as a titled magnate and wealthy landowner in her own right. Related to King Henry VIII by both birth and marriage, Margaret's position as a royal kinswoman allowed her at times to enjoy great favor at the Tudor court. However, her Yorkist ancestry often attracted jealousy and hostility from the Crown on other occasions as well. The Countess of Salisbury's large brood of offspring also brought her grief at times, especially her son **Reginald Cardinal Pole**, whose harsh criticism of the **Henrician Reformation** greatly annoyed both King Henry and his chief

minister, **Thomas Cromwell**. When two of her sons became embroiled in the so-called Exeter conspiracy of 1538, Lady Margaret Pole was arrested and imprisoned for a few years and was then executed on the block as a traitor at the **Tower of London** in May 1541.

Margaret Pole was born in summer 1473 at Farleigh Castle near Bath in Somerset. She was the daughter of George Plantagenet, the first Duke of Clarence (and the brother of Yorkist kings Edward IV and Richard III), and Clarence's wife, Isabel Neville, who was the eldest daughter of Richard Neville, the "kingmaker" Earl of Warwick. Margaret Plantagenet and her brother Edward were orphaned at an early age, and after **Henry VII** seized the English throne in 1485, he married the children's cousin **Elizabeth of York** and then took the two youngsters into the Tudor household as royal wards. Well aware of young Margaret's Yorkist ancestry, King Henry arranged in 1487 (or possibly 1491) her marriage to his own cousin Sir Richard Pole, a man closely allied to the House of Tudor. In 1501, Henry VII installed Sir Richard as chief chamberlain to his son and heir, **Arthur** Tudor, while Margaret Pole was assigned to **Katherine of Aragon**, Arthur's new bride, as a lady-in-waiting. This latter appointment allowed Lady Margaret to develop a close relationship with the Spanish princess, but Arthur's death in 1502 prompted King Henry to dissolve Katherine's household and dismiss most of her attendants. Meanwhile the Poles produced five children together before Sir Richard died prematurely of an illness in 1505. That left Margaret Pole a destitute widow with five mouths to feed and few prospects for an advantageous remarriage.

She partially overcame these challenges by entrusting the support and career of her son Reginald to the church and then by taking up residence in the Brigittine nunnery of Syon Abbey near London, where her expenses were very few. Margaret Pole returned to royal favor in 1509, when the Tudor succession passed to Henry VIII, who again appointed her to serve his new queen, Katherine of Aragon, as lady-in-waiting. In 1512, King Henry elevated Margaret to the Earldom of Salisbury, a title and collection of estates that had once belonged to her father, Duke George of Clarence. She thus became one of just a few women in Tudor England to possess a titled peerage, one whose landed income ranked her among the wealthiest magnates in the realm. The Countess of Salisbury's children also prospered during these years at court. Her eldest son, Henry, was created Lord Montagu and represented the Pole family in the House of Lords, while her second son, Arthur, a client of **Edward Stafford**, third Duke of Buckingham, survived the duke's precipitous downfall in 1521 to marry well, take possession of extensive lands, and father four children.

Henry VIII's high regard for his relative Margaret Pole began to fade, however, by the time the Tudor king approached the 20th year of his reign. The countess's close relationship with and loyalty to Katherine of Aragon and her daughter, **Mary** Tudor, irked Henry a great deal once he took the initial steps to replace his Spanish queen with **Anne Boleyn**. In addition, Margaret Pole's scholarly third son, Reginald, who had earlier researched the validity of the king's remarriage plans, now changed his allegiance and fled abroad to lead opposition to Henry VIII's second queen and his supremacy over the English Church. Reginald Pole accepted a cardinal's hat from Pope **Paul III** and then wrote to encourage **Henry Courtenay**, the Marquis of Exeter, to raise a revolt against the dissolution of the **monasteries** in the southwest of England in 1538. Outraged by this so-called Exeter conspiracy, King Henry had his chief minister, Thomas Cromwell arrest not only Exeter himself but also the Countess of Salisbury and her sons Henry Lord Montagu and Geoffrey Pole to retaliate against the seditious meddling of their exiled kinsman.

Lord Montagu was executed with the Marquis of Exeter for treason in December 1538, but Geoffrey Pole was pardoned the following month for having testified against his own mother and brother. Margaret Pole was confined fairly comfortably in the Tower of London for some 30 months—and even accepted gifts of clothing from Queen **Katherine Howard**—before she was told she was to suffer a traitor's death on the morning of 27 May 1541. She bravely climbed onto the scaffold in the tower

precincts, where an inexperienced headsman required multiple axe blows (reportedly hacking wildly at her head and shoulders) to end her life. Margaret Pole, the Countess of Salisbury and one of the last remaining members of the House of York, was buried in the Tower of London's Peter ad Vincula Chapel and was beatified toward Catholic sainthood by Pope Leo XIII in 1886.

POLE, REGINALD CARDINAL (1500–1558). A cardinal of the Roman Church in Henry VIII's lifetime and later archbishop of Canterbury under Henry's daughter Queen **Mary I**, Reginald Pole was descended from the royal House of York and as such threatened the Tudor claim to England's throne with his very existence. As one of the most scholarly men of his age, Pole studied at many of Europe's finest universities and was mentored by (or knew) many of the greatest minds of the Renaissance. Although he did not formally take holy orders until some 20 months before his death, he collected multiple ecclesiastical livings and accepted a cardinal's hat from Pope **Paul III** while still only 36 years of age. Pole lived in exile in Italy during the heyday of the **Henrician Reformation**, hurling harsh criticism at Henry VIII and his Church of England but also playing a prominent role in the early stages of the reformist Council of Trent. After King Henry's death in 1547, Cardinal Pole remained in exile and only returned to England when Catholic Mary Tudor acceded to the English throne in 1553. He served the new queen as her chief advisor and archbishop of Canterbury and notoriously promoted the persecution and burnings of the Marian martyrs, an iniquity with which he is principally associated today.

Reginald Pole was born the third son of Sir Richard and **Margaret Pole** at Stourton Castle in Staffordshire. Because his mother was the daughter of George Plantagenet, the first Duke of Clarence, Reginald was thus the great-nephew of both Edward IV and Richard III, the two 15th-century Yorkist kings of England. He received his earliest education from the **Carthusian** friars at Sheen priory just west of London, then entered Magdalen College at **Oxford University** in 1512, where he studied with humanist masters William Latimer and **Thomas Linacre**. After graduating with his baccalaureate degree in 1515, Pole embarked on a career in the church that yielded several lucrative sinecures in various dioceses, even though he had not yet professed his vows as a priest. In 1521, he traveled to Italy, where he began a course of study at Padua University under Renaissance scholars Pietro Bembo; Gianpietro Carafa (the future pope); Pier Paolo Vergerio; and Peter Martyr Vermigli, the eminent theologian and future reformer. A fellowship at Oxford's Corpus Christi College in 1523 provided Pole with enough financial support to continue his studies in Italy until 1527. That year, he returned to his native England, and sporting his Yorkist ancestry and impressive academic credentials, he soon attracted the notice of Henry VIII and his chief minister, **Thomas Cardinal Wolsey**. In 1529, the king and cardinal sent Pole to Paris to find theological solutions to King Henry's **"Great Matter,"** the campaign to free him from his first marriage so that he might wed another.

Reginald Pole returned from France in 1530 with the scriptural evidence Henry VIII desired but found that Wolsey in the meantime had lost the king's favor and had been dismissed from court. King Henry offered Wolsey's old dioceses of either Winchester or York to Pole, but the youthful theologian was by now entertaining doubts about the validity of his royal master's attempts to set aside Queen **Katherine of Aragon**. Henry and Pole quarreled; the former exploded with anger, while the latter wept, and although they soon reconciled, Pole decided to go abroad again to resume his studies in Padua. While Pole was away, Henry VIII appointed a new archbishop of Canterbury, had him annul his first marriage, and then married his mistress **Anne Boleyn** and had her crowned queen of England. In 1534, Pope **Clement VII** condemned the Tudor king's second marriage as unlawful, a decree that prompted an enraged Henry to split from Roman obedience and declare himself the supreme head of his own Church of England.

Seeking to win Pole's approval for his new wife and church, Henry VIII ordered his new chief minister, **Thomas Cromwell**, to solicit the exiled scholar's thoughts on England's recent break with Rome. Pole replied with his treatise *Pro ecclesiasticae unitatis defensione* (*For the Defense of the Unity of the Church*), a scathing denunciation of King Henry's union with Queen Anne and his claim to supremacy over the English Church. The relationship between king and theologian was now quite acrimonious and became even more strained when Pope Paul III added Pole to the papal curia as a new cardinal in December 1536. Henry VIII took his revenge by having members of the exiled cardinal's family arrested in 1538 for plotting with **Henry Courtenay**, the Marquis of Exeter, against the Tudor government. Although the charges against them were essentially baseless, Reginald Pole's brother Henry and his mother, Margaret, the Countess of Salisbury, both died on the block as traitors in 1539 and 1541, respectively.

Understandably, Cardinal Pole remained in exile on the Continent through the remainder of the reign of Henry VIII and through that of his son Edward VI. Pope Paul selected him to preside over two early sessions of the Council of Trent, and he nearly won election as pope himself at the conclave that met following Paul III's death in 1549. He did not attempt a return to England until the accession of Queen Mary in 1553, although his disapproval of her marriage to Prince Philip of Spain prevented his actual arrival on English soil until November 1554. The new queen—a devoted daughter of the Church of Rome—quickly appointed Pole to her royal council, a position that allowed him to guide the restoration of papal authority, Roman religious rites, and England's old heresy laws through **Parliament**. After Archbishop **Thomas Cranmer** suffered a martyr's death at the stake in Oxford as a heretic, Cardinal Pole finally took holy orders in March 1556 and then was appointed archbishop of Canterbury by Pope Paul IV (Pole's old tutor Gianpietro Carafa) two days later. His health was in decline by the end of Mary's short reign, and he died in London of influenza only 12 hours after the death of the queen herself on 17 November 1558. His tomb is still to be seen in Canterbury Cathedral today.

POPINCOURT, JANE OR JEANNE (c. 1484–c. 1530).

A French courtesan and language tutor to the royal children of King **Henry VII**, Popincourt spent at least 18 years in England during the youth and early reign of Henry VIII. Some scholars believe that she and the lusty second Tudor king carried on an affair between 1514 and 1516, although evidence of this remains circumstantial and thus inconclusive. King Henry is known to have enjoyed the extramarital pleasures of more than a dozen women (not including his wives), however, so the likelihood that Jane Popincourt was among them should not be lightly dismissed.

Jane Popincourt's date of birth in France is unknown, as is the date when she arrived in England, but by 1498, she was employed in the Tudor royal household to instruct the Princesses **Margaret** and **Mary** Tudor (and perhaps seven-year-old Prince Henry) in the French language. She must have been at least 14 years old as a royal tutor, making her some 7 years older than the future king of England. In 1502, Popincourt became a lady-in-waiting to Prince Henry's mother, Queen **Elizabeth of York**, and in 1509, she was named a maid of honor to **Katherine of Aragon**, Henry VIII's first wife and queen.

Still unmarried by around the age of 30, Popincourt ruined her chances for an advantageous match when she entered into a romantic dalliance with a French lover. During King Henry's **French invasion of 1513–14**, English forces captured Louis, duc de Longueville, a scion of the **noble** House of Orléans. Taken to England as a hostage and held there under comfortable house arrest, Longueville began a love affair with his compatriot Jane Popincourt soon after his arrival at the Tudor court. Meanwhile the French nobleman also served as a useful diplomatic liaison once hostilities with France ended and peace talks began. It was Longueville who arranged for Princess Mary Tudor to wed the aged, toothless King **Louis XII** of France as part of the Treaty of London and suggested that Popincourt accompany her across the English Channel as her maid of honor. Believing the French woman to be promiscuous, however, King Louis rejected this overture, and so Mademoiselle Popincourt remained in England when both Princess Mary and the duc de Longueville embarked for France in 1514.

By this time, of course, King Henry had known Jane Popincourt since childhood as a royal tutor, but now, at age 23, it seems that his relationship with the 30-year-old French courtesan may have changed. After Longueville's departure, rumors swirled that the king had taken Popincourt as his lover. She did not have a wealthy family or belong to a powerful court faction to complicate their relationship, and she was French, a cultural attribute that King Henry often found most attractive. Still, if they did become lovers at this time, the only evidence we possess for their affair today is purely suggestive. During Christmas celebrations at Eltham Palace in 1514, King Henry chose Jane Popincourt as his dance partner over many other ladies of much higher rank; he also bestowed a hefty parting gift of £100 upon Mademoiselle Popincourt when she finally left England in May 1516. Returning to France, she took up with Longueville once again and then promptly disappeared from the historical record. *See also* BLOUNT, ELIZABETH OR BESSIE (c. 1497–1540); BOLEYN, MARY (CAREY; c. 1499–1543); SHELTON, MARGARET OR MADGE (c. 1505–c. 1553); STAFFORD, ANNE, LADY HASTINGS, COUNTESS OF HUNTINGDON (c. 1483–1544).

R

REFORMATION OF HENRY VIII. *See* HENRICIAN REFORMATION (1531–47).

RESTRAINT OF APPEALS, ACT IN. *See* ACT IN RESTRAINT OF APPEALS (1533).

RICH, RICHARD, LORD CHANCELLOR, FIRST BARON RICH OF LEIGHS (c. 1496–1567). Richard Rich's ability to dissemble, shift loyalties, perjure himself, and even torture alleged enemies of the Crown has earned him one of the blackest reputations in English history. A social and economic climber, Rich came to prominence in the 1530s for testifying against Sir **Thomas More** and Bishop **John Fisher** of Rochester, for enriching himself during the campaign to dissolve the **monasteries**, and for his duplicitous treatment of Henry VIII's chief minister **Thomas Cromwell**. Rich was lord chancellor during most of the reign of young **Edward VI**, and he supported Queen **Mary I** when she tried to return her kingdom to the religious obedience of Rome. His sinister character in Robert Bolt's play and the later film version of *A Man for All Seasons* has led most readers of Tudor history to despise the man who almost single-handedly (according to Bolt) brought the saintly Thomas More to a traitor's death on the block.

Although Richard Rich may have been the son of one Richard Rich and Joan Dingley Rich of London, he was more probably born around 1496 in Basingstoke, Hampshire, to Agnes and John Rich, whose family claimed descent from a long line of London mercers. Young Richard likely attended **Cambridge University** during his teens and then matriculated in 1516 at the Middle Temple of the **Inns of Court** law schools in London. There he acquired a solid legal education before seeking the patronage of **Thomas Cardinal Wolsey**, who appointed him commissioner of the peace in 1528 for the counties of Essex and Hertfordshire. At around the same time, Rich befriended **Thomas Audley**, the speaker of the House of Commons, who helped the young lawyer secure a seat in **Parliament** in 1529 representing the town of Colchester in Essex. Four years later, Rich accepted a knighthood and became solicitor general of England and **Wales**, an office that authorized him to draft legislative bills for both houses of Parliament.

By 1533, Audley had succeeded Sir Thomas More as lord chancellor, while his friend Richard Rich had entered the service of Thomas Cromwell, the influential royal secretary and soon-to-be lord privy seal of Henry VIII. Following the king's second marriage to **Anne Boleyn**, Cromwell engineered the parliamentary passage of the **Act of Succession** and the **Act of Supremacy** in 1534. Both statutes required (on pain of treason) that all English subjects swear their loyalty to the heirs of Henry and Anne and also publicly acknowledge the king as supreme head of the English Church. Bishop John Fisher refused outright to swear these oaths, as did Sir Thomas More, but the latter (as a lawyer himself) simply remained silent rather than voice his dissent and thus invite treason charges. At their respective trials, Richard Rich testified that each man had privately expressed opposition to the succession and supremacy laws—even though More had very likely said nothing at all—and so sent them both to their deaths as traitors in summer 1535.

Ever eager to profit from the ongoing **Henrician Reformation**, Sir Richard persuaded Cromwell in 1536 to appoint him chancellor of the Court of Augmentations, which gave him control over (and access to) the newly created holding account for suppressed monastic assets. Rich was roundly hated by many as Cromwell's chief agent and was named (along with his master) in the articles of grievance drawn up by the **Pilgrimage of Grace** insurgents in autumn 1536. When Cromwell fell from royal favor and was put on trial as a traitor and heretic in June 1540, Richard Rich abruptly turned on and offered damaging testimony against his former employer that soon led to his execution on the block. Rewarded with a seat on the royal council, Rich supervised the interrogation and torture in 1541 of **Thomas Culpepper** and Francis Dereham, both of whom stood accused of adulterous affairs with King Henry's fifth queen, **Katherine Howard**.

Sir Richard had seemingly supported (and had certainly profited from) religious reforms during the 1530s, but after Henry VIII restored most of the doctrines and ceremonies of Rome in the early 1540s, Rich actively pursued "heretical" Protestants and saw to their arrest, imprisonment, and punishment. While helping conservative Crown ministers and bishops investigate King Henry's reformist consort **Katherine Parr** in 1546, Rich took part in the heresy trial of **Anne Askew**, a young religious reformer with reputed ties to ladies within the inner circle of the queen. When Bishop **Stephen Gardiner** of Winchester ordered the defiant Askew tortured to extract the names of her associates, Rich and Lord Chancellor **Thomas Wriothesley** actually operated the rack themselves when others would not. At Henry VIII's death in January 1547, Richard Rich hid away his conservative religious views and openly turned Protestant again to survive as a royal councilor into the more radically reformed reign of Edward VI.

Always an opportunist, Sir Richard was soon created Baron Rich of Leighs one month

after the new king's accession, and in March 1547, he succeeded Thomas Wriothesley as lord chancellor, an office he would retain for the next five years. He outwardly championed the reformed religious settlement and other progressive policies of Lord Protector **Edward Seymour**, Duke of Somerset, but shifted his allegiance to **John Dudley**, Earl of Warwick (and soon Duke of Northumberland), when Somerset fell from grace and perished on the block in 1552. Although he helped imprison several Catholic bishops in the **Tower of London** during King Edward's reign, Queen Mary I retained Rich on her expanded royal council. He was in poor health after 1554 and, retired to his estates in Essex, rarely traveled to London or attended much to Crown affairs for the rest of his life. He died in Rochford, Essex, on 12 June 1567 and was laid to rest in the nearby Felsted parish church, where a reclining effigy marks his grave today.

ROME, SACK OF (MAY 1527). The "eternal city" of Rome was captured and plundered by imperial forces as part of the ongoing Italian Wars waged in the 1520s between France, Spain, and the Holy Roman Empire. Although Emperor **Charles V** was not directly in command of the rogue imperial army that sacked the Holy See, the brutal treatment of the city's population and wanton theft of its treasures shocked the rest of Christendom and temporarily darkened the reputation of Charles as a champion of the Roman Church. The presence of his troops in Rome allowed the emperor to control the movements and decisions of Pope **Clement VII**, however, who was then under pressure to free Henry VIII from his first marriage. The pope denied the English king's request, which led in turn to the fall from favor and eventual death of King Henry's chief minister, **Thomas Cardinal Wolsey**, in 1530.

Following the catastrophic defeat and capture of the French king **François I** at the Battle of Pavia in 1525, Emperor Charles V stood triumphant in northern Italy and was thus in excellent position to threaten parts of Tuscany, the Papal States, and the kingdom of Naples as well. Fearing potential domination of all Italy by the emperor, Pope Clement

VII joined Florence, Venice, and France in the League of Cognac in May 1526 to oppose any further imperial territorial expansion in the region. When members of the Colonna family revolted against the pope in central Italy early in 1527, Emperor Charles sought to undermine the Cognac alliance by sending his garrison commander in Milan, Charles duc de Bourbon, to reinforce the rebels with a sizable German and Spanish army.

Young Bourbon accordingly assembled his troops, most of whom were hungry and unpaid, and with them marched south amid much destruction to join the Colonna insurgents. When his ragged force finally arrived at Rome's outer gates on 6 May 1527, Bourbon was killed in an initial assault that left his unruly soldiers leaderless and free to loot the possessions and rape and murder the terrified inhabitants of the Holy See. Pope Clement VII was forced to flee across the Tiber River to safety in the papal stronghold of Castel Sant'Angelo to avoid being killed himself. Emperor Charles was at this moment away in Spain, but the pillaging of Rome took place under his banner, and so his enemies—chiefly King **François I** of France—quickly laid blame for the devastation of the papal capital at his door.

In an odd coincidence, Cardinal Wolsey had just arrived in May 1527 to petition (and probably bribe) the pontiff for an annulment of his master Henry VIII's marriage with **Katherine of Aragon**, who, in another coincidental twist, happened to be the aunt of Holy Roman Emperor Charles V. With Pope Clement now under the control of Charles's soldiers in Rome, he dared not grant the English king's requested annulment for fear that the emperor, as his absentee jailer, might punish him personally and perhaps put his territory of the Papal States to the sword. Wolsey was thus sent home empty handed, and when the pope finally did regain his freedom in December 1527, his halfhearted authorization of a legatine court to try King Henry's annulment suit in England eventually came to nothing. Wolsey was banished from the Tudor court in disgrace and soon died, leaving Henry VIII still married to Queen Katherine and in search of other ways to free himself from his Spanish spouse.

The wars in Italy continued after the sack of Rome when the League of Cognac was revived, King François invaded Lombardy with a fresh French army, and a Genoese fleet commanded by Andria Doria laid siege to Naples, all by the end of 1527. Doria soon switched sides, however, and imperial troops twice defeated the French, resulting in the peace of Cambrai and a new alliance between the pope and the emperor by 1530. With all hope of obtaining a papal marriage annulment now dead, King Henry started down the long and painful road toward eventual separation of his kingdom from the Church of Rome.

ROPER, MARGARET MORE (1505–44).

This daughter of Sir **Thomas More** and wife of lawyer William Roper was well known even in her own day as an accomplished scholar and as one of the best-educated nonroyal women in Europe. The most gifted pupil among many in the More household, Margaret became her father's trusted confidante over time and in many ways his best friend as well. Some of Europe's most celebrated humanist scholars knew and corresponded with her, and a few even dedicated writings to her or noted her intellectual attributes in their dialogues and poetry. Although much of Roper's own literary output is lost to us, we do possess a few of her more important pieces, along with several of the many letters she exchanged with her father. Margaret Roper frequently visited with Sir Thomas More during his imprisonment in the **Tower of London** and, following his execution, lovingly recovered his remains and helped preserve his writings for posterity.

Margaret More was the first of four children born to Thomas More and his first wife, Joanna "Jane" Colt More, in the Bucklersbury district of central London. The death of her mother in 1511 and her father's remarriage to Alice Middleton More just one month later seems to have caused a great deal of distress among all the More children. Perhaps to distract them, Thomas More created a dedicated schoolroom, later known as the academia, or school of More, where his own offspring and other young relations and wards might receive the foundations of a good education.

Accordingly, he hired such prominent scholars as John Clement (the future physician), the classicist William Gonell, and the astronomer Nicholas Kratzer to tutor his brood of young students. More himself set the curriculum with a grounding in Latin and Greek, followed by immersion in such subjects as grammar, rhetoric, poetry, logic, history, mathematics, philosophy, astronomy, theology, and the medical arts. The Mores also kept an exotic menagerie (including a monkey) to stimulate the curiosity of the children, who were encouraged to perform skits, learn musical instruments, and play games and jests together as well. Margaret More soon blossomed in this intellectually fertile environment, earning great praise from her father's close friend **Desiderius Erasmus** whenever he visited the More home in London.

After she met the promising young barrister Will Roper around 1518, Margaret married him in early July 1521, a few months before her 16th birthday. The Ropers continued to live with Thomas and Alice More in their Bucklersbury home until the family moved to a spacious manor house and estate in Chelsea in 1524. By this time, Margaret had already published her first scholarly work, an English rendering of Erasmus's *Precatio dominica*, which she translated as *A Devout Treatise upon the Paternoster*, in 1523. Well pleased, Erasmus dedicated his essay on the hymn of Prudentius to the teenaged Margaret Roper later the same year. Similarly, the eminent Spanish humanist and educator Juan Luis Vives also referenced her learning and intelligence in his *Instruction of a Christian Woman*. She and her husband went on to have five children of their own, one of whom, the middle child Mary Roper (later Basset), became a competent scholar and translator herself.

Sir Thomas More and his daughter Margaret (or usually just Meg) enjoyed a very close relationship that featured not only reverent filial affection but heady intellectual discourse as well. The many letters they exchanged reveal a depth of mutual understanding and a shared respect for one another that neither father nor daughter ever managed to cultivate with their respective spouses. In 1527, the renowned

German artist **Hans Holbein** the Younger produced a More family portrait, and although the finished painting no longer exists, his pen-and-ink planning sketch has survived to show Margaret More Roper occupying a prominent position at the side of her proud father. When Margaret contracted the dreaded **sweating sickness** in 1528, Sir Thomas prayed fervently for her recovery but promised to enter a monastery if God chose that time to take his daughter from him. Meg survived the "sweate," and More became Henry VIII's lord chancellor of England in October 1529.

The next phase in the lives of Sir Thomas More and Margaret More Roper is well known thanks in part to Robert Bolt's 20th-century stage play and film *A Man for All Seasons*. More was a reluctant lord chancellor at best and resigned his chain of office in May 1532 rather than support Henry VIII's marriage annulment plans and his bid to control the English Church. After the king married **Anne Boleyn**, he required all his subjects to swear allegiance to their future children as royal heirs and to uphold a general condemnation of the pope in Rome. Sir Thomas More avoided the oath by keeping an unwavering silence and soon found himself imprisoned in the Tower of London in April 1534. Margaret Roper often wrote to and visited her father during his 15-month incarceration, and when he also offered only silence in place of the supremacy oath, his daughter begged him to save himself and submit to the Crown's demands. This he resolutely refused to do, which led to his trial, conviction, and decapitation on Tower Hill as a traitor on 6 July 1535.

Margaret could not bring herself to attend her father's execution, but she accepted his headless corpse soon afterward and had it properly buried in the Chapel of St. Peter ad Vincula inside the Tower of London. More's head was displayed on a London Bridge pike for a time, until Margaret bribed a watchman to remove it and place it in her care. A few years later, Will Roper was arrested by Crown officials and asked to produce Thomas More's papers, but he surrendered nothing and was eventually released. Margaret More Roper died (possibly in childbirth) during the summer of

1544 and was buried in the local parish church at Chelsea. Her husband lived on until 1578; when he died, he was interred in the Roper family crypt in St. Dunstan's Church in Canterbury, along with the decaying remains of Sir Thomas More's severed head.

ROSES, WARS OF THE. *See* WARS OF THE ROSES (1455–1485).

RUTHALL, THOMAS, BISHOP OF DURHAM, LORD PRIVY SEAL (c. 1465–1523). An influential prelate, royal councilor, and diplomat in the early-Tudor period, Thomas Ruthall (alternately Rowthall) is best known today for his service to the English Crown and the Roman Church as prince bishop (viceroy in the north) of Durham. He was a friend and colleague of **Thomas Cardinal Wolsey** and Sir **Thomas More**, and he succeeded Bishop **Richard Fox** of Winchester in several ecclesiastical and governmental offices. Though less prominent a figure in Tudor times than some of his more famous associates, Bishop Ruthall still took part in or was an eyewitness to most of the major events of King Henry VIII's early reign.

Thomas Ruthall's date of birth is unknown, but the award of his undergraduate degree and the time of his ordination suggest a possible birth date sometime around 1465. According to later-16th-century sources, Ruthall was a native of Cirencester in Gloucestershire and was probably a younger son (judging from his church career) of John Ruthall and his wife, Alicia Avelyng Ruthall. Young Thomas evidently received a solid grammar school education because he is known to have attended **Oxford University**, where he earned his baccalaureate degree in canon laws in 1488. Ruthall became a priest two years later and, named as a doctor of degrees in a 1493 papal dispensation, then accepted a teaching fellowship at **Cambridge University** in 1500. As was the custom in late-medieval England, Ruthall was an unapologetic pluralist (holder of multiple church livings) who collected two prebendary stalls (cathedral sinecures), one parish rectory, three deaneries, and one archdiaconal post between 1495 and 1506.

Thomas Ruthall also attracted the attention of the Crown at the same time and, by the late 1490s, was already serving **Henry VII** as a personal secretary and a member of the royal council. In 1499, he accompanied Bishop Fox of Durham and other diplomats on an embassy to negotiate a peace treaty with the new king of France **Louis XII**. The first Tudor king later nominated Ruthall to the vacant diocese of Durham, but the old king died, and so his successor Henry VIII was left to reconfirm the appointment in 1509. The youthful new king kept Ruthall on as a secretary and councilor and ordered him to recruit and equip 100 soldiers for his planned **French invasion in 1513–14**. When King Henry sailed with his army to France, the Prince bishop of Durham hurried back to his diocese to fortify Norham Castle against the impending invasion of King **James IV** of Scots. After helping Bishop Richard Fox negotiate the Treaty of London that ended the 1513 French and Scottish wars, Ruthall accompanied King Henry's youngest sister, **Mary** Tudor, to Paris for her wedding with the decrepit old Louis XII in autumn 1514.

Having already followed in Richard Fox's footsteps as a Crown diplomat, a royal councilor, and a prince bishop of Durham, Thomas Ruthall became lord privy seal when Fox resigned that post in April 1516. Now working as Cardinal Wolsey's chief governmental lieutenant, Ruthall took part in talks to wed Henry VIII's daughter **Mary** Tudor to the dauphin of France in 1518 and then accompanied the English contingent to **Calais** to attend the **Field of Cloth of Gold** summit meeting with King **François I** in 1520. Known to contemporaries as a hard-working and detail-oriented administrator, Prince Bishop Ruthall played the crucial role of recording secretary during the May 1521 treason trial of **Edward Stafford**, the third Duke of Buckingham. After renovating his northern palace of Bishop Auckland and contributing significantly to the grammar school in his native Cirencester, Thomas Ruthall died of unknown causes on 4 February 1523 at his Durham Place residence in London. His remains were interred in a tomb in the Chapel of St. John in Westminster Abbey.

S

SAVOY, MARGARET OF. *See* MARGARET OF AUSTRIA, DUCHESS OF SAVOY AND REGENT OF THE NETHERLANDS (1480–1530).

SCOTLAND. *See* JAMES IV, KING OF SCOTLAND (1473–1513; r. 1488–1513); JAMES V, KING OF SCOTLAND (1512–42; r. 1513–42); MARGARET (TUDOR), QUEEN OF SCOTLAND, COUNTESS OF ANGUS AND METHVEN (1489–1541).

SEVEN SACRAMENTS, DEFENSE OF THE. *See ASSERTIO SEPTEM SACRAMENTORUM (DEFENSE OF THE SEVEN SACRAMENTS*; 1521).

SEYMOUR, EDWARD, FIRST EARL OF HERTFORD, FIRST DUKE OF SOMERSET (c. 1500–1552). This powerful magnate was the eldest brother of **Jane Seymour**, Henry VIII's third wife and queen, and was thus the uncle of their son and heir, **Edward** Tudor, who acceded to the English throne as Edward VI in 1547. Seymour acquired many landed estates and progressively more prestigious titles as rewards from a grateful sovereign for service he rendered as a royal councilor and military commander. Well trusted by both King Henry and his nephew the Prince of **Wales**, Earl Edward Seymour of Hertford was in a favorable position to become young Edward VI's lord protector when the old king died in January 1547. Created Duke of Somerset early in the new reign, Seymour tried to improve conditions for England's commoners, but his ambition and arrogance aroused much hostility in

his **noble** rivals, and he was overthrown and executed for high treason in January 1552.

Edward Seymour was born at Wolf Hall around 1500 (alternately but improbably in 1506) to Sir John Seymour, the Lord of Hatch Beauchamp manor in Somersetshire, and his wife, Margery Wentworth Seymour, whose family traced its roots back to King Edward III. Young Edward Seymour was the oldest of eight Seymour children, a brood that included his sister Jane, the future queen of Henry VIII, and his brother **Thomas Seymour**, the future lord high admiral and eventual husband of King Henry's dowager queen, **Katherine Parr**. We know little of Edward Seymour's early years, but at age 14 (as a page of honor), he accompanied Princess **Mary** Tudor, Henry VIII's younger sister, overseas for her wedding to King **Louis XII** of France. When the sickly French ruler dismissed most of Mary's English entourage, Seymour returned home and probably attended **Oxford** or **Cambridge University** for a few years to acquire some academic polish. In 1518, he married Katherine Fyllol, a young heiress with lands in Essex and Dorset, but their union was not a happy one, and she died 17 years later to release him for a second marriage.

Edward Seymour rode with his father, Sir John, and **Charles Brandon**, the Duke of Suffolk, on King Henry's second **French invasion of 1523–24** and was knighted during the campaign by the duke for his conspicuous courage on the battlefield. Henry VIII appointed him esquire of the king's body in 1524, and the following year, he became master of the horse (worth £60 per annum) in the household of **Henry Fitzroy**, Henry's bastard son. In 1527, Sir Edward traveled abroad with **Thomas Cardinal Wolsey** to find scriptural grounds for an annulment of King Henry's first marriage, but this enterprise yielded few results and eventually led to Wolsey's precipitous downfall two years later. With no other connection to the cardinal, Seymour sidestepped Wolsey's fall and then set about acquiring multiple estates in Somersetshire and Wiltshire, thanks in part to a loan he procured from the king for £2,000 in 1532. Sir Edward cast off his adulterous first wife in 1533, and when she died a few years later, he married Anne Stanhope, who went on to give him no fewer than 10 children.

As Henry VIII grew increasingly weary of his second queen, **Anne Boleyn**, in the mid-1530s, his wandering eye fell on one of her ladies-in-waiting, the quiet and amiable Jane Seymour, Sir Edward's younger sister. The king spent more and more time with Mistress Jane until, following Queen Anne's execution for adulterous treason on 19 May 1536, he hastily married the younger Seymour woman just 11 days later. One week after the wedding, Henry elevated Edward Seymour to the peerage as Viscount Lisle, then granted him the Earldom of Hertford a few days after the birth of Prince Edward in October 1537. His sister Queen Jane soon died from childbirth complications, however, but the Earl of Hertford remained in royal favor nonetheless. King Henry came to rely on Seymour even more after **Thomas Cromwell**, the king's chief minister since 1532, abruptly fell from grace and died on the block as a traitor and heretic in July 1540.

Henry VIII continued to place great trust in Hertford during the final years of his long reign. In 1542, Seymour was appointed warden of the Scottish marches, and when Edinburgh repudiated a peace treaty and marriage alliance with England, an insulted King Henry sent the earl north with an army to ravage southern Scotland two years later. During his final **French invasion of 1544–45**, the English king made Hertford lieutenant of the realm under his queen regent Katherine Parr, then named him governor and defender of the captured citadel of Boulogne in France. The earl acquitted himself well in this role by thwarting a determined French attempt to retake the town in 1545. He returned to military action the following year with another destructive raid into Scotland and another tour as Boulogne's garrison commander until King Henry's failing health hastened Hertford's return to court in October 1546. The old king died in late January 1547, leaving Edward Seymour to take custody of his nephew Edward VI and proclaim himself lord protector of England as the leading member of the boy-king's new privy council.

Quite comfortable with this arrangement at first, young King Edward rewarded his uncle by granting him the Duchy of Somerset in February 1547. Seymour had kept his reformist Protestant views to himself during King Henry's return to religious conservatism in the 1540s, but now, with his fiery Calvinist nephew on the throne, the new Duke of Somerset let his true evangelical sympathies be known. He sponsored repeal of King Henry's punitive **Act of Six Articles**, authorized the publication of Archbishop **Thomas Cranmer**'s *Book of Common Prayer*, and standardized English religious practices under the Act of Uniformity. Somerset also tried to ameliorate peasant hardships by restricting arable land **enclosures** and taxing sheep to slow tenant evictions, but these measures had little effect and only turned many of England's most powerful nobles against him. When his **coinage** debasement triggered a major uprising in summer 1549, Somerset's chief rival **John Dudley**, the Earl of Warwick, convinced young King Edward to have his uncle arrested and imprisoned in the **Tower of London**. There Somerset remained on and off for more than two years until, finally tried and convicted of treason, he was beheaded on Tower Hill on 22 January 1552.

SEYMOUR, JANE, QUEEN OF ENGLAND (c. 1509–37). The third queen of Henry VIII, Jane Seymour was the only royal wife who successfully delivered the living son and heir that King Henry had longed for his entire reign and had discarded two earlier wives and the

Roman Church in order to obtain. It was (and still is) widely believed that Queen Jane was the wife Henry VIII loved most dearly, perhaps because she finally bore him his coveted male heir or perhaps because her demure and acquiescent personality suited his domineering character the best. When the old king died in late January 1547, he left instructions that his remains be entombed next to those of his beloved Queen Jane.

Jane Seymour was likely born around 1509 (the date is uncertain) to Sir John and Margery Wentworth Seymour at their ancestral home of Wolf Hall in Wiltshire. Jane was the eldest daughter among eight Seymour children, a group that included her brothers **Edward Seymour** (later Viscount Lisle, Earl of Hertford, and Duke of Somerset) and **Thomas Seymour** (later lord high admiral), both of whom would end their lives on the block as convicted traitors. Jane's early life is fairly obscure, but we do know that, thanks to the influence of her kinsman Sir Francis Bryan, she was appointed as lady-in-waiting to Henry VIII's first wife, Queen **Katherine of Aragon**, at some point in 1529. King Henry may have first noticed the 25-year-old Jane when he visited Wolf Hall in September 1534 at the end of his royal progress that summer, although some sources claim she was away from her family residence at the time. Already remarried to Queen **Anne Boleyn**, the king's wandering eye nevertheless fell on Jane Seymour sometime during 1534–35, when rumors of his growing infatuation with her began to circulate around the court. Wishing to keep Jane close, King Henry had her installed as one of Queen Anne's ladies-in-waiting later in 1535, an appointment that infuriated the king's jealous and hot-tempered second wife. As Queen Anne continued to alienate herself from Henry and fell ever farther from royal favor, Jane quietly remained in the background and even humbly refused the king's awkward attempts to win her affections with gifts of jewelry and venison.

We do not know exactly when Henry VIII decided to abandon Queen Anne in order to remarry, but now convinced that his second wife was a philandering witch, the king had her arrested on 2 May 1536 and incarcerated in the **Tower of London**. Jane Seymour, meanwhile, kept well away from court during Anne's imprisonment and trial, staying at the home of her brother Sir Edward Seymour and only receiving the king a few times when members of her family were present. On 17 May, Archbishop **Thomas Cranmer** dissolved the marriage of Henry VIII and Anne, and two days later the unfortunate daughter of the House of Boleyn was executed. Thus free to marry again, King Henry wasted no time and hastily wed his third queen just 11 days after the death of his second.

Jane Seymour was just the kind of virtuous, docile, and agreeable new wife King Henry needed at this point in his life. Despite her lengthy residence at the promiscuous Tudor court, most contemporaries assumed that Jane had entered into matrimony with the king at age 27 as a virgin. She had not been raised to marry royalty, so she was not well educated and reputedly was only able to recognize and sign her own name. Jane was of medium height with a pale complexion and rather plain features. The imperial ambassador **Eustace Chapuys** remarked in 1536 that "nobody thinks she has much beauty," an impression reinforced by the portrait **Hans Holbein** the Younger painted of her the same year. No, Henry VIII had other reasons to wed the meek Jane; as one of eight children, she could be counted on to bear many royal offspring, and she was the complete opposite of the flirtatious, opinionated, and tempestuous queen that Anne Boleyn had proven to be.

Jane Seymour's married life lasted just under 17 months, but she still left a significant mark on Henry VIII's reign and on the Tudor dynasty itself. She was largely responsible for reconciling her new husband to his eldest daughter, **Mary** Tudor, the Catholic princess Queen Katherine had given him some two decades before and who had been banished from court in recent years by the unforgiving and petty Anne Boleyn. Queen Jane prevailed upon the reluctant Mary to accept King Henry's supremacy over the Church of England, a submission that duly restored the princess to royal favor during the autumn of 1536. Jane Seymour's greatest achievement as queen came when she gave birth to the healthy male child the king was convinced would finally secure the English throne for his Tudor successors. Clearly with child by spring 1537, the queen's pregnancy progressed normally through the summer and inspired astrological predictions that the expected infant would be a boy. Jane went into labor on 9 October and, after several days of agony, presented an overjoyed king with his seemingly robust son Prince Edward. All seemed well with mother and child at first, but within one week of the birth, Queen Jane developed puerperal fever; by 23 October, she was delirious, and during the night of 24 October, she breathed her last. Although King Henry was thrilled to have his first legitimate son and royal heir, he was so grief-stricken with the loss of his third queen that he would not enter into matrimony again for almost three years. Queen Jane Seymour was laid to rest on 12 November 1537 in the Chapel of St. George at Windsor Castle.

SEYMOUR, SIR THOMAS, LORD HIGH ADMIRAL, FIRST BARON SEYMOUR OF SUDELEY (c. 1508–49).

The brother of Henry VIII's third queen and so the Tudor king's kinsman by marriage, Thomas Seymour owed his high place at court largely to his siblings and to his own boundless ambition. He served King Henry as an international diplomat between 1538 and 1543, then distinguished himself on the battlefield and later as a successful military administrator. Under his brother **Edward Seymour**, the first Duke of Somerset and young **Edward VI**'s lord protector, Thomas Seymour was raised to **noble** rank and assumed command of most of England's **navy** as well. After marrying **Katherine Parr**, the widowed queen dowager of Henry VIII, Seymour ingratiated himself with the youthful King Edward, flirted with Princess **Elizabeth** Tudor, and eventually plotted to overthrow his own brother Somerset. He was arrested in January 1549, and tried and convicted as a traitor, he died on the block two months later outside the **Tower of London**.

Thomas Seymour was born the fourth son of Sir John Seymour and his wife, Margery Wentworth Seymour, at their ancestral home of Wolf Hall in Wiltshire. Little is known of young Thomas's early upbringing or education. He first appeared in the historical record as a messenger on a diplomatic mission to France with Sir Francis Bryan in 1532. Four years later, Seymour's fortunes rose dramatically when his younger sister Jane attracted the amorous attentions of Henry VIII. Following the precipitous downfall and execution of **Anne Boleyn** in May 1536, King Henry made Jane Seymour his third wife and queen and so welcomed her brothers Edward and Thomas into the royal family. Preferment soon followed for Thomas Seymour, who entered the king's service as a chamberlain and then accepted a knighthood in the Order of the **Garter** in summer 1537. When his sister Jane presented the Tudor king with his long-desired son and male heir Prince Edward the next autumn, Sir Thomas attended the infant's christening as one of his honored uncles and guardians.

Queen Jane died unexpectedly only 12 days after her son's birth, but Thomas Seymour and his brother Edward retained Henry VIII's confidence and continued to bask in the king's good graces. Drawing on his previous diplomatic experience in France, Sir Thomas traveled to Paris to represent his Tudor master at the court of King **François I** in 1538. He was present at **Calais** in December 1539 to greet **Anne of Cleves**, Henry VIII's intended fourth bride, before she set sail for England and her royal nuptials the following month. Seymour spent the next two years in Vienna at the court of Emperor **Charles V** negotiating an alliance with the Habsburg ruler and fighting in the imperial army against the invading Turks.

Briefly back in London in 1542, Sir Thomas became romantically involved with Lady Katherine Parr, an attractive widow of 30 years whose second husband had just recently passed away. When King Henry's eye fell on the eligible Lady Katherine, he arranged for Seymour to join another embassy to Brussels to clear the way for his own matrimonial advances. While still resident in **Flanders**, Sir Thomas commanded a detachment of imperial troops that stormed, captured, and demolished two fortresses near the town of Boulogne in France. Although this action took place under a foreign flag, an impressed (and now newly married) Henry VIII made Seymour his master of royal ordnance and warden of the Cinque Ports in 1544–45.

Sir Thomas traveled widely for two more years but then returned to England during the final declining days of the old Tudor king in January 1547. After Henry's death, Seymour was created Baron Sudeley and was granted the office of lord high admiral by his brother Edward, now the Duke of Somerset and lord protector of the child-king Edward VI. The younger Seymour soon fell out with his brother, however, over which of them would become the personal governor of their adolescent royal nephew. He also hastily married his former sweetheart Katherine Parr just four months after Henry VIII's death and then worked to win King Edward's trust with flattery and extra pocket money.

The real break with Somerset came in spring 1548, when Thomas Seymour began indecently romping about with his wife's 15-year-old stepdaughter Elizabeth Tudor in the teenager's private bedchamber. When rumors spread that he planned to kidnap his royal nephew and niece and then overthrow Somerset's regime entirely, King Edward's privy council ordered Seymour's arrest in January 1549. An extended investigation into the lord admiral's affairs followed, and finally convicted of treason by **parliamentary** act of attainder, he was taken to Tower Hill and there beheaded on 20 March 1549. Seymour was laid to rest—as were so many other victims of the headsman's axe in Tudor times—in the Chapel of St. Peter ad Vincula within the precincts of the Tower of London.

SHELTON, MARGARET OR MADGE (c. 1504–c. 1553). One of Henry VIII's many mistresses, Margaret (known by her family and close associates as Madge) Shelton was a first cousin of and lady-in-waiting to Queen **Anne Boleyn**. Shelton was caught up in the court intrigues and gossip of the mid-1530s and was briefly thought to be a candidate to become King Henry's fourth wife and queen following her cousin's execution. Although most historians have generally identified Madge as the

Tudor king's lover, recent scholarship has suggested that her younger sister Mary may have been Henry's actual paramour instead.

Margaret Shelton drew her first breath at Shelton Hall in Norfolk sometime between 1501 and 1506 and was one of nine children born to Sir John Shelton and his wife, Lady Anne Boleyn Shelton, the sister of Sir **Thomas Boleyn** and so the aunt of the future queen Anne Boleyn. Little is known of Madge's upbringing or education, but some early sources suggest that she was pretty, not overly intelligent, and quietly docile as a child. When Madge's cousin Anne Boleyn married King Henry in June 1533 and then gave birth to Princess **Elizabeth** Tudor the following September, the new queen's aunt Lady Anne Shelton became the infant's governess, while her daughters Madge and Mary Shelton accepted positions as Queen Anne's attending ladies. Henry VIII's second wife loathed **Mary** Tudor, the king's daughter by his first wife, **Katherine of Aragon**, and insisted that Lady Anne Shelton treat the teenaged Tudor daughter harshly for her refusal to acknowledge Princess Elizabeth's claim to the throne. Lady Anne obeyed these orders for a time but later relented and nursed Princess Mary back to health when she fell ill early in 1536.

As King Henry's passion for his willful and jealous second queen began to cool, members of the Boleyn faction introduced him to Madge, by now a beautiful woman in her late 20s who may have possessed the fair good looks of the king's earlier mistress **Mary Boleyn**, Queen Anne's older sister. Once Henry believed that his queen was again with child—her third pregnancy in two years—he began an affair with Madge Shelton in spring 1535 that lasted for around six months. It may have been that, as a kinswoman, Queen Anne trusted Madge to keep her royal husband safely satisfied until the delivery of her next child would allow the king into her bed once again. However, the ambitious Boleyn family may have seen Madge as a safety net of sorts, a candidate for King Henry's hand should Anne miscarry or give birth to a second disappointing daughter.

Unlike some of Henry VIII's other lovers, such as **Bessie Blount** and possibly Mary

Boleyn, Madge Shelton did not give the king any illegitimate children. After Henry discarded her in autumn 1535, Shelton was briefly betrothed to Sir **Henry Norris** and then enjoyed a flirtatious dalliance with Sir Francis Weston, both courtiers who were soon to die with Queen Anne Boleyn for high treason. Madge often spelled her name Marg, and because the Tudor letters *g* and *y* looked somewhat alike, a few modern scholars have supposed that Mary Shelton, and not Madge, was actually the real mistress of King Henry VIII. There also exists a sketch by **Hans Holbein** the Younger of one Lady Mary Heverington (Mary Shelton's married name), but the existence of this piece by the famous royal portraitist does not necessarily confirm or refute either sister's claim to have shared King Henry's bed. Madge Shelton eventually married Sir Thomas Wodehouse and with him produced no fewer than eight children before her death from unknown causes at some point between 1552 and 1555. One of their descendants, P. G. Wodehouse, later authored the popular Bertie Wooster and Jeeves tales during the 20th century. *See also* POPPINCOURT, JANE OR JEANNE (c. 1484–c. 1530); STAFFORD, ANNE, LADY HASTINGS, COUNTESS OF HUNTINGDON (c. 1483–1544).

SHRINES AND PILGRIMAGES (c. AD 650–1539).

Shrines and the journeys of pilgrims to visit them were important components of popular devotional practice in England during the Middle Ages and into the reign of King Henry VIII. Shrines were sanctified places—usually churches, **monastic** abbeys, or crypts—that housed blessed relics believed to have some connection to saints or other holy persons of the Roman Church. Often small body parts, bone fragments, or bits of hair and clothing, these relics were thought to be powerful sources of divine grace that in turn could cure the sick, mend the crippled, and speed penitent sinners on their way to heaven. Over time, however, greedy churchmen began to exploit popular interest in shrines by displaying fraudulent relics and collecting lucrative admission fees from gullible pilgrims. By the 16th century, abuses of this kind were widespread,

causing Henry VIII to order the closure and destruction of nearly all the shrines in England at the same time the monasteries were being dissolved during the **Henrician Reformation**.

The religious phenomena of relics, shrines, and pilgrimages had their origins in the cult of saints that arose during the heyday of the Christian persecutions under the Emperor Diocletian in the late third and early fourth centuries AD. When Christian martyrs died in Roman prisons or arenas, their followers often recovered and then venerated their corpses as precious receptacles of divine grace. Once the bodies of such holy martyrs were entombed in underground catacombs or beneath altars in churches, devout believers increasingly pushed forward to pray over and even touch the sacred remains to benefit from their saving and healing properties. These relics were later encased in reliquaries to protect them from frequent human contact and were stored in buildings called shrines that in turn were inhabited, administered, and jealously controlled by members of the Christian **clergy**.

Already popular in the Mediterranean world, shrines began to appear in England once Roman Christianity reestablished itself in the island's Anglo-Saxon and Frisian kingdoms during the seventh century AD. One of the first English shrines founded in this period memorialized the life of St. Alban, a Christian convert who had suffered martyrdom in the town of Verulamium (later St. Albans) during the Roman occupation of Britain. Another early shrine appeared in the 10th century at Bury St. Edmunds in Suffolk, where invading Vikings had murdered King Edmund of East Anglia in 869. These two holy places soon attracted large crowds of pilgrims each year and led to the establishment of sprawling Benedictine monasteries above the graves of both martyrs in later centuries. Other important medieval shrines included Our Lady of Glastonbury, which claimed (improbably) Joseph of Arimathea as its founder; Our Lady of Walsingham, where the Virgin Mary had appeared in 1061; and Thomas à Becket, the slain archbishop of Canterbury whose elaborate tomb in that city's cathedral became England's most popular pilgrimage destination. Like St. Thomas, the shrines of other holy

English men, such as St. Edward the Confessor (Westminster), St. Swithun (Winchester), and St. Cuthbert (Durham), were all located in special tombs or crypts in each of their home cathedrals.

After **Henry VII** seized the throne of England in 1485, he visited and worshipped at his realm's more prominent shrines, as had most of his royal predecessors. Famously pious, the first Tudor king ordered images of himself placed near the Canterbury and Walsingham shrines in his will to remind the holy saints in each place to pray for his soul. Henry VIII was (like his father) conventionally religious and is known to have made several pilgrimages to major and even minor English shrines during the first two decades of his reign. His first visit to Walsingham as king took place in 1511 at the birth of his short-lived son Henry; he later donated money there to maintain a votive candle and pay for improvements to the shrine's fabric. Over the next decade, King Henry attended and made offerings at the sacred tombs of Edward the Confessor in Westminster and St. Swithun in Winchester and also journeyed to the smaller shrines of John Shorne at North Marston, Our Lady of Ipswich, and the Rood of Grace at Boxley. In 1520, the king once again undertook a pilgrimage to Walsingham, this time in the company of his imperial guest **Charles V**, and when the emperor returned to England two years later, both men traveled to Canterbury to pray at the shrine of the martyred Thomas à Becket.

Thus devoted to the cult of saints during his early years, Henry VIII abruptly changed course once he began his campaign to separate his kingdom and subjects from the Roman Church. After declaring himself supreme head of the English Church, the king was gradually convinced by his new vicegerent in spirituals (religious director) **Thomas Cromwell** that England's shrines were (like her monasteries) riddled with corruption. Cromwell claimed that the clerical guardians of most English shrines were charging admission fees and were selling souvenir badges that visitors wore on their caps and hoods to advertise the number of pilgrimage sites they had visited. The irritated king also learned that animal bones or vials of

duck's blood were routinely being passed off at such shrines as the so-called relics of this-or-that saint. Even worse, shrine custodians were shamelessly broadcasting tales of their relics' healing miracles to attract even larger groups of impressionable and fee-paying pilgrims.

When Cromwell's agents discovered that scheming monks were using hidden wires to move the image of Christ on the Rood (crucifix) of Boxley, King Henry finally lost his temper and ordered all his kingdom's shrines closed down as part of the ongoing suppression of the monasteries. Scores of shrines were accordingly shuttered and dismantled between 1537 and 1539, including that of Thomas à Becket at Canterbury, where Crown agents secretly reburied the saint's bones and then smashed his tomb and reliquary to pieces. Today a rough inscription on the Canterbury Cathedral floor indicates the spot where Becket was martyred, while a solitary candle several meters away marks the location of his shrine before it was demolished.

SIX ARTICLES, ACT OF. *See* ACT OF SIX ARTICLES (1539).

SKELTON, JOHN (c. 1460–1529). John Skelton was a poet and satirist who served between 1496 and 1501 as the "scolmaster," or tutor, of young Henry Tudor, then Duke of York and later King Henry VIII. Skelton is best known today in literary circles for incorporating a series of rhythmic speech patterns into his poetry, but he also composed a short guide to princely conduct entitled *Speculum principis* (1501) that he hoped would instruct and inspire the youthful Prince Henry.

Skelton's birth and early life are obscure, but he was probably born either in Norfolk or perhaps in Yorkshire in the early 1460s. He was educated first at **Cambridge University** and then attended **Oxford University**, where he was honored with the title poet laureate in 1488. He finished his education at Louvain University in **Flanders** and was there awarded a second laureate in 1492. Skelton, a client of Lady **Margaret Beaufort**, entered royal service under her son King **Henry VII** as a court poet in 1488. In 1498, he was ordained a priest and later accepted a church living in 1502 as rector of Diss parish in Norfolk, which he retained (mainly as an absentee) for the rest of his life. When King Henry VIII appointed him *orator regius* (royal speaker) in 1512, Skelton moved to London to write poetry for his former pupil. During this period, he aimed a few of his more satirical barbs at **Thomas Cardinal Wolsey**, King Henry's chief minister and a notorious pluralist, but the two managed to patch up their quarrel by 1522. Skelton died in June 1529 (possibly in Westminster Abbey) and was buried in St Margaret's Church in London.

Skelton gained an early reputation for his translations of classical works and in 1499 even earned the admiration of Dutch humanist **Desiderius Erasmus**, who called him the "light and glory of English letters." As a royal tutor, he mostly instructed Prince Henry in Latin grammar and other European languages. Skelton also composed his *Speculum principis* (*A Princely Mirror*) to help his young charge avoid the pitfalls of vice, seek the solace of a constant wife, and heed the advice of loyal counselors. His earliest known work of poetry was his 1489 "Elegy on the Death of the Earl of Northumberland." Two of Skelton's other more important offerings included the poem "The Bowge of Courte" ("The Prizes of Court," 1498), a stinging critique of courtly ambition, and the play *Magnyfycence* (1516), a lampoon of **noble** self-importance.

SOLWAY MOSS, BATTLE OF. *See* JAMES V, KING OF SCOTLAND (1512–42; r. 1513–42).

SPAIN. *See* FERDINAND II OF ARAGON (1452–1516) AND ISABEL I OF CASTILE (1451–1504), KING AND QUEEN OF SPAIN (r. 1474–1516).

STAFFORD, ANNE, LADY HASTINGS, COUNTESS OF HUNTINGDON (c. 1483–1544). The sister of one of England's most powerful **nobles** and a lady-in-waiting to Queen **Katherine of Aragon**, Anne Stafford was the first of many mistresses to share the bed of Henry VIII over the course of his lengthy reign. Unlike a few of the king's other lovers—namely **Bessie Blount** and possibly **Mary**

Boleyn—Anne did not give Henry any illegitimate children. His affair with her prompted angry reactions from Queen Katherine and from Anne's brother and husband, which resulted in her withdrawal from court and seclusion for a time in a remote convent. She was twice married, and although her first union was childless, she and her second husband produced eight offspring, five of whom reached maturity and had families of their own.

Anne Stafford was born in the castle of Ashby-de-la-Zouch, Leicestershire, in 1483 (or 1484) to Henry Stafford, the powerful second Duke of Buckingham. His wife (Anne's mother) was Katherine Woodville Stafford, the aunt of Queen **Elizabeth of York** and so the great-aunt of the future Henry VIII. Anne's father had been a supporter of Richard III but then rebelled against the Yorkist king and died on the block as a traitor in the year his daughter Anne was born. Anne Stafford had two brothers, Edward (later the third Duke of Buckingham) and Henry (later the first Earl of Wiltshire), along with a sister, Lady Elizabeth Fitzwalter, whose eventual marriage made her the Countess of Sussex.

The daughter of one of the most prestigious noble houses in England, young Anne Stafford probably learned to read and write, ride and hunt, dance, play musical instruments, and do needlework, although little is known with much certainty about her early life. In 1503, she married Sir Walter Herbert, a bastard son of William Herbert, the first Earl of Pembroke, but their union was barren, and four years after their wedding, Sir Walter died. Now a widow, Anne went to live with her brother Duke Edward Stafford of Buckingham and his wife, Eleanor Percy Stafford, at Thornbury Castle in Gloucestershire. Buckingham quickly arranged a second match for his sister, and in 1509, she married Lord George Hastings, a minor noble who, quite close in age to Henry VIII, soon became one of the teenaged king's boisterous inner circle of companions. When King Henry married Katherine of Aragon in summer 1509, Anne Stafford Hastings and her elder sister, Elizabeth Stafford Fitzwalter, both entered the queen's service as two of her most prominent attending ladies.

Queen Katherine was already pregnant with her "honeymoon" child by autumn 1509, an event that occasioned much rejoicing at court but effectively barred the lusty King Henry from her bed. During his first years on the throne, Henry seems to have cultivated a taste for somewhat older women; his queen Katherine was six years his senior, while Anne Stafford Hastings and his next paramour, **Jane Popincourt**, were both 7 to 8 years older than the teenaged king. In spring 1510, rumors began to circulate that one of Henry VIII's rowdy young courtiers, Sir William Compton, was having an illicit affair with the attractive Lady Hastings. Many at court believed, however, that Compton was merely running interference for his royal Tudor master, who in fact was enjoying the favors of the lovely Lady Anne himself. It may be that Anne told her sister Lady Fitzwalter of her liaisons with Compton, the king, or both, or perhaps one of Queen Katherine's other ladies shared this gossip with Luis Caroz, the Spanish ambassador. However it might have leaked out, the news of his sister's alleged infidelities soon reached the ears of the Duke of Buckingham, who was understandably outraged. Reacting almost immediately, he intercepted Compton on his way to Lady Anne's bedchamber and, delivering a severe tongue lashing, declared that his sister was not a suitable plaything for the likes of a lowborn knight or, for that matter, even a Tudor king!

This exchange was quickly reported to Henry VIII, who summoned Buckingham and scolded him for his ill-considered remarks, then banished him from court for the next several months. Quite embarrassed himself, Lord George Hastings packed up his wife, Lady Anne, and hastily retreated with her to a rural location some 60 miles distant from London. There he deposited her in a convent to ponder her recent indiscretions and wait for the scandal to blow over. At the same time, Katherine of Aragon was herself incensed by the affair and thoroughly chastised her husband for having violated their marital vows. The stress of this angry encounter and the tension that then crept into her marriage with Henry may well have brought on Queen Katherine's premature labor and delivery of a stillborn daughter in April 1510.

Lord George Hastings remained close to King Henry and served him as a soldier and diplomat until a grateful sovereign created him first Earl of Huntingdon in 1529. Over time, George Hastings appears to have forgiven his wife, for their later letters display much mutual affection, and they managed over time to produce a large brood of children together. During their last years, the Earl and Countess of Huntingdon resided in the household of Princess **Mary** Tudor, Henry VIII's only surviving child by Katherine of Aragon, and they died in the same year (1544) in Buckinghamshire of unknown causes. *See also* SHELTON, MARGARET OR MADGE (c. 1504–c. 1553).

STAFFORD, EDWARD, THIRD DUKE OF BUCKINGHAM (1478–1521). One of England's most powerful **nobles** during the early reign of Henry VIII, Buckingham possessed a genuine but dormant claim of his own to the English throne that gradually eroded his relationship with his insecure young Tudor sovereign. The great duke also nursed a deep loathing for **Thomas Cardinal Wolsey**, Henry's lord chancellor, whom Buckingham regarded as a lowborn political climber. The Duke of Buckingham detested any and all things French and did everything in his power to scuttle the **Field of Cloth of Gold** summit meeting with King **François I** in 1520. When rumors surfaced implicating the duke in plots against Henry and Wolsey, the king's suspicions reached the breaking point, and he had Buckingham arrested, convicted of treason, and executed in May 1521.

Edward Stafford was born in Brecon Castle in **Wales** on 3 February 1478. He was the eldest son and heir of Henry Stafford, the second Duke of Buckingham, and his wife, Katherine Woodville Stafford, who was a younger sister of Elizabeth Woodville, the wife and queen of King Edward IV. Edward Stafford's father was descended from the seventh and youngest son of King Edward III, Thomas of Woodstock, an ancestry that settled claims of royalty upon both the senior Stafford and his firstborn son. When the elder Buckingham led a revolt against King Richard III in 1483, the second Duke of Buckingham was captured and beheaded for treason by the angry Yorkist king, who also used an act of attainder to strip away the rebel's ducal title.

After King Richard's death at Bosworth Field, the newly crowned **Henry VII** restored the Duchy of Buckingham to Edward Stafford in 1485 to reclaim the loyalty of his wealthy and influential family. The young third Duke of Buckingham then became a ward in the household of Lady **Margaret Beaufort**, Countess of Richmond and the mother of the new Tudor king. Buckingham grew up with three siblings, one of whom, Henry Stafford, was later ennobled as the Earl of Wiltshire, while a younger sister, **Anne Stafford**, briefly became one of Henry VIII's many mistresses.

Raised and trained to be a soldier, Buckingham entered the chivalrous Order of the **Garter** at age 17 and fought with Crown forces to suppress the great Cornish uprising of 1497. In 1500, he married Eleanor Percy, the eldest daughter of the Earl of Northumberland, and with her sired four children, including Elizabeth Stafford, who later wed **Thomas Howard**, the Earl of Surrey and future third Duke of Norfolk. In 1501, Buckingham cut a fashionable figure at the wedding of Prince **Arthur** Tudor and **Katherine of Aragon**, and he starred as a champion of the celebratory **joust** and feast that followed. When Henry VIII acceded to the throne in 1509, Buckingham almost immediately joined the young king's royal council, but over the next dozen years, he attended meetings only infrequently. In 1510, when the 32-year-old duke discovered his youngest sibling **Anne Stafford**'s affair with the amorous Tudor king, Buckingham quickly ended their dalliance by having his naïve sister packed away to virtual exile for a time in the countryside.

Despite the fact that Buckingham rode with Henry VIII's army during the first **French invasion of 1513–14**, the duke never grew close to the king and generally absented himself from the political intrigues of the royal court. In 1518, his son and heir Henry Stafford married into the House of Pole, a family who also entertained a distant but clear claim

to the English throne. If issue came from this union, King Henry probably reasoned, the resulting offspring would own a rival royal claim that perhaps eclipsed the tenuous hold on the Crown of the Tudors themselves. In addition, the arrogant duke openly showed contempt for Henry's lord chancellor, Cardinal Wolsey, whom Buckingham saw as an uncouth upstart with too much influence over the king and too much affluence for a base-born butcher's son. The two men traded insults and threats, but because the cardinal had Henry's ear, the king became increasingly jealous of the duke's extraordinary wealth and ever more suspicious of his royal pretentions. An avowed Francophobe and thus an opponent of Wolsey's attempted rapprochement with France, Buckingham grudgingly attended the Field of Cloth of Gold summit near **Calais** in June 1520 but afterward did little to hide his hatred of Wolsey and his policies.

Early in 1521, the duke requested leave from court to raise his feudal levies along the Welsh marches, but Henry saw this as a potential plan to foment revolt against the Crown and so turned him down. Then when Cardinal Wolsey produced an anonymous letter accusing the great duke of treasonous intent, the unsuspecting Buckingham was met on 16 April in the Thames River on his barge by a contingent of royal yeoman guards and was there arrested and taken to the **Tower of London**. A hasty investigation was launched on King Henry's command, and after Buckingham was brought to trial for treason in mid-May before a court of 17 peers of the realm, Thomas Howard, the second Duke of Norfolk, tearfully pronounced the inevitable sentence of death upon his good friend. On 17 May 1521, the Duke of Buckingham was led through a jeering London throng to Tower Hill, where his head was struck off with three blows of the headsman's axe.

THE STEELYARD (c. 1280–1598). The Steelyard was the London headquarters of the merchants of the Hanseatic League, a trade association of mostly independent towns that stretched across northern Europe from England and **Flanders**, along the German coastline to Scandinavia, the Baltic states, and Russia. The merchants of the Steelyard were mostly ethnic Germans, and because they connected England to the far-flung trading network of the Hansa consortium, they enjoyed special tax exemptions and legal privileges that increasingly annoyed and then angered their English mercantile counterparts. The Steelyard merchants gradually lost their privileged status during the reigns of King Henry VIII's successors and were officially expelled from England entirely near the end of the life of Queen **Elizabeth I**.

The Hanseatic League, also known as the Hansa trade association, derived its name from the medieval German word *Hanse*, meaning guild or company, a term that (thanks to the presence of the league) eventually came to identify the coastal region of northern Germany as well. By the 12th century, such emergent Baltic ports as Lübeck, Danzig, Visby (on the Swedish island of Gotland), Riga, and Novgorod were dominating trade in the area; by the 13th and 14th centuries, their commercial contacts had spread west and south to Bremen, Hamburg, and Cologne and then into the North Sea to Bruges and Antwerp and across to London and King's Lynn in England. The enterprising merchants of the original German trade towns began to join together in *Hanse*, or commercial guilds, during the later-medieval period, granting each other commercial concessions and reserving properties in their harbors for visiting merchants to use as bases of operation. At its height around 1370, the Hanseatic League included 37 towns scattered across some 1,500 miles of sea and river-borne trade routes and encouraged a lively exchange between its members of commodities like timber, iron ore, pitch, rope, furs, flax, grain, fish, wax, and woolen cloth. The league also coordinated efforts to sweep pirates from the waters of the Baltic and North Seas and constructed lighthouses across its trading network to guide ships safely into fellow Hansa harbors.

The earliest record of Hansard trade in England dates from the reign of King Edward I in the late 13th century, though it is likely German and Flemish traders were operating in London well before that. Once established there, these "easterling" (from the east) merchants of the Hanseatic League situated their headquarters on the north bank of the Thames River, just west of London Bridge, on the site occupied by the 19th-century Cannon Street railway station today. The place came to be called the Steelyard (from the German *Stahlhof*, meaning steel house or strong house) and featured warehouses to store trade goods, an inn to accommodate visiting merchants, a weigh house, a chapel, and several counting offices. A stout wall enclosed the entire Steelyard compound to keep xenophobic Londoners away from the Hansa traders and to prevent the visiting Germans from falling prey to English thieves and prostitutes.

Because of the lucrative foreign commerce the Steelyard attracted to London, the Hansards enjoyed wide-ranging exemptions from customs duties and English laws and were granted monopolies on the import and export of various continental goods. During the **Wars of the Roses**, King Edward IV extended additional trade concessions to the Steelyard merchants to win their support against his enemies. In the 1530s, Hansa officers commissioned **Hans Holbein** the Younger to paint several company portraits, and impressed with his work, they retained the famous German artist to create his allegorical *Triumph of Riches* and *Triumph of Poverty* artworks for their Steelyard guildhall. As the English economy worsened in the mid-16th century, however, competing London merchants increasingly resented the presence of the Steelyard in their midst and prevailed upon the Crown to curtail and then eliminate the customs and legal exemptions the resident German traders had been enjoying for centuries. Finally, when Queen Elizabeth I undertook a trade war against the Holy Roman Empire in 1598, she evicted the Hansa merchants from London altogether and permanently closed their Steelyard headquarters.

STOKESLEY, JOHN, BISHOP OF LONDON
(c. **1475–1539**). This important English prelate carved out an episcopal career during the 1530s that sometimes supported and at other times opposed certain elements of the

Henrician Reformation. John Stokesley was primarily a religious conservative who remained loyal to the doctrines of the Roman Church and who earned a reputation as an active hunter of Protestant heretics. However, the bishop of London outwardly supported Henry VIII's rejection of his first queen and then christened the daughter of her successor **Anne Boleyn**. Much like **Stephen Gardiner**, bishop of Winchester, who tended to bend with the political winds of the moment, Stokesley managed to placate King Henry and his chief minister, **Thomas Cromwell**, long enough to avoid the deadly fates of many of his conservative contemporaries.

John Stokesley was born in Collyweston, Northamptonshire, and was educated at **Oxford University**'s Magdalen College, where he accepted a teaching fellowship at the young age of 20. In 1504, he was ordained a priest and then became a lecturer in philosophy and vice president of his Oxford alma mater as well. Between 1504 and 1507, a corruption scandal at the university saw him accused by his academic enemies of theft, adultery, heresy, and even witchcraft, but he was cleared of any wrongdoing by investigating agents of Bishop **Richard Fox** of Winchester, Magdalen College's official visitor, or overseer. Through the likely influence of Bishop Fox, Stokesley then joined the royal council when young Henry VIII acceded to the English throne in 1509.

Stokesley's diplomatic career began in June 1520, when he accompanied the royal court to the **Field of Cloth of Gold** summit meeting in France, and he was a member of King Henry's entourage one month later at a meeting with Emperor **Charles V** in **Flanders**. In 1529, he traveled (with **George Boleyn**, brother of future Queen Anne) to the court of King **François I** of France to try to derail an impending Franco-Scots alliance. The following year he visited Italy to search out learned legal precedents for King Henry's attempted annulment of his marriage with **Katherine of Aragon**. Afterward, Stokesley coauthored *The Determinations of Famous and Most Excellent Universities*, a treatise that summarizes the juridical opinions he had gathered on his journeys. The English king was so impressed with Stokesley's

research, diplomacy, and book that he elevated the 55-year-old priest to the diocese of London as its new bishop in autumn 1530.

Never wavering from his support for the king's annulment and remarriage to Anne Boleyn, Stokesley attended Archbishop **Thomas Cranmer** in May 1533 at Dunstable when the latter pronounced the king's desired "divorce" from Queen Katherine. He also performed the christening of the Princess **Elizabeth** Tudor the following September at **Greenwich Palace** and loudly protested when Pope **Paul III** granted a cardinal's hat to religious exile **Reginald Pole** a few years later. The bishop of London was steadfastly opposed, however, to any attempts to reform the teachings of the Roman Church, and he only reluctantly accepted the king's lordship over the English Church with the additional phrase "as far as the law of Christ allows." Along with Sir **Thomas More**, Stokesley was a zealous foe of heresy who later claimed responsibility for executing more than 30 Lutheran believers during his tenure as London's bishop. Once Thomas Cromwell began to infuse the English Church with reformist doctrines, Stokesley found himself under investigation in 1538 for his devotion to Rome and only escaped the headsman's axe by throwing himself on the mercy of King Henry. The bishop of London died in his bed on his birthday the following year and was buried in the Chapel of St. George in St. Paul's Cathedral.

SUBMISSION OF THE CLERGY AND SUPPLICATION AGAINST THE ORDINARIES

(1531–32). These two legal devices—one passed by the Southern **Convocation of Bishops** and the other by the House of Commons in **Parliament**—signaled the start of King Henry VIII's campaign to break from Rome and establish his own separate Christian church in England. The Supplication against the Ordinaries was a legislative petition from Parliament that complained about and sought to clean up corruption among the English **clergy** along with abuses in the ecclesiastical court system. Shortly after passage of the supplication, Convocation formally acquiesced in the Submission of the Clergy that declared King

Henry the sole overlord of the English Church. Both measures weakened the power of the Roman Church and greatly restricted papal authority in England, thus igniting the spark that led to the **Henrician Reformation** just a few years later.

The failure of **Thomas Cardinal Wolsey** in 1529–30 to secure Henry VIII's long-awaited marriage annulment prompted an angry king to exile his former lord chancellor, but not yet satisfied, he then turned on the rest of the English clergy to assuage his pent-up frustrations. When the 19 bishops of the Southern Province met in Convocation in January 1531, Henry fined the gathered prelates £100,000 for having violated the 14th-century statute of praemunire (limiting papal authority in England) by accepting Wolsey as the pope's legatine representative during the annulment trial of **Katherine of Aragon**. The king then insisted that a committee of Crown officials and selected bishops be empowered to review canon (religious) laws before their passage by Convocation. Finally, Henry demanded that the assembled prelates acknowledge him as "sole protector and supreme head of the English Church," a concession that, if approved in Convocation, would effectively transfer control of all ecclesiastical affairs in England from the pope to the king. Alarmed, Archbishop **William Warham** of Canterbury dismissed Convocation before the bishops could fully discuss or, even worse, accept King Henry's demands.

While Convocation was on hiatus through the rest of 1531, a related matter arose in the House of Commons that called for additional restrictions on the prerogatives of the English clergy. Since 1529, House members had complained about the arbitrary rulings dispensed by church courts; the use of excommunications for minor religious offenses; the exorbitant fees collected by clerics for sacramental duties; the abusive nepotism, pluralism, and absenteeism of appointments to church livings; and the redundant number of holy days in the liturgical calendar. Fueled by deep sentiments of anticlericalism then sweeping the realm, the House debates on these issues had been lively and at times heated for a few years, but no reforming legislation had been enacted.

However, when Parliament reconvened in March 1532, the anticlerical climate in England had reached a fever pitch, prompting Commons to petition Henry VIII for swift correction of the worst vices of the English clergy. Having received this Supplication against the Ordinaries (clerics with ordinary ecclesiastical jurisdiction), the king turned it over to Archbishop Warham the following month to share with the Southern Province of English Bishops.

Predictably, the episcopal ordinaries resented the Commons' allegations of corruption and issued their own Answer to the Supplication that challenged the petition's underlying assumptions and protested physical attacks on the clergy by a hostile laity. On 30 April 1532, King Henry handed the answer to **Thomas Audley**, speaker of the House, who carried it to the Commons for review and then led a vote to ratify the original supplication's grievances against the clergy. The answer thus rejected, episcopal resistance to lay criticism collapsed in Convocation, and on 15 May 1532, the seven assembled bishops (most stayed away) voted to surrender to the king's earlier demands in the Submission of the Clergy. Henry VIII's supremacy over the English Church was made contingent, however, on the addition of "as far as the law of Christ allows," a qualifying phrase the king grudgingly but prudently accepted. The day after the prelates' submission to Henry, his lord chancellor, Sir **Thomas More**, resigned his chain of office and retreated to his Chelsea estate to take up the life of a private citizen and scholar once again. Intertwined as they were, the supplication and the submission marked the beginning of the legislative break with Rome and the creation of the Church of England that followed a few years later.

SUCCESSION, ACT OF. See ACT OF SUCCESSION (1534).

SUPREMACY, ACT OF. See ACT OF SUPREMACY (1534).

SWEATING SICKNESS OR THE "SWEATE" (1485–1551). Also known as *sudor anglicus* or the "English sweate," this virulently contagious disease ravaged England on five separate occasions during the early-Tudor period. The mortality rate of the sweate was exceedingly high, and it seemed to contemporaries that young people and especially members of the **noble** and **gentry** classes were more vulnerable to the disease than were other age and social groups. Medical practitioners in Tudor times did not understand the origins or causes of this strange malady, and because it disappeared in England almost as suddenly as it had broken out, modern science remains just as baffled by the nature of the sweating sickness today. The sweate caused King Henry VIII much anxiety during his **"Great Matter,"** prompting him to quarantine **Anne Boleyn** and send royal physicians to assist her, while he continually traveled to avoid contacting the illness himself. It may well have been the care and affection the king showered on Mistress Boleyn during the 1527–28 sweating sickness outbreak that helped convince her of Henry's true romantic and even matrimonial interest in her.

Although its causes are still a mystery, the sweate usually first presented with body chills, limb and neck pains, and debilitating headaches, symptoms that typically lasted three or four hours. Then victims experienced hot flashes, heart palpitations, profuse sweating, and delirium that often ended in their deaths after only 4 to 18 hours, though patients who survived a full 24 hours usually recovered completely. England was violently struck by sweating sickness in 1485, 1508, 1517, 1527–28, and 1551; some of these outbreaks were so deadly (especially in filthy London) that they sometimes carried off scores of people each day. Only in 1520–28 did the sweate reach the Continent, where it claimed thousands of lives from **Calais**, Antwerp, and Hamburg, across northern Europe to Scandinavia and even to Poland. The best surviving description of the malady comes to us from the Shrewsbury physician John Caius (1510–73), whose *Book or Counsel against the Disease Commonly Called the Sweate* appeared in 1552 following the final English occurrence of the disease.

Our earliest accounts of the sweating sickness date to 1485, when, following the Battle of Bosworth in the **Wars of the Roses**, thousands perished of the deadly but as-yet-unknown illness in London over the course of just 70 days. Prince **Arthur** Tudor, the heir of King **Henry VII** and Henry VIII's older brother, died in 1502 of what was likely consumption (tuberculosis), but many contemporaries blamed the sweate for the sudden demise of the royal teenager instead.

Perhaps the most memorable occurrence of the contagion took place in June 1527, during Henry VIII's courtship of Anne Boleyn known as the king's "Great Matter." The sweate struck London fiercely that summer, prompting King Henry to abandon the capital with Queen **Katherine of Aragon** and most members of his court for the safety of various country estates. He ordered his paramour Anne Boleyn to retreat to the safety of her ancestral home at Hever Castle in Kent, but on 20 June, she displayed early symptoms of the sweate, and the king was greatly alarmed. Having written her often during his recent travels, he now penned another more urgent letter assuring Mistress Boleyn of his unwavering affection and promising to send her his "second best" doctor, **William Butts** of Norfolk, because his most able physician, Dr. John Chamber, was then unavailable. In the meantime, Anne's father, **Thomas Boleyn**, and her brother **George Boleyn** both contracted the illness but survived, while dozens died of it in the households of Archbishop **William Warham** of Canterbury and **Thomas Cardinal Wolsey**. When news reached Henry that his "good sweetheart" had also survived and was now recovering from the dreaded disease, the king was overjoyed and continued to shower Anne with gifts and more romantic letters. Ironically, it may have been the deadly threat posed by the sweating sickness that inspired Henry VIII to proclaim his true feelings for his mistress, thus transforming what had been a royal infatuation into more serious considerations of matrimony and dynastic change.

T

TALBOT, GEORGE, FOURTH EARL OF SHREWSBURY (1468–1538). George Talbot was a prominent magnate who served the first two Tudor kings as a reliable soldier, able diplomat, and loyal Crown official. Inheriting his earldom at a tender age, Shrewsbury grew up to take part in the coronation of King **Henry VII** and fought at his side against Yorkist pretenders to the English throne. He was close to all the Tudor children, standing as godfather to one and investing another with royal titles and regalia. Shrewsbury went on to serve Henry VIII with equal devotion as a royal councilor, battlefield commander, household officer, and trusted ambassador. He attended the younger King Henry on campaign and at diplomatic conferences, and he supported his Tudor master's attempts to annul his first marriage with **Katherine of Aragon**. Active in royal service well into old age and infirm health, the Earl of Shrewsbury made a significant mark on the first half-century of the Tudor age.

George Talbot was born in the market town of Shifnal in Shropshire to John Talbot, the third Earl of Shrewsbury, and his wife, Katherine Stafford, the daughter of Duke Humphrey Stafford of Buckingham. When the third Earl of Shrewsbury passed away in 1473, little George succeeded to his father's title and estates and at the age of just five was enrolled as a knight of the Bath as well. After the death of Richard III at Bosworth Field in August 1485, young Shrewsbury carried the ceremonial sword of state before Henry VII at the new king's coronation a few months later. Around 1486, he married Anne Hastings, the daughter of Lord William Hastings (murdered by order of King Richard in 1483), and with her sired no fewer than 11 children. The earl marched with King Henry's army against the royal pretensions of Lambert Simnel and helped defeat the Irish lad and his Yorkist supporters at the Battle of Stoke in June 1487. At age 20, Shrewsbury accepted a knighthood in the prestigious Order of the **Garter**, and the following year, he served as godfather to Henry VII's firstborn daughter, **Margaret** Tudor. In 1492, he took part in the French invasion—and was present at the signing of the subsequent Treaty of Étaples—that brought an extortionate windfall of cash into the English royal treasury. Clearly a trusted client of the House of Tudor, George Talbot played an important role in the investiture ritual that elevated little Prince Henry to the Duchy of York in 1494.

When that young prince became Henry VIII in 1509, the Earl of Shrewsbury was immediately appointed to the royal council and then joined the new king's household as its lord high steward and chief exchequer official as well. After representing the Crown on diplomatic missions to Rome and Spain in 1511–12, he accompanied King Henry on his **French invasion of 1513–14**. Shrewsbury distinguished himself during the campaign at the sieges of Thérouanne and Tournai and rode at the side of the English king during the cavalry skirmish later known as the Battle of the Spurs. In 1514, the earl was supposed to travel with another embassy to Rome, but he developed the first of many dangerous fevers and had to excuse himself from undertaking so strenuous a journey. Shrewsbury subsequently remained on his estates in England for several years until Henry VIII insisted he attend the opulent **Field of Cloth of Gold** summit with the French near **Calais** in 1520. The king next appointed him lord lieutenant of the north two years later, but his recurring fevers flared up on his way to the Scottish border, and he was forced to withdraw from royal service once more.

His poor health did not, however, completely prevent the ever-loyal Shrewsbury from participating in certain Crown affairs and courtly intrigues over the next few decades. He backed Henry VIII's campaign to replace his first queen with another, and he signed a petition urging Pope **Clement VII** to grant the marriage annulment his Tudor master had been energetically seeking for several years. When **Thomas Cardinal Wolsey** fell from royal favor, Shrewsbury signed the articles that condemned him and then hosted the disgraced lord chancellor at Sheffield Castle on his way back to London to face treason charges in November 1530. The earl briefly commanded guardsmen on the Scottish frontier in 1532, but illness forced his return to his estates in the Midlands shortly thereafter. In 1536, the **Pilgrimage of Grace** broke out, and resident at the time near the uprising's epicenter, Shrewsbury received orders from the Crown to raise a body of troops against the insurgents. This he did, then joined with **Thomas Howard**, the third Duke of Norfolk, to negotiate an emergency truce with the rebel leader Robert Aske. Shrewsbury acquired the estates of several religious houses during the dissolution of the **monasteries** in the late 1530s, but his health continued to deteriorate, and he died at age 70 on 26 July 1538 at Wingfield Manor in Derbyshire. In accordance with his will, he was buried in the Sheffield Castle chapel (now Sheffield Cathedral) beneath a marble slab that, still visible today, bears the images of himself (in Garter robes) and his wife, Anne Hastings Talbot.

TEN ARTICLES OF FAITH (1536). These statements of religious belief were designed to achieve a doctrinal compromise during the **Henrician Reformation** between the conservative and evangelical factions of the newly formed Church of England. Partly reflecting the Lutheran views of Henry VIII's chief minister, **Thomas Cromwell**, and Archbishop of Canterbury **Thomas Cranmer**, the Ten Articles also catered to the more "old church" sensibilities of believers like Bishop **Stephen Gardiner** of Winchester and even King Henry himself. These few articles were not meant to establish a sweeping program of religious reform but rather to clarify certain doctrines that by 1536 still remained as points of theological contention in the English Church. The Ten Articles were largely the editorial creation of Cromwell, from 1535 Henry VIII's vicegerent in spirituals (lay superintendent of religious affairs), and initiated a partial reformation of the Church of England following the mostly political split from Rome two years earlier.

Once **Parliament** had proclaimed Henry VIII the supreme head of his own church in 1534, the authority of the pope in Tudor England was instantly dissolved, but otherwise English Christians believed and practiced their faith as they had done before. Thomas Cromwell, meanwhile, an ardent but (until the mid-1530s) under-the-radar evangelical Lutheran, was anxious to bring the Church of England into closer theological accord with the more fully reformed Lutheran churches on the Continent. By the spring of 1536, King Henry was distracted by his marital concerns and, having appointed Cromwell his chief religious administrator, granted him a free hand to run and make adjustments to the English Church as he saw fit. Accordingly, Cromwell sent a delegation of English clerics to Wittenberg (the epicenter of Martin Luther's Reformation) to negotiate a religious and political treaty in spring 1536 with the Protestant princes of northern Germany. Although the hoped-for alliance eluded them, the English delegates did return to London with a systematic statement of Lutheran doctrine called the Wittenberg Articles. This document especially appealed to the reform-minded Cromwell and Cranmer, who thought to use it as a starting point for a full theological overhaul of the Church of England. When the vicegerent and archbishop presented the articles to **Convocation of Bishops** in June 1536, however, the mostly conservative churchmen swiftly and decisively rejected the Wittenberg proposals out of hand.

It now fell to Thomas Cromwell to draft a more balanced set of faith principles that would reflect essential Lutheran tenets but might still prove acceptable to England's prelates and even her traditionalist Tudor king. The vicegerent deftly reworked the Wittenberg Articles and, after securing King Henry's assent, submitted them to the assembled bishops in Convocation for their consideration and (hopefully this time) their endorsement. Cromwell's amended Ten Articles of Faith are divided into two sections: The first five articles address matters of doctrine, while the last five deal with ecclesiastical ceremonies and institutions. Following a wordy preamble assigning all religious authority in England to the supreme head, the opening article declares that Scripture and the Christian creeds are the sole sources of divine truth. The next three articles more closely define the sacraments, reducing them to just three in number (versus the seven of Rome) but interpreting each conservatively as soul-saving baptism, real eucharistic presence, and sin remission through auricular confession. The final doctrinal article upholds salvation through grace and faith alone (Lutheran) but insists that good works (Roman) are necessary demonstrations of heavenly election. The second set of five articles preserves the institution of sainthood (but not relics, **shrines**, or pilgrimages); church images and ceremonies as worship aids; and prayers (but not indulgence purchases) for the souls of the dead. Because these Ten Articles feature both evangelical and conservative components and had already been sanctioned by King Henry himself, the bishops of Convocation quickly discussed and ratified them in August 1536. Cromwell then issued injunctions ordering all parish clergy in England to preach the Ten Articles henceforth from their pulpits on Sundays.

Passage of the Ten Articles of Faith signaled the start of a tentative religious reformation in the Church of England. It was a statement of theological principles that clarified acceptable beliefs and practices for English Christians and paved the way for other reformed measures, such as the **monastic** dissolution and the publication of the **Great Bible** in English a few years later. Although the Ten Articles officially introduced Lutheran teachings for the first time into the English Church, they only remained in force for a mere three years. The **Act of Six Articles**, passed by Parliament in 1539 at the direction of conservative Henry VIII, restored most of the doctrines of the Roman Church and brought back the old heresy laws to suppress any potential opposition to them. Thomas Cromwell fell from royal favor and died on the block as a traitor and heretic the following year, thus delaying true reformation of the English Church until the reign of King Henry's son and successor, **Edward VI**, in the late 1540s.

TOWER OF LONDON (1066–). Originally constructed by England's first Norman king in the 11th century, the Tower of London has guarded the eastern approaches to the capital for more than 950 years and is today one of Britain's best-known tourist attractions. The tower, initially only a bastion of defense, became over time a complex of buildings and towers that also served as a royal residence, a mint, a prison, and a storage house for government records and the Crown jewels. Although Henry VIII upgraded the defenses and renovated some of the royal apartments of the tower, he is more famous for having imprisoned and executed several of his political enemies there, along with two of his allegedly unfaithful queens. The Yeoman Warders, originally royal Tudor bodyguards, were first installed at the tower by Henry VIII and remain in service there today as the castle's garrison and tour guides.

Although the Romans and King Alfred of Wessex both maintained fortifications on the site, King William I the Conqueror ordered the construction of a stout timber tower on the north bank of the Thames River at the southeastern corner of London just after his victory over the Saxons at Hastings in 1066. His aim was to control overland and river-borne access to the capital from an easterly direction while also establishing a local stronghold to suppress opposition to the Norman occupation from restive Saxon Londoners. Between 1078 and 1100, the Conqueror and his successor, William II Rufus, replaced the wooden tower with a more permanent edifice that, built of light-colored limestone from Normandy, came to be (and is still) known as the White Tower.

Subsequent English rulers added other such structures as the Wardrobe Tower (completed in 1199), the Bell Tower (1210), the Wakefield and Lanthorn Towers (mid-13th century), and a protective curtain wall that incorporated parts of the old Roman ramparts at its base. This crenellated wall enclosed the inner ward, which boasted several additional towers; a great hall; extensive kitchens; a munitions warehouse; the Chapel of St. Peter ad Vincula; and Tower Green, the site of most of the private executions of royalty before and during the reign of Henry VIII. The entire castle was encircled in the later Middle Ages by an outer ward, another curtain wall, and the notorious Traitor's Gate, a Thames-side passageway through which condemned prisoners entered the tower but almost never emerged. Located between the outer ward and the city wall of London was Tower Hill, the place of execution where many nonroyals of distinction were destined to meet their ends on the headsman's block.

King Henry VIII was quick to seek the security of the Tower of London when his father, **Henry VII**, died in 1509; indeed, the first act of his reign was signed and sealed from the fortress on 23 April of that same year. Early on, the teenaged Tudor king also ordered a contingent of his royal bodyguard, the Yeomen Warders, to garrison the tower on a permanent basis. These guardsmen were later nicknamed Beefeaters because, as privileged protectors of the Crown, they enjoyed an extravagant beef-rich diet unavailable to most common Londoners. The uniforms sported by the Yeomen Warders today reflect the same style of soldierly dress as that worn by Tudor-era Beefeaters some five centuries ago. King Henry renovated the royal apartments known as the Queen's House in 1532–33 as a wedding gift for his second wife and queen, **Anne Boleyn**, and then had **Thomas Cromwell** import thousands of tons of Norman stone to repair the castle's outdated defenses a few years later.

More famously, perhaps, the Tower of London is best known today for the stunning array of Tudor luminaries who were imprisoned and executed in or near the fortress during the reign of Henry VIII. Bishop **John Fisher** of Rochester and Sir **Thomas More**, King Henry's former lord chancellor, were both imprisoned in the tower and beheaded on Tower Hill in summer 1535 for refusing to swear the **Act of Succession** and **Act of Supremacy** oaths. Religious reformers **John Frith**, **Hugh Latimer**, and **Anne Askew** all spent time in the tower in the 1530s and 1540s and were all eventually burned alive as heretics by order of the Crown. Two of King Henry's queens, Anne Boleyn and **Katherine Howard**, also languished in the tower and died on the block on Tower Green just six years apart following their respective convictions for adulterous treason. And Thomas Cromwell, the chief minister who had engineered the deaths of so many of the tower's earlier victims, was himself jailed in the fortress and then beheaded on Tower Hill in July 1540 as a traitor and heretic. After King Henry's death in 1547, the Tower of London continued to serve the Tudor, Stuart, and Hanoverian monarchies as England's most infamous prison, a reputation the castle still retains today to attract millions of curious visitors each year.

TREASONS, ACT OF. *See* ACT OF TREASONS (1534).

TUDOR, ARTHUR. *See* ARTHUR (TUDOR), PRINCE OF WALES (1486–1502).

TUDOR, EDWARD. *See* EDWARD VI (TUDOR), PRINCE OF WALES AND KING OF ENGLAND (1537–53; r. 1547–53).

TUDOR, ELIZABETH. *See* ELIZABETH I (TUDOR), QUEEN OF ENGLAND (1533–1603; r. 1558–1603).

TUDOR, MARGARET. *See* MARGARET (TUDOR), QUEEN OF SCOTLAND, COUNTESS OF ANGUS AND METHVEN (1489–1541).

**TUDOR, MARY, QUEEN OF FRANCE, DUCH-
ESS OF SUFFOLK.** *See* MARY (TUDOR),
QUEEN OF FRANCE, DUCHESS OF SUF-
FOLK (1496–1533).

**TUDOR, MARY I, PRINCESS AND QUEEN
OF ENGLAND.** *See* MARY I (TUDOR), PRIN-
CESS AND QUEEN OF ENGLAND (1516–58;
r. 1553–58).

**TUNSTALL,   CUTHBERT,   BISHOP   OF
DURHAM   AND   LONDON   (1474–1559).**
Cuthbert Tunstall was an important Tudor-era
bishop who reluctantly accepted Henry VIII's
supremacy over the English Church but who
later suffered deprivation and imprisonment
as one of England's most conservative religious leaders. A friend of English humanist
scholars in his youth, Tunstall was a trusted
ambassador who traveled widely on the Continent on important diplomatic missions for
the Tudor Crown. He served on the staff of
an English archbishop for a number of years
before accepting his first episcopal appointment to the diocese of London in 1522. As a
bishop, Tunstall actively opposed both **Lollard**
and Lutheran heretics and did his best to suppress religious dissent and keep English Bible
translations out of the capital. He became
prince bishop of Durham in 1530, a remote
northern diocese that allowed him to retain
his conservative beliefs without antagonizing
the architects of the **Henrician Reformation**
back in London. Although he quietly lived out
the final years of King Henry's reign, Bishop
Tunstall was alternately defrocked and jailed,
then released and restored to prominence, and
finally deprived and confined again by Henry
VIII's three children and successors.

Cuthbert Tunstall (also spelled Tonstall
or Tunstal) was born out of wedlock in Hack-
forth, Yorkshire, to Thomas Tunstall and the
woman (name unknown) who later became
his second wife. Young Tunstall was a kitchen
boy at a local manor in his earliest years, then
acquired a solid enough grammar school education to win admittance to Balliol College at
Oxford University in 1491. There he met and
befriended **Thomas More**, **William Grocyn**,
Thomas Linacre, and **John Colet**, all of whom

soon became the leading lights of the early
English Renaissance. An outbreak of plague
forced Tunstall's flight to Trinity College at
Cambridge University in 1493. There he continued to study Latin, Greek, Hebrew, the ancient classics, theology, and mathematics, the
last of which became his favorite subject. He
did not take a degree at either English university but traveled instead to Italy, where he met
the Venetian printer Aldous Manutius before
earning his doctorate in law at Padua University in 1501. Returning to England four years
later, he began a long church career by accepting his first parish living in County Durham
despite his not yet being in holy orders.

Thus acquainted with some of England's
most prominent scholars, Cuthbert Tunstall
came to the attention of Archbishop **William
Warham** of Canterbury in 1508. Warham took
the ambitious clerk on as an archdiocesan
chancellor, saw him finally ordained into the
priesthood, and then instituted him to successive rectories and several cathedral prebends
(chorus stalls) over the next several years.
Tunstall rose quickly in the archbishop's service, and promoted in 1511 to the post of
commissary general, he began to accompany
Warham into the privileged world of the Tudor
royal court. King Henry noticed Tunstall's
learning and wisdom as well and in 1515 sent
him off with Thomas More to **Flanders** to negotiate a new commercial treaty with the representatives of Emperor **Maximilian I**. He took
part in multiple other diplomatic missions over
the next several years, one of which returned
him to Brussels, where he met and briefly
shared lodgings with the great Dutch humanist
Desiderius Erasmus.

Cuthbert Tunstall's interest in mathematics
resulted in the publication of his treatise *De
arte supputandi libri*, or *A Book on the Art
of Computation*, in London in 1522. Later the
same year, Henry VIII and Archbishop Warham
agreed to name Tunstall the next bishop of
London following the death of the city's episcopal incumbent. This was a challenging first
assignment for a new prelate, for London had
been a hotbed of religious dissent ever since
the1514–15 **Richard Hunne** scandal had undermined public confidence in the English

clergy. In 1523, Tunstall met with **William Tyndale**, the reformist scholar who at that moment was busy translating the New Testament into English. Tyndale hoped a fellow scholar like Tunstall would support his project, but the bishop of London instead banned his English Scriptures and charged their translator with heresy. Tyndale fled to Germany, where he completed his translation, had it published, and then helped his friend **Simon Fish** smuggle hundreds of copies back into England. Bishop Tunstall retaliated against both Fish and Tyndale, suppressing the former's anticlerical pamphlet *Supplication of the Beggars* while purchasing as many copies of the latter's New Testament as possible and having them all burned.

As Henry VIII's campaign to cast off **Katherine of Aragon** took center stage at court in the late 1520s, the beleaguered Spanish queen asked Tunstall to serve as one of her legal and spiritual advisors. Likely prompted by the king's chief minister, **Thomas Cardinal Wolsey**, the bishop of London listened sympathetically to Katherine but counseled her against appealing her case to the pope in Rome. When she ignored his advice, the annulment proceedings broke down, and Wolsey fell from royal favor. With the king's "**Great Matter**" still unresolved, Cuthbert Tunstall was translated (in effect, exiled) to the far northern diocese of Durham in 1530. There he continued to operate as one of England's more conservative bishops, although (like Bishop **Stephen Gardiner** of Winchester) he offered almost no opposition to the **Act of Supremacy** when **Parliament** enacted it in 1534. In fact, the prince bishop of Durham actually scolded several **Carthusian** monks for denying the royal supremacy prior to their execution in 1535, and he denounced papal authority in a sermon he delivered before the king and his entourage three years later.

In 1537, Tunstall became president of the Council of the North, but its peacekeeping duties did not suit his scholarly temperament, and he resigned the office the following year. In 1538, he also joined an editorial board to review and approve the English **Great Bible** that (ironically) was based on the Tyndale

text Tunstall had condemned 12 years before. Still a religious conservative, however, he was pleased to vote in Parliament the next year for the **Act of Six Articles** that restored much of Rome's doctrines and practices to the English Church. During the 1540s, the prince bishop of Durham continued to serve the Crown as guardian of the Scottish marches and as a diplomat in negotiations to secure a new peace treaty with France.

The fortunes of Cuthbert Tunstall began to change rather dramatically after the death of the old king in January 1547. Although he officiated at the coronation of young **Edward VI** the following month, the new king and his regents soon pushed Tunstall aside as they implemented a fully Protestant reform program in England. When the septuagenarian prelate was asked to support King Edward's church supremacy, he refused, a stand that led to his diocesan deprivation and imprisonment in the **Tower of London**. Catholic Queen **Mary I** freed the old prisoner and reinstated him in his Durham see at the start of her reign, but Tunstall found himself deprived again when **Elizabeth I** succeeded her half-sister five years later. This time the 85-year-old Tunstall was comfortably housed with Elizabeth's new archbishop of Canterbury at Lambeth Palace in London, where he finally passed away on 18 November 1559. He was buried in the nearby archepiscopal chapel of St. Mary-in-Lambeth, which today still stands but has been converted to secular use. *See also* CONVOCATION OF BISHOPS (c. AD 690–).

TYNDALE, WILLIAM (c. 1492–1536). Arguably the "father of the English Bible," this evangelical reformer was the first to translate the entire New Testament from the original Greek into English. A gifted linguist, Tyndale (alternately Huchyns) later rendered parts of the Old Testament into English, thus providing a starting point or template for all subsequent vernacular editions of Holy Writ. Unfortunately for Tyndale, his English Bible appeared before the ecclesiastical authorities in England were ready to accept it, so he was forced to remain in exile in **Flanders** and was there betrayed, arrested, convicted of heresy, and burned at the stake in 1536. After his death, ironically, the essential elements of the Tyndale translation formed the core text for the first officially authorized **Great Bible** in 1539 and eventually for the King James version of Scripture in 1611.

William Tyndale was certainly not born in North Nibley, where his statue has stood for many years, but more probably in Slimbridge in Gloucestershire, a part of England that had once been home to an active group of **Lollard** heretics. While attending Magdalen Hall (later Hertford College) at **Oxford University**, he earned baccalaureate (1512) and master's (1515) degrees and entered holy orders as a priest, then moved on to **Cambridge University** to study Greek with the eminent classical scholar Richard Croke in 1518. In 1522, Tyndale was hired to tutor the children of Sir John Walsh in Little Sodbury, Gloucestershire, but his increasingly reformed views on religion aroused local hostility, and he left Sir John's household to seek secretarial work and a chaplaincy with **Cuthbert Tunstall**, the bishop of London. When Tunstall turned him down, Tyndale met and befriended Lutheran activist **John Frith** and wealthy merchant Humphrey Monmouth in London before leaving for Germany early in 1524 to fulfill his dream of translating the Scriptures into English.

Briefly taking up residence in Hamburg and supported there by Monmouth, Tyndale soon made his way to Wittenberg, where he matriculated at the university under the name William Daltin (Tyndale backward) and made the acquaintance of Martin Luther himself. Early in 1525, he engaged an amanuensis, William Roye, and together they produced a manuscript copy of the New Testament in English that they then took to Cologne to publish the following summer. The local Catholic authorities got wind of the project, however, forcing Tyndale and Roye to flee to the Lutheran city of Worms, where they revised their New Testament, had it printed, and then arranged to smuggle it back into England hidden in bales of woolen broadcloth. By spring 1526, Tyndale's Scripture translation was selling briskly in London, and in order to facilitate additional print runs and take advantage of regular

smuggling routes across the North Sea, Tyndale relocated to Antwerp, where commercial ties to his homeland were still very strong. **Thomas Cardinal Wolsey**, Archbishop **William Warham**, and Sir **Thomas More**, all conservative guardians of the orthodox Roman Church in England, were greatly alarmed by the huge number of Tyndale Bibles flooding into London and soon were busy (with King Henry's blessing) collecting and destroying as many of the illicit black-market Scripture translations as they could lay their hands on.

Angered by this open assault on his "life's work," Tyndale fired off several polemical tracts that lambasted the corrupt Roman clergy, denounced the authority of the pope, and called for lay access to vernacular Scripture all across Christian Europe. In 1527, his *Parable of Wicked Mammon* rejected the teachings of Rome for those of the Lutherans, while his 1528 *Obedience of a Christian Man* declares that secular princes—and not the pope—should rule over churches in their domains. In *The Practice of Prelates* (1530), Tyndale condemns Cardinal Wolsey, who in recent years had been negotiating with the pope to end King Henry VIII's marriage to Queen **Katherine of Aragon**. Tyndale also exchanged vitriolic barbs with Sir Thomas More, responding to the English scholar's 1528 *Dialogue Concerning Heresies* with his own *Answer unto Sir Thomas More's Dialogue* the following year. Splitting time between Hamburg and Antwerp to avoid capture by his enemies, Tyndale worked in 1530 with Miles Coverdale, the future compiler of the Great Bible, to translate the first five books of the Old Testament, the Pentateuch, from the original Hebrew (Tyndale had taught himself the language two years earlier) into vernacular English.

Still Humphrey Monmouth's client by 1533, Tyndale finally settled permanently into the protective "English House" of the Merchant Adventurers (a London commercial guild) in Antwerp. There he continued to revise his English Bible by adding glosses and commentaries that hurled abusive criticism at the doctrines and institutions of Rome. Also at this time, Tyndale befriended one Henry Phillips, the charming but penniless son of a Dorset landowner, who had sold his surveillance services to the Catholic government of the Holy Roman Empire in return for ready cash. Phillips laid a trap for the trusting reformer, and on the evening of 21 May 1535, imperial agents seized Tyndale and imprisoned him in Vilvorde Castle, an imposing stronghold located north of Brussels. There he busied himself translating more of the Old Testament into English, but in August 1536, Tyndale was brought to trial and convicted of heresy by a court of the Inquisition for his defense of Luther's *solafideism* (salvation by faith alone) doctrine. Two months later, imperial officers took the unfortunate Bible translator to a place of execution, secured him to a stake, and strangled him (an act of mercy) before setting fire to his limp body. As he died, he was heard to gasp, "Lord, open the king of England's eyes!" The legacy of William Tyndale of course lies with his authoritative English editions of the New and parts of the Old Testament. These pioneering works provided his protégé Miles Coverdale with a foundation for his own 1539 vernacular Scriptures, the Great Bible, the first fully authorized (legal) version of the Holy Book to be made available to lay believers in their own language in English history.

UNIVERSITIES. *See* CAMBRIDGE UNIVER-
SITY (1209–); OXFORD (c. 1167–).

V

VERGIL, POLYDORE (c. 1470–1555). Best known today for his magisterial history of England, *Anglicae historiae*, Polidoro Virgili (later Anglicized to Polydore Vergil) was an Italian humanist author and an unabashed church pluralist who lived in England for 48 years and devoted much of his life to serving the interests of King **Henry VII** and his successor, King Henry VIII. Vergil's English history was a principal source for the later histories of **Edward Hall** and Raphael Holinshed, whose works in turn informed the history plays of William Shakespeare. In 1582, a royal decree made Vergil's *Anglicae historiae* required reading in all English schools for its unapologetic celebration of the achievements and reputation of the early-Tudor monarchy.

Polydore Vergil was born and grew up in Urbino in the Papal States of north-central Italy and went on to study at the Universities of Padua and Bologna. He served as a secretary to Guidobaldo Montefeltro, Duke of Urbino, and worked in the chancery office under Pope Alexander VI before he was ordained a priest sometime prior to 1496. Vergil began his scholarly career at this time with the 1498 publication of *Proverbiorum libellus* (*The Little Book of Adages*) and his 1499 *De inventoribus rerum*, a treatise describing the origins of human institutions, activities, and even everyday objects. In 1502, he followed his kinsman Adrian Cardinal Castelli to England to assist in the collection of "peter's pence," money the English Crown paid annually to Rome to retain the favor of the pontiff. Between 1503 and 1513, Vergil collected several lucrative church benefices (income-generating appointments) that included the parish of Church Langston in Leicestershire; the archdeaconry of Wells; and prebends (choir stall pensions) in Lincoln, Hereford, and St. Paul's Cathedrals.

Upon his arrival in England, Vergil was somewhat surprised that his scholarly fame had preceded him, and welcomed into the kingdom's intellectual community, he was able to make the acquaintance of both **Desiderius Erasmus** and **Thomas More**. In 1505, **Richard Fox**, bishop of Winchester and Henry VII's lord privy seal, persuaded Vergil to begin researching and composing an updated history of England that would for the first time cover events since the accession of the Tudors in 1485. Vergil went to work immediately on the project and, over the next five years, felt so comfortable in England that he applied for and became a naturalized subject of his adopted country. However, when a letter he penned in 1514 was intercepted and found to heap abuse on Henry VIII's lord chancellor, **Thomas Wolsey**, the irate royal minister had Vergil arrested and briefly imprisoned in the **Tower of London**. Soon released, the Italian humanist went to work again to edit and publish an early history by the sixth-century AD Scottish monk Gildas in 1525 and followed this up the next year by producing *Dialogus de prodigiis*, a philosophical discussion of the meaning of supernatural phenomena and mystical omens.

Polydore Vergil's masterwork, however, was his *Anglicae historiae*, which he published in 1534 in an edition of 26 books, or chapters, contained in two large folio volumes with illustrations by the Flemish artist **Hans Holbein** the Younger. The first seven books treat the earliest history of England from ancient times to the Norman conquest and draws on such classical (and fairly unreliable) authors as Julius Caesar, Polybius, and Tacitus for source material. Books 8–26 then address the reigns of the other English rulers down to and including the time of Henry VIII. Most of the pre-1450 content in *Anglicae historiae* borrows from medieval accounts by Gildas, Bede, Geoffrey of Monmouth, William of Malmesbury, and the like. The rest of the book, however, is based on Vergil's interviews with living witnesses and his careful review of extant manuscript and printed materials, modern methods that helped him produce a balanced history we would be proud to read today. Thus, although he was obliged to please Henry VII by justifying his seizure of the English throne in 1485, Vergil also gives credit to his royal patron's slain enemy King Richard III, who is depicted in the book as having died bravely in battle at Bosworth Field. Less fairly, however, Vergil severely disparages Cardinal Wolsey in the final book of his history for the rough treatment he had received from the lord chancellor some 20 years before.

The *Anglicae historiae* appeared in subsequent editions in 1546 and 1555 and eventually covers events in the reign of Henry VIII through 1537. Vergil continued to live quietly for much of the remainder of his life within the precincts of St. Paul's Cathedral in London, where he managed to avoid wholly committing himself either to the old Roman Church or to the newly reformed Church of England. He finally returned to Italy in 1553, purchased and lived in a villa near Urbino, and died there two years later. Vergil is often regarded today as one of the great pioneers of modern historiography, and his work is still consulted as an important primary source for the reigns of the first two Tudor kings.

W

WALES (1485–1547). Of all the non-English countries in the British Isles, Wales boasted the most direct connection to the ruling House of Tudor. Tracing his roots back to Owen Tudor, the knight from Wales who married into the Lancastrian royal family, King **Henry VII** recruited Welsh troops to help him seize the English throne in 1485 and then created each of his sons Prince of Wales as his designated heirs. The Welsh, who regarded the Tudors as fellow countrymen, acquiesced when Henry VIII established firmer English control over the Welsh marches (border regions) during the 1520s. The second Tudor king also extended the rule of English law and the use of the English language for governmental and religious purposes under the Act of Union in 1536.

Wales, the broad peninsula that juts into the Irish Sea off the western coast of Britain, has a long, colorful, and at times tumultuous history. Originally populated by indigenous prehistoric peoples, Wales was later settled by Celtic immigrants and then played host to the Romans beginning in the first century AD. Following their departure some 350 years later, Anglo-Saxon invaders occupied most of England but generally avoided the rugged mountains and infertile rocky soil of the Welsh heartland. With the Norman conquest and Plantagenet succession in England during the Middle Ages, several military incursions into Wales resulted in the recognition of English kings as Welsh overlords, although native Celtic leaders continued to rule the more remote northern and western regions of the peninsula. Welsh chieftains styled themselves Princes of Wales for nearly two centuries until King Edward I (r. 1272–1307) subjugated the entire country, built massive castles in north Wales to control his new territories, and then appropriated the title Prince of Wales for his eldest son and heir.

At the end of the 14th century, Henry of Lancaster overthrew and murdered his predecessor to become King Henry IV and establish his Lancastrian line of succession on the English throne. His son Henry V married a French princess, Katherine of Valois, but he died in 1422 while on campaign and was survived by his young widow and an infant son, the future Henry VI. Following her royal husband's death, Queen Katherine began a secret affair with a handsome Welsh courtier named Owen Tudor, whom she eventually married around 1431 and with whom she had four children before her own death at age 36 in 1437. Edmund Tudor, the couple's eldest son, grew up to wed Lady **Margaret Beaufort**, a descendant of the House of Lancaster, and together they also produced a son, Henry Tudor. After arriving in Wales and summoning native soldiers to his banner, this youngest Tudor triumphed over King Richard III in battle in 1485 to secure his own royal line of succession on the throne of England. Thus, the first Tudor king Henry VII was the grandson of a Welsh gentleman and a French princess, an ancestry that gave Henry ap Tyddor (as the Welsh knew him) and his progeny a level of acceptance in Wales that no earlier English ruling house had ever enjoyed.

Not surprisingly, Henry VII advanced the fortunes of fellow Welshmen by ennobling his uncle Jasper Tudor as the Duke of Bedford and hiring David Cecil, later the grandfather of Elizabethan chief minister William Cecil, as one of his royal secretaries. The new king also reconstituted the Council of the Welsh Marches, an advisory body created by the Yorkist kings to maintain order and dispense justice in the English-Welsh border region. In addition, King Henry gave his firstborn son and heir the Welsh name **Arthur** and appointed him Prince of Wales at the age of 15. He and his Spanish consort, **Katherine of Aragon**, lived briefly together at Ludlow Castle near the Welsh frontier before the prince succumbed to an illness and died early in April 1502. Aggrieved but unbroken, the English king passed the principality of Wales on to his next son and heir, Henry, who wore the mantle of Welsh royalty proudly until his own accession as King Henry VIII in 1509.

The second Tudor king undertook measures to assert his authority over Wales soon after the conclusion of his **French invasion of 1513–14**. He ordered his chief minister, **Thomas Cardinal Wolsey**, to strengthen the centralizing powers of the Council of the Welsh Marches, and he issued charters to Welsh lords permitting them to own estates and hold offices in England. Once **Thomas Cromwell** rose to prominence at court, King Henry had him shire Wales (divide the principality into counties) and then appointed sheriffs and royal justices to maintain the king's peace there. In 1536, Cromwell persuaded **Parliament** to pass the Act of Union (alternately, the Laws in Wales Act), a statute that replaced Welsh with English law, granted 26 seats in the English Parliament to Welsh representatives, and mandated the English language for exclusive use in Welsh courts and Crown offices. This last element of the act was difficult to implement because most natives of Wales at that time spoke and understood only Welsh. The **Henrician Reformation** also came to Wales when its four bishops were forced to accept King Henry's supremacy over the English Church, and the Welsh **monasteries** were shuttered and sold off just as they had been in England. The reformed religion was slow to win converts in Wales because the same Welsh language barrier impeded the spread of the service and liturgical texts in English for several centuries to come.

WARHAM, WILLIAM, ARCHBISHOP OF CANTERBURY (c. 1450–1532). This long-lived "primate of all England" enjoyed a successful career as a lawyer, diplomat, and churchman during the reigns of the first two Tudor kings. A trusted Crown minister and prelate under King **Henry VII**, Warham receded into the political background once the exuberant young Henry VIII inherited the English throne in 1509. One reason for this was the archbishop's own advancing age, but another was the dominating presence of **Thomas Cardinal Wolsey** in all aspects of church and state governance. Wolsey did his best to render Warham irrelevant, all the while hoping for the old man's death so he might seize the archiepiscopal dignity of Canterbury for himself. Warham outlived Wolsey, only to become ensnared in battles between Henry VIII and the English **clergy** during the early stages of the **Henrician Reformation**. Weary of this struggle, Archbishop Warham died in his bed at around age 82, a merciful end when compared to the more violent deaths of many of his contemporaries.

William Warham was born the son of Robert Warham, a minor **gentry** landowner in the Hampshire village of Church Oakley around 1450. He was a pupil at Winchester College before studying at New College in **Oxford University**, where he became a teaching fellow following his baccalaureate graduation in 1475. Warham earned a doctorate in civil law and then administered Oxford's legal studies program until 1488, when he left academia to practice law in the ecclesiastical courts of London. Following his ordination in the early 1490s, Warham embarked on a lucrative church career that brought him beneficed (income-generating) clerical livings in Barley, Huntingdon, Cottenham, and the diocese of Wells. He also began serving the Crown during these years as master of the rolls (royal archivist) and as an ambassador who helped negotiate several important treaties with Spain, France, and the Holy Roman Empire. Well pleased, King Henry VII successively created Warham bishop of London (1501), archbishop of Canterbury (1503), and lord chancellor of England (1504). By the time the old king died in April 1509, Warham stood supreme as the chief royal minister and as the archiepiscopal leader of the Roman Church in England.

After presiding at the coronation of Henry VIII and his queen consort, **Katherine of Aragon**, William Warham joined the new king's royal council along with **Richard Fox**, the bishop of Winchester, and other holdovers from the previous reign. In 1512, he and Fox quarreled over Warham's encroachments on diocesan judicial rights, and after Henry VIII intervened in Fox's favor, the two prelates avoided each other for the rest of their time in government service. The year 1512 also brought another challenge to Archbishop Warham's authority when Thomas Wolsey, the ambitious royal chaplain, became an influential member of King Henry's council and his inner circle. The brilliant and hard-working Wolsey soon swept the aging archbishop aside by helping organize the king's **French invasion of 1513–14** and by negotiating the treaty that ended the conflict the following year. Increasingly ignored and forgotten, Warham surrendered the lord chancellor's chain of office in 1515 just as Wolsey accepted a cardinal's hat from Rome and then claimed the vacant lord chancellorship for himself as well. Already the archbishop of York by 1514, Cardinal Wolsey also coveted the more prestigious Canterbury archdiocese but was thwarted in this ambition by William Warham's stubborn longevity.

Despite his declining interest in politics or affairs at court, Warham did attend the **Field of Cloth of Gold** summit meeting in France in 1520, and he supported Wolsey's "amicable grant" scheme to raise money for King Henry's second **French invasion of 1523–24**. In 1525, the archbishop of Canterbury met with **Elizabeth Barton**, the Holy Maid of Kent, whose strange seizures and prophetic visions he believed were miraculous expressions of divine favor. When Henry VIII first sought to replace Queen Katherine with **Anne Boleyn** in 1527, Warham joined Cardinal Wolsey on a commission to investigate the validity of the king's first marriage to his brother's widow. The archbishop had little taste for such work, and after he became Queen Katherine's chief legal counsel in 1528, he did almost nothing for her and even refused to offer her any advice. He

thereafter removed himself completely from Henry's martial affairs, including the papal tribunal that Wolsey convened in 1529 to hear the king's annulment case against his Spanish queen.

The final (and perhaps most important) events in Warham's archiepiscopal career took place in the early 1530s, when he actively opposed King Henry's attempts to control all religious affairs in England. In January 1531, the Tudor king fined the bishops in **Convocation** £100,000 for violating the law of praemunire (acknowledging papal authority) and then ordered the assembled prelates to name him "sole protector and supreme head of the English Church." As the metropolitan (leader) of Convocation, Warham wisely sent the bishops home rather than surrender to or even discuss Henry's demands. Meanwhile, the House of Commons in **Parliament** passed the Supplication against the Ordinaries, a measure asking the king to suppress clerical corruption and eliminate wasteful ecclesiastical practices. Using the supplication to apply additional pressure, Henry VIII again demanded that his earlier fine be paid and his new title be approved when the bishops reassembled in Convocation in May 1532. This time, Warham and his episcopal colleagues gave in to the king—the so-called **Submission of the Clergy**—but amended Henry's new "supreme head" title with the phrase "as far as the law of Christ allows." By now an octogenarian, suffering from illness, and worn out by recent events, Archbishop Warham died while visiting his nephew (also named William Warham) on 22 August 1532 in the Kentish village of Hackington. He was laid to rest in the north transept of Canterbury Cathedral, where his tomb can still be seen today.

WARS OF THE ROSES (1455–85). This bloody English civil war was fought by armies of overmighty **nobles** to determine which royal house—Lancaster or York—would rule England in the late 15th century and beyond. In reality a series of violent clashes punctuated by long periods of peace, the Wars of the Roses occurred in four distinct battle phases in 1455, 1460–61, 1470–71, and 1485. The white and red roses, symbols invented in the 16th century by historians and playwrights, were never used to identify combatants in the respective Lancastrian and Yorkist armies. Rather, troops sported the livery (colors and heraldic insignia) of the magnates for whom they fought, thus causing a good deal of confusion (and often casualties from friendly forces) in battles that took place in bad weather. The Wars of the Roses had a profound impact on the reign of Henry VIII for two reasons: First, they ended with the enthronement of the first Tudor ruler of England; and second, they demonstrated the vulnerability of the Tudor succession if King Henry VIII failed to produce an undisputed male heir.

The causes of the Wars of the Roses were rooted in the reign of Henry VI (r. 1422–61), the third king of the Lancastrian dynasty. This 15th-century King Henry was saintly, overly generous, and gullible, and by 1450, he had amassed more than £300,000 of Crown debt while alienating (giving away) many royal estates at the same time. In 1445, he married Margaret of Anjou, a French princess of imperious will who ruled her timid husband and manipulated the decisions he made with an iron hand. When Henry VI went temporarily insane in August 1453 and then his queen gave birth to a son and heir two months later, a regency regime was needed to rule England while the king was incapacitated. Queen Margaret believed she should dominate that regency, but Duke Richard of York, another powerful magnate with his own claim to the throne, insisted that he serve as the king's lord protector instead. York and the queen uneasily shared power for a year until King Henry VI regained his senses in February 1455, a development that then prompted Margaret to push her Yorkist rival out of the regency government. Incensed, Duke Richard called up his feudal levies, and encountering a small Lancastrian force in St. Albans in May 1455, an unintended street-to-street battle took place to mark the opening stage of the Wars of the Roses.

The second phase of the conflict opened in 1460, when Richard of York tried to persuade **Parliament** to recognize his royal claims and hand him the English Crown. The assembled lords hesitated, however, and then only agreed to make him Henry VI's heir by passing the Act of Accord in October 1460. Two months later, Duke Richard was killed while leading a sortie against Lancastrian besiegers at Wakefield Castle, which left leadership of the Yorkist cause in the hands of the duke's teenaged son Earl Edward of March. He and his ally Richard Neville, the Earl of Warwick, decisively defeated the Lancastrians at Mortimer's Cross and Towton early the next year and then occupied London, where Warwick (as "the kingmaker") crowned the youthful Earl of March King Edward IV. Queen Margaret, her unstable husband, and their eight-year-old son scurried into exile in Scotland, but after the Yorkists unexpectedly chanced upon and captured Henry VI a few years later, the Lancastrian queen was forced to flee with her son to her relatives in France.

The third phase of the war was caused by jealousy within the ranks of the ruling House of York in 1470–71. In 1464, Edward IV had impetuously married Elizabeth Woodville, an alluring but otherwise lowborn widow whose large, greedy family had then convinced the young Yorkist king to enrich them all with estates, offices, noble titles, and advantageous marriages. King Edward's younger brother George of Clarence, along with Warwick "the kingmaker," felt excluded from this royal largess and traveled in summer 1470 to France to join forces with their former foe, the exiled Queen Margaret of Anjou. Reinforced with French money and troops, the Lancastrian queen and her rebel Yorkist allies landed in England in autumn 1470, occupied London, and placed the still-unsteady Henry VI upon his throne. This unexpected reversal in turn caused Edward IV to flee to **Flanders**, where he raised an invasion force of his own and then returned to England in spring 1471. After defeating Margaret's forces at Barnet (April) and Tewkesbury (May) and killing both Warwick and the young Lancastrian prince, King Edward captured Henry VI and drove his queen back to France. Clarence was temporarily forgiven his treachery (but later executed), while the hapless Henry VI was again taken to London, incarcerated, and shortly thereafter murdered.

The final phase of the Wars of the Roses ended with a single battle that changed the ruling dynasty and set the first Tudor king on the English throne. In April 1483, King Edward IV died, leaving his two adolescent sons by Queen Elizabeth Woodville to succeed him. King Edward's youngest brother, Duke Richard of Gloucester, seized control of his royal nephews, locked them away in the **Tower of London**, and then proclaimed himself king of England in their place. The two Yorkist princes mysteriously disappeared in autumn 1483 and were believed by most contemporaries to have been murdered. Over the next few years, Richard III managed to alienate a large number of mighty English lords (along with most of the Woodvilles), causing many to flee to France to join the entourage of a royal pretender named **Henry** Tudor, the Earl of Richmond. Although Richmond's claim to the throne of England was patently weak, he nonetheless attracted considerable support as the chief rival of King Richard and as the last best hope of the Lancastrian cause.

After assembling his English exiles and accepting another infusion of French assistance, Richmond set sail with his makeshift army and landed in **Wales** in August 1485. Following a sharp clash of arms at Bosworth Field near Leicester, Henry Tudor defeated and killed Richard III to claim the English Crown for himself as King Henry VII. His victory in the final battle of the Wars of the Roses paved the way for his son Henry VIII to succeed him but also impressed upon his Tudor successor the need for an undisputed male heir to avoid similar bloodshed and dynastic conflict in the future.

WESTMINSTER PALACE (c. 1050–1547). Originally built by the Saxon and Norman kings of England as their primary place of residence in London, Westminster Palace was gradually enlarged during the Middle Ages to house various government offices, the kingdom's principal **judiciary**, and (by Tudor times) both Houses of **Parliament**. Aside from its spacious Westminster Hall, the palace became over time an extensive complex of buildings that collectively projected the power and majesty of the English monarchy. In 1512, fire destroyed much of the residential, or privy, apartments of the palace, an event that forced Henry VIII to seek alternate royal lodgings elsewhere in the capital. The second Tudor king also designated Westminster Palace as the permanent home of the House of Commons, where its members met continuously until an even more devastating fire destroyed most of the palace's remaining medieval fabric in the 19th century. Today the name Westminster generally refers to the entire government of the United Kingdom because of the palace's long association with British royalty and Parliament.

As early as the 11th century, King Canute first took up residence on what was then Thorney Island on the north bank of the Thames River, just outside London's western wall. Later the pious Edward the Confessor built a more permanent royal residence on the island site and then erected Westminster Abbey close by to provide access to a holy place of worship. Because of its proximity to Westminster (western church or cathedral) Abbey, the palace naturally came to be known over time by the same name. William I the Conqueror held his lavish coronation and Christmas and Easter feasts there, while his son William II Rufus built an enormous new banquet and audience chamber—Westminster Hall—that measured 240 feet by 70 feet and soon became the social and ceremonial focal point of the palace. Over the next two centuries, English rulers erected such outbuildings as the privy palace and prince's palace living quarters, the decorative painted chamber council meeting room, an administrative center housing the exchequer (treasury) and the Crown courts of King's Bench and Common Pleas, and the 14th-century Chapel of St. Stephen. Richard II, the last Plantagenet king, thoroughly renovated Westminster Hall between 1393 and 1399 by installing an impressive hammerbeam ceiling, replacing the old Norman columns with gothic arches, and enlarging all the windows to flood the interior space with more natural light. He further commissioned the carving of 12 statues of his royal predecessors to stand in niches along the perimeter of the hall, but only 6 of these have survived to stand guard along the chamber's south wall today.

When Henry VIII acceded to the English throne in April 1509, he married **Katherine of Aragon** a few months later, and the couple then occupied the royal apartments of Westminster Palace whenever they were resident in London. Three years into Henry's reign, however, fire destroyed the complex's privy palace living quarters, which compelled the king and his consort to stay at the uncomfortable **Tower of London** until alternate lodgings could be found. Suitable accommodations finally became available when York Place, the London residence of **Thomas Cardinal Wolsey**, was acquired by the king following the former lord chancellor's fall from favor, exile, and death in 1530. Henry VIII quickly set about renovating his new royal house, renamed it **Whitehall** to reflect its brilliant exterior stone masonry, and then used it as his principal London residence from 1532 through the end of his reign. In the meantime, Westminster Palace continued to function as the kingdom's chief governmental center until, near death early in January 1547, King Henry saw fit to relocate the House of Commons from the chapter house (monastery) of Westminster Abbey to the Chapel of St. Stephen within the palace precinct. This became the established home of the Commons until another more massive fire in October 1834 destroyed nearly all of Westminster Palace. The only structures to survive were the medieval Westminster Hall; St. Stephen's Chapel; and the fortified Jewel Tower, which for centuries had provided secure storage for the precious Crown regalia. Careful to recreate the high-gothic architectural style of the original medieval complex, Parliament authorized and financed the reconstruction of Westminster Palace between 1837 and 1860 to serve as a permanent meeting place for both Houses of Parliament, a governmental role it still fulfills today.

WHITEHALL PALACE (c. 1506–1698). This

sprawling property served as the principal London residence of the Tudor and Stuart royal families from 1530 until its destruction by fire at the end of the 17th century. Located on the western bank of the Thames River some 700 yards south of Westminster Abbey and covering an area of about 23 acres, Whitehall featured more than 1,500 rooms in its heyday and was—until the palace of Versailles was completed in France—the largest royal residence in Europe. Whitehall ranked among the favorite palaces of King Henry VIII because he enjoyed exercising in the various sporting and gaming facilities he had installed on its grounds. The king married two of his six wives at the palace, and he died there in January 1547. Although the fire of 1698 destroyed most of its original buildings, Whitehall gave its name to the district of London where it once stood and that houses many administrative offices of the British government today.

The center of royal government since before the Norman Conquest was **Westminster**, an abbey church and palace constructed outside the western wall of London by Edward the Confessor during the mid-11th century. In the 13th century, the archbishop of York built his own London residence called York Place near Westminster to afford easier access to the king and his royal council. This modest structure was first enlarged and then completely overhauled in the 14th and 15th centuries before **Thomas Cardinal Wolsey** took possession of it as the new archbishop of York in 1514. Later responsible for constructing **Oxford University**'s Cardinal College and the palace of **Hampton Court**, Wolsey set about expanding York Place until it became one of the largest and most lavish episcopal dwellings in the capital. When Cardinal Wolsey fell from royal favor and then died in 1530, King Henry VIII took over York Place and turned it into his principal place of residence whenever he visited London.

The king was also an enthusiastic builder and soon began his own renovation of York Place, which he renamed Whitehall in 1532 to reflect the white stonework adorning the exterior of much of his new construction. Wolsey's magnificent Great Hall was kept as a place to stage royal banquets and **pageants**, while tennis courts, bowling greens, **jousting** yards, and a cockpit (for rooster fights) were added to accommodate the need of King Henry and his courtiers for competitive sport. The king employed the Flemish painter and architect Anton van den Wyngarde (father of the topographical artist of the same name) to design many of Whitehall's new structures, while **Hans Holbein** the Younger, the Tudor court's most prodigious portraitist, was set to work providing interior decoration. King Henry later added a large brick wine cellar and then reconditioned Wolsey's orchard garden to include more formal walks, shrubbery beds, landscaped hedges, and neoclassical sculpture ensembles.

Henry VIII secretly wed **Anne Boleyn** in the royal chapel at Whitehall Palace just before dawn on 25 January 1533, but less than three years later, the anxious king was again at Whitehall awaiting the artillery discharge from the **Tower of London** that announced her execution. Within 11 days of Queen Anne's death, Archbishop **Thomas Cranmer** married **Jane Seymour** and Henry VIII in the queen's closet at Whitehall Palace, a very private ceremony that was then followed by a very public feast in the Great Hall to honor the king's newest consort. Finally, and once again in residence at Whitehall, King Henry breathed his last on 28 January 1547 in the presence of Queen **Katherine Parr** and Archbishop Thomas Cranmer. He was laid to rest next to his beloved Queen Jane three weeks later in the Chapel of St. George at Windsor Castle.

WOLSEY, THOMAS CARDINAL, ARCHBISHOP OF YORK, LORD CHANCELLOR (c. 1473–1530).

The wealthiest and most powerful man in England (aside from Henry VIII himself) at the height of his career, Thomas Wolsey was a brilliant and tireless administrator who faithfully served both Crown and church for many years before his fall from royal grace and death in 1529–30. Emerging from obscurity, Wolsey rose quickly in the service of Bishop **Richard Fox** of Durham and King **Henry VII** before accepting a cardinal's hat and becoming lord chancellor of England during the early reign of Henry VIII. He brought fairness and reform to the English **judiciary**, steered his country toward a pacifist foreign policy, founded and built several palaces and colleges, and raised powerful armies and substantial revenues for his royal master. Wolsey's ostentatious wealth and hauteur, his hostility toward England's great **nobles**, his seething hatred of Lutheran reformers both home and abroad, and his shameless collection of lucrative church livings earned the "Great Cardinal" (as his detractors called him) the enmity of both common folk and privileged elites alike. Despite the dedicated service he gave Henry VIII through the first half of his reign, an ungrateful king eventually discarded his talented chief minister when the latter failed to secure the longed-for papal annulment of Henry's first marriage to Queen **Katherine of Aragon**.

Thomas Wolsey was born sometime between 1471 and 1475 to Robert Wolsey of Ipswich and his wife, Joan Daundy Wolsey. Although later enemies whispered that Thomas's father was a common butcher, in fact, Robert Wolsey was a yeoman farmer and tavern owner who raised and sold cattle, while Thomas's mother was descended from a family of successful merchants. Thomas's uncle Edmund Daundy paid for his education at Magdalen College, **Oxford University**, from which the "boy-bachelor" graduated in the late 1480s at the age of just 15 years. He accepted a position as a teaching fellow at Magdalen and then became the school's bursar (financial officer) before his ordination as a priest in 1498. In that year, Richard Fox, the prince bishop of Durham and official visitor (overseer) of Magdalen College, noticed the bright young priest and took him on as a personal secretary. Clearly impressed with his diligence and intellect, Bishop Fox commended Wolsey in 1501 to the service of Henry Deane, the new archbishop of Canterbury. Deane died two years later, and following a brief secretarial stint in **Calais**, Wolsey came to the attention (thanks to Fox) of King Henry VII himself, who welcomed the ambitious priest into the royal household as a chaplain.

When the teenaged Henry VIII acceded to the English throne in April 1509, it only took him a few months to find a place for Wolsey on his staff as a chaplain and almoner (charity director). He proved his worth to the young king so quickly that within three years he was promoted to membership on the royal council, where Bishop Fox (now of Winchester) needed his support against some of their common conciliar opponents. Wolsey soon overtook his mentor Fox as one of the Crown's most valued advisors and then earned his sovereign's long-term trust by stepping forward to organize King Henry's massive **French invasion of 1513–14**. The royal councilor now became a quartermaster, assembling a vast stockpile of military equipment and 40,000 soldiers on England's southern coast in spring 1513 in preparation for the sea voyage to France. When King Henry finally landed at Calais with his invasion force, he advanced inland to capture two French towns and won a cavalry skirmish before a fast-approaching winter cut the campaign short. Wolsey then helped Bishop Fox hammer out the Treaty of London in summer 1514 that formally ended hostilities between France and England. Greatly pleased with Wolsey's ability to execute his royal will, the king showered his councilor with appointments as the new bishop of Tournai (a captured French town) and Lincoln and then as archbishop of York, before naming Wolsey his lord chancellor in 1515.

The common-born priest from Ipswich was thus already a powerful statesman and prince of the church, but he soon added the diocese of Bath and Wells (1518) and the monastery of St. Albans (1521) to his beneficed (income-producing) holdings as well. In 1515, Pope **Leo X** made Wolsey a cardinal of the church, and within three years, the same pontiff elevated him to the dignity of legate a latere (papal representative) in England. Eventually Wolsey also became the prince bishop of Durham (1523) and bishop of Winchester (1528), running his total ecclesiastical income to a staggering £35,000 per annum, or about $38 million a year in today's American currency. Still not satisfied, Wolsey longed to become the archbishop of Canterbury, but the aged incumbent **William Warham** ended up outliving the acquisitive cardinal. When Pope Leo died in 1521, followed by his successor Adrian VI two years later, Wolsey twice tried to make himself pope, but the enormous bribes he paid out to his fellow cardinals came to

nothing when they cast their votes in conclave for a different candidate.

The Great Cardinal (Wolsey eventually weighed well over 300 pounds) loved to display his wealth by hosting sumptuous banquets and gorgeous entertainments. Whenever he went on progress or processed through London, he had acolytes precede him and his entourage with the symbols—a tall silver cross and four silver columns—of his archiepiscopal and legatine offices. Comporting himself at times in grander estate than even King Henry himself, most of England's great magnates despised the upstart lord chancellor; chief among them was **Edward Stafford**, the third Duke of Buckingham, who went out of his way to put the powerful prelate in his place. When rumors about a potential Buckingham plot against King Henry surfaced in April 1521, Wolsey produced corroborating evidence that eventually led to the execution of the great duke for treason the following summer.

Aside from some of his less-admirable qualities, Cardinal Wolsey did have a significantly positive impact on the reign of Henry VIII as well. He was a great builder who renovated his London residence of York Place (later **Whitehall Palace**) and constructed the sprawling **Hampton Court** complex for his own use before King Henry confiscated it in 1529. The brilliant lord chancellor was also an avid educationalist who endowed and built the magnificent Cardinal College (later Christ Church College) at Oxford University in 1524–25. At the same time, Wolsey was in a sense a builder of careers who employed in his household such future Tudor luminaries as Sir **Thomas More**, **Thomas Cromwell**, **Stephen Gardiner**, **Thomas Audley**, and **George Cavendish**, the last of whom was the cardinal's later biographer. In addition, he reconstructed parts of England's judiciary by personally overseeing (and often attending sessions of) the Courts of Chancery and Star Chamber, and he created the new Court of Requests, a "poor man's" tribunal that eliminated rampant bribery and streamlined judicial decisions. Finally, Wolsey established a commission to regulate the **enclosure** of common lands, a practice that encouraged profitable sheepherding but often evicted peasant farmers from their feudal land holdings in the process.

In the field of foreign affairs, Lord Chancellor Wolsey promoted the cause of peace when he could yet ably supported his sovereign's yearning for military glory when required to do so. The **Field of Cloth of Gold** peace summit between Henry VIII and King **François I** of France in June 1520 was entirely orchestrated by Thomas Wolsey. However, when those talks broke down, he arranged a new alliance with Emperor **Charles V** and then assembled supplies and troops for his master's second **French invasion in 1523–24**. This campaign was even less successful than the king's first incursion into France, leaving the Crown in debt and prompting Wolsey to raise funds through his extortionate and wildly unpopular amicable grant policy of 1524–25. Religiously, the Great Cardinal was a staunch opponent of the Lutheran Reformation, one who may have helped Henry VIII compose his *Assertio septem sacramentorum* against the renegade German monk and who sponsored a public burning of Luther's writings in London in May 1521. Always the fiscal conservative, Wolsey tried with his **Eltham Ordinances** in 1526 to restrict expenditures and eliminate overstaffing in King Henry's court, but the political winds blew hard against him, and so this initiative ultimately came to nothing.

Despite his great administrative abilities and the immense power and wealth he had accumulated by the late 1520s, Thomas Cardinal Wolsey finally fell prey to Henry VIII's need for a legitimate male heir and his fiery infatuation with Mistress **Anne Boleyn**, in an episode known euphemistically as the king's "**Great Matter.**" By 1525, Queen Katherine of Aragon had not provided her royal husband with a son, and when the king's roving eye fell on the darkly attractive Boleyn daughter—the younger sister of one of Henry's earlier mistresses—he began to seek release from his first marriage in order to wed Anne and with her sire his longed-for male heir.

Accordingly, Cardinal Wolsey traveled to Rome to convince Pope **Clement VII** to annul his master's union with his Spanish queen, but the pontiff was at that moment a virtual prisoner of Emperor Charles V—Katherine of Aragon's nephew—and so flatly rejected Wolsey's petition out of hand. When the pope finally did gain his freedom from the emperor, he sent **Lorenzo Cardinal Campeggio** to England in 1528 to try King Henry's annulment suit through a legatine court with Cardinal Wolsey. The trial got underway in summer 1529, but when Queen Katherine began planning to appeal her case back to Pope Clement in Rome, Campeggio abruptly dissolved the court and then made preparations to leave England. King Henry was beside himself with rage, blamed Wolsey for failing to secure the annulment, and then stripped his chief minister of his chancellor's chain of office and his palaces of Hampton Court and York Place.

Cynically reminding the absentee prelate that he had never set foot in his archdiocese of York, the king ordered Wolsey to travel there to minister to his neglected flock in November 1529. The disgraced cardinal took his time on the journey until an exasperated King Henry changed his mind and ordered Wolsey back to London to face his royal wrath and possible charges of treason. Stopping to rest at an Augustinian friary in Leicester on his way south, the sick and despondent Cardinal Wolsey passed away on 29 November 1530 (possibly from a heart attack) and was laid to rest in an unassuming tomb on the monastery's grounds. Sir Thomas More succeeded Wolsey as lord chancellor in 1529, and within a few years, Thomas Cromwell took his place as King Henry's chief minister.

WOOL TRADE. *See* FLANDERS (c. 1384–1547).

WORDE, WYNKYN DE (c. 1452–1535). Originally an immigrant from western Europe, Wynkyn de Worde was the protégé and successor of England's first printer, William Caxton, who established and operated his press in London in the late 15th century. Wynkyn was recruited by Caxton to serve as his apprentice printer and then became a partner in the business before the founder of the press passed away and left the print shop to his younger associate. Once he became the master of his own press, Wynkyn relocated the business to another London district and then introduced innovative type styles and volume sizes to promote the sale of his books. His smaller and cheaper editions of hundreds of titles brought the printed word to many thousands of readers and contributed significantly to higher rates of literacy in early-Tudor England.

Wynkyn de Worde's date of birth has never been accurately established, although backtracking the years from his probable date of arrival in England and death date suggest a likely birth year in the early 1450s. Equally mysterious to us today is the location of his birth, which has variously been assigned to one of two continental towns named Wörth, one lying in the Netherlands and the other in the Rhine Valley region of Alsace. In addition, he has been associated with the town of Worth in Kent, England, where he may have spent his adolescence and possibly first made the acquaintance of William Caxton, himself a Kentish resident for much of his early life. The name of Wynkyn de Worde has also caused some confusion among scholars over the years. Wynkyn seems to have been a diminutive form of the Dutch name Winand or Willem, while later references to John Wynkyn suggest that his given name was really Jan, as in Jan de Wynkyn, a supposition reinforced by his son's known name of Richard Wynkyn. Worde might have been a corrupted form of a place name, such as Wörth in Europe or Worth in Kent, so that Wynkyn de Worde or Jan Wynkyn de Worde may simply have indicated his hometown and not, as some believe, his later profession as a purveyor of printed words.

Whatever his real name, date, and place of birth may have been, it appears that young Wynkyn befriended William Caxton in either Cologne or Bruges in **Flanders** and then followed the enterprising Englishman to London, where they set up the capital's first printing press in the district of Westminster around 1476–77. There the Caxton press turned out many editions of more than 100 titles in Latin and English, including works on saints' lives, chivalric and romantic tales, historical chronicles, translations, and popular fables. The Westminster print shop also earned a goodly income from the reproduction of government documents and court records for **Parliament** and the Crown. Before he died, Caxton willed the print business to Wynkyn, who took over sole ownership and control of the press following his partner's death in 1491–92.

Over the next eight years, Wynkyn honored his deceased mentor by reproducing many of Caxton's own writings, translations, and more popular offerings in new editions. Some of the works he printed in these early years in Westminster included Caxton's own *Lives of Our Fathers* (1492), Walter Hilton's mystical *Scale of Perfection* (1494), Geoffrey Chaucer's *Canterbury Tales* (1498), and Sir Thomas Malory's *Morte d'Arthur* (1498). Wynkyn lacked the **noble** patrons who had backed Caxton's operation, however, so in 1500, he moved his print shop across London to Fleet Street, where he could market books to a much wider reading public. In order to attract less-wealthy buyers, Wynkyn lowered his production costs and thus his prices by using cheaper English paper and reducing the size of the volumes he printed. He was soon so successful that he opened a sales outlet away from Fleet Street in St. Paul's Churchyard, which later became the center of the flourishing London book trade.

Wynkyn also began to garner lucrative episcopal and royal commissions around this time, publishing the devotional *Contemplacyon of Synners* for Bishop **Richard Fox** of Winchester in 1500 and later issuing copies of the eulogy delivered by Bishop **John Fisher** of Rochester at the 1509 funeral of King **Henry VII**. He managed to increase the number of volumes sold and thus his income by producing sturdy yet affordable editions of such popular favorites as the anonymous *Treatise of Love*, Sir John Mandeville's *Travels*, and the *Aurea Legenda* of Jacobus de Voragine. Wynkyn was the first printer in England to incorporate Hebrew, Arabic, and italic type into his English editions, and he was the first to employ moveable type to print musical scores as well. Expanding his repertoire to include romances, satires, and grammars and illustrating them with finely engraved woodcuts, Wynkyn de Worde produced some 800 editions of more than 400 different titles during his 42-year career as a master printer. Probably well into his 80s, he died during the winter of 1534–35 and was buried in the graveyard of St. Bride's Church close to the site of his Fleet Street press.

WRIOTHESLEY, THOMAS, FIRST EARL OF SOUTHAMPTON, LORD CHANCELLOR
(1505–50). Thomas Wriothesley was an important courtier, diplomat, and Crown official who rose to prominence during the later years of Henry VIII's reign. Like other men of substance in 16th-century England, Wriothesley survived the religious and political upheavals at the Tudor court by switching allegiances and often avoiding the dangers that claimed the careers and lives of so many of his contemporaries. Wriothesley was a religious conservative who nevertheless supported King Henry's supremacy over the English Church and who shamelessly acquired multiple **monastic** properties when the religious houses were closed during the **Henrician Reformation**. Later a persecutor of reformist believers, Wriothesley also took part in the unsuccessful plot to bring down Queen **Katherine Parr** in 1546 just before Henry VIII's death. He fell afoul of the regency council early in **Edward VI**'s reign and then died at the young age of just 45 years.

Thomas Wriothesley was born in December 1505 in London and was the eldest of four children in the family of William Wriothesley, a college-of-arms herald, and his wife, Agnes Drayton Wriothesley. As a youth, Thomas studied at St. Paul's School in London, where he probably received some instruction in theology and the classics from the great English humanist **John Colet**. In 1522, he entered Trinity Hall at **Cambridge University** and studied there under the future bishop and Crown minister **Stephen Gardiner**, but he left after only two years and did not earn a degree. Instead, he went to work as an underclerk to **Thomas Cromwell**, then a secretary himself in the service of **Thomas Cardinal Wolsey**. In 1530, Wriothesley joined the staff of his old teacher Stephen Gardiner as an officer of the signet, or keeper of the signet ring that authorized royal writs in the absence of the great or privy seals. The next few years

found him traveling on diplomatic missions to **Flanders** and France, after which he entered Gray's Inn, one of the prestigious law schools among the **Inns of Court** in London. In 1533, Wriothesley married Jane Cheney and with her produced six surviving children over the course of their union together.

When Thomas Cromwell became King Henry's vicegerent in spirituals (director of church affairs) early in 1535, he ordered Wriothesley to assess the wealth of England's monasteries to prepare for their dissolution beginning in 1536. He was rewarded for this work with extensive estates in the southern county of Hampshire, and although a religious conservative himself, he outwardly supported Henry VIII's schism with Rome and personally supervised the destruction of the **shrine** of St. Swithun in Winchester Cathedral in 1538. As one of Cromwell's chief overseas emissaries, he helped arrange the king's marriage to **Anne of Cleves** in 1540, but when that union cost Cromwell his position in government and eventually his life, Wriothesley briefly endured imprisonment himself but was soon released without charge. He recovered quickly from this incident to become a member of King Henry's privy council, a position that authorized him to interrogate the alleged lovers of Queen **Katherine Howard** and offer evidence of her infidelities at her treason trial late in 1541.

Having thus become a major Crown official, Thomas Wriothesley found himself allied once more with his former teacher Stephen Gardiner, since 1531 the bishop of Winchester and now the leader of the religiously conservative party that dominated the royal government in the 1540s. Wriothesley was much trusted during these years by the king, who appointed him lord chancellor when **Thomas Audley**, his predecessor in the office, passed away in April 1544. Wriothesley enthusiastically participated in Gardiner's campaign to track down and punish evangelical believers as heretics and personally tortured the outspoken religious dissident **Anne Askew** on the rack in summer 1546. When he appeared with an armed escort to arrest Queen Katherine Parr as a suspected heretic, however, King Henry turned on his lord chancellor and angrily dismissed him amid a torrent of insults. Still, he managed to retain the royal confidence and favor, even as his commanding presence at court began to attract growing hostility from many of his jealous colleagues. One of his principal political rivals was **Edward Seymour**, the soon-to-be Duke of Somerset, who stepped up to head the regency privy council as lord protector once the old king breathed his last in January 1547.

Henry VIII's will elevated Wriothesley to the Earldom of Southampton, but the haughty Duke of Somerset was not about to share power with his political adversary and so deprived the lord chancellor of his chain of office in March 1547. Wriothesley duly took his seat in the House of Lords, however, and then helped bring Somerset down in 1549 by supporting the coup d'état of his ambitious rival **John Dudley**, the future Duke of Northumberland. Thomas Wriothesley made out his will only a few days before his untimely death on 30 July 1550 from an unknown malady (possibly the **sweating sickness**) at Lincoln House in Holborn, Derbyshire. His remains were entombed in St. Andrew's Church in Holborn but were later transferred to the chapel at his country estate of Titchfield in Hampshire.

WYATT, SIR THOMAS (1503–42).

A courtier, ambassador, poet, and alleged lover of Henry VIII's second queen, **Anne Boleyn**, Sir Thomas Wyatt is best remembered today for his translations of the sonnets of Francesco Petrarch into English and for his authorship (with Henry Howard, the Earl of Surrey) of a poetry collection that finally appeared in print some 15 years after his death. Some modern literary scholars credit Wyatt with having introduced the poetic form of the sonnet (with its final verses in rhyming couplets) to England and ultimately to William Shakespeare himself. Wyatt also enjoyed successful careers as a courtier and diplomat during his lifetime, despite the fact that he was twice incarcerated in the **Tower of London** on suspicion of treason. After managing to avoid execution on both occasions, the mercurial Tudor poet died of natural causes at the youthful age of just 39 years in Dorsetshire.

Thomas Wyatt was born to Henry and Anne Wyatt in Allington Castle near the town of Maidstone in Kent. His father occupied a seat on the royal council of King **Henry VII**, a position he retained when the youthful Henry VIII acceded to the English throne in 1509. Young Thomas followed his father to court and was selected to serve as a royal page at the christening of Princess **Mary** Tudor early in 1516. He attended St. John's College at **Cambridge University** in his midteens, and in 1520, he married Elizabeth Brooke, the daughter of Thomas Brooke, Lord Cobham of Reigate in Kent. The Wyatts had a son (also Thomas) in 1521; this lad would later grow up to lead a revolt against Queen Mary I in spring 1554, a rash undertaking for which he eventually paid with his life.

The senior Thomas and his wife meanwhile did not get along and were estranged and then separated from one another by 1525. A tall, muscular, and comely man, Thomas Wyatt was well-liked at King Henry's court and used his rising popularity to join an embassy to France in 1526 and then another to Rome in 1527. While traveling in Italy, he fell into the hands of Spanish troops near Ferrara but was soon able to persuade his captors to release him. For the next four years, he resided in **Calais** on the French coast, where he commanded the town's garrison as its high marshal. It was during these years on the Continent that Wyatt became fascinated with the work of Petrarch and with that of his near-contemporary Ludovico Ariosto, the cynical Italian humanist, playwright, and satirist.

It was also around this time that the youthful courtier and diplomat made the acquaintance of Anne Boleyn, the darkly pretty and flirtatious daughter of a Kentish knight who had returned from royal service in France to catch the eye of King Henry himself. Wyatt likely met Boleyn at the English court before he left for France in 1526, but he was almost certainly present in Calais when Henry VIII and Mistress Anne visited that port town in 1532. The next year, he returned to England, and after the Tudor king had freed himself from his first union with **Katherine of Aragon**, Wyatt attended the formal wedding of Henry and

Anne—and the latter's coronation—in June 1533. The new royal consort and the handsome, poetic courtier grew to be close during the first few years of Boleyn's marriage to King Henry, who considered Wyatt a friend and saw fit to bestow a knighthood upon him in 1535.

It seems unlikely in hindsight that Sir Thomas and Queen Anne ever shared a romantic relationship of any kind, but by 1536, Henry VIII was growing weary of his demanding second queen and so began to cast about for ways to be rid of her. **Thomas Cromwell**, the king's chief minister and an avowed enemy of the **Boleyn** family, quickly went to work to oblige his royal master. In spring 1536, he sent agents to gather evidence against six men he believed had committed adultery with the queen, a group that included her minstrel; several courtiers; Sir Thomas Wyatt; and even her own brother **George Boleyn**, Lord Rochford. These six individuals, along with Queen Anne herself, were all arrested and committed to the Tower of London to await their trials for treason. All the accused men were condemned on 12 May 1536, but only five of them died as traitors a few days later. Strangely, Sir Thomas Wyatt was returned to the tower to fret over an unknown but possibly bloody fate before being released one month later. History does not record the reason Sir Thomas was spared the headsman's axe this time, but some sources suggest that Henry VIII never took the charges against his friend too seriously. Later the same year, the Tudor king promoted Wyatt to several lucrative posts, including sheriff of Kent, to reward him for raising 350 soldiers to help put down the **Pilgrimage of Grace** uprising in autumn 1536.

Having thus been restored to royal favor, Sir Thomas spent the next few years in Germany and Spain as King Henry's ambassador to the court of Holy Roman Emperor **Charles V**. One of the English embassy's members, an experienced diplomat, and future bishop named **Edmund Bonner** accused Wyatt of insulting the English king in order to win favor with the emperor's Roman Catholic envoys. Bonner renewed his criticism of Sir Thomas after their return to England in 1540 and this time persuaded King Henry's councilors to have the unlucky poet arrested and locked away in the Tower of London for a second time. The eloquent Wyatt sent a passionate repudiation of Bonner's charges to the king, and perhaps also aided by a request for mercy from Queen **Katherine Howard**, Sir Thomas was pardoned and then released from the tower late in 1541. He accepted appointments as the steward of a royal manor in Kent and as a fleet vice admiral during his final year of life, which ended abruptly when he contracted and died from a fever on 11 October 1542.

As a poet and author, Sir Thomas Wyatt rendered many of Francesco Petrarch's sonnets into cleverly worded English verse, though his rhyming schemes were usually somewhat different from those of the 14th-century Florentine humanist. He also composed sonnets of his own, many of which were published (along with 10 Plutarch translations) in 1557 as *Songes and Sonnettes* in *Tottel's Miscellany*, an anthology he shared with Henry Howard, the Earl of Surrey. One of those poems, "Whoso List to Hunt," is today widely believed to reflect Wyatt's confession of romantic interest in Anne Boleyn. Most of his work appeared in print posthumously, including his seven penitential *Certaine Psalms* and three satires entitled *On the Mean and Sure Estate*, *Of the Courtier's Life*, and *How to Use the Court and Himself*. In modern times, Sir Thomas Wyatt has often been accorded the honorific title "Father of the English Sonnet."

Bibliography

CONTENTS

ARCHIVAL MANUSCRIPT PRIMARY SOURCES

British Library, London

Additional Manuscripts

5758, f. 8. Opening of Henry VIII's First Parliament, 1510.

6113, f. 61. Ceremony Creating Henry Fitzroy Duke of Richmond, 1525.

———, f. 72. Nobles Who Did Homage to Henry VIII at His Coronation, 1509.

15387, f. 25. Letter from Henry VIII to Pope Leo X, 1514.

19398, f. 644. Letter from Henry VIII to Thomas Wolsey, 1521.

21481. King's Book of Household Payments, 1509–18.

25114, ff. 162–65, 175–77, and 191. Three Letters from Thomas Cromwell to Bishop Stephen Gardiner of Winchester, 1536.

27402, f. 47. A List of Executions during Henry VIII's Reign, 1548.

45131, ff. 37–41. Description of the Funeral of Arthur, Prince of Wales, 1502.

———, ff. 41–47. Description of the Funeral of Queen Elizabeth of York, 1503.

———, ff. 48–54. Description of the Funeral of King Henry VII, 1509.

45716, ff. 12–13. Arrangements for the Christening of Prince Edward, 1537.

46348, ff. 168–71. Inventory of Queen Katherine Parr's Jewels in 1546.

48000, ff. 590–594. Marriage Treaty between Prince Henry and Katherine of Aragon, 1503.

Cottonian Manuscripts

Caligula B I, f. 232. Letter from Queen Margaret of Scotland to Henry VIII, 1519.

Caligula B VI, f. 35. Letter from Queen Katherine to Thomas Wolsey, 1513.

———, f. 76. Letter from James IV of Scots to Henry VIII, 1513.

Caligula D VI, ff. 92–84. Letters from Queen Katherine to Thomas Wolsey, 1513.

———, ff. 149, 176, and 184. Letters from Charles Brandon, Duke of Suffolk, to Henry VIII and Thomas Wolsey, 1514–15.

Cleopatra E IV, ff. 101–4. Letter from Thomas Cromwell to Bishop John Fisher of Rochester, 1534.

Faustina E VIII, f. 6. Battle Order for King Henry's French Invasion, 1513.

Julius B XII, ff. 91–110. Creation of Prince Henry as Duke of York, 1494.

Nero C X, ff. 6. Letter Draft from Queen Katherine Parr to Prince Edward, 1546.

——— (4), f. 6. Letter from Prince Edward to Henry VIII, 1546.

Otho C X. Annulment of Henry VIII's Marriage to Anne of Cleves, 1540.

Tiberius E VIII, f. 100. Order of Henry VIII's Coronation Ceremony, 1509.

Titus B I, f. 94. Letter from Thomas Howard, the Duke of Norfolk, to the Privy Council as Written in the Tower of London, 1546.

———, f. 104. Letter from Thomas Wolsey to Bishop Richard Fox, 1511.

Titus B II (25), f. 51. Letter Announcing the Death of Henry VIII, 1547.

Vespasian C VI, f. 375. Treaty between Henry VIII and Ferdinand of Spain, 1513.

Vespasian F III, f. 15. Letter from Queen Katherine to Henry VIII, 1513.

———, f. 44. Letter from Henry Fitzroy, Duke of Richmond, to Thomas Wolsey, 1526.

———, f. 73. Letter from Henry VIII to Thomas Wolsey, 1518.

Vespasian F XIII, f. 60. Letter from Lady Margaret Beaufort to Henry VII, 1501.

———, f. 191. Letter from Thomas Cromwell to Thomas Audley, Lord Chancellor of England, 1534.

Vitellius B II, ff. 56 and 69. Letters from Pope Leo X to Henry VIII, 1513–14.

Vitellius B IV, ff. 84 and 96. Letters from Richard Pace to Thomas Wolsey Regarding the Treasonous Guilt of Edward Stafford, the Duke of Buckingham, 1521.

Vitellius B XI, f. 207. Letter from Pope Clement VII to Thomas Cardinal Wolsey, 1529.

Vitellius C I, f. 65. Prince Edward's Household Arrangements, 1539.

Egerton Manuscripts

616, f. 5. Letters from Arthur, Prince of Wales, to Queen Katherine of Aragon, 1499.

———, ff. 29–30. Letter from Katherine of Aragon to King Ferdinand of Spain, 1506.

———, f. 43. Letter from Henry VIII to Ferdinand of Spain, 1509.

985, f. 33. Prince Edward's Christening Arrangements, 1537.

Harleian Manuscripts

281, f. 75. Announcement of the Birth of Princess Elizabeth, 1533.

787, f. 58. Letter from Henry VIII to James IV of Scots, 1513.

3504, f. 232. Christening of Princess Mary, 1516.

5087, f. 17. Letter from Prince Edward to Queen Katherine Parr, 1546.

6148, f. 81. Letter from Thomas Cromwell to Archbishop Thomas Cranmer of Canterbury, 1534.

6079, f. 36. Account of Celebratory Joust with Combatants' Scores, 1511.

7039, f. 34. Letter from Prince Henry of Wales to His Grandmother, Margaret Beaufort, 1507.

King's Manuscript

9, ff. 66 and 231. Undated Expressions of Love between Henry VIII and Anne Boleyn in a *Book of Hours.*

Lansdowne Manuscript

1236, f. 9. Letter from Queen Katherine Parr to Henry VIII, 1544.

Royal Manuscripts

2 A, XVIII. Lady Margaret Beaufort's *Book of Hours.*

7 D, X. Queen Katherine Parr's *Prayers and Meditations,* Translated by Princess Elizabeth into Four Languages and Dedicated to Henry VIII, 1545.

14 B, XXXIX. Expenses of Katherine of Aragon's Journey and Escort from Exeter to London for Her Wedding to Prince Arthur, 1501.

Stowe Manuscripts

163, f. 3. The Treason Trial of Edward Stafford, the Duke of Buckingham, 1521.

396, f. 8. Treason Trial of Henry Howard, the Earl of Surrey, 1546.

Hampshire Record Office, Winchester

Register Richard Fox, 21 M 65: A1/17–21.

Huntington Library, San Marino, California

HM 745. Henry VII's Funeral Expenses, 1509.

HM 813. Betrothal of Princess Mary Tudor to Prince Charles of Castile, 1508.

Lambeth Palace Library, London

Archepiscopal Registers of William Warham and Thomas Cranmer (no classifications).

CM 51/115. Archbishop Warham's License for the Marriage of Henry VIII and Katherine of Aragon, 1509.

MSS 2341:2. Legal Opinions on the Validity of Henry VIII's Marriage to Katherine of Aragon, 1529.

The National Archives (Formerly the Public Record Office) at Kew

Exchequer Records

E 23/3. Last Will and Testament of King Henry VII, 1509.

E 23/4/1. Last Will and Testament of Henry VIII, 1546.

E 36/209, ff. 8v and 12v. Purchases of Clothing for Prince Henry, 1498.

E 36/217, f. 41. Revels Account of the Joust at Westminster, 1511.

E 101/424/5. Queen Katherine Parr's Expenses, 1546–47.

Prerogative Court of Canterbury

PCC. Prob 11/34, f. 13. Will of Thomas Wriothesley, Earl of Southampton.

———, 11/40. Will of Bishop Stephen Gardiner of Winchester.

State Papers

SP 1/1/3. General Pardon Issued upon the Accession of Henry VIII, 1509.

SP 1/1/18. Letter from King Ferdinand of Spain to Henry VIII, 1509.

SP 1/1/43. Letter from Ferdinand of Spain to Katherine of Aragon, 1509.

SP 1/1/45. Formal Pronouncements at Henry VIII and Katherine of Aragon's Wedding, 1509.

SP 1/2/119. Letter from Thomas Howard, the Earl of Surrey, to Thomas Wolsey, 1512.

SP 1/7/80. Letter from Thomas Lord Darce to Thomas Wolsey, 1514.

SP 1/47/166–67 and 1/50/81–82. Two Letters from Thomas Cromwell to Thomas Cardinal Wolsey, 1528.

SP 1/57/92–93. Letter from Thomas Cromwell to Thomas Cardinal Wolsey, in 1530.

SP 1/69/41–42. Letter from Thomas Cromwell to Bishop Stephen Gardiner of Winchester, 1532.

SP 1/80/51–52. Letter from Thomas Cromwell to Henry VIII, 1533.

SP 1/82/98. Letter from Thomas Cromwell to Henry VIII, 1534.

SP 1/83/98–99. Letter from Thomas Cromwell to Archbishop Thomas Cranmer of Canterbury, 1534.

SP 1/86/58. Letter from Thomas Cromwell to the Privy Council, 1534.

SP 1/126/62–65. Letter from Thomas Cromwell to the Council of the North, 1537.

SP 1/138/156–57. Letter from Thomas Cromwell to His Commissioners for the Suppression of the English Monasteries, 1538.

SP 1/161/173–74. Letter from Thomas Cromwell to the Royal Council, 1540.

SP 1/217. Letters and Documents, Spring 1546.

SP 4. Documents, 1545–47.

SP 6/6/4, ff. 38–43. Letter from Thomas Cromwell to the English Clergy on Doctrinal Reform, 1536.

SP 10/1/17. Instructions for the Funeral of Henry VIII.

PUBLISHED PRIMARY SOURCES

Allen, P. S., and H. M. Allen, eds. *The Letters of Richard Fox, 1486–1527*. Oxford, UK: Clarendon Press, 1929.

Ascham, Roger. *The Whole Works*. 3 vols. Edited by J. A. Giles. 1535. New York: AMS Press, 1965.

Ashmole, Elias. *The Institutions, Laws and Ceremonies of the Most Noble Order of the Garter*. 1672. London: Frederick Muller, 1971.

Beilin, Elaine, ed. *The Examinations of Anne Askew*. 1546. Oxford, UK: Oxford University Press, 1996.

Bergenroth, G. A., ed. *Calendar of Letters, Dispatches and State Papers Relating to Negotiations between England and Spain*. 13 vols. London: His Majesty's Stationery Office, 1862–1954.

Bergenroth, G. A., and Rawdon Brown, eds. *Calendar of State Papers: Spanish and Venetian*. London: Longman, Green, 1485–1526, 1862–64.

Bradford, W., ed. *Correspondence of the Emperor Charles V and His Ambassadors at the Courts of England and France*. New York: AMS Press, 1971.

Brown, Rawdon, ed. and trans. *Four Years at the Court of Henry VIII: Selections from Dispatches Written by Sebastian Guistinian 1515–1519*. 2 vols. London: Smith and Elder, 1854.

Byrne, Muriel St. Clare, ed. *Letters of King Henry VIII 1509–46*. New York: Funk and Wagnalls, 1968.

———, ed. *The Lisle Letters: An Abridgement*. 1533–42. Chicago: University of Chicago Press, 1981.

Caius, John. *A Boke or Counseill against the Sweate*. 1552. New York: Scholars' Facsimiles and Reprints, 1937.

Campbell, William, ed. *Materials for a History of the Reign of Henry VII*. London: Rolls Series LX:I, 1873.

Cavendish, George. "The Life and Death of Cardinal Wolsey." In *Two Early Tudor Lives*, ed. Richard S. Sylvester and Davis P. Harding. New Haven, CT: Yale University Press, 1962.

Chitty, Henry, ed. *Registra Stephani Gardiner et Johannis Poynet*. Oxford, UK: Canterbury and York Society, 1930.

Cook, George Henry, ed. *Letters to Cromwell and Others on the Suppression of the Monasteries*. 1535–40. London: J. Baker, 1965.

Cranmer, Thomas. *Miscellaneous Writings and Letters of Thomas Cranmer*. Edited by John

Edmund Cox. Cambridge, UK: Parker Society, 1846.

Cromwell, Thomas. *On Church and Commonwealth: Selected Letters 1523–40.* Edited by Arthur J. Slavin. New York: Harper and Row, 1969.

Dascent, John F., ed. *Acts of the Privy Council of England.* 46 vols. London: Her Majesty's Stationery Office, 1890–1964.

Douglas, David C., ed. *English Historical Documents.* Vol. 5, *1485–1558.* New York: Routledge, 2010.

Ellis, Henry, ed. *Original Letters Illustrative of English History.* 4 vols. 1827. New York: AMS Press, 1970.

Elton, Sir Geoffrey, ed. *The Tudor Constitution.* Cambridge, UK: Cambridge University Press, 1972.

Elyot, Sir Thomas. *The Book Named the Governor.* 1531. New York: Dutton, Everyman's Library, 1962.

Erasmus, Desiderius. *The Complete Works.* 19 vols. Edited and translated by R. J. Schoeck et al. Toronto: University of Toronto Press, 1974–2016.

Feuillerat, Albert, ed. *Documents Relating to the Office of the Revels.* 1597. Louvain, Belgium: Uystpruyst, 1908.

Fish, Simon. *A Supplication for the Beggars.* Edited by Edward Arber. 1529. New York: AMS Press, 1967.

Fisher, John. *The English Works of John Fisher.* 9 vols. Edited by John E. Mayor. 1489–1533. Oxford, UK: Early English Text Society, 1867.

———. *De Veritiate Corporis et Sanguinis in Christi Eucharistia, per Reverendum in Christo Patrem, ac Dominum D. Johanem Rossensem Episcopum, adversus Johannem Oecolampadium.* Coloniae, 1527. CCC, XII, c. 13.

Foxe, John. *History of the Acts and Monuments of the Church.* 8 vols. Edited by S. R. Cattley and George Townsend. London: Seeley and Burnside, 1841.

Fulman, William. *Academiae Oxoniensis Notitia.* Oxford, UK: W. H. Impensis and R. Davis, 1665.

Furnivall, E. J., ed. *Ballads from Manuscripts: Ballads on the Condition of England in Henry VIII's and Edward VI's Reigns.* London: Ballad Society, 1868–72.

Gairdner, James, ed. *Letters and Papers Illustrative of the Reigns of Richard III and Henry VII.* London: Rolls Series XXIV:1 and 2, 1861.

Gairdner, James, R. H. Brodie, and J. S. Brewer, eds. *Letters and Papers, Foreign and Domestic of the Reign of Henry VIII.* 36 vols. London: Her Majesty's Stationery Office, 1862–1932.

Gardiner, Stephen. *De Vera Obedientia.* 1535. Leeds, UK: Scholar Press Facsimiles, 1966.

Gee, Henry, and William Hardy, ed. *Documents Illustrative of English Church History.* New York: Macmillan, 1896.

Haddon, Arthur W., and William Stubbs, eds. *Councils and Ecclesiastical Documents Relating to Great Britain and Ireland.* 3 vols. Oxford, UK: Clarendon Press, 1969–78.

Hall, Edward. *The Union of the Two Noble and Illustre Fameles of Lancastre and York, or Chronicle.* Edited by Henry Ellis. 1548. London: J. Johnson et al., 1809.

Halliwell-Phillips, J., ed. *The Love Letters of Henry VIII to Anne Boleyn.* 1526–36. New York: John W. Luce, 1907.

Harpsfield, Nicholas. *Historia Anglicana Ecclesiasticus.* 1558. Douai, France: Mark Wyon, 1622.

———. *The Life and Death of Thomas More, Knight.* Vol. 197. Edited by E. V. Hitchcock and R. W. Chambers. 1557. Oxford, UK: Early English Text Society, 1935.

———. *A Treatise on the Pretended Divorce between Henry VIII and Katherine of Aragon.* Edited by Nicholas Pocock. 1556. London: Camden Society, 1878.

Harrison, William. *A Description of England in Shakespeare's Youth.* Edited by Frederick J. Funival. 1586. London: Trubner for the New Shakespeare Society, series VI:1, 1877.

Heath, J. B., ed. *An Account of the Materials Furnished for the Use of Queen Anne Boleyn.* Vol. 7. 1534. London: Philobiblon Society, 1863.

Henry VIII. *Assertio septem sacramentorum.* Edited and translated by Raymond de

Souza. 1521. Conyngham, PA: Saint Gabriel Communications International, 2007.

Herbert, Henry W., ed. *Memoirs of Henry the Eighth of England*. 1509–47: Miami: Hard-Press, 2013.

Hinds, Allen B., ed. *Calendar of State Papers and Manuscripts Existing in the Archives and Collections of Milan*. Vol 1., *1485–1618*. London: His Majesty's Stationery Office, 1912.

Holinshed, Raphael. *Chronicles of England, Scotland and Ireland*. 1577. London: J. Johnson et al., 1807.

Hughes, Paul L., and James F. Larkin, eds. *Tudor Royal Proclamations*. 3 vols. New Haven, CT: Yale University Press, 1964.

Jerdan, William, ed. *The Rutland Papers: Original Documents Illustrative of the Courts and Times of Henry VII and Henry VIII*. Vol. 21. London: J. B. Nichols and Sons for Camden Society, 1842.

Journals of the House of Lords. 65 vols. London: His Majesty's Stationery Office, 1834.

Kipling, G., ed. *Receipt of the Lady Katherine*. 1501. London: Early English Text Society, 1990.

Lacey, T. A., ed. *The King's Book, or a Necessary Doctrine and Erudition for any Christian Man*. 1543. London: Society for Promoting Christian Knowledge, 1932.

Leland, John. *Leland's Itinerary of England and Wales 1535–1543*. Edited by Lucy Toulmin Smith. London: Centaur Press, 1964.

Lloyd, Charles, ed. *Formularies of Faith Put Forth by Authority during the Reign of Henry VIII*. Oxford: Clarendon Press, 1825.

Lupsett, Thomas. *The Life and Works of Thomas Lupsett*. Edited by John Archer Gee. New Haven, CT: Yale University Press, 1928.

Maxwell-Lyte, H. C., ed. *Calendar of Close Rolls*. 61 vols. London: His Majesty's Stationery Office, 1895–1963.

———, ed. *Calendar of Patent Rolls*. 54 vols. London: His Majesty's Stationery Office, 1901–16.

More, Sir Thomas. *Complete Works*. 15 vols. 1513–35. New Haven, CT: Yale University Press, 1963–97.

———. *The Correspondence of Sir Thomas More*. Edited by Elizabeth Francis Rogers. Princeton, NJ: Princeton University Press, 1947.

Muller, James A., ed. *The Letters of Stephen Gardiner*. Cambridge, UK: Cambridge University Press, 1933.

Mumby, Frank Arthur, ed. *The Youth of Henry VIII: A Narrative in Contemporary Letters*. 1513. London: Forgotten Books, 2016.

Nichols, John Gough, ed. *The Chronicle of Calais in the Reigns of Henry VII and Henry VIII to the Year 1540*. London: Camden Society, 1846.

———, ed. *A Collection of Ordinances and Regulations for the Government of the Royal Household, Made in Diverse Reigns from King Edward III to King William and Queen Mary*. London: Society of Antiquities of London, 1790.

———, ed. *Memoir of Henry Fitzroy, Duke of Richmond*. Vol. 61. 1535. London: Camden Society, 1855.

———, ed. *Narratives of the Days of the Reformation*. London: Camden Society, 1859.

Nicolas, Harris, ed. *Proceedings and Ordinances of the Privy Council of England*. 7 vols. London: His Majesty's Printing Office, 1835.

Nicolas, Harris, ed. *The Privy Purse Expenses of King Henry the Eighth from MDXIX to MDXXXII*. London: Forgotten Books, 2016.

Norton, Elizabeth, ed. *The Anne Boleyn Papers*. 1504–36. Gloucestershire: Amberley Press, 2013.

Nott, George F., ed. *The Works of Henry Howard, Earl of Surrey and Sir Thomas Wyatt the Elder*. 2 vols. 1526–46: London: T. Bensley, 1815–16.

Paget, William. *The Letters of William Lord Paget of Beaudesert*. London: Camden Society, 1974.

Parker, Matthew. *De Antiquitate Britannica Ecclesiae et Privilegiis Ecclesiae Cantauriensis*. 1572. London: William Bower, 1729.

Parr, Katherine. *Complete Works and Correspondence*. Edited by Janel Mueller. 1528–48. Chicago: University of Chicago Press, 2011.

Pocock, Nicholas, ed. *Records of the Reformation: The Divorce, 1527–1533.* 2 vols. Oxford: Clarendon Press, 1870.

Pollard, A. F., ed. *The Reign of Henry VII from Contemporary Sources.* 3 vols. London: Longmans, Green, 1913.

———. *Tudor Tracts.* New York: E. P. Dutton, 1903.

Richards, G. C., ed. *The Dean's Register of Oriel.* Oxford, UK: Oxford Historical Society at the Clarendon Press, 1926.

Robinson, Hastings, ed. *Original Letters Relating to the English Reformation.* Cambridge, UK: Parker Society, 1846.

Roper, William. "The Life of Sir Thomas More, Knight." In *Two Early Tudor Lives,* edited by Richard S. Sylvester and Davis P. Harding. New Haven, CT: Yale University Press, 1962.

Rymer, Thomas, ed. *Foedera, Conventiones, Litterae, et Cujuscunque Generis Acta Publica, Inter Reges Angliae, et Alios Quosuis Imperatores, Reges, Pontifes, Principes, etc.* Vols. 12–13. London: J. Tonson, 1735.

Sanders, Margaret, ed. *Intimate Letters of England's Queens.* Stroud, UK: Amberley Press, 2014.

Skelton, John. *The Poetical Works.* Edited by Alexander Dyce. 1490–1523. New York: AMS Press, 1970.

Stapleton, Thomas, ed. *The Plumpton Correspondence: A Series of Letters, Chiefly Domestick, Written in the Reigns of Edward IV, Richard III, Henry VII and Henry VIII.* Vol. 4. London: Camden Society, 1839.

Statutes of the Realm. 11 vols. London: His Majesty's Stationery Office, 1810–22.

Steele, R. R., ed. *A Bibliography of Tudor and Stuart Royal Proclamations, 1485–1714.* Oxford, UK: Clarendon Press, 1910.

Stow, John. *The Annals of England.* Edited by Edmund Howes. 1592. London: Impensis Richardi Meighen, 1631.

———. *Survey of the Cities of London and Westminster.* 2 vols. Edited by Charles L. Kingsford. 1598. Oxford, UK: Clarendon Press, 1971.

Strype, John, ed. *Ecclesiastical Memorials Relating Chiefly to Religion and the Reformation of It.* 3 vols. Oxford, UK: Clarendon Press, 1822.

———, ed. *Memorials of Archbishop Cranmer.* 3 vols. 1554. Oxford, UK: Ecclesiastical History Society, 1852.

Sturtz, J., and V. Murphy, eds. *The Divorce Tracts of Henry VIII.* 1528–33. Angers, France: Moreana, 1988.

Tyndale, William. *The Obedience of a Christian Man.* Edited by Richard Lovett. 1528. Columbus, OH: Vintage Archives, 1999.

———. *The Practice of Prelates.* Vol. 43. Edited by Henry Walter. 1521. Cambridge: Parker Society, 1849.

Valor Ecclesiasticus temp. Henry. VIII. 6 vols. 1535. London: His Majesty's Stationery Office, 1810; Ann Arbor, MI: University Microfilms International, 1978.

Vergil, Polydore. *Anglicae Historiae.* Vol. 74. Edited by Denis Hay. 1536. London: Royal Historical Society, 1950.

Vives, Juan Luis. *On the Education of a Christian Woman.* Edited and translated by Charles Fantazzi. 1531. Chicago: University of Chicago Press, 2007.

Wilkins, David, ed. *Concilia Magnae Britanniae et Hiberniae.* 4 vols. London: R. Gosling, 1737.

Wood, Anthony. *History and Antiquities of Oxford.* 1674. Oxford, UK: Clarendon Press, 1786.

Wright, Thomas, ed. *Three Chapters of Letters Relating to the Suppression of the Monasteries.* Vol. 26. 1535–40: London: Camden Society, 1843.

Wriothesley, Charles. *A Chronicle of England during the Reigns of the Tudors from A.D. 1485 to 1559.* Edited by William D. Hamilton. 1560. London: Camden Society, 1875.

PUBLISHED SECONDARY SOURCES

General Works on the Tudor Age

Ackroyd, Peter. *The Tudors.* New York: St. Martin's Press, 2012.

Bernard, G. W. *Power and Politics in Tudor England.* Oxford, UK: Routledge, 2017.

Bingham, Jane. *The Tudors: England's Golden Age.* London: Arcturus, 2018.

Brigdon, Susan. *New Worlds, Lost Worlds: The Rule of the Tudors*. New York: Viking, Penguin, 2000.

De Lisle, Leanda. *Tudor: The Family Story*. London: Chatto and Windus, 2013.

Doran, Susan. *The Tudor Chronicles*. London: Quercus, 2008.

Elton, Sir Geoffrey. *England under the Tudors*. London: Methuen, 1955/62.

Griffiths, Ralph A., and Thomas Rogers. *The Making of the Tudor Dynasty*. Gloucestershire, UK: Sutton, 1998.

Guy, John. *Tudor England*. Oxford, UK: Oxford University Press, 1980.

Kinney, Arthur F. *Tudor England: An Encyclopedia*. London: Routledge, 2010.

Lockyer, Roger. *Tudor and Stuart Britain 1471–1714*. New York: St. Martin's Press, 1985.

McGurk, John. *The Tudor Monarchies 1485–1603*. Cambridge, UK: Cambridge University Press, 1999.

Meyer, G. J. *The Tudors: A Most Notorious Dynasty*. New York: Random House, 2010.

Ridley, Jasper. *The Tudor Age*. London: Constable and Robinson, 2002.

Skidmore, Chris. *The Rise of the Tudors*. New York: St. Martin's Press, 2013.

The Forebears of King Henry VIII

Alexander, Michael. *The First of the Tudors: Henry VII and His Reign*. Lanham, MD: Rowman and Littlefield, 1980.

Amin, Nathen. *The House of Beaufort: The Bastard Line That Captured the Crown*. Gloucestershire, UK: Amberley, 2018.

Bacon, Francis. *The History of the Reign of King Henry VII*. 1622. Cambridge, UK: University Printing House, 1951.

Breverton, Terry. *Henry VII: The Maligned Tudor King*. Gloucestershire, UK: Amberley, 2016.

Cavill, P. R. *The English Parliaments of Henry VII 1485–1504*. Oxford, UK: Oxford University Press, 2009.

Chrimes, S. B. *Henry VII*. Berkeley: University of California Press, 1972.

Cunningham, Sean. *Henry VII*. London: Routledge, 2007.

Grant, Alexander. *Henry VII*. London: Routledge, 2015.

Hicks, Michael. *The Wars of the Roses*. New York: Oxford University Press, 2012.

Jones, Michael K., and Malcolm G. Underwood. *The King's Mother: Lady Margaret Beaufort, Countess of Richmond and Derby*. Cambridge, UK: Cambridge University Press, 1992.

Licence, Amy. *Elizabeth of York*. Gloucestershire, UK: Amberley, 2013.

Norton, Elizabeth. *Margaret Beaufort: Mother of the Tudor Dynasty*. Gloucestershire, UK: Amberley, 2010.

Penn, Thomas. *Winter King: Henry VII and the Dawn of Tudor England*. New York: Simon and Schuster, 2011.

Rees, David; *The Son of Prophecy: Henry Tudor's Road to Bosworth*. London: Black Raven Press, 1985.

Royle, Trevor. *Lancaster against York: The Wars of the Roses and the Foundation of Modern Britain*. New York: St. Martin's Press, 2014.

Simons, Eric N. *Henry VII, the First Tudor King*. London: Frederick Muller, 1968.

Tallis, Nicola. *The Uncrowned Queen: Lady Margaret Beaufort*. New York: Basic Books, 2020.

Thompson, Benjamin, ed. *The Reign of Henry VII: Symposium Papers*. Stamford, UK: Paul Watkins, 1995.

Weir, Alison. *Elizabeth of York*. London: Vintage Books, 2014.

Biographies of King Henry VIII

Betteridge, Thomas, and Thomas Freeman. *Henry VIII and History*. Aldershot, UK: Ashgate, 2012.

Bingham, Jane. *Henry VIII*. London: Wayland, 2013.

Butterfield, Moira. *Henry VIII*. London: Franklin Watts, 2013.

Fletcher, David. *Henry VIII*. New York: St. Martin's Press, 1977.

Graves, Michael A. *Henry VIII*. New York: Longman, 2003.

Guy, John. *Henry VIII*. London: Alan Lane, 2014.

Hutchinson, Robert. *The Last Days of Henry VIII*. New York: HarperCollins, 2015.

———. *Young Henry: The Rise of Henry VIII*. New York: St. Martin's Press, 2012.

Lipscomb, Suzannah. *The King Is Dead: The Last Will of Henry VIII*. New York: Pegasus Books, 2016.

Loades, David. *Henry VIII*. London: History Press, 2011.

MacCulloch, Diarmaid. *The Reign of Henry VIII*. Basingstoke, UK: Macmillan, 1997.

Matusiak, John. *Henry VIII: The Life and Rule of England's Nero*. Cheltenham, UK: History Press, 2013.

Oliver, Marilyn Tower. *Henry VIII*. San Diego: Lucent Books, 2004.

Pollard, A. F. *Henry VIII*. 1902. London: Harper and Row, 1966.

Ridley, Jasper. *Henry VIII: The Politics of Tyranny*. New York: Fromm International, 1985.

Scarisbrick, J. J. *Henry VIII*. London: Cambridge University Press, 1968.

Smith, Lacey Baldwin. *Henry VIII: Mask of Royalty*. Boston: Houghton Mifflin, 1971.

Starkey, David. *Henry: The Prince Who Would Turn Tyrant*. London: Harper, 2009.

———. *The Reign of Henry VIII*. London: Vintage, 2002.

Weir, Alison. *Henry VIII: The King and His Court*. New York: Ballantine Books, 2001.

Wilson, Derek. *A Brief History of Henry VIII*. London: Constable and Robinson, 2009.

Wooding, Lucy. *Henry VIII*. London: Routledge, 2009.

Government of the Realm

Anglo, Sydney. *Images of Kingship*. London: Seaby, 1992.

———. *Spectacle, Pageantry and Early Tudor Policy*. Oxford, UK: Oxford University Press, 1997.

Bindoff, S. T., ed. *The History of Parliament: The House of Commons 1509–58*. London: Secker and Warburg, 1982.

Challis, Christopher E. *The Tudor Coinage*. Manchester, UK: Manchester University Press, 1978.

Claire Cross, David Loades, and J. J. Scarisbrock, eds. *Law and the Government under the Tudors*. Cambridge, UK: Cambridge University Press, 1988.

Dietz, Frederick C. *English Government Finance 1485–1558*. London: Frank Cass, 1964.

Elton, Sir Geoffrey. *The Tudor Revolution in Government*. Cambridge, UK: Cambridge University Press, 1969.

Goodman, Anthony. *The New Monarchy: England 1471–1534*. Oxford, UK: Basil Blackwell, 1989.

Gunn, Steven. *Early Tudor Government 1485–1558*. Basingstoke, UK: Palgrave Macmillan, 1995.

Lehmberg, Stanford E. *The Later Parliaments of Henry VIII*. Cambridge, UK: Cambridge University Press, 1977/2008.

Loach, Jennifer. *Parliament under the Tudors*. Oxford, UK: Clarendon Press, 1991.

Loades, David. *The Tudor Court*. Oxford, UK: Davenant Press, 2003.

Schofield, R. *Taxation under the Early Tudors 1495–1547*. Oxford, UK: Oxford University Press, 2004.

Thurley, S. *Houses of Power: The Places That Shaped the Tudor World*. London: Black Swan, 2017.

Williams, Penry. *The Tudor Regime*. Oxford, UK: Clarendon Press, 1979.

Wilson, Derek. *In the Lion's Court of Henry VIII*. New York: St. Martin's Press, 2001.

Henry VIII's Brother and Sisters

Bryson, Sarah. *La Reine Blanche: Mary Tudor, A Life in Letters*. Gloucestershire, UK: Amberley, 2018.

Carson, D. R. "Royal Tutors in the Reign of Henry VII." *Sixteenth Century Journal* 22, no. 2 (1991): 253–79.

Clegg, Melanie. *Margaret Tudor: The Life of Henry VIII's Sister*. Yorkshire, UK: Pen and Sword History, 2018.

Cunningham, Sean. *Prince Arthur*. Gloucestershire, UK: Amberley Press, 2016.

Gunn, Steven, and Linda Monckton, eds. *Arthur Tudor, Prince of Wales: Life, Death, and Commemoration*. Woodbridge, UK: Boydell Press, 2009.

Lloyd, David. *Arthur, Prince of Wales, 1486–1502*. Ludlow, UK: St. Lawrence, 2002.

Loades, David. *Mary Rose: Tudor Princess*. Gloucestershire, UK: Amberley Press, 2014.

Perry, Maria. *The Sisters of Henry VIII*. New York: St. Martin's Press, 1998.

Richardson, Walter. *Mary Tudor: The White Queen*. Seattle: University of Washington Press, 1970.

Watkins, Sarah-Beth. *Margaret Tudor, Queen of Scots*. London: John Hunt, 2013.

Henry VIII's Queens

Bernard, G. W. *Anne Boleyn*. New Haven, CT: Yale University Press, 2010.

———. "Anne Boleyn's Religion." *Historical Journal* 36 (1993): 1–20.

———. "The Fall of Anne Boleyn." *English Historical Review* 106 (July 1991): 420.

Bordo, Susan. *The Creation of Anne Boleyn*. Boston: Houghton Mifflin, 2014.

Chapman, Henry W. *Anne Boleyn*. London: Jonathan Cape, 1974.

Darsie, Heather R. *Anna, Duchess of Cleves*. Gloucestershire, UK: Amberley, 2019.

Denny, Joanna. *Anne Boleyn*. Cambridge, MA: Da Capo, Perseus, 2004.

Fletcher, Catherine. *The Divorce of Henry VIII*. New York: Palgrave Macmillan, 2012.

Fraser, Antonia. *The Six Wives of Henry VIII*. New York: Random House, 1993.

Ives, E. W. *Anne Boleyn*. Oxford, UK: Basil Blackwell, 1986.

———. *The Life and Death of Anne Boleyn*. Oxford, UK: Blackwell, 2005.

James, Susan. *Katheryn Parr: The Making of a Queen*. Aldershot, UK: Ashgate, 1999.

Licence, Amy. *Anne Boleyn*. Gloucestershire, UK: Amberley, 2018.

———. *Catherine of Aragon*. Gloucestershire, UK: Amberley, 2016.

Lindsey, Karen. *Divorced, Beheaded, Survived*. New York: HarperCollins, 1995.

Loades, David. *The Boleyns: The Rise and Fall of a Tudor Family*. Gloucestershire, UK: Amberley, 2012.

———. *Catherine Howard*. Gloucestershire, UK: Amberley, 2012.

———. *Henry VIII and His Queens*. Gloucestershire, UK: Sutton, 2001.

———. *Jane Seymour*. Gloucestershire, UK: Amberley, 2013.

Mattingly, Garrett. *Catherine of Aragon*. Boston: Little, Brown, 1941/63.

Morris, Sarah, and Natalie Grueninger. *In the Footsteps of Anne Boleyn*. Gloucestershire, UK: Amberley, 2013.

Norton, Elizabeth. *Catherine Parr*. Gloucestershire, UK: Amberley, 2011.

Paget, Hugh. "The Youth of Anne Boleyn." *Bulletin of the Institute of Historical Research* 55 (1981).

Porter, Linda. *Katherine the Queen*. New York: St. Martin's Press, 2010.

Russell, Gareth. *Young and Damned and Fair: The Life of Katherine Howard*. New York: Simon and Schuster, 2016.

Smith, Lacey Baldwin. *Catherine Howard: A Tudor Tragedy*. London: Jonathan Cape, 1961.

Starkey, David. *Six Wives: The Queens of Henry VIII*. London: Chatto and Windus, 2003.

Tremlett, Giles. *Catherine of Aragon: Henry's Spanish Queen*. London: Faber and Faber, 2010.

Trewin, John C., and Rosemary A. Sisson. *The Six Wives of Herny VIII*. London: Elek, 1972.

Warner, J. Christopher. *Henry VIII's Divorce: Literature and the Politics of the Printing Press*. Woodbridge, UK: Boydell Press, 1998.

Warnicke, Retha. *The Marrying of Anne of Cleves*. Cambridge, UK: Cambridge University Press, 2000.

———. *The Rise and Fall of Anne Boleyn*. Cambridge, UK: Cambridge University Press, 1989.

Watkins, Sarah-Beth. *Anne of Cleves: Henry VIII's Unwanted Wife*. Washington, DC: Chronos Books, 2018.

Weir, Alison. *The Lady in the Tower: The Fall of Anne Boleyn*. Toronto: Emblem Books, 2010.

———. *The Six Wives of Henry VIII*. New York: Grove Weidenfeld, 1991.

Wilkinson, Josephine. *The Early Loves of Anne Boleyn*. Gloucestershire, UK: Amberley, 2009.

Williams, Patrick. *Katherine of Aragon*. Gloucestershire, UK: Amberley Press, 2013.

Henry VIII's Royal Children

Alford, Stephen. *Kingship and Politics in the Reign of Edward VI*. Cambridge, UK: Cambridge University Press, 2002.

Edwards, John. *Mary I: England's Catholic Queen*. New Haven, CT: Yale University Press, 2011.

Guy, John. *The Children of Henry VIII*. Oxford, UK: Oxford University Press, 2013.

Hilton, Lisa. *Elizabeth: Renaissance Prince*. London: Weidenfeld and Nicolson, 2016.

Jordan, Wilbur K. *Edward VI*. London: Allen and Unwin, 1970.

Loach, Jennifer. *Edward VI*. New Haven, UK: Yale University Press, 1999.

Loades, David. *Elizabeth I*. London: Hambledon, 2003.

———. *Mary Tudor: A Life*. Oxford: Blackwell, 1989.

MacCaffrey, Wallace. *Elizabeth I*. London: Arnold, 2004.

MacCulloch, Diarmaid. *The Boy King: Edward VI and the Protestant Reformation*. New York: Palgrave, St. Martin's, 2001.

Norton, Elizabeth. *The Temptation of Elizabeth Tudor*. New York: Pegasus Books, 2017.

Porter, Linda. *The First Queen of England: The "Myth" of Bloody Mary*. New York: St. Martin's Press, 2008.

Rex, Richard. *Elizabeth I: Fortune's Bastard?* Gloucestershire, UK: Amberley, 2003.

Skidmore, Chris. *Edward VI*. New York: St. Martin's Press, 2007.

Starkey, David. *Elizabeth: Struggle for the Throne*. New York: HarperCollins, 2001.

Thomas, Melita. *The King's Pearl: Henry VIII's Daughter Mary*. Gloucestershire, UK: Amberley, 2019.

Weir, Alison. *The Children of Henry VIII*. New York: Ballantine Books, 1996.

———. *The Life of Elizabeth I*. New York: Random House, 2013.

Whitelock, Anne. *Mary Tudor: Princess, Bastard, Queen*. New York: Random House, 2009.

Henry VIII's Mistresses and Their Offspring

Baldwin, David. *Henry VIII's Last Love: The Extraordinary Life of Katherine Willoughby*. Gloucestershire, UK: Amberley, 2015.

Beauclerk-Dewar, Peter. *Royal Bastards: Illegitimate Children of the British Royal Family*. Gloucestershire, UK: History Press, 2008.

Carlton, Charles. *Royal Mistresses*. London: Routledge, 1991.

Hart, Kelly. *The Mistresses of Henry VIII*. Gloucestershire, UK: History Press, 2009.

Hobden, Heather. *Tudor Bastard: King Henry VIII's Son, Henry Fitzroy, Duke of Richmond and Somerset, and His Mother, Elizabeth Blount*. Lincoln, UK: Cosmic Elk, 2001.

Jones, Philippa. *The Other Tudors: Henry VIII's Mistresses and Bastards*. New York: Sterling, New Holland, 2009.

Licence, Amy. *In Bed with the Tudors: The Sex Lives of a Dynasty*. Gloucestershire, UK: Amberley, 2012.

Murphy, Beverly A. *Bastard Prince: Henry Fitzroy*. Gloucestershire, UK: Sutton Books, 2001.

Norton, Elizabeth. *Bessie Blount: Mistress to Henry VIII*. Gloucestershire, UK: Amberley, 2013.

———. *The Boleyn Women: The Tudor Femmes Fatales*. Gloucestershire, UK: Amberley, 2014.

Weir, Alison. *The Lost Tudor Princes*. London: Vintage, 2015.

———. *Mary Boleyn: The Mistress of Kings*. New York: Ballantine Books, 2013.

Wilkinson, Josephine. *Mary Boleyn: The True Story of Henry VIII's Mistress*. Gloucestershire, UK: Amberley, 2010.

Chief Ministers of Henry VIII

Beckingsale, Bernard W. *Thomas Cromwell: Tudor Minister*. London: Macmillan, 1978/2014.

Borman, Tracy. *Henry VIII and the Men Who Made Him*. New York: Atlantic Monthly Press, 2018.

———. *Thomas Cromwell*. London: Hodder and Stoughton, 2014.

Davies, C. S. L. "The Cromwellian Decade: Authority and Consent." *Transactions of the Royal Historical Society* 6, no. 7 (1997): 177–95.

Elton, Sir Geoffrey. *Policy and Police: Enforcement of the Reformation under Thomas Cromwell*. Cambridge, UK: Cambridge University Press, 1972.

Everett, Michael. *The Rise of Thomas Cromwell*. New Haven, CT: Yale University Press, 2015.

Ferguson, Charles W. *Naked to Mine Enemies: The Life of Cardinal Wolsey*. Boston: Little, Brown, 1958.

Gunn, Steven. *Henry VIII's New Men and the Making of Tudor England*. Oxford, UK: Oxford University Press, 2016.

Gunn, Steven, and P. G. Lindley, eds. *Cardinal Wolsey: Church, State and Art*. Cambridge, UK: Cambridge University Press, 1991.

Gwyn, Peter. *The King's Cardinal: The Rise and Fall of Thomas Wolsey*. London: Pimlico, 1992.

Harvey, Nancy L. *Thomas Cardinal Wolsey*. New York: Macmillan, 1980.

Hutchinson, Robert. *Thomas Cromwell*. London: Phoenix, 2008.

Loades, David. *Cardinal Wolsey*. Oxford, UK: Davenport Press, 2008.

———. *Thomas Cromwell*. Gloucestershire, UK: Amberley, 2013.

MacCulloch, Diarmaid. *Thomas Cromwell: A Life*. London: Penguin, 2018.

Matusiak, John. *Wolsey*. London: History Press, 2014.

Ridley, Jasper. *Statesman and Saint: Cardinal Wolsey, Sir Thomas More and the Politics of Henry VIII*. New York: Viking, 1983.

Schofield, John. *The Rise and Fall of Thomas Cromwell*. London: History Press, 2008.

Wabuda, Susan. "Cardinal Wolsey and Cambridge." *British Catholic History* 32 (2015): 280–92.

Prominent Nobles

Bernard, G. W. *The Power of the Early Tudor Nobility: The Earls of Shrewsbury*. Sussex, UK: Harvester Press, 1985.

Childs, Jessie. *Henry VIII's Last Victim: Henry Howard, Earl of Surrey*. New York: St. Martin's Press, 2006.

Davies, Jonathan. *Thomas Audley and the Tudor "Arte of Warre."* Farnham, UK: Pike and Shot, 2002.

Emerson, Kate. *Secrets of the Tudor Court: At the King's Pleasure*. New York: Gallery Books, 2012.

Gibbons, Geoffrey. *The Political Career of Thomas Wriothesley, First Earl of Southampton, 1505–1550*. Lewiston, NY: Edwin Mellen Press, 2001.

Gunn, Steven. *Charles Brandon: Henry VIII's Closest Friend*. Gloucestershire, UK: Amberley, 2015.

Harris, Barbara J. *Edward Stafford, Third Duke of Buckingham*. Palo Alto, CA: Stanford University Press, 1986.

Loades, David. *John Dudley, Duke of Northumberland*. Oxford, UK: Davenport Press, 2002.

MacCulloch, Diarmaid. *Suffolk and the Tudors*. Oxford, UK: Oxford University Press, 1986.

Miller, Helen. *Henry VIII and the English Nobility*. Oxford, UK: Basil Blackwell, 1989.

Rawcliffe, Carole. *The Staffords: Earls of Stafford and Dukes of Buckingham*. New York: Cambridge University Press, 2008.

Robinson, John M. *The Dukes of Norfolk*. Chichester, UK: Phillimore, 1995.

Scard, Margaret. *Edward Seymour: Lord Protector*. London: History Press, 2016.

Starkey, David. *Rivals in Power: Tudor Noble Dynasties*. New York: Grove Weidenfeld, 1990.

Tucker, M. J. *The Life of Thomas Howard, Earl of Surrey and Second Duke of Norfolk 1443–1524*. The Hague: Mouton, 1964.

Wilson, Derek. *Uncrowned Kings of England: The Black Legend of the Dudleys*. London: Constable, 2013.

Intellectual Life and Scholarship

Ackroyd, Peter. *The Life of Thomas More*. New York: Doubleday, Dell, 1998.

Brigden, Susan. *Thomas Wyatt: The Heart's Forest*. London: Faber and Faber, 2014.

Carley, James P. *The Libraries of Henry VIII*. London: British Library, 2000.

Dickens, A. G., and Whitney Jones. *Erasmus the Reformer*. London: Methuen, 2000.

Dowling, Maria. *Humanism in the Age of Henry VIII*. London: Croom Helm, 1986.

Emden, A. B. *A Biographical Register of the University of Cambridge to A.D. 1500*. Cambridge, UK: Cambridge University Press, 1963.

———. *A Biographical Register of the University of Oxford, A.D. 1501–1540*. Oxford, UK: Clarendon Press, 1974.

———. *A Biographical Register of the University of Oxford to 1500*. Oxford, UK: Clarendon Press, 1959.

Fox, Alistair, and John Guy. *Reassessing the Henrician Age: Humanism, Politics and Reform*. Oxford, UK: Basil Blackwell, 1986.

———. *Thomas More: History and Providence*. Oxford, UK: Basil Blackwell, 1984.

Gleason, J. B. *John Colet*. Berkeley: University of California Press, 1989.

Guy, John. *A Daughter's Love: Thomas More and His Dearest Meg*. Boston: Houghton Mifflin Harcourt, 2009.

———. *Thomas More*. New York: Oxford University Press, 2000.

Jardine, Lisa. *Erasmus: Man of Letters*. Princeton, NJ: Princeton University Press, 1993.

Kinney, A. F. *John Skelton: Priest as Poet*. Chapel Hill: University of North Carolina Press, 1987.

Maddison, Francis. *Essays on the Life and Work of Thomas Linacre*. Oxford, UK: Oxford University Press, 1977.

Marius, Richard. *Thomas More*. New York: Alfred Knopf, 1984.

Martz, Louis L. *Thomas More: The Search for the Inner Man*. New Haven, CT: Yale University Press, 1992.

McConica, James. *English Humanists and Reformation Politics under Henry VIII and Edward VI*. Oxford, UK: Clarendon Press, 1965.

Paisey, D., and G. Bartrum. "Hans Holbein and Miles Coverdale." *Print Quarterly* 26 (2009): 227–53.

Walker, Greg. *John Skelton and the Politics of the 1520s*. Cambridge, UK: Cambridge University Press, 2002.

Wilson, Derek. *Hans Holbein: Portrait of an Unknown Man*. London: Weidenfeld and Nicolson, 1996.

Foreign Rulers and Their Kingdoms

Baumgartner, Frederic J. *Louis XII*. New York: St. Martin's Press, 1996.

Cameron, Jamie. *James V: The Personal Rule 1528–1542*. Edinburgh, UK: John Donald, 2011.

Cummings, Anthony M. *The Lion's Ear: Pope Leo X*. Ann Arbor: University of Michigan Press, 2012.

Edwards, John. *Ferdinand and Isabella*. London: Routledge, 2014.

Fernández-Armesto, Felipe. *Ferdinand and Isabella*. New York: Dorset, 1991.

Fichtner, Paula S. *Emperor Maximilian I*. New York: Oxford University Press, 2011.

Frieda, Leonie, *Francis I: The Maker of Modern France*. New York: HarperCollins, 2018.

Hackett, Francis. *Francis the First*. New York: Greenwood, 1968.

Knecht, Robert J. *Francis I*. New York: Cambridge University Press, 1982.

Macdougall, Norman. *An Antidote to the English: The Auld Alliance 1295–1560*. East Linton, UK: Tuckwell Press, 2001.

———. *James IV*. East Linton, UK: Tuckwell Press, 1997.

———. *James V 1512–1542*. East Linton, UK: Tuckwell Press, 1998.

Maltby, William. *The Reign of Charles V*. Basingstoke, UK: Palgrave, 2002.

McKendrick, Melveena. *Ferdinand and Isabella*. London: Cassell, 1969.

Noel, Gerard. *The Renaissance Popes*. London: Constable, 2016.

Norwich, John Julius. *Four Princes: Henry VIII, Francis I, Charles V and Suleiman the Magnificent*. London: John Murray, 2017.

Parker, Geoffery. *Emperor: A New Life of Charles V*. New Haven, CT: Yale University Press, 2019.

Reiss, Sheryl E. *The Pontificate of Clement VII: History, Politics and Culture*. London: Routledge, 2017.

Richardson, Glenn. *Renaissance Monarchy: The Reigns of Henry VIII, Francis I and Charles V.* New York: Oxford University Press, 2002.

Wilson, Peter H. *Heart of Europe: A History of the Holy Roman Empire.* Cambridge, MA: Harvard University Press, 2016.

Religion and the Reformation

Alsop. J. D. "Cromwell and the Church in 1531." *Journal of English History* 31 (1980): 327–30.

Aston, Margaret. *Broken Idols of the English Reformation.* Cambridge, UK: Cambridge University Press, 2016.

———. *England's Iconoclasts.* Oxford, UK: Clarendon Press, 1988.

Bernard, G. W. *The King's Reformation: Henry VIII and the Remaking of the English Church.* New Haven, CT: Yale University Press, 2005.

Bobrick, Benson. *Wide as the Waters: The English Bible.* New York: Simon and Schuster, 2002.

Brigden, Susan. *London and the Reformation.* Oxford, UK: Clarendon Press, 1989.

Clark, J. G. "Humanism and Reform in Pre-Reformation English Monasteries." *Transactions of the Royal Historical Society* 6, no. 19 (2009): 57–93.

Clark, Peter D. "Canterbury as the New Rome." *Journal of English History* 64 (2013): 20–44.

Coby, J. Patrick. *Henry VIII and the Reformation Parliament.* 2006. Chapel Hill, NC: Reading Consortium, 2019.

Cross, Claire. *The Church and the People, 1450–1660.* Atlantic Highlands, NJ: Humanities Press, 1999.

Dickens, A.G. *The English Reformation.* New York: Schocken Books, 1964/89.

———. *Late Monasticism and the Reformation.* London: Hambledon Press, 1994.

Drees, Clayton J. *Authority and Dissent in the English Church: The Prosecution of Heresy and Religious Non-Conformity in the Diocese of Winchester, 1380–1547.* Lewiston, NY: Edwin Mellen Press, 1997.

Duffy, Eamon. *Reformation Divided: Catholics, Protestants and the Conversion of England.* London: Bloomsbury, 2017.

———. *Stripping of the Altars: English Traditional Religion 1400–1580.* New Haven, CT: Yale University Press, 1992.

Elton, Sir Geoffrey. *Reform and Reformation: England, 1509–1558.* Cambridge, MA: Harvard University Press, 1977.

Eppley, Daniel. *Defending Royal Supremacy and Discerning God's Will in Tudor England.* London: Routledge, 2016.

Gray, J. M. *Oaths and the English Reformation.* Cambridge, UK: Cambridge University Press, 2013.

Haigh, Christopher. *English Reformations.* Oxford, UK: Clarendon Press, 1993.

Heal, Felicity. *Of Prelates and Princes: A Study of the Economic and Social Position of the Tudor Episcopate.* Cambridge, UK: Cambridge University Press, 1980.

Houlbrooke, Ralph A. *Church Courts and the People during the English Reformation 1520–1570.* Oxford, UK: Oxford University Press, 1979.

Hudson, Anne. *The Premature Reformation: Wycliffite Texts and Lollard History.* Oxford, UK: Clarendon Press, 1988.

Kaufman, Peter Iver. *The "Polytyque Church": Religion and Early Tudor Political Culture, 1485–1516.* Macon, GA: Mercer University Press, 1986.

Lehmberg, Stanford E. *The Reformation Parliaments 1529–1536.* Cambridge, UK: Cambridge University Press, 1970.

Le Neve, John, ed. *Fasti Ecclesiae Anglicanae.* 3 vols. Oxford, UK: Oxford University Press, 1854.

Logan, F. D. "Thomas Cromwell and the Vicegerency in Spirituals: A Revisitation." *English Historical Review* 103 (1988): 558–67.

Marshall, Peter, and Alec Ryrie. *The Beginnings of English Protestantism.* Cambridge, UK: Cambridge University Press, 2007.

———. *Heretics and Believers: A History of the English Reformation.* New Haven, CT: Yale University Press, 2017.

Moorhouse, Geoffrey. *The Last Divine Office: The Dissolution of the Monasteries.* New York: Bluebridge, 2008.

Rex, Richard. "The Early Impact of Reformation Theology at Cambridge University 1521–1547." *Reformation and Renaissance Review* 2 (December 1999): 38–71.

———. *Henry VIII and the English Reformation*. New York: St. Martin's Press, 1993.

———. *The Lollards*. New York: Palgrave, 2002.

Ryrie, Alec. *The Age of Reformation in England and Scotland*. New York: Pearson Longman, 2009.

———. *The Gospel and Henry VIII: Evangelicals in the Early English Reformation*. Cambridge, UK: Cambridge University Press, 2003.

Scarisbrick, J. J. *The Reformation and the English People*. Oxford, UK: Blackwell, 1985.

Shagan, E. H. *Popular Politics and the English Reformation*. Cambridge, UK: Cambridge University Press, 2003.

Teems, David. *Tyndale*. Nashville, TN: Thomas Nelson, 2012.

Telford, Lynda. *Tudor Victims of the Henrician Reformation*. Barnsley, UK: Pen and Sword History, 2016.

Thomson, J. A. F. *The Later Lollards, 1414–1520*. Oxford, UK: Oxford University Press, 1965.

Tyacke, Nicholas, ed. *England's Long Reformation 1500–1800*. London: Taylor and Franics, 1998.

Wilson, Derek. *The English Reformation*. London: Constable and Robinson, 2012.

Youings, J. *The Dissolution of the Monasteries*. London: Allen and Unwin, 1971.

Zahl, Paul F. M. *Five Women of the English Reformation*. Grand Rapids, MI: William B. Eerdmans, 2001.

Religious Figures

Ayris, P. "The Public Career of Thomas Cranmer." *Reformation and Renaissance Review* 4 (December 2000): 75–125.

Bradshaw, Brendan, and Eamon Duffy, eds. *Humanism, Reform and the Reformation: The Career of Bishop John Fisher*. Cambridge, UK: Cambridge University Press, 1989.

Chibi, Andrew A. *Henry VIII's Bishops*. Oxford, UK: James Clarke, 2003.

Daniell, D. *William Tyndale: A Biography*. New Haven, CT: Yale University Press, 1994.

Darby, Harold S. *Hugh Latimer*. Eugene, OR: Wipf and Stock, 2018.

Drees, Clayton J. *Bishop Richard Fox of Winchester: Architect of the Tudor Age*. Jefferson, NC: McFarland, 2014.

Maas, Korey D. *The Reformation and Robert Barnes*. Woodbridge, UK: Boydell Press, 2010.

MacCulloch, Diarmaid. *Thomas Cranmer: A Life*. New Haven, CT: Yale University Press, 1996.

Mayer, T. E. *Reginald Pole: Prince and Prophet*. Cambridge, UK: Cambridge University Press, 2000.

Redworth, Glyn. *In Defense of the Church Catholic: The Life of Stephen Gardiner*. London: Basil Blackwell, 1990.

Rex, Richard. *The Theology of John Fisher*. Cambridge, UK: Cambridge University Press, 1991.

Ridley, Jasper. *Thomas Cranmer*. Oxford, UK: Clarendon Press, 1962.

Riordan, M. and A. Ryrie. "Stephen Gardiner and the Making of a Protestant Villain." *Sixteenth Century Journal* 34, no. 4 (2003): 1039–63.

Teems, David. *Tyndale: The Man Who Gave God an English Voice*. Nashville, TN: Thomas Nelson, 2012.

Yaxley, Susan. *Thomas Bilney 1495–1531*. Dereham, UK: Larks Press, 1995.

Wars, Revolts, and Diplomacy

Bernard, G. W. *War, Taxation and Rebellion in Early Tudor England: Henry VIII, Wolsey and the Amicable Grant of 1525*. New York: St. Martin's Press, 1986.

Bush, M. L. *The Pilgrimage of Grace*. Manchester, UK: Manchester University Press, 1996.

Cruickshank, Charles. *Henry VIII and the Invasion of France in 1513*. Gloucestershire, UK: Sutton, 1994.

Fletcher, Anthony, and Diarmaid MacCulloch. *Tudor Rebellions*. 6th ed. London: Routledge, 2016.

Hoyle, Richard W. *The Pilgrimage of Grace and the Politics of the 1530s.* Oxford, UK: Oxford University Press, 2010.

Jansen, Sharon. *Dangerous Talk and Strange Behavior: Women and Popular Resistance to the Reforms of Henry VIII.* New York: St. Martin's Press, 1996.

Licence, Amy. *1520: The Field of Cloth of Gold.* Stroud, UK: Amberley, 2020.

Loades, David. *The Fighting Tudors.* Kew, UK: National Archives, 2009.

———. *The Tudor Navy.* Aldershot, UK: Ashgate, 1992.

Loughlin, Susan. *Insurrection: Henry VIII, Thomas Cromwell and the Pilgrimage of Grace.* Gloucestershire, UK: History Press, 2016.

MacKay, Lauren. *Inside the Tudor Court through the Writings of the Spanish Ambassador Eustace Chapuys.* Gloucestershire, UK: Amberley, 2014.

Marsden, Peter. *The Mary Rose: Your Noblest Ship.* Oxford, UK: Oxbow Books, 2015.

McElvogue, Douglas. *Tudor Warship Mary Rose: Anatomy of the Ship.* Annapolis, MD: Naval Institute Press, 2015.

Moorhouse, Geoffrey. *Great Harry's Navy.* London: Phoenix, Orion, 2005.

———. *The Pilgrimage of Grace.* London: Phoenix, Orion, 2002.

Raymond, James. *Henry VIII's Military Revolution.* New York: Macmillan, 2007.

Richardson, Glenn. *The Field of Cloth of Gold.* New Haven, CT: Yale University Press, 2013.

Russell, Joycelyne G. *The Field of Cloth of Gold.* London: Routledge and Kegan, 1969.

Thomas, Paul. *Authority and Disorder in Tudor Times.* Cambridge, UK: Cambridge University Press, 2004.

Wall, Alison D. *Power and Protest in England 1525–1640.* New York: Oxford University Press, 2000.

Society and Geography

Ackroyd, Peter. *London: The Biography.* New York: Random House, 2000.

———. *Thames: The Biography.* New York: Doubleday, 2007.

Alford, Stephen. *London's Triumph: The Merchant Adventurers and the Tudor City.* London: Penguin, 2017.

Clark, Peter. *Migration and Society in Early Modern England.* London: Hutchinson, 1987.

Coster, Will. *Family and Kinship in England 1450–1800.* London: Pearson, 2001.

Cressy, David. *Birth, Marriage and Death: The Life Cycle in Early Modern England.* Oxford, UK: Oxford University Press, 2002.

Ekwall, Eilert, ed. *The Concise Oxford Dictionary of English Place-Names.* 4th ed. Oxford, UK: Clarendon Press, 1936/64.

Harris, Barbara J. *English Aristocratic Women 1450–1550.* Oxford, UK: Oxford University Press, 2002.

Hutton, Ronald. *The Rise and Fall of Merry England.* Oxford, UK: Oxford University Press, 2011.

Kintgen, Eugene R. *Reading in Tudor England.* Pittsburgh, PA: University of Pittsburgh Press, 1996.

Norton, Elizabeth. *The Hidden Lives of Tudor Women: A Social History.* New York: W. W. Norton, 2018.

Orme, Nicholas. *Medieval Schools: From Roman Britain to Tudor England.* New Haven, CT: Yale University Press, 2006.

Plowden, Alison. *Tudor Women: Queens and Commoners.* Gloucestershire, UK: Sutton, 2002.

Rowse, A. L. *Court and Country: Studies in Tudor Social History.* Brighton, UK: Harvester Press, 1987.

Sim, Alison. *Pleasures and Pastimes in Tudor England.* Gloucestershire, UK: History Press, 2011.

Victoria History of the Counties of England. London: Constable, 1902–12.

INTERNET STARTING POINTS

Biography. https://www.biography.com/.

Britannica. https://www.britannica.com/.

British Library. https://www.bl.uk/sacred-texts/articles/henry-viii.

BritRoyals. https://www.britroyals.com/kings.asp?id=henry8.

Catholic Encyclopedia. https://www.newadvent.org/cathen/04024a.htm.

Christianity. https://www.christianity.com/church/church-history/.

Christianity Today. https://www.christianitytoday.com/history/.

Daily History. https://dailyhistory.org/.

Encyclopedia. https://theodora.com/encyclopedia/.

English Heritage. https://www.english-heritage.org.uk/learn/histories/.

English History. Tudor. https://englishhistory.net/tudor.

Google Scholar. https://scholar.google.com/.

Henry VIII Timeline. https://www.henryviiithereign.co.uk/henry-viii-timeline.html.

Historical Journal. https://www.cambridge.org/core/journals/historical-journal/.

Historic Royal Palaces. https://www.hrp.org.uk/.

Historic UK. https://www.historic-uk.com/HistoryUK/HistoryofEngland/.

History Extra. Tudor. https://www.historyextra.com/period/tudor.

History Learning Site. https://www.historylearningsite.co.uk/.

History on the Net. https://www.historyonthenet.com/henry-viii/.

History Press. https://www.thehistorypress.co.uk/.

Luminarium Encyclopedia. http://www.luminarium.org/encyclopedia/.

National Archives. https://www.nationalarchives.gov.uk/.

Oxford Dictionary of National Biography. https://www.oxforddnb.com/.

Reformation 500. https://reformation500.csl.edu/.

Smithsonian Magazine. https://www.smithsonianmag.com/history/.

Spartacus Educational. https://spartacus-educational.com/Tudors.htm.

Thought Company. https://www.thoughtco.com/.

Totally Timelines. https://www.totallytimelines.com/henry-viii-1491-1547/.

Tudor Place. http://www.tudorplace.com.ar/.

Tudors Dynasty. https://tudorsdynasty.com/.

Tudor Travel Guide. https://thetudortravelguide.com/.

Wikipedia. https://en.wikipedia.org/.

World History Encyclopedia. https://www.worldhistory.org/.

Index

About the Author

Clayton J. Drees earned his doctorate from the Claremont Graduate School in California in 1991 after teaching high school for seven years, including a two-year stint with the Peace Corps in Sierra Leone, West Africa. He is professor of history at Virginia Wesleyan University, where he teaches courses in medieval and early modern European, African, and Islamic history. A two-time recipient of VWU's Samuel Nelson Gray Distinguished Teaching Award (1998, 2015), Drees has also served his university as director of the General Education Program (1999–2005) and as dean of the School of Social Sciences (2005–2011). His other published books include *Authority and Dissent in the English Church* (1997), *The Late Medieval Age of Crisis and Renewal* (2001), and *Bishop Richard Fox of Winchester: Architect of the Tudor Age* (2014). He has lived in Virginia Beach for 30 years with his wife, Val.